For Free Press and Equal Rights

For Free Press and Equal Rights

Republican Newspapers in the Reconstruction South

RICHARD H. ABBOTT

Edited by John W. Quist

THE UNIVERSITY OF GEORGIA PRESS
Athens and London

© 2004 by the University of Georgia Press
Athens, Georgia 30602
All rights reserved
Set in Minion by Bookcomp, Inc.
Printed and bound by Maple-Vail
The paper in this book meets the guidelines for permanence and durability
of the Committee on Production Guidelines for Book Longevity of the
Council on Library Resources.
Printed in the United States of America
08 07 06 05 04 C 5 4 3 2 1

Library of Congress Cataloging-in-Publication Data

Abbott, Richard H.
For free press and equal rights : Republican newspapers in the
Reconstruction South / Richard H. Abbott ; edited by John W. Quist.
p. cm.
Includes bibliographical references and index.
ISBN 0-8203-2527-9 (alk. paper)
1. American newspapers—Southern States—History—19th
century.   2. Journalism—Southern States—History—19th century.
3. Republican Party (U.S. : 1854–)   I. Quist, John W., 1960–   II. Title.
PN4893.A24 2004
071'.5'09034—dc22   2003019206

British Library Cataloging-in-Publication Data available

To my grandchildren: Charlie, Hayden, Ike, Katie, and Logan

Contents

Preface, *ix*

Introduction, *1*

1. Origins of the Southern Republican Press, *7*

2. Limited Expansion, *24*

3. The White South Confronts the Republican Press, *40*

4. Patronage Saves the Republican Press, *56*

5. The Geographic Breadth of the Southern Republican Press, *70*

6. The Ideology of the Republican Press, *95*

7. Differences in Approach, *117*

8. Continuing Factionalism, *143*

9. The Two-Edged Sword of Patronage, *164*

Appendix: Republican Newspapers by State, 1865–1877, *187*

Notes, *203*

Index, *255*

Preface

Richard Henry Abbott, known informally as "Hank," spent most of his career teaching at Eastern Michigan University. Despite a heavy teaching load, Hank was a productive and widely known scholar, authoring *Cobbler in Congress: The Life of Henry Wilson, 1812–1875* (1972), *The Republican Party and the South, 1855–1877: The First Southern Strategy* (1986), and *Cotton and Capital: Boston Businessmen and Antislavery Reform, 1854–1868* (1991), as well as numerous articles and book reviews. Hank had completed a draft of the present volume and submitted it for publication in December 1998. Before he received a response, however, physicians diagnosed Hank with a disease that would claim his life a year later. Although his manuscript was nearly ready for publication, Hank lacked the strength to make revisions.

Richard Goff and Michael Sinclair began the work of shepherding Hank's manuscript toward publication. In January 2002 they entrusted me with this responsibility—one that I eagerly accepted, as Hank had been a trusted friend and mentor during my three years at Eastern Michigan University. As editor I have tightened the manuscript's prose, conformed inconsistent usage, and corrected minor errors while leaving the book's structure and argument undisturbed. Hank certainly would have performed these tasks differently—including those revisions that many authors make as their work nears publication.

Regrettably, the librarians and historians who aided Hank as he prepared this book must remain unrecognized. I must thank Richard Goff, Michael Sinclair, and Marie Richmond-Abbott for their confidence. R. Charles Loucks's talents have been indispensable. A devoted graduate-school friend of Hank's, Charles generously read the manuscript several times, always utilizing his vigilant eye for detail. Michael Fitzgerald and Heather Cox Richardson recognized this book's importance and made numerous suggestions that improved the final product. Derek Krissoff at the University of Georgia Press offered wisdom, flexibility, good humor, and subtle reminders about deadlines. Sarah McKee and Sally Antrobus, also at the University of Georgia Press, ably copyedited and improved the book.

Chapter 1 originally appeared in a slightly different form as "Civil War Origins of the Southern Republican Press," *Civil War History* 43 (1997), 38–58. It is reprinted here with the editor's permission.

For Free Press and Equal Rights

Introduction

From the earliest years of the American republic, political parties had forged close alliances with newspapers. Publishers and editors often held important posts in party organizations and sometimes ran for political office themselves. Their papers fed party doctrine to the faithful, refuted the heresies of their opponents, and endeavored to convert the uncommitted. During the ubiquitous political campaigns, publishers sold candidates space in their columns, printed candidates' handbills, and disseminated news of local, state, and national conventions and platforms. In these ways editors helped solidify party organization and loyalty, and on election days they worked to ensure a large turnout of their followers. The number of a party's newspapers became a measure of its strength, and rival partisan organizations vied to achieve newspaper representation in every city and important town, particularly county seats. In turn, the newspapers received support from the political parties they advocated. To secure favorable publicity, parties sometimes resorted to gifts and loans to newspapers or even outright ownership of presses, and they paid party newspapers to post political advertisements and lists of candidates. The parties' most important assistance to their newspapers was the dispensation of printing patronage to local, state, and national governments. Partisan presses came to depend heavily on this subsidy.[1]

The conviction of nineteenth-century newspaper editors that they substantially influenced public opinion proves difficult to evaluate. Like preachers, teachers, public officials, and other community leaders, editors certainly helped mold political attitudes. This was especially true of rural editors, whose readers depended on them for condensed news and opinions from the large city dailies. A community's habitual newspaper readers were people of position and power who helped shape the views of others. For an editor to be influential, he needed to retain such readers' confidence and could not afford to stray too far from the generally accepted community views and mores. Consequently, editors not only molded but also reflected, reinforced, and legitimized the attitudes that they discerned around them.[2]

Southern editors figured more prominently than their Northern counterparts in shaping public opinion. Newspapers constituted the only mass medium for the South, which lacked the North's increasingly common publishing houses, magazines, lyceums, libraries, and schools. For most Southerners, their local newspaper was the only source of information from the outside world. In addition, more Southern than Northern newspapers were politically active. In 1860, 74 percent of the nation's newspapers reported a political affiliation, but in the South, the figure jumped to 83 percent.[3] Increasingly, as tensions over slavery pushed the nation toward Civil War, these partisan Southern editors deployed their influence to unite readers against outside threats. As staunch sectional defenders, they tolerated less and less dissent from the prevailing commitment to slavery, white supremacy, and state rights. These protagonists thereby hastened the transformation of their region into a closed society, which, as one historian of Southern journalism has observed, "reflected a closed press reinforcing and reiterating community views."[4]

This intolerance of divergent opinion and dissent characterized the South from the 1850s through the end of Reconstruction and constituted a major roadblock for Republicans hoping to organize in that section. Their party, which emerged in the North in 1854, had initially represented only Northern concerns. As critics of Southern domination of the federal government, Republican spokesmen had called for curbing the expansion of slavery and for legislation advancing Northern economic interests. Hence the vast majority of Southern whites had strongly opposed the Republicans, and after the Republican presidential candidate Abraham Lincoln won the 1860 election, eleven Southern states had seceded from the Union, precipitating a four-year Civil War. Most Republicans, however, hoped theirs would eventually become a national rather than a sectional party. Even before hostilities began they were attempting to build partisan support in the South. By 1860, the party had established weak organizations in the border slave states of Missouri, Maryland, Kentucky, Delaware, and Virginia, but aside from the Old Dominion, had generated no support in the states that eventually formed the Confederacy. During the Civil War, however, Republicans found opportunities to establish footholds in a number of these states, creating a basis for anticipated postwar expansion.[5]

After Appomattox the odds against establishing the party in the ex-Confederate states appeared overwhelming. Republicans were identified with the war to save the Union and with the slaves' emancipation that had occurred during that conflict. The Republican-controlled postwar Congresses further antagonized Southern whites by recognizing the former slaves' citizenship and right to vote. Southern white newspaper editors played a leading role in rallying sectional and racial loyalties against the Republicans. Traveling through the South in the fall of 1865, Northern journalist Sidney Andrews found that the region's papers were "all local in character, and most of them are intensely Southern in tone." After Republicans gained control of most Southern states by capitalizing on the newly enfranchised freedmen's votes, the region's Democratic editors treated these new regimes with hostility and contempt, condemning them for elevating the freedmen to citizenship and calling on whites to unite against them. The editor of South Carolina's *Laurensville Herald* spoke for many of his Democratic colleagues by vowing to use his paper to denounce and ridicule Republicans, "hold the white men together and prevent the weak-kneed from going over to the enemy." Historian Thomas Clark, a close observer of the Southern press, contended that it was the Southern editor more than any other individual "who implanted the idea that the South could maintain its regional integrity only through the predominance of the Democratic party."[6]

Given the close nineteenth-century connection between parties and newspapers, Southern Republicans could hardly hope to survive without a party press that would perform all the functions that a party press provided in the North. But in the South, a Republican party press faced considerable obstacles not encountered north of the Mason-Dixon line. There, Republicans could take for granted the right to organize, rally supporters, and contend for control of government. In the South, however, as challengers of deeply ingrained sectional and racial loyalties, Republicans faced hostile whites who refused either to recognize their party's right to exist or to accord legitimacy to the state and local governments that Republicans controlled.[7] Establishing and maintaining a party press was one way for Republicans to claim this legitimacy, and to achieve that goal, Southern Republican journalists, unlike their Northern counterparts, had to make a case for freedom of press, speech, and expression.

In that bristling Southern climate, Republican editors faced many problems that did not exist in the North. Mobs destroyed numerous Republican presses in the ex-Confederate states, threatened or physically assaulted their editors, and even murdered a few of them. Everywhere Republican publishers had difficulty generating advertising support and building subscription lists among a party constituency that was largely poor, black, and illiterate. Editors were constantly on the defensive, trying to counter the power and influence of opposition editors who routinely slandered Republican candidates and distorted their positions. Because of this antipathy to their party and its followers, Southern Republican editors played a greater role than their Northern counterparts in building a sense of community that would empower resistance to harassment and repression. Finally, the South's Republican editors faced a greater challenge than those in the North because they sought support from voters of both races. Although Northern African Americans voted Republican, they represented a tiny fraction of the party's total count. In the South, African Americans comprised the party's majority. Hence the greatest challenge facing the Republican party and its editors was enlisting sufficient white membership to accord it legitimacy and a chance for survival, as reliance on black votes alone spelled doom.

The lack of legitimacy for the Republican press in the South invites comparison with the press of other nineteenth-century American parties and movements whose challenges to the status quo engendered hostility. Newspapers speaking for third parties, for instance, faced some of the same problems Republican editors experienced. In the late nineteenth-century South and West, a powerful third-party movement, the Populists, formidably challenged existing social, economic, and political institutions. Elites in both sections loathed the Populists. Papers of both major parties ridiculed and distorted their principles and ideas, triggering the publication of independent newspapers. A student of the Populist press, Jean Folkerts, contends that these newspapers served three purposes for their party: they disseminated information ignored by mainstream newspapers, engendered a sense of community among party members, and sought to legitimize the party in the eyes of its opponents. These are precisely the functions provided by the Republican press in the South.[8]

Given the importance and magnitude of the problems facing Republican editors, historians have accorded them surprisingly little attention. Only one statewide study of the Republican press exists.[9] The few characterizations of Southern Republican journalists as a whole are generally unfavorable, reflecting older interpretations of Reconstruction. E. Merton Coulter's history of the South during Reconstruction has little to say about newspapers, Democratic or Republican, except to ridicule the latter. Coulter incorrectly labels almost all of them as being "carpetbagger" edited or owned, and characterizes two of them as "offensive" and "rabid." Hodding Carter, in his history of the Southern press during the Civil War and Reconstruction, was equally scornful of Republican editors, claiming that they did not constitute responsible voices of dissent. Among the Republican papers, the total number of which he put at somewhat over one hundred, a significant undercount, Carter concluded that "only two . . . can be considered reputable, unselfish, and honest." The others, such as Jason Clarke Swayze's *American Union* and John Emory Bryant's *Loyal Georgian,* he characterized as "vicious, wholly self-seeking journals, that cared not to make the South a truly integrated part of the nation." While rejecting these stereotypes of Reconstruction Republicans, Eric Foner's landmark study of Reconstruction has almost nothing to say about the Republican press. Mark

Summers's examination of Reconstruction-era newspapers and politics offers a brief and informative chapter on the Southern Republican press, but he underestimates its strength, claiming that Republicans were able to establish only a "scattering" of newspapers across the section.[10]

This study of the Southern Republican press during Reconstruction has several goals. My initial purpose was to learn how Republican editors handled racial issues; in particular I wanted to determine how they hoped to attract whites into a party numerically dominated by African Americans. This raised the question of how many Republican newspapers operated in the South during Reconstruction. Ultimately I identified some 430 such papers that appeared in the ex-Confederate states from 1857 to 1877. Chapter 5 compares these Republican newspaper totals with the Democratic press and analyzes the numbers and distribution of Republican papers state by state. The appendix tabulates Republican papers in the Reconstruction South and indicates their often brief durations. If this work accomplishes nothing else, I hope it will draw attention to these papers; their importance as a resource for researching Reconstruction history has been overlooked.

This monograph also incorporates a general history of the Republican press in the Reconstruction South from its Civil War origins to its demise in the later 1870s. This material, which is found in chapters 1–5 and 9, includes a discussion of the many problems facing Republican publishers during the period and stresses the role of patronage in building a party press. Patronage proved to be both an aid and a handicap, however, as the competition for printing contracts exacerbated factionalism within the Republican party, and the waste and corruption associated with its dispensation gave hostile Democratic editors ammunition for condemning Republican regimes. Finally, I have sought to characterize the ideology of the Republican editors—that is, the body of ideas and proposals that they advocated in the hope of earning regional legitimacy for their party and convincing white voters to cross the color line and vote with the Republicans. These issues are taken up in chapters 6, 7, and 8, which also analyze disagreements within the Republican press over how to build the party and which explore how editors' concerns and emphases changed over time.

The Republican party that struggled to survive in the Reconstruction South owed much to its editors. They challenged the intolerant atmosphere that stifled the free exchange of opinions and championed the principles of free speech and press. They strove to create a sense of group solidarity and community among Republicans that would help them to cope with ostracism and violence. Some Republican newspapermen were undoubtedly corrupt and filled their pockets at state expense. Many others, however, ran their papers at a loss, hoping thereby to help sustain a party representing principles they took seriously, particularly the commitment to equal rights. They were willing to challenge the South's rampant white racism and to encourage whites and blacks to put aside the issue of color and support a party that they believed would work for the best interests of people of both races. This was their greatest legacy.

CHAPTER ONE

Origins of the Southern Republican Press

Prior to the Civil War, the only Republican papers existing in the future Confederate States of America were in northwestern Virginia. That mountainous area, with almost no slaves, had little in common with the rest of the state. In the late 1850s, John C. Underwood, a transplanted New Yorker and slavery opponent who had moved to Virginia in 1846, organized a fledgling Republican Party presence there. In 1858, with Northern Republican financial aid, Underwood and his friends secured control of the *Wheeling Intelligencer* and three other smaller papers in western Virginia. In the presidential election of 1860, almost two thousand of the region's voters cast ballots for Republican candidate Abraham Lincoln.[1]

The Civil War offered Republicans opportunities to expand their influence in Virginia and also to gain a foothold for their party and its newspapers in other Confederate states. As Union armies advanced into the South, their presence had a decided influence on the journalistic climate. Military authorities believed that Southern editors had been instrumental in whipping up support for secession and the Confederacy. In response, they jailed these editors, closed their newspapers, and confiscated their presses or suspended their papers until the offenders exorcised rebel sentiments from their columns.[2] Not content with stifling the rebel press, Union officers also encouraged newspapers that would support the Union cause. Before the war's end, a number of Unionist papers appeared in the occupied portions of the Confederate states. A few of them would survive, thanks primarily to federal printing patronage. U.S. Army officers established some of these papers; Northern civilians accompanying the army initiated others, while a third group was founded by Southern whites who supported the Union. Since the Republican Party did not emerge in most Southern states until after the war, one cannot always identify these Unionist papers with that party. Wartime Unionists, however, provided the most reliable source of white recruits for the Republican Party when it did appear in the South, and most of the Unionist papers that survived the war eventually endorsed the Republicans.

During the war U.S. Army units established at least one hundred papers in the occupied South, and military officers usually edited them. Often they published their papers on presses seized from Confederate proprietors. Circulations sometimes reached into the thousands. A few of these papers served as the personal organs of the commanding generals in their districts; for instance, both Benjamin Butler in Norfolk and New Orleans and Nathaniel Banks in the latter city helped found newspapers to support their military administrations. These army publications kept their readers informed of major wartime developments, carried some news from home, and clipped items from both Northern and Southern papers. Their editors praised the Union, condemned the secessionists, sometimes criticized slavery, and when voicing political preferences generally favored Lincoln's Republican administration. All of these papers were short-lived; most survived only a few months, and they all disappeared at the war's close. That they existed at all spoke to Union soldiers' yearning for diversion, information, and entertainment, and they underscore the importance of newspapers in mid-nineteenth-century American life. The proliferation of these sheets also illustrates the relative ease of launching a paper.[3]

Northern civilians accompanying Union armies also began publishing Unionist newspapers in occupied areas of the South. Frequently these men were federal treasury agents or postal officers. Others were correspondents covering the war for Northern newspapers. Often they too published their papers on presses seized from Confederate owners. These publications tended to last longer than the sheets produced by the Union Army and were more overtly political in their commentaries, usually defending the Lincoln administration.

Native white Southerners or, in the case of New Orleans, native free blacks established the third category of Unionist newspapers to emerge behind Union lines in the Confederate states. Although they all espoused the Union cause and condemned the secessionists, these black publishers held diverse views on slavery and politics. A few opposed emancipation and not all of them endorsed the Lincoln administration. Some black editors who backed Lincoln cannot be clearly identified as Republican because the party did not exist in most Southern states until after the war's end. Nevertheless, a number of such papers eventually became staunch Republican sheets.

Publishers of these Unionist papers struggled to keep them afloat. Newsprint was hard to obtain in the wartime South, and material and labor costs escalated. In most areas of the occupied South, business owners hesitated to advertise in these papers, and subscription lists were short. The Union Army often provided the chief means of sustaining these sheets. Local commanders turned over presses and materials to the publishers and placed military notices and advertisements in their columns. Union soldiers stationed in the towns where the papers were published often bought copies, and the army sometimes purchased additional ones for troops stationed elsewhere. The War Department also paid these papers for job work, which involved printing up government broadsides, general orders, and other official pronouncements.[4]

The U.S. government had other means of sustaining some of these Unionist newspapers. Federal treasury agents who followed the Union armies into the South turned to friendly papers to advertise sales of properties seized for unpaid federal taxes. The government in Washington also contracted with some papers to publish the U.S. laws. The official responsible for publishing these laws, the secretary of state, was empowered to select two papers per state to receive this patronage. Since 1789, the government had relied on this system to inform people in every section of the country about the actions of Congress. Successive administrations utilized this patronage to reward newspapers for their political support. After Lincoln's Republican administration came to power, the new secretary of state, William H. Seward, assigned printing privileges to Republican newspapers across the North as well as to western Virginia's fledgling Republican papers. In the South, however, no Republican papers existed, and the ones that Seward did select lost the patronage as their states seceded from the Union. Therefore, as Union armies penetrated into the Confederacy, Seward sought recommendations for Unionist papers from commanding generals in the South.[5]

Soon after hostilities began, Union publications appeared in the wake of federal penetrations of the Confederate frontier. In the spring of 1861, Union troops occupied Alexandria, Virginia, across the Potomac River from Washington. Although sentiment in the city had been opposed to secession, its leading paper, the *Alexandria Gazette,* supported the Confederacy. Federal authorities interrupted its publication, and in February 1862, a mob that included Union soldiers sacked its office. In May, it resumed publication under the watchful eyes of federal authorities.[6] In October 1862, the first issue of the *Virginia State Journal* appeared in that city, edited by W. J. Cowing, a Northerner. This paper supported Virginia's Unionist government organized by loyal citizens at Wheeling in the northwestern section of the state. President Lincoln recognized this Wheeling government and its chief executive, Francis H. Pierpont, as constituting the state's only legal authority. Virginia's handful of Republicans helped create the Pierpont regime and supported it during the war. In August 1863, after the northwestern counties had seceded to form the new state of West Virginia, Pierpont moved his government to Alexandria, where it remained until the war was over. In December 1863, at Pierpont's urging, Seward granted the

Journal U.S. printing patronage. The paper also became the official newspaper of the Pierpont regime. The governor granted it whatever printing patronage he could provide. This included the contract to publish the journal of the 1864 state constitutional convention that Pierpont convened in Alexandria and the right to publish one thousand copies of the constitution itself. In that convention, Pierpont's forces agreed to abolish slavery in the state and to enact strict disfranchisement laws to bar Confederate sympathizers from power.[7]

In May 1862, Union forces occupied Norfolk and Portsmouth at the southern end of Chesapeake Bay. This was another Virginia area where some inhabitants had opposed secession, although the majority embraced the Confederacy. By the time federal forces arrived, only one newspaper, the *Norfolk Day Book*, still operated in the area. Because of its Confederate sympathies, U.S. officials suppressed it. In June, Union officers established the *Norfolk Union*, using the press of one of the previous local papers. This army paper lasted only two months. In the summer of 1863, Portsmouth Unionists established a daily, the *Old Dominion*, which they moved to Norfolk later in the war. Following the recommendations of Governor Pierpont and Cowing of the *State Journal*, Seward granted the *Old Dominion* U.S. printing privileges for the first session of the Thirty-eighth Congress. The paper supported the Lincoln administration and called for the president's reelection. In February 1864, General Benjamin Butler, the local Union military commander, established the *New Regime* in Norfolk and persuaded Seward to transfer patronage from the *Old Dominion* to Butler's paper. This switch elicited complaints from local Unionists and Republicans; when the *New Regime* suspended publication in 1865, Seward returned the printing to the *Old Dominion*.[8]

In the meantime, other Unionist papers were appearing on the Confederacy's coastal fringes wherever combined Union naval and army expeditions could establish footholds. In November 1861, Union forces operating in South Carolina's Sea Islands seized Port Royal, Hilton Head Island, and the town of Beaufort and thereafter controlled these areas. In March 1862, a Unionist newspaper, the *New South*, appeared in Port Royal. Its publisher, Joseph Sears, was a Northerner who also ran the local post office and a store. Eventually Sears moved the *New South* to Beaufort, where it survived the war. He distributed his paper mainly to Union soldiers, and by September 1863, it had a circulation of almost ten thousand copies. For the most part Sears avoided political commentary.[9]

In January 1863, three U.S. treasury agents, James M. Latta, Lyman Stickney, and Harrison Reed, established Beaufort's second Unionist paper, the *Free South*. These men subsidized their paper by advertising large numbers of tax sales in its columns; in 1863 the paper received around $1,350 from the Treasury Department. James G. Thompson, a Philadelphia native, edited the paper. In its columns Thompson excoriated secessionists, condemned slavery, and pronounced the state irredeemable until it was remodeled like Massachusetts. In August 1864, complaining that his paper's defense of emancipation and the Union had "retarded its prosperity," Thompson asked Seward for the right to publish U.S. laws. Before he obtained that right, Stickney and Reed sold the *Free South* and bought a Florida paper. Their former paper struggled until November 1864, when it ceased publishing; the federal printing contract went to the *New South* instead. In March 1864, Port Royal secured a third Unionist paper, the *Palmetto Herald*, published by S. W. Mason, a wartime journalist for the *Boston Herald*, but at year's end Mason shifted his press to Savannah, Georgia. After Charleston fell to Union forces early in 1865, military authorities seized the *Charleston Courier* and turned it over to two Northern journalists attached to the Union Army. This pair published the *Courier* as a Union paper until November, when it passed back to its original owners.[10]

Early in 1862, after Union general Ambrose Burnside's forces occupied portions of North Carolina's Outer Banks, Burnside established a Union paper in New Bern, appropriating both the office and name of the *Newbern Daily Progress*. George Mills Joy, a Massachusetts sergeant, edited the paper, which supported Lincoln's efforts to organize a Unionist government under Edward Stanly in eastern North Carolina. Joy assured conservative North Carolina Unionists that Lincoln's goal was restoring the Union, not abolishing slavery, and he criticized Charles Foster, a local Unionist congressional candidate, for supporting abolition. Late in 1863, Joy renamed his paper the *North Carolina Times;* by then Lincoln had embraced emancipation as a war aim and Joy now supported this goal in North Carolina. He successfully appealed to Seward for a government printing contract, pointing out that his paper was the state's only loyal publication. Joy backed Lincoln for reelection and urged loyal North Carolina voters to overthrow the slave aristocracy that controlled the state. In 1865 Joy opened another paper, the *Old North State,* in Beaufort, and secured printing for it as well.[11]

In February 1865, after the coastal city of Wilmington fell to the Union, federal authorities seized a local secessionist paper's facilities and turned them over to H. H. Munson and Thomas M. Cook, who began publishing the *Herald of the Union*. Munson, a Wilmington businessman and publisher, had supported the Confederacy, but once Union forces occupied his city he switched sides. Cook, a *New York Herald* correspondent, had accompanied the invading Union armies. The two men successfully petitioned Seward for federal printing patronage, vowing to use their paper to support the Union and the Lincoln administration. For some eight months the *Herald of the Union* was the region's only paper.[12]

In Florida, thanks to the Union Navy, federal forces kept control of Pensacola and Key West throughout the war. Pensacola hosted a Unionist paper, the *Observer*, which survived the war years and became a Republican sheet after the party was organized in the state in 1867. In Key West, Union and Confederate sympathizers were evenly divided. In May 1861, Union authorities shut down a secessionist paper, *Key of the Gulf*, and turned its press over to a Union regiment. A New Yorker, Richard B. Locke, edited and published the paper, which was subsidized by the Union Army. An abolitionist, Locke used his paper to urge the few hundred slaves in Key West to declare themselves free. He also hoped his paper would rekindle Unionist sympathies in the Keys, but it folded in less than a year.[13]

In March 1862, Union forces captured Jacksonville and soon seized control of nearby St. Augustine and Fernandina. Jacksonville would not be occupied permanently until December 1863, but Fernandina and St. Augustine stayed in Union hands for the war's duration. In April 1863, the first issue of the Fernandina *Peninsula* appeared, published weekly by James M. Latta, who had just arrived in Florida after selling the *Free South* of Beaufort, South Carolina. In September Latta sold the *Peninsula* to William C. Morrill, apparently a local Unionist. Lyman Stickney, the treasury agent earlier associated with Latta's Beaufort paper, financed the purchase and controlled the paper, for which he obtained the State Department's printing contract. Stickney used the *Peninsula* to advocate abolition and to champion the presidential aspirations of Lincoln's treasury secretary, Salmon P. Chase, until the Chase boom collapsed.[14] Stickney, who was eager to organize the Jacksonville area Unionists, transferred the paper there in 1864 after the Union Army had returned to the city. It appeared along with the *Jacksonville Herald*, which was published as a Union paper after U.S. forces arrived. In September 1864, Morrill and Stickney bought control of the Jacksonville *Florida Union*, and the *Peninsula* disappeared; the U.S. government transferred its printing to the *Florida Union*, which Stickney and Morrill used to back Lincoln's reelection and to garner support for the Thirteenth Amendment, abolishing slavery.[15]

Just up the coast from Jacksonville, two Unionist papers appeared in Savannah, Georgia, before the war's end. In December 1864, after the city fell to General William T. Sherman, the Union Army seized the *Savannah Republican* and assigned control to John E. Hayes, a Massachusetts journalist who was covering the war for the *New York Tribune*. Hayes bought the press and printing materials of the Beaufort *Free South* and was soon publishing the *Savannah Daily*

Republican. Early in January 1865, S. W. Mason arrived from the Sea Islands with the press of the *Palmetto Herald,* moved into the offices of the *Savannah News,* and began publishing the *Daily Herald.* The *Savannah Daily Republican* and the *Daily Herald* benefited from War Department patronage, strongly supported the Union war effort, and encouraged Georgians to declare their loyalty to the federal government. Eventually Hayes's sheet backed the Republicans, while Mason supported the Democrats, but in 1865 neither paper took a partisan stand and neither editor asked Seward for printing patronage.[16]

In April 1862, the Union Navy penetrated Confederate defenses near the mouth of the Mississippi River and landed a force that occupied New Orleans. With the encouragement of Generals Benjamin Butler and Nathaniel P. Banks, Louisiana Unionists soon organized a government and began publishing several Unionist newspapers. Both generals were eager to build a base for the Republican Party in the state, and before the war's close, the party had emerged in Louisiana. Butler, who took command of the occupation forces in 1862, quickly became involved in newspaper operations. He suspended several papers for short intervals and shut down the *Crescent* and *Commercial Bulletin,* both of which resumed after the war. Butler also seized the *Daily Delta* press, turning it over to military officers, who published it until February 1863. At that point two Northern journalists, A. C. and A. G. Hill, took over its offices and began publishing the *New Orleans Era.* The Hills ardently supported General Butler's successor as Louisiana's military governor, General Nathaniel P. Banks, in his efforts to establish a Unionist and Republican government in the state.[17]

Early in 1863, Louisiana Unionists formed a Free State General Committee to secure the restoration of a loyal Louisiana. The most prominent spokesman for the Free State movement, Thomas J. Durant, hoped not only to abolish slavery in the state but also to enfranchise its black inhabitants. Eagerly he and his followers pressed Banks's subordinate in New Orleans, General George F. Shepley, to register loyal voters and to call for an election to a constitutional convention to reorganize the state. Finding the *Era*'s editors suspicious of their efforts, Durant and his followers established the *New Orleans Times* in September 1863. The paper's chief proprietor was Thomas P. May, a wealthy Unionist planter. George Denison, a treasury agent, also invested in it, and John R. Hamilton, a former *New York Times* correspondent, became its editor.[18]

In December 1863, eager to facilitate the organization of a loyal government in Louisiana, President Lincoln announced a Reconstruction plan. Lincoln's plan would allow a new government to assume power if as few as 10 percent of the state's voters would take an oath of future loyalty and vote for new state officials. Lincoln also gave Banks complete control of Louisiana's Reconstruction process, thereby undercutting Durant and his Free State party. Consequently Louisiana's Free State movement split into two wings, with Durant on one side and Banks's supporters on the other. The Banks men hoped to stage a constitutional convention and then elect one of their own, Michael Hahn, as governor. The distinction between the two groups was not too clear: both favored emancipation, supported Lincoln, and could be regarded as Republican. The Durant wing favored enfranchising the freedmen, a step the more moderate Banks-Hahn Republicans were reluctant to take.[19]

In January 1864, New Orleans acquired another Unionist paper when Hahn, who had been a journalist before the war, bought control of the *Daily True Delta*. When Secretary of State Seward asked Banks which Louisiana papers should get federal printing, the general named the *Era* and the *True Delta*. Both papers backed Banks and voiced opposition to Durant and his supporters, often by appealing to white racial prejudices. This white supremacist rhetoric irritated May and Denison, the proprietors of the *New Orleans Times*. Although their paper sought to be neutral regarding the party split, occasionally the *Times* read like a radical sheet, publishing speeches of Massachusetts senator Charles Sumner, for example, and criticizing Lincoln's lenient amnesty program. By the summer of 1864, however, the *Times* began steering closer to the Hahn camp. Its editors warned against elevating the freedmen too rapidly and claimed that since blacks would remain "hewers of wood and drawers of water," their education should be limited to self-supporting industrial schools. The paper eventually supported Banks and the 1864 Free State constitution his followers drew up. In the gubernatorial election that followed, the Banks forces easily elected Hahn over the candidate of the Durant wing of the Free State party. The victors indicated their support of Lincoln and the Republicans by sending to the party's 1864 national convention a delegation pledged to renominating and reelecting the president.[20]

Disappointed with the *Times*'s editorial stance, Durant and his radical followers looked to the free African Americans of New Orleans for journalistic support. The city had the Deep South's largest free black community. Its members were mostly light-skinned descendants of black women and French settlers, and many were well educated and wealthy. In September 1862, a small group of free blacks had founded *L'Union*, a French-language paper that became the first black newspaper outside the North. Its chief editor Paul Trevigne, a free man of color, boldly championed equal rights for the city's free blacks. Early in 1863, white French immigrant Jean-Charles Houzeau began writing for it and soon obtained a voice in its management. At his urging the paper began publishing in English as well as French. Durant started to publish political announcements in *L'Union,* and after the Free State movement split, the paper supported the radical proposal to recognize suffrage for the state's freedmen. This position incurred the wrath of General Banks, who ordered the army occupation forces to stop subsidizing the paper. Local whites talked openly of destroying *L'Union*'s printing plant, but this proved unnecessary. The paper's readership remained small, limited chiefly to the French-speaking free colored community in New Orleans. Deprived of U.S. printing patronage, the paper published its last issue on July 19, 1864.[21]

Two days after *L'Union*'s collapse a new black newspaper appeared, the *New Orleans Tribune,* edited first by Trevigne and then by Houzeau. Although Houzeau was white, the paper's owners, who had purchased the press and other equipment from *L'Union,* came from New Orleans's free colored community. The founder and principal owner of the *Tribune,* Dr. Louis Charles Roudanez, was a native-born Louisiana mulatto who had obtained his medical education in France. On October 4, 1864, Houzeau began publishing a daily edition, making the *Tribune* the nation's first African American daily. The *Tribune* quickly established itself as an outspoken advocate of freedmen's rights. Its editors harshly criticized General Banks's labor policies and faulted Lincoln's Reconstruction plan, the 1864 Louisiana Constitution, and the Hahn government. They also defended Durant, whose ideas significantly influenced the economic program that Houzeau championed in their columns.[22]

So strong were the *Tribune*'s attacks on Thomas Conway, the head of Louisiana's Freedmen's Bureau, that he encouraged military authorities to suppress the paper. Failing in this, Conway and other federal officials helped finance a short-lived publication, the *Black Republican.* Its editor, S. W. Rodgers, was a former slave, while one of its associate editors, Caesar Carpentier Antoine, a member of the city's free black community, had been a member of the 7th Louisiana Colored Infantry. Antoine was subsequently elected the state's lieutenant governor. The paper, first issued April 15, 1865, lasted only a few weeks. It defended the U.S. government and Banks's labor policy and advocated impartial, rather than universal, suffrage.[23]

Two German-language newspapers published in New Orleans supported the Unionist cause during the war. The *Louisiana Staats-Zeitung* backed Durant and the radicals and attempted to tar the other German-language paper, the *Deutsche Zeitung,* as pro-Confederate. The *Staats-Zeitung* disappeared in 1864, leaving its rival with a monopoly of German-language newspaper readers. The *Deutsche Zeitung*'s political position shifted several times in the next few years, perhaps as a function of fluctuating government patronage. Eventually it backed the Republicans.[24]

During the war, Louisiana's Unionist government exerted little influence beyond New Orleans, its environs, and the sugar-producing regions south of the city. The only Republican papers were published in New Orleans, and by the war's end their numbers were diminishing. In September 1864, Thomas May retired from the *Times* and sold it to conservatives who withdrew the paper from the Republican camp. The proprietors of the *True Delta* and the *Era*, proving incapable of building circulation or advertising, survived on patronage from the federal government and the Unionist Louisiana state government. The 1864 Louisiana constitutional convention spent $7,000 for printing and $4,237 for purchasing newspapers for its delegates. To the disgust of those at the *Times*, most of this largesse accrued to the *True Delta*, which the *Times* alleged was "without circulation, position, or influence." After becoming governor, Hahn made the *True Delta* the state's official organ and its editor, William A. Fish, state printer. A. C. Hill of the *Era* purchased an interest in the *True Delta* and tried unsuccessfully to merge it with his paper; the *Era* then disappeared. In January 1865, after Louisiana's legislature elected Hahn to the U.S. Senate, he sold the *True Delta*. Under its new owners the paper embraced conservative policies, and it disappeared early in 1866. This left only the *New Orleans Tribune* supporting the Republican Party, which barely clung to existence in the state.[25]

The centers of Unionist strength that emerged during the war in Virginia, North and South Carolina, Georgia, Florida, and Louisiana were generally located in urban areas along waterways controlled by the Union Navy or along those states' coastal peripheries. Cities such as Alexandria, Norfolk, Jacksonville, Savannah, and New Orleans had large numbers of Northern natives who were indifferent or hostile to the Confederacy. Many of them were businessmen eager to restore Northern trade connections. Most of the Unionist papers in these areas were established by Northerners—army officers, treasury agents, or journalists. In contrast to New Orleans and its vicinity, however, these Atlantic Coast enclaves were too small to sustain effective Union governments. Lincoln sent emissaries to the east coasts of Florida and North Carolina to attempt organizing Unionist governments in those states, but such efforts collapsed. Among the Confederate states on the Atlantic Coast, only Virginia had a Unionist government, and its influence was limited to Alexandria and Norfolk.[26]

In a number of Confederate states, pockets of Unionist strength emerged among the native whites in interior counties. Most of these Southern Unionists lived in the mountainous regions of western Virginia and North Carolina, eastern Tennessee, northern Georgia and Alabama, and northwest Arkansas. Counties in these areas were isolated from the rest of their states; they had few slaves or plantations, and many of their inhabitants had opposed secession. Before the war's end, these regions of the South would furnish at least three-quarters of the approximately one hundred thousand Southern whites who enlisted in the Union Army. Unfortunately for such Southern white Unionists, the Union Army was slow to reach them, and hence they remained relatively unorganized and at the mercy of Confederate forces. Very early in the war, Union troops did move into counties in northwestern Virginia, and with their protection local Unionists managed to separate from the Old Dominion and establish and control the new state of West Virginia. Not until later in the war, however, did Union forces penetrate other parts of the Appalachian chain reaching south from Wheeling into the heart of the Confederacy.[27]

In April 1862, at the same time Union forces were occupying New Orleans, federal armies operating in central Tennessee seized Nashville, the state's capital. During the remainder of the war, Union officers published ten military newspapers in central Tennessee, but none lasted very long. Shortly after Union forces arrived in Nashville, the city acquired two papers that promoted Tennessee's restoration to the Union, the *Daily Nashville Union* and the *Daily Press*. Both were established with help from Andrew Johnson, an eastern Tennessee Unionist senator whom Lincoln would shortly appoint state military governor. To edit the *Union*, Johnson imported S. C. Mercer from Kentucky, and Johnson's longtime friend and private secretary, Benjamin C. Truman, edited the *Press*. Johnson secured a federal printing contract for the *Union*. At the end of 1863, Mercer left the *Union* to edit a new paper, the *Daily Times and True Union*, which began publication in February of the following year. At Johnson's request, Seward transferred U.S. printing patronage from the *Union* to Mercer's new paper. All three papers supported Johnson's efforts to organize a state government based on "Unconditional Unionists" who had consistently opposed secession and the Confederate government.[28]

After Memphis, Tennessee, fell to Union troops early in 1862, several army papers appeared there, none of which lasted. In April 1863, federal authorities seized control of the few newspapers still publishing in the city. They turned over the *Memphis Bulletin* to J. B. Bingham, a local journalist and friend of Andrew Johnson. Bingham used it to support Johnson's efforts at restoring the state on a loyal basis. Germans in Memphis also established a Unionist paper, *Die Neue Zeit*. The city's most outspoken Unionist newspaper was the *Memphis Weekly Republican*, which was the only paper in Tennessee to declare affiliation with the Republican Party before the war's end. Its editor, B. F. C. Brooks, was a Mississippi doctor who had arrived in Memphis in 1854. In 1861 Brooks's open anti-secession stance incited a mob that chased him from the city. After Union forces occupied Memphis, he resumed publication of his paper, using its columns to chastise the rebels. In 1864 Brooks recommended the radical Republican congressman Thaddeus Stevens for the presidency.[29]

Despite Union occupation of Nashville and Memphis, Union sentiment in these cities was not as strong as it was in the eastern third of Tennessee. Most inhabitants of this region had strongly resisted secession, and even under Confederate occupation, many remained loyal to the Union. Union troops did not occupy this area until the end of 1863, and in the meantime eastern Tennessee suffered heavily from internal conflicts between Union and Confederate guerrilla bands. These often savage conflicts created deep-seated animosities that outlived the war and shaped the politics of the region and the state. Many of these beleaguered Unionists would eventually become Republicans.[30]

In October 1863, William G. Brownlow, an ardent Unionist editor from Knoxville whose denunciation of the Confederacy had led to his arrest and expulsion from the state early in 1862, returned home with the occupying Union Army. Federal officers helped him revive his paper, renamed the *Knoxville Whig and Rebel Ventilator*, by providing him with a new printing press, type, and $1,500. Brownlow filled his columns with denunciations of the rebels, and at Johnson's request, Seward rewarded him with a U.S. government printing contract. In February 1864, under similar federal protection, Chattanooga Unionist editor James R. Hood reopened his paper, the *Gazette*, which he had earlier been forced to abandon. Both Brownlow and Hood helped organize a Unionist party in eastern Tennessee.[31]

Divisions soon appeared in Tennessee Unionist ranks. Conservative Unionists criticized Johnson for interfering in elections, especially for attempting to limit the franchise through test oaths. They also opposed Johnson's efforts to abolish slavery in the state. One Unionist newspaper, the Nashville *Daily Press*, now under Edwin Paschal's editorship, echoed these views. In 1864, many of the conservative Unionists, including Paschal, backed the Democratic presidential candidate, George B. McClellan. Their opponents, known as Unconditional Unionists, sent delegates to the Republican national convention in Baltimore and supported its nominees, Lincoln and Johnson. The following September, when Tennessee's Unionists convened in Nashville, the Unconditionals denounced their conservative opponents as "copperheads" and expelled them from the assembly.[32] Except for the Nashville *Press*, the Unionist papers all supported the Unconditionals. All of them endorsed emancipation and advocated stringent disfranchisement to prevent former slaveholders and Confederates from gaining power in the state. After the 1864 presidential election, Mercer, Bingham, Brownlow, and Hood endorsed a convention in Nashville the following January. The session abolished slavery in Tennessee and arranged for elections to organize a new state government. In the ensuing election, Brownlow was chosen governor, along with a legislature firmly in Unionist hands. To cement their hold on power, Unionist legislators passed a voting registration law disfranchising supporters of the Confederacy.[33]

Like Tennessee, Arkansas harbored a significant Unionist minority that had opposed secession. Unionists tended to predominate in the state's more mountainous northwestern counties. Soon after the war began, a peace society emerged in this area. The strains of the war, and particularly Confederate conscription, contributed to unrest, and by mid-1863 organized resistance to the Confederacy also began appearing in the southwestern counties of Arkansas. Northwest Arkansas Unionists were often victims of partisan raids and guerrilla attacks similar to those experienced by their Tennessee counterparts.[34]

The Union Army's advance into Arkansas encouraged Unionists to come forward. On September 1, 1863, Union forces arrived in Fort Smith, near the western border, and soon two Union papers appeared there. The first, the *Fort Smith Union*, edited by an army attaché, soon disappeared; but the other, the *Fort Smith New Era*, survived for twenty-two years. Its editor, Valentine Dell, was an 1846 German immigrant who had moved to Fort Smith in 1859. His first issue appeared on October 8, 1863. Dell denounced the Southern aristocracy that he claimed had precipitated the war, and he played a leading role in organizing the state's Unionist party.[35] The Arkansas capital, Little Rock, fell to Union forces a week after Fort Smith, and two weeks later Dr. C. V. Meador, who in 1860 had supported Democrat Stephen A. Douglas's presidential candidacy, began publication of the *National Democrat*. On January 23, 1864, a second Unionist paper appeared in Little Rock, the *Unconditional Unionist*, controlled by William M. Fishback and edited by T. D. Yonley, both Union veterans. A fourth Unionist paper, the *Western Clarion*, appeared in Helena in eastern Arkansas just as the war ended.[36]

As in Louisiana and Tennessee, so also in Arkansas the federal troops' arrival encouraged the formation of a party seeking readmission to the Union. In Arkansas, too, the Unionist movement divided, with the more conservative members opposing the radical wing's call for emancipation and large-scale disfranchisement of former Confederates. In this split, Meador and his *National Democrat* supported the conservatives, while the *Unconditional Unionist*, *New Era*, and *Western Clarion* backed the radicals. As in Tennessee, these issues were settled in Arkansas by a state convention. The Arkansas convention assembled in January 1864. Its members, who included Valentine Dell, abolished slavery and provided for elections the following March to staff a Unionist government for the state. The voters chose Isaac Murphy, a Unionist leader from north Arkansas, as governor. Foreshadowing Tennessee developments, the Unconditional Unionist legislators secured their hold on power by disfranchising voluntary supporters of the Confederacy. Supportive of the Arkansas radicals, the United States government provided printing patronage to the *Unconditional Unionist* and the *Western Clarion*. That summer the Unconditionals sent delegates, including Dell, to the Republican national convention that renominated Lincoln. Not until 1867, however, did the Republican Party organize in Arkansas.[37]

During the war, the Confederacy faced significant internal opposition in a number of other Southern states where Unionist governments were not organized. This opposition came from several sources, only one of which was actual or latent loyalty to the Union. As the war proceeded, more and more Southerners became alienated from the Confederate government because of its policies of conscription, impressment, imposition of taxes in kind, and occasional suspension of the writ of habeas corpus. Disillusioned with the lack of Confederate victories, many simply wanted an end to the war.

Such discontent with the Confederacy was notable in North Carolina, and U.S. authorities hoped to tap support there for the Union. Like Tennessee and Virginia, the Tarheel State also suffered from internal divisions sharpened by the Civil War. Most North Carolinians did not own slaves, and many in the western counties resented the fact that the state's legislative apportionment and taxation systems favored the wealthier east, where slaveholders dominated. Although North Carolina eventually furnished more volunteers to the Confederate Army than any other state, dissatisfaction with the Confederate government rose as the war progressed. As early as 1861, a secret society called the Heroes of America emerged in the North Carolina Piedmont counties. This group and others like it, such as the Red Shirts, encouraged desertions from the Confederate Army and sought protection for Union sympathizers. W. I. Vestal, an associate editor of the New Bern *North Carolina Times*, helped found the Heroes of America. Organized war resistance also surfaced in North Carolina's western mountains, where conditions verged on anarchy.[38]

By 1863, two Raleigh newspapers were expressing dissatisfaction with the war and exploring possibilities for peace. One of them, the Raleigh *Weekly Progress*, was edited by J. L. Pennington, a North Carolinian and former slaveholder. This paper apparently had been published in both Raleigh and New Bern until Union occupiers of the latter town turned its offices over to George Mills Joy. Although a secession opponent, Pennington had stuck by his state after it left the Union. But by 1863 he was disillusioned with the war, bitterly critical of the Confederate administration in Richmond, and ready to explore the possibility of taking

North Carolina out of the war. The editor of the second Raleigh paper, William Holden of the *North Carolina Standard,* was more outspoken than Pennington in his criticism of the Confederacy. Holden had played a leading role in the state Democratic Party prior to the war, when he had ardently defended Southern rights. His sympathies for the common man and his party's western nonslaveholding members, however, led him to oppose secession. Like Pennington, he acquiesced in North Carolina's decision to leave the Union but soon became alienated from the Confederate government. Although Holden had no connection with the Heroes of America, his overt opposition to the Confederacy alienated him from the state's white majority. In 1863, a mob led by Confederate soldiers sacked his press, but he soon resumed publication, and in 1864 he ran for governor on a platform calling for North Carolina's negotiated withdrawal from the war. The voters overwhelmingly rejected Holden; what support he received came largely from counties around Raleigh and in the central Piedmont and northwest.[39]

In South Carolina, there was almost no discernible Unionist activity away from the seacoast. This state was the first to secede, and its white population appeared more united behind the Confederacy than that in any other state. Although the vast majority of Georgia's whites supported the Confederacy, significant Unionist sentiment existed in the northern counties. Yet many people in this area were not so much pro-Union as anti-war or anti-Confederacy. The region was full of army deserters, and a peace movement also appeared in some of these counties. Dissatisfaction with the war grew as the conflict wore on, and armed bands, plundering without concern for anyone's political loyalties, plunged parts of northern Georgia into near anarchy. No one like Holden emerged in Georgia, however, to organize Unionist discontent. Although Sherman's army marched through northern Georgia in 1864 en route to Atlanta, the general did not occupy much of the region, and no Unionist party or newspaper appeared there. Not until Sherman reached Savannah in December did two Unionist papers, the *Republican* and the *Herald,* appear in the state.[40]

Distinct geographical differences also divided Alabama. Prior to the war, the state's central counties, which contained most of Alabama's plantations and slaves, dominated the state economically and politically. Nonslaveholders in the northern counties and in the Wiregrass area of southeastern Alabama resented this domination. Opposition to secession was especially strong in the north, and once hostilities began, signs of disaffection from the Confederacy—particularly desertions from its army—surfaced there. Early in 1862, federal forces occupied Alabama counties north of the Tennessee River. Although the occupation troops destroyed rebel printing presses there, no Unionist press emerged in this region until after the end of the war. As in parts of North Carolina, sections of Alabama verged on anarchy, and hostilities sharpened by these events helped shape the state's postwar politics. Many Alabama Unionists would become Republicans.[41]

Union forces also occupied Mississippi's northernmost counties and eventually obtained control of river towns like Vicksburg and Natchez. These forces occasionally destroyed presses, and in Vicksburg and Natchez they seized rebel papers and published them as Union sheets until the war's end. Vicksburg had harbored a small Unionist band since the beginning of the war, and once Union troops arrived, a number of prominent citizens took an oath of allegiance to the federal government. In 1864, Ira Batterton, a Union Army veteran from Illinois, began publishing the *Vicksburg Herald*, which he touted as the state's only Unionist daily. When asked by Seward to recommend a Mississippi paper for publishing the U.S. laws, General Nathaniel Banks named the *Herald*, and in January 1865 Seward awarded this patronage to Batterton. Vicksburg had little contact with the growing war disaffection that swept the central part of Mississippi, where large numbers of Confederate deserters gathered and resistance to Confederate authority was widespread. Much of this disloyalty to the Confederacy in Mississippi could not, however, be equated with loyalty to the Union. More likely it was a reflection of the persistently independent attitudes of backwoods Mississippians.[42]

During the war, Lincoln made no attempt to organize Unionist governments in Georgia, Alabama, or Mississippi. He did try to establish a Union regime in the Confederacy's westernmost state, Texas. That state also produced a significant amount of dissent from the Confederacy. One estimate is that only a third of whites in Texas were ardent Confederate supporters. Texas was also beset by internal geographical divisions. The east-central counties that were home to most of the state's plantation agriculture had dominated the prewar government, creating jealousies in regions to the north, east, and west, areas that were less developed and lacked adequate communications. Disagreements over secession exacerbated these divisions. Prior to the war, the state's governor, Sam Houston, had organized a Union party in an attempt to keep Texas from leaving the United States. After the war began, disaffection quickly appeared in the northern counties, which had a few slaves and a number of Northern immigrants, and it soon spread into other parts of Texas. Prominent Unionists faced abuse and violence that drove a number of them out of the state. Others attempted to remain neutral during the conflict; a few, loyal to their state, joined the Confederate effort.[43]

One of the Texas émigrés was Andrew Jackson Hamilton, an attorney and former congressman who fled the state to avoid arrest by Confederate authorities. In the North he gained the attention of President Lincoln, who appointed him Texas military governor in 1862. Unfortunately for Hamilton and his fellow Unionists, U.S. forces had little success in occupying any portion of the state, and the move to establish a Unionist government there fizzled, to be revived after Appomattox. In December 1864, when Secretary Seward inquired about loyal papers in Texas, General Banks claimed there were none.[44]

Thus, as the war ended, Republican prospects for converting Unionist sentiment into support for their party varied considerably from state to state, depending in large part upon how well organized the local Unionists were. Clearly, however, these wartime Unionists had created the basis for a Republican press in the South. By the time the guns fell silent at Appomattox, at least twenty-seven Unionist papers existed in the states of the former Confederacy. Most of these papers were located in states that had experienced significant divisions regarding secession: there were seven in Tennessee, five in North Carolina, and four in Arkansas; Florida had three, and Virginia, Georgia, and Louisiana two each. There was one Unionist paper in South Carolina, one in Mississippi, and none in Alabama or Texas. Of these publications, at least seven were backing the Republican Party in 1865: the Alexandria *Virginia State Journal*, Norfolk *Old Dominion*, Beaufort *New South*, the *Jacksonville Herald*, Jacksonville *Florida Union*, *New Orleans Tribune*, and *Memphis Weekly Republican*. Another ten of these papers, four from Tennessee, became Republican after the party was organized in their states.[45] Most of the rest disappeared within a year or two.[46] Only four, the *Nashville Union*, Raleigh *Weekly Progress*, *Vicksburg Herald*, and *Savannah Daily Herald*, eventually opposed the Republicans.[47]

CHAPTER TWO

Limited Expansion

At the end of the war, the number of Southern white Unionists, many of whom would become a major source of white Republican recruits in the former Confederacy, varied considerably from state to state. The states with the strongest wartime Unionist movements were those that had been deeply divided over secession in 1861, had subsequently experienced wrenching internal conflict between Confederate and Union supporters, and had undergone some period of federal occupation. The foremost example of this was Tennessee, followed by Arkansas, and Unionists were in control of both states. Unionists also controlled the reconstructed governments of Louisiana and Virginia, where their power was based in cities like New Orleans, Alexandria, and Norfolk. Pockets of Unionist sentiment of varying degrees of intensity existed in the seven other former Confederate states, but because of Lincoln's inability to organize loyal governments in any of them before the war's end, Unionists there were disorganized and politically powerless. With the exception of William Holden's Raleigh *North Carolina Standard,* the few Unionist publications in these states were located on the coastal fringes of the Carolinas, Georgia, and Florida, and only a couple of these could be considered Republican in 1865. The future did not look bright for the Republican Party in the South.

Of the four ex-Confederate states with Unionist governments at the end of the war—Tennessee, Virginia, Louisiana, and Arkansas—only Tennessee had more than a handful of whites who could claim loyalty to the Union throughout the war. These "Unconditional" or "straitest sect" Unionists hoped to control their states either by disfranchising those who had sustained the Confederacy or by bidding for the votes of reluctant Confederates who were also willing to swear future loyalty to the Union. A small but growing minority of Republican Unionists pushed a third alternative, arguing that only by enfranchising the freedmen could Unionists keep their states out of the hands of former secessionists. Although postwar freedmen's conventions in some Southern states endorsed this approach, it found little favor among white Unionists until late in 1866.

In Tennessee, Virginia, and Arkansas, Unionist leaders had opted for disfranchisement before the war ended and had either written such provisions into their constitutions or passed legislation to the same effect. Louisiana Unionists decided not to follow this course. The state's lieutenant governor, James Madison Wells, who became acting governor after the legislature sent Michael Hahn to the U.S. Senate, sought to broaden the Unionists' base by appointing ex-Confederates to office and extending the vote to anyone swearing an oath of future loyalty to the government. Consequently, returning ex-Confederates easily gained control of the state legislature in November 1865.[1]

Virginia's Unionist government headed by Francis Pierpont had a base as limited as Wells's in Louisiana. West Virginia's wartime secession had reduced Pierpont's jurisdiction to Virginia's Eastern Shore and the Alexandria and Norfolk environs. His government drew support primarily from Unionist Whigs and a few Democrats as well as the Old Dominion's handful of Republicans. Only two Unionist newspapers, the Alexandria *Virginia State Journal* and the Norfolk *Old Dominion*, survived the war, and they both supported the Republican Party. To the despair of the Alexandria *State Journal*'s editor, at the war's close Pierpont, like Wells, sought to expand his limited base by appealing to men who had been cool to secession but had supported the Confederacy. Hence he convinced the Unionist legislature to eliminate the state's voting disqualifications. In the October 1865 elections, a flood of ex-Confederate ballots easily defeated almost all the Unionist candidates for the state legislature and Congress, just as they had in Louisiana.[2]

In Arkansas, Isaac Murphy's Unionist government chose not to follow Wells's and Pierpont's course; after the war it continued to deny the vote to ex-Confederates. In December 1865, however, the Arkansas Supreme Court dealt the Murphy government a fatal blow by declaring the state's disfranchising laws unconstitutional. In the August 1866 elections, Unionists lost control of the legislature and most state offices other than the governorship. This left Tennessee as the only Southern state in Unionist hands. There Governor Brownlow maintained control of the state through measures disfranchising ex-Confederates and giving himself power to appoint voting registrars.[3]

The future of civil governments in the remaining seven former Confederate states depended on Lincoln's successor, President Andrew Johnson, who in the summer of 1865 announced his plan to restore them to the Union. His program appeared to offer hope to the Unionists in these states. Johnson had created his own political career in Tennessee by campaigning against slaveholding aristocrats, and he hoped to use Reconstruction in these states to bring to power a new Unionist leadership based on yeoman farmers. Johnson appointed provisional governors to administer these seven states until they had reorganized their governments and held elections for state and congressional officials. Although Johnson opened these elections to anyone who would swear future loyalty to the Union, he exempted from this amnesty major Confederate officials and owners of property worth more than $20,000. Unconditional Unionists in the South were pleased by this, for they too wanted to displace the "slaveocracy" that they claimed had dominated their states and led them into secession.[4]

In South Carolina, Florida, Georgia, and Mississippi, wartime Unionists were too weak to have much impact on the fall 1865 elections for state office and for Congress. In these states, the few Unionist papers that had appeared during the war had little influence. In South Carolina the Beaufort *New South* circulated mainly among a few literate blacks and the handful of Northerners in the Sea Islands. In Georgia, Savannah's two Unionist papers showed more signs of life, but like the Jacksonville *Herald* in Florida, they had little influence among the masses of white voters in their states. Ira Batterton, editor of the Unionist *Vicksburg Herald*, died in 1865, robbing Unionists in that state of any effective newspaper voice until the Republican Party organized there in 1867. The 1865 elections in these four states proved disappointing to Unionists, as voters returned to state and congressional office candidates who had been secession opponents but who had supported the Confederacy after the war began.[5]

In the months following Appomattox, Unionists began stirring in Alabama, especially in the northern part of the state. In July 1865, they obtained a newspaper voice with the appearance of the *Huntsville Advocate*. William Figures, its editor and publisher, was a native Alabamian who had learned the newspaper business at an early age. Before the war he had been Huntsville's mayor, and in 1861 he was editor and proprietor of the Huntsville *Southern Advocate*. A former Whig, Figures had backed Stephen A. Douglas in the 1860 presidential election and had opposed secession. Subsequently he supported the Confederacy and was elected to the Alabama state senate. Union forces arriving in Huntsville suspended his paper for the duration of the war. When the conflict ended, Figures resumed publication, using his paper to urge Northern Alabamians to wrest control of the state from the Black Belt aristocrats who had controlled it at their expense.[6] In 1865, Alabama voters elected as governor Robert M. Patton, an antebellum Whig from northern Alabama. During the war Patton had raised money for the Confederacy, but he had also maintained contacts with the state's wartime Unionists. Five of the six congressmen elected by Alabamians had opposed secession in 1861 but had subsequently supported the Confederacy. A number of consistent Unionists protested some of these results, claiming that power was slipping away from them. Most accepted the new conditions, however, and threw their support behind Johnson's Reconstruction program.[7]

At the war's conclusion, North Carolina and Texas Unionists appeared to have at least a fighting chance of gaining control of their states. In North Carolina Johnson had appointed Unionist leader William Holden provisional governor. Holden used the power of his office to withhold pardons and make appointments, hoping to build a reliable Unionist organization that would elect him governor in November 1865. His own paper, the Raleigh *North Carolina Standard,* championed his candidacy, as did two Unionist papers founded in 1865, the Salisbury *Daily Union Banner* and the *Wilmington Herald.* He also gained support from the Charlotte *Western Democrat.* Unfortunately for Holden's chances, his appointment policies alienated as many as they pleased, and he was already very unpopular with large numbers of North Carolinians who had supported the Confederacy. In November, Jonathan Worth, a former Whig Unionist who had been a member of the state's Confederate government, easily defeated Holden for the governorship.[8]

Holden and his Unionist party remained alive, however, and continued to struggle for newspaper support. In 1866, the Salisbury and Wilmington papers that had backed him the previous year disappeared, and J. L. Pennington sold his Raleigh *Progress* to more conservative publishers. In May 1866, however, Holden gained a new journalistic ally in western North Carolina when Alexander H. Jones established the *Henderson Pioneer.* During the war, Jones, a former Whig, had twice run for the state legislature as a peace candidate and had been impressed into Confederate service and then imprisoned. He had managed to escape and with his son joined the Union Army. He was North Carolina's only 1865 congressional candidate who could take the test oath and was elected to that office both then and in the following year. By the late fall, two other Unionist papers in the state, the New Bern *Weekly Times* and the *Rutherford Star,* also endorsed Holden's Unionist party. In November 1866, however, the Unionists passed over Holden and nominated Jones as their gubernatorial candidate. Jones lost to Worth by a three-to-one margin.[9]

At the end of the war, Texas Unionists also mounted a bid to control their state. Johnson's appointee as its provisional governor, Andrew Jackson Hamilton, was a tried and true Unionist who in 1864 had campaigned for Lincoln in the North. Hamilton and his Unionist followers hoped to revive the prewar coalition opposed to the dominance of east-central Texas and ride that coalition into power. Unfortunately, divisions caused by the war cut across these regional lines, and Hamilton was a poor choice to overcome them. His blustering, intense personal style, similar to Brownlow's in Tennessee and Holden's in North Carolina, generated as many enemies as friends. Aware of his lack of support, Hamilton was able to delay a state election until June 1866 and used the intervening time to organize his Unionist following more effectively. Although his backers wanted to run him for governor, Hamilton refused, and they turned to former governor E. M. Pease. The Pease-Hamilton Unionists opposed ex-Confederate participation in the state's Reconstruction and they stood ready to accept basic civil rights for the freedmen. Pease faced J. W. Throckmorton, the nominee of a coalition of more conservative Unionists and former secessionists who opposed any rights for the former slaves.[10]

By 1866, Hamilton could rely on the support of several newspapers: *Flake's Bulletin* in Galveston, the *Southern Intelligencer* in Austin, the *San Antonio Express*, and the *Freie Presse fur Texas*, published in the same city. The men associated with these papers were all immigrants, although they had lived in Texas for years. Ferdinand Flake, editor of the Galveston paper, had immigrated to that city from Germany in 1843 and established two German-language newspapers there. Unlike many Germans in Texas, Flake was not opposed to slavery and even owned a slave. He was dismayed, however, by the increasingly pro-slavery position of the state Democratic Party and left it in 1859. The following year Flake backed Houston's Union party and supported Stephen A. Douglas for president. During the secession crisis, he was a conditional Unionist, claiming that Texans should wait to see what course Lincoln would take toward the South. This position did not satisfy Texan fire-eaters, who stormed his office in January 1861 and wrecked his press. Flake decided to submit to the will of his neighbors, and during the war remained in Galveston, where he warned against Northern domination of the South. In June 1865, he began publishing *Flake's Bulletin* and used its columns to champion Hamilton's Union party.[11]

Another German, August Siemering, who had arrived in Texas around 1849, founded the San Antonio *Freie Presse fur Texas* in 1865 and the *Express* the following year. Although opposed to slavery, Siemering had joined the Confederate Army and thus did not experience the hostility that Flake endured. Yet a *Freie Presse* associate editor, Theodore Herzberg, had been forced to flee the state during the war because of his antislavery views. The proprietor of the fourth Unionist paper, the Austin *Southern Intelligencer*, was the Norwegian-born, Ohio-raised A. B. Norton. Norton had come to Texas sometime before 1855, where he became associated with the *Intelligencer*. Three times he was elected to the state legislature. A strong Unionist, he too backed Sam Houston in 1860. When the war began he went back to Ohio but returned to Texas afterward to resume publishing his Austin paper.[12]

All of these papers took part in the 1866 campaign; the *McKinney Messen-*

ger, which was also edited by a prewar Unionist, backed Pease as well. Pease's supporters appealed to whites outside central Texas by emphasizing loyalty to the Union, support for railroads into the state's underdeveloped regions, and protection for the western frontier against Indians. They denigrated Throckmorton's backers as secessionists who were still resisting U.S. authority, accusing them of planning to drive Union men out of the state and of restoring some semblance of slavery. For their part, Democrats and conservative Unionists characterized Hamilton and his followers as radicals bent on revolutionizing the state. Conservatives won an overwhelming electoral victory, proving that the Unionists had failed to create an effective coalition. The legislature chosen at that time generated patronage for Democrats and secessionists, enacted Black Codes restricting freedmen's rights, and redistricted the state so as to weaken the Unionist position further.[13]

By the summer of 1866, it was clear that outside the South's mountainous regions, the political reorganization of the former Confederate states had not created a new political leadership to replace their prewar elites. Only Tennessee's government remained in the hands of Unionists who had refused to support the Confederacy. Most of the congressmen elected from Tennessee, Virginia, and Arkansas could take the iron-clad oath that they had never aided the Confederacy, but in the lower South anti-secessionist Whigs who had supported the Confederacy dominated state governments and congressional delegations. Newly elected state legislatures passed Black Codes severely restricting the freedmen's rights. The overwhelming majority of Southern whites were satisfied with these developments and hoped to gain rapid readmission to the Union. President Johnson, despite his initial interest in placing Southern yeoman farmers in power, decided to endorse these new state governments and urged Congress to accept them without further conditions. The Republican congressional majority, however, refused to seat the Southern delegations, established a committee to review the Reconstruction process and make policy recommendations, and began preparing legislation to protect freedmen's rights.[14]

In the Southern states, Unionists were divided over how to proceed. Some, fearing Congress would turn to radical Reconstruction measures such as enfranchising blacks or confiscating ex-Confederate property, preferred Johnson's plan to restore their states. Many more Unionists were greatly disappointed with the fruits of Johnson's program but were not in agreement regarding an alternative. Comprising a small minority of voters in most Southern states, they feared revenge from former Confederates once federal troops departed. Virginia's former Unionist governor Francis Pierpont warned that once the Southern states were readmitted and the U.S. Army withdrawn, "you would not have a loyal paper in ninety days south of Mason and Dixon's line" except in North Carolina and portions of Tennessee and Kentucky. Most Southern loyalists now hoped that the congressional Republicans would protect them as well as the freedmen from the retribution of their old enemies.[15]

Although the Unionist editors whose papers had appeared during and shortly after the war were preoccupied with the fate of other whites who, like themselves, had stood by the U.S. flag, they also addressed issues of concern to blacks. They supported emancipation, not so much because slavery oppressed the slave as because they believed it retarded the South's economic growth and was harmful to nonslaveholding whites. Most agreed that emancipation would destroy the foundation of the slaveholding aristocracy that they believed had dominated and exploited the nonslaveholders. As James Hood of the *Chattanooga Gazette* explained, Tennesseans had to eradicate slavery "not because we love the negro, but because we love the government and hate the domineering, fiendish spirit which slavery breeds." Valentine Dell used the first issues of his *Fort Smith New Era* to claim that slavery was "a curse to the white man" and to urge his fellow Arkansas Unionists to abolish it in the state.[16]

After the war, a few Unionist editors were unsympathetic or even hostile toward the freedmen. Some predicted that African Americans would eventually disappear as a race or revert to a savage condition. Governor Brownlow recommended settling blacks in a separate territory, a view endorsed by the editor of the Greeneville *New Era*. According to the editor of the Jonesborough *Union Flag*, the freedmen had "but crude ideas of freedom," were indolent and thriftless, and would require close supervision. The *New Bern Times* editor recommended educating the former slaves "up to the point that will make them intelligent and useful free laborers" but also believed that some compulsory system of labor must replace slavery. In the fall of 1865, Lyman Stickney hired a conservative ex-Confederate, Holmes Steele, to edit his Unionist publication, the Jacksonville *Florida Union*. Steele warned that unless the freedman remained under the control of "his natural master, the white man," he would relapse into "his heathenish nature."[17]

Most Unionist journalists, however, opposed colonization or any compulsory labor system and contended that the freedmen would prove to be reliable and productive workers. They praised the former slaves' eagerness to learn and urged opening schools for them. Unionist editors were among the few white Southerners who criticized the Black Codes enacted by most states to restrict rights of the freedmen severely; the editor of the Austin *Southern Intelligencer* charged that the Texas codes were designed "to fetter the limbs of labor and enslave the poor." In Nashville, both the *Press and Times* and the *Daily Union* strongly supported the freedmen's right to testify in court. Other Unionist editors advocated recognizing former slaves' civil rights and sometimes spoke well of the Freedmen's Bureau at a time when such views were decidedly unpopular in the South. Unionist papers also condemned violence against the freedmen and gave full attention to race riots occurring in Memphis and New Orleans in the summer of 1866.[18]

Desperate for allies who would help them gain control of their state governments, some Unionists concluded that it would be necessary to enfranchise the freedmen, who would surely vote to return loyal men to office. As Valentine Dell expressed it, in order to "keep down the rebels," Unionists would have to allow the freedmen to vote. Conventions of blacks that met in several Southern states in 1865 and 1866 were already calling for enfranchisement, as were a number of Northern Republicans. Enfranchising blacks was a hard pill for many white Unionist editors to swallow, for their readers were strongly Negrophobic. Nonetheless, expediency eventually compelled most of them to side with the congressional Republicans in their struggle with Johnson over control of Reconstruction, for it would have to be the Republicans, not the president, who would demand black suffrage in the South.[19]

As the gap between President Johnson and the Congress widened in 1866, Unionist and Republican newspapers in the states the president had reconstructed were taking sides. Lyman Stickney, the Jacksonville *Florida Union* publisher who had denounced the Confederacy while in charge of the Fernandina *Peninsula*, began moderating his views. Now that the war was over, he announced, Florida should be restored to the Union as quickly as possible. To that end, he supported Andrew Johnson's lenient Reconstruction program. He hoped the president would organize a moderate party between the extremes of secessionist Democrats and radical Republicans. His editor, Holmes Steele, who contended that ex-Confederates could be trusted with office, was soon elected Jacksonville's mayor and a state legislator as well. Steele used the *Union*'s columns to chastise the editor of the *Jacksonville Herald* for advocating enfranchisement of the freedmen. In December 1865, the *Herald* disappeared when Harrison Reed, the former treasury agent who was now holding a post office appointment, bought the paper and began publishing a new one, the Jacksonville *Florida Times*. Reed pronounced himself satisfied with the state's newly elected governor and legislature. He condemned the idea of enfranchising the freedmen and backed Johnson's efforts to get Florida readmitted to the Union. After a few months Reed sold the *Times* to a group of Florida loyalists, and in May 1866, its new editor, W. H. Christy, began complaining that former rebels were running the state. He urged Florida Unionists to form a party with Yankee immigrants and secure control of the state, but few supported his efforts.[20]

In Georgia, the editors of the two Unionist papers founded in the last months of the Civil War also denounced the secessionists and called for loyal men to organize to control the state. John Hayes, editor of the *Savannah Daily Republican,* followed a course similar to Lyman Stickney's in Florida, urging President Johnson to build a Union party drawing support from moderate Northern Republicans, Southern loyalists, and Democratic backers of the Union war effort. S. W. Mason of the *Savannah Daily Herald* also backed Johnson and, by the summer of 1866, was condemning the Republicans and expressing support for the Democratic Party.[21] Both editors opposed enfranchising the freedmen, but a newspaper that supported such a move appeared in Georgia in October 1865, when African Americans in Augusta established the state's first avowedly Republican paper, the *Colored American.* Its proprietor, John T. Shuften, used the publication to promote civil and political equality for the state's freedmen. Early in 1866, the Georgia Equal Rights Association bought control of Shuften's paper and reissued it as the *Loyal Georgian.* The only white man to join the association, John Emory Bryant, a former Freedmen's Bureau agent from Maine, became the paper's editor.[22]

In South Carolina, the only discontent with the state's government established by President Johnson emerged in the Sea Islands and in Charleston, where blacks and a few white Northern missionaries and Freedmen's Bureau agents began to call for recognizing ex-slaves' rights. In September 1865, meetings of blacks at St. Helena and in Charleston petitioned the state's constitutional convention for the right to vote, and in November a Charleston Colored People's Convention condemned South Carolina's legislature for adopting severely restrictive Black Codes.[23]

In 1865, Northerners in South Carolina established two papers that joined the Beaufort *New South* in championing black rights. In July the *New Era* appeared in Darlington, edited by Benjamin F. Whittemore, who had spent four years in the state as a chaplain of a regiment from Massachusetts, his home state. Whittemore, who was to play an important role in the state's Republican Party, urged his readers to put away their old pro-slavery, state rights doctrines, to cooperate with the government, and to recognize the citizenship rights of the newly freed slaves. Since the Republican Party did not exist in the state, the *New Era* did not formally endorse it, but Whittemore eulogized Lincoln on his death. Printers from the 49th Pennsylvania Volunteers helped establish the second paper, the *South Carolina Leader,* which appeared in Charleston in October 1865. The paper's motto was "Free Labor and General Reform." Its editors advocated equal rights for all and informed readers that theirs was not a white man's country or government. The paper had a precarious existence, going through several changes of ownership. In March 1866, its proprietors replaced an editor who had criticized President Johnson for vetoing congressional legislation to protect the freedmen, and its columns took on a more conservative tone. In the summer of 1866, two blacks who had attended the Charleston Colored People's Convention the year before, Richard Harvey Cain and Alonzo Ransier, secured control of the paper and used it to support the Republican Party and African American suffrage. Both men had been born free, Ransier in Charleston and Cain in Virginia; Cain had arrived in Charleston as an African Methodist Episcopal missionary in 1865. The *Leader* was the city's only Republican journal until two other blacks, B. F. Randolph and E. J. Adams, founded the *Charleston Journal* in September 1866. Randolph, who had been born free in Kentucky and educated in the North, had taken part in the Charleston convention in 1865. He used the *Journal*'s columns to call for equal civil and political rights for blacks and criticized the state governor's conservative views on race.[24]

In Texas, Hamilton's supporters began to move away from Congress and toward Johnson; some began to accept the need for black suffrage. A. B. Norton of the *Southern Intelligencer* and Ferdinand Flake of *Flake's Bulletin* were not ready to take this step, however, hoping to find some position between the former secessionists backing Johnson, on the one hand, and radical Republicans on the other.

North Carolina's only Unionist paper to defend Johnson was the *New Bern Times*, but again the president's critics could not agree on what solutions to recommend. On September 30, 1865, Edward P. Brooks, a Wisconsin Union Army veteran living in Raleigh, published the first issue of his *Journal of Freedom*, calling for equal rights, including the vote, for the state's freedmen. Brooks anticipated that his views would be unpopular among whites in the state, a fact reflected in the absence of any advertisements in his columns. After struggling for a month, his paper disappeared. The only other North Carolina paper to advocate suffrage for blacks, Albion Tourgee's *Greensboro Union Register*, did not publish its first issue until late in 1866. The Raleigh *Daily Progress* opposed suffrage for African Americans, as did Holden's *North Carolina Standard*, the *Rutherford Star,* and the *New Bern Times*.[25]

In Alabama, William Figures used the columns of his *Huntsville Advocate* to urge his fellow Unionists to ally with congressional Republicans, but he opposed giving blacks the right to vote. In December 1865, the state's first avowedly Republican paper, the Mobile *Nationalist*, appeared, and its editors supported suffrage for the freedmen. African Americans in Mobile owned the paper and staffed its board of directors. Two white carpetbaggers, John Silsby and then Albert Griffin, edited the paper, but many others who worked for it were black and went on to become involved in Reconstruction politics. Silsby, a Wisconsonite, was a Union Army veteran who had come to Alabama as a missionary for the American Missionary Association; he was also a Freedmen's Bureau agent. Griffin, who took over the editorship in April 1866, had lived in Georgia before the war but because of his antislavery views opted to leave for the North. After the war he moved to Mobile and began a law practice. Along with the *New Orleans Tribune*, the *Nationalist* soon became one of the South's leading newspaper advocates of freedmen's rights, including suffrage.[26]

Unionists in Arkansas, Louisiana, and Virginia also struggled to unite on a policy that would enable them to regain control of their states. In Arkansas, only Valentine Dell's *Fort Smith New Era* backed suffrage for the freedmen. In Louisiana, radical Republicans led by Thomas Durant renewed their campaign for black suffrage. They gained support from a handful of Northerners led by Henry Clay Warmoth, who had arrived in the state with the Union Army, together with some conservative Louisiana Unionists who had earlier supported Hahn and who now agreed that universal suffrage was essential for their regaining power in the state. In September 1865, these groups met to revive Louisiana's Republican Party. At this point the only paper to support them was the *New Orleans Tribune*, which called itself the official organ of the state's Republican Party. In January 1866, Louisiana Republicans gained another editorial voice when Northern Methodists established the *New Orleans Advocate*.[27]

Virginia's Unionist papers were divided over Johnson's program. James W. Lewellen, who began publishing the Richmond *Republic* in the summer of 1865, avoided any partisan commitment. Yet like many other Unionists he supported the president's Reconstruction policies. Lewellen hoped Johnson could steer a middle course between the Democrats, who he believed encouraged sectional animosity, and Republican radicals "who wanted to establish a despotism over the South." This was a view shared by John Clark of Norfolk, formerly associated with Benjamin Butler's *New Regime;* in the summer of 1865, Clark began publishing the *Norfolk Post*, using it to back Johnson's policies.[28]

Virginian Unionists of a more radical bent, most of whom were Republicans, opposed President Johnson's course and sought to establish newspapers supporting their views. In 1865, state Republican leader John C. Underwood consulted with General Alfred H. Terry, who commanded federal occupation troops in Virginia, about the possibility of confiscating the press of one of Richmond's papers and using it to publish a Republican sheet. Terry, however, opposed this course. Underwood and U.S. Supreme Court Justice Salmon P. Chase then urged African American leader Frederick Douglass to establish a newspaper in Virginia, but Douglass demurred. In March 1866, radical Unionists finally obtained a newspaper voice in Richmond with the appearance of the *New Nation*, edited by James W. Hunnicutt, a South Carolina clergyman who had lived in Fredericksburg, Virginia, for many years. Hunnicutt had moved to Richmond right after the war to open a Unionist newspaper but had published only one issue before closing, for the city proved quite hostile to his endeavors. Bearing a letter of introduction from John Underwood, he had journeyed to the North and soon obtained enough money to reopen his paper the following year, using the offices of the defunct Richmond *Republic*. Hunnicutt initially opposed enfranchising the freedmen, fearing they would be controlled by their former owners, but by the summer of 1866 he had accepted the need for such reform and soon established himself as the most outspoken of the state's Republican editors.[29]

Outside Richmond there appeared several newspapers that adopted a more radical tone. In November 1865, former New York Union Army officer D. B. White established a Republican paper, the *True Southerner,* in Hampton. Unable to make ends meet, White transferred his paper to Norfolk early in 1866. Joseph T. Wilson, a free black man from Massachusetts, edited the publication. He condemned President Johnson for vetoing the Freedmen's Bureau and civil rights bills that Congress had passed to protect the former slaves. He too called for enfranchising the state's black males. Two months after White's arrival in Norfolk, a mob angered by his paper's outspoken views had broken into its office and destroyed its press. Wilson, the first African American to edit and publish a Virginia paper, established the *Union Republican* in Norfolk a few months after the demise of the *True Southerner,* but it too was short-lived.[30]

Two other Virginia papers opposed to Johnson's policies, both edited by native white Virginians, appeared in the Shenandoah Valley. This region of Virginia had been divided over secession; strong pockets of Unionism existed in some of its counties and there had even been some prewar opposition to slavery. In September 1865, A. M. Crane began publishing the *Winchester Journal*. That city had changed hands repeatedly during the war. In the summer of 1864, General Philip Sheridan finally drove the Confederates from the area and also destroyed much property in the valley. Crane had rejoiced in Sheridan's success, and he insisted that ex-Confederates must not be allowed to control Virginia. In February 1866, Dr. G. K. Gilmer of Harrisonburg began publishing the *American Union*. Claiming that as an Unconditional Union man he had faced "rebel hate and venom," he agreed with Crane that former Confederates must be dislodged from power in the state. Crane, Gilmer, and White joined W. J. Cowing, editor of the Alexandria *Virginia State Journal*, in attacking President Johnson's policies. In May 1866, the four men attended a convention in Alexandria that organized the state's Union Republican party. The editors disagreed, however, about the need to enfranchise the freedmen; White and Cowing favored this move, while Crane and Gilmer hesitated to endorse it.[31]

By early 1866, Tennessee was home to at least a dozen Unionist papers, far more than in any other Southern state. Their editors, however, could not agree on how to respond to Johnson's program and to the possibility of ex-Confederates' regaining power in Nashville. By the fall of 1866, only a few Unionist papers, including the *Memphis Bulletin* and two publications in Greeneville, the *New Era* and the *National Union*, continued to defend the president and his Reconstruction program. The editor of the *Bulletin* also favored allowing the state's ex-Confederates to vote. Most Unionist sheets supported continued disfranchisement of the former rebels, but realizing that this proscriptive policy could not be maintained forever, some editors began debating the advisability of enfranchising blacks. The state's only African American newspaper backed the idea. Its proprietor and editor, William B. Scott, was a free black who had moved from North Carolina to eastern Tennessee before the war. There, befriended by Quakers, he established a successful harness and saddle business. At the war's end, he and his son moved to Nashville, and in May 1865, they began publication of the *Colored Tennessean*, using its columns to promote African American suffrage. Some white Unionist editors, however, spoke against the idea. In March 1865, the editor of the *Memphis Bulletin* voiced his opposition to black suffrage, and in December the editor of the Jonesborough *Union Flag* sarcastically advocated running black leader Frederick Douglass for president, claiming that with his election "the Anglo-Saxons of every name and tongue, would crowd to the overshadowing ensign of Ethiopian domination." The editor of the Greeneville *New Era* also ridiculed the idea of enfranchising black Tennesseans.[32]

In the summer of 1864, James Hood of the *Chattanooga Daily Gazette* had characterized African American enfranchisement as "a political monstrosity," but as early as January of the following year he had expressed a willingness to let loyal blacks vote to offset rebel ballots. The following summer, S. C. Mercer, whose paper had just merged with the *Nashville Press* to form the *Daily Press and Times*, speculated about the wisdom of enfranchising the freedmen. By January 1866 he was backing the idea. Since Mercer's paper was the state capital's chief voice for the Brownlow administration, this was a significant indication that the Tennessee governor was heading in the same direction. As early as October 1865, Brownlow advised the legislature that "although negro voting cannot suit my natural prejudices of caste," if rebels were to regain the vote he would advocate enfranchising the former slaves. The following April he proposed allowing certain classes of blacks to vote. The editor of the Greeneville *New Era* warned that Brownlow could not "cram [black suffrage] down the throats of Tennesseans," but the governor picked up newspaper support from the Memphis *Weekly Republican* and from the *Memphis Morning Post*, founded in January 1866 by John Eaton, a Northerner, Union veteran, and former Freedmen's Bureau official. The cautious editor of the Shelbyville *Republican* endorsed qualified black suffrage as an act of justice to the freedmen but condemned universal suffrage as "unwise and inexpedient."[33]

By the summer of 1866, the few Unionist and Republican papers that championed suffrage for blacks were solidly opposed to Johnson and eager for Congress to intervene in Reconstruction. With congressional elections coming up in the fall, however, Northern Republicans were not eager to enfranchise the freedmen as they feared white voters' backlash. Instead Republicans submitted a Fourteenth Amendment to the states, which recognized blacks' citizenship and deprived leading Confederates of the right to hold office. It also provided a compromise on the question of African American suffrage, leaving that decision in the states' hands but penalizing those states that did not enfranchise blacks by reducing their congressional representation. Most Unionist papers in the South rallied around the amendment. Some, like Holden's *North Carolina Standard* and the *Rutherford Star*, claimed the amendment would head off stronger measures such as confiscation of Southern property or enfranchisement of blacks, while others hoped it would pave the way for black enfranchisement. In the summer of 1866, Brownlow persuaded the Tennessee legislature to ratify the Fourteenth Amendment; it was the only Southern state to do so before 1868. In return Congress agreed to seat Tennessee's representatives, thus readmitting the state to the Union.[34]

A few Unionist papers stood with Johnson, endorsing the organization of a National Union Party in the late summer of 1866 and supporting the president's efforts to readmit the Southern states without subjecting them to further requirements such as the Fourteenth Amendment. These papers included the Jacksonville *Florida Union*, the Greeneville *New Era*, the *Memphis Bulletin*, and the *Savannah Herald*. Although sympathetic to Johnson and deeply suspicious of Republican radicals, the editors of the *New Bern Times*, the *Savannah Republican*, and the Austin *Southern Intelligencer* eventually opted to support the Fourteenth Amendment.[35]

In his efforts to build Southern newspaper support for his Reconstruction program, Johnson utilized federal printing patronage. Distribution of this patronage fell to Secretary of State Seward, who appointed newspapers to publish the laws of the Thirty-Ninth Congress. Congress also appropriated $15,000 to permit two newspapers in each of the seven ex-Confederate states that had not had wartime Union governments to publish the laws of the two preceding Civil War Congresses.[36] Seward made most of his decisions about awarding this patronage late in 1865, while seven of the ex-Confederate states were still under provisional governors. In most cases he allowed the governors to designate the papers to do the printing. This explains why lucrative contracts for publishing the laws of the Civil War Congresses went to William Holden's *North Carolina Standard* and to two Texas Unionist papers that were supporting Governor Hamilton, *Flake's Bulletin* and the *San Antonio Express*. At the time Seward made the awards, these papers had not broken with Johnson. The only other Unionist or Republican papers to receive federal patronage in the South were the *Huntsville Advocate,* the *Florida Times,* and the Norfolk *Old Dominion,* all supporters of the president at the time the awards were made. Seward did receive recommendations and requests for various radical papers, including the Mobile *Nationalist* and the Norfolk *True Southerner,* but ignored them. In Arkansas, Fort Smith's mayor wrote to Seward endorsing the *Fort Smith Herald* and warning Seward not to appoint Dell's *New Era,* which was "a radical sheet of the Sumner-Stevens stripe." Needless to say, Dell did not get the printing; in addition, Johnson removed him from his post as a federal treasury agent. Texas Unionists were particularly dismayed when Seward assigned some of the printing in their state to the Austin *Texas State Gazette,* edited by ex-Confederate president Jefferson Davis's former secretary. In Tennessee, where Brownlow had already broken with the president, Seward assigned the printing for the Thirty-Ninth Congress to two anti-Brownlow journals.[37]

In September, as the fall congressional elections drew nigh, Northern Republicans decided to hold a convention in Philadelphia. They invited Southern loyalists to attend, hoping to encourage them to campaign against Johnson's Reconstruction program and for the Fourteenth Amendment. Unionists and Republicans from every ex-Confederate state except South Carolina sent at least a handful of delegates to Philadelphia. Many of them hoped to convince congressional Republicans to enfranchise their states' freedmen. Northerners, however, refused to go beyond the terms of the Fourteenth Amendment. A number of Southern Unionists remained in the North after the convention to campaign for Republican congressional candidates.[38]

After congressional Republicans won a resounding victory in the fall elections, Tennessee became the first Southern state to enfranchise blacks. With this action, party lines in the state crystallized. Mercer, editor of the Nashville *Daily Press and Times,* had referred to the Tennessee "Radicals" as Republicans as early as March of 1866, although Brownlow's Radical Unionist Party did not embrace the name Republican until the summer of 1867. Emboldened by Republican victories in the North, Southern Unionists increased their pressure on Congress. In December, Unconditional Unionists in Arkansas organized a state Republican Party and sent a delegation asking Congress to abolish the South's existing state governments and to reorganize them on the basis of loyal voters, black and white. At the same time Southerners who had attended the Philadelphia convention organized the Southern Republican Association to urge congressional approval of the Arkansans' proposal. In North Carolina, Unionist leaders William Holden and Alexander H. Jones also decided the time had come to call for enfranchising the freedmen.[39]

Southern developments over the past year, including election of ex-Confederates to office, enactment of Black Codes, and brutal race riots in Memphis and New Orleans, had already convinced Republican congressmen that Johnson's program had been a failure. In March 1867, emboldened by their overwhelming victory in the 1866 congressional elections, they responded to Southern Unionists' pleas by enacting a new Reconstruction program. In the First Reconstruction Act of 1867, Congress declared the Johnson governments provisional and put them under the supervision of military commanders. Military government in the South would end after states ratified new constitutions enfranchising the freedmen and ratified the Fourteenth Amendment.[40] Tennessee, now back in the Union, was the only ex-Confederate state not affected by the new Reconstruction program, but it was already in the hands of Brownlow's party. The establishment of black suffrage in the rest of the South now provided an opportunity for the Republican Party to organize—and, they hoped, to control—every other state in the former Confederacy. A key element in this organizational drive would be a Republican press, which began rapidly expanding in the South.

CHAPTER THREE

The White South Confronts the Republican Press

By the time congressional Reconstruction began in 1867, the Republicans had already established a number of papers in the South. In January 1867, the *Great Republic,* the national organ of the Union League—an organizing arm of the Republican Party—published a list of twenty-three papers it claimed were supporting more radical Reconstruction measures. It could have cited at least another eighteen that fell into that category.[1] Many of these papers were avowedly Republican, and the rest would become so after the advent of congressional Reconstruction. They were not well distributed across the South, however. The majority were in states that had had wartime Unionist governments or had a sizable minority of white Unionists. There were twelve Republican newspapers in Tennessee, six each in Virginia and North Carolina, four in Texas, three each in Florida and Georgia, and two each in Alabama, Louisiana, and Arkansas. South Carolina had only one Republican newspaper in early 1867 and Mississippi none. Most of these papers were in cities; only a few existed in rural areas. Almost all of these newspapers were in shaky financial condition.

Prospects for a rapid expansion of newspapers of any political persuasion in the postwar South were not encouraging. Although in the 1850s the number of newspapers in the future Confederate states had grown rapidly, advancing from 503 to 847 between 1850 and 1860, their numbers lagged behind those in the North. In 1860 these states, with one third of the nation's white population, had only an eighth of its newspapers. Three Northern states—New York, Pennsylvania, and Massachusetts—each had at least one newspaper with a circulation greater than the total in the eleven Confederate states; the circulation of several New York newspapers was three times as large.[2]

The Civil War had dealt the Southern newspaper business a heavy blow. Large numbers of publishers, editors, printers, and printers' assistants had joined the Confederate Army, leaving their papers to languish. Two-thirds of Mississippi's newspapermen enlisted. Due to the Union blockade newsprint was scarce, and its cost skyrocketed. Proprietors often abandoned their presses when the Union

Army arrived, and occupation forces often destroyed printing establishments. Advertisers stopped advertising and subscribers ceased subscribing. Before the war was over, Georgia had lost fifty-three newspapers; of the approximately twenty-three Florida papers existing in 1860, only ten survived. A mere 17 of Virginia's approximately 120 papers at the beginning of the war survived its first two years. Fifty of the sixty Texas newspapers suspended within a year after the firing on Fort Sumter. Mississippi began the war with forty-one papers, but only fourteen remained at its end. By the time of Appomattox, Tennessee retained only eleven weeklies. One Southern newspaper estimated that when Lee surrendered, only twenty-two dailies were still being published in the entire South, whereas there had been sixty-six prior to the war. The number of weeklies had dropped from 633 to 182.[3]

After the war ended, however, newspaper publishing in the South began to revive. By 1870, the ex-Confederate states boasted about a third more dailies than they had enjoyed a decade earlier and over one hundred more weeklies. This rate of growth still lagged behind that in the rest of the nation, since in the United States as a whole the number of papers rose almost 50 percent during the decade. Throughout the Reconstruction years, newspaper publishing remained a risky business, as it had been before the war. Of the 5,871 journals reported in the 1870 United States census, 1,904 disappeared within the next ten years. The year 1880 saw the establishment of 85 dailies and 1,042 weeklies, but in the same year proprietors suspended 56 dailies and 777 weeklies.[4]

The increase in the number of postwar newspapers in the South, despite the section's relative poverty, indicated that establishing one was not difficult. A prospective publisher needed scant education to edit a paper and little skill to run a press. Although steam presses had emerged in the printing business in the 1850s, they were expensive, costing upward of $1,000; in 1865 the publisher of a New Bern paper said he had to pay $2,000 for a cylinder press. Due to this high cost, many printers continued to rely on cheap hand presses. By 1880, when steam drove 37 percent of the country's newspaper presses, only 15 percent of the presses in the South had steam power. In Alabama, Mississippi, North Carolina, and Texas, the figure was under 10 percent. Typically a newspaper proprietor produced a sheet with a small staff using an ancient hand press and a few boxes of type. Most publishers also obtained a foot-treadle press for job printing.[5]

Estimates range widely as to the cost of starting up a paper. One historian who has studied Piedmont newspapers in the Carolinas during the 1850s found that the price of most printing plants advertised for sale there averaged $1,000–$1,600. After the Civil War, the cost rose for either starting a high-quality newspaper or acquiring an existing one. In 1867, Republican editor Edward M.

Cheney paid $3,000 to take control of the Jacksonville *Florida Union*. The editor of the Elizabeth City *North Carolinian,* who published an attractively printed paper, claimed in 1871 that it would cost between $3,000 and $5,000 to start up a newspaper like his. When the editor of the Macon *American Union* advertised his paper for sale in 1872, he valued his presses and equipment at $9,500. These three papers were weeklies; dailies required even more capital investment. Agents for the Republican Party in the South who hoped to establish daily newspapers for their party provided cost estimates ranging from $10,000 to $35,000 for starting a paper and $40,000 to $60,000 for buying existing newspapers with large circulations.[6]

One could start a paper with a much smaller capital investment. After the Civil War an Arkansas editor claimed he had bought a half interest in a paper for $25; another said he purchased a paper for $400, putting only $25 down. In 1866, a fire in Darlington, South Carolina, consumed the local paper; its proprietors had insured its press and office furniture for $500. Looking at a somewhat later period, one historian has found that from 1880 to 1914 many African American editors started papers with an initial investment of less than $1,000; Robert Abbott began publishing his *Chicago Defender* with only $25.[7] The papers with the least invested in them looked cheap, however, and did not last long.

Operating costs for Southern newspapers could run higher than the national average. After the war Southern publishers had trouble locating skilled printers, and they usually paid more for newsprint than did Northern operators. Southern paper mills produced only 5 percent of the nation's newsprint, and importing it raised its price. In 1860, the *New York Tribune* paid eight cents a pound for newsprint; in the North and South Carolina Piedmont, newsprint prices ranged from eight to fourteen cents a pound. Prices rose steeply during and after the war. In December 1865, William G. Brownlow complained that the cost of newsprint had risen by 100 percent since the previous August. By 1866, the cost of the *Tribune*'s newsprint had more than doubled from its antebellum level, rising to seventeen cents. Prices the New York paper paid then slowly declined, reaching the eight-cent level again in 1874.[8]

Operating costs for publishers varied widely, depending on the newspaper's frequency of issue, the size and number of its pages, and the number of copies printed. The nation's largest newspaper, the *New York Herald,* spent $4,000–$5,000 a day. John Forsyth, editor of Alabama's leading Democratic paper, the Mobile *Daily Register,* put his cost per week at $2,250. By 1871, Republicans were publishing two dailies in Austin, Texas; one editor estimated his expenses at $1,200 a week, and the other put his at $20,000 per year. The editor of the *Savannah Daily Herald* claimed his weekly expenses averaged almost $1,000. Samuel

Bard, who published a number of Republican papers in several states during Reconstruction, claimed that it cost him $600–700 per week to bring out his Atlanta *Daily New Era* in 1868. James Dugan put the cost of publishing his daily *Vicksburg Republican* at a much lower figure, $250 per week. Weekly newspapers cost less to run. The publisher of the *Louisiana State Register* estimated his annual expenses at $3,000, while the editor of a Mississippi weekly put his monthly running cost at $350. George Ruby, an African American who played an important role in the Texas Republican Party, said his weekly expenses for publishing the *Galveston Standard*, a small semiweekly, were not less than $150. Another black publisher, James T. Rapier, said it cost him about $50 per week to print one thousand copies of his paper.[9]

The typical Southern newspaper was a weekly published in a small or medium-sized town. Larger metropolitan dailies also often published weekly editions, which cost them little to print because they contained material already appearing in the daily editions. Hence they were formidable competitors to the rural weeklies. The development of "ready-print" after the war helped these smaller presses survive. Syndicates mass-produced newsprint prepared in four sheets, with either the outside or inside pages already printed with undated material and advertisements that could be used at any time. Small-town editors could buy this paper and print their own local news, editorials, and advertisements on the blank pages. An Arkansas newspaper historian reports that a Democratic editor who had prepared political matter for one of his blank pages then sold the paper to a Republican, who printed his party's propaganda on the other page and distributed the result. The utilization of ready-print, or "patent outsides," as they were sometimes called, expanded greatly in the 1870s, helping explain the phenomenal increase of over 100 percent in the number of American newspapers during the decade.[10]

To make ends meet, publishers depended upon job printing, advertising, subscriptions, and government printing patronage. Job printing, particularly for proprietors who issued weeklies, probably generated about half their income. Of revenue derived directly from newspaper publishing, somewhat less than half came from advertising and the rest from subscriptions and government patronage. Most papers carried some national advertising, particularly if they used patent outsides, but they received no income from the ads placed there. In 1875, editors in the Mississippi Valley tried to join forces in order to require suppliers of ready-print to give them either ad-free copy or a percentage of the revenues derived from advertisements contained therein. Almost all newspapers carried columns of advertisements for various patent medicines, but these generated little revenue. The publisher of the *Louisiana State Register* estimated that if he filled his entire paper with patent medicine ads for a year, the resulting income would amount to about a third of his annual operating expenses. Hence newspaper proprietors depended heavily on selling advertising space to local business owners and professionals. Particularly in small towns, publishers constantly complained that small-minded merchants did not see the importance of advertising, and the papers frequently included articles proclaiming its virtues.[11]

By the time of the Civil War, a number of advertising brokers were selling space in local newspapers to national advertisers. By 1869, the most important of these firms, George P. Rowell's, made annual contracts for newspaper space, which they retailed to advertisers. In negotiating advertising rates and in finding advertisers, Rowell needed to know the approximate circulation of newspapers with which he dealt. He began collecting information about newspapers, which he published in an annual directory beginning in 1869. This publication listed newspapers by state, city, or town and identified their publishers, editors, and political affiliation. Rowell also published each newspaper's approximate circulation.[12]

Publishers were understandably reluctant to provide circulation estimates, for they understood that merchants would prefer to advertise in papers with large numbers of readers. Additionally, in cities with several dailies, the post office awarded the paper with the largest circulation the right to publish lists of undelivered mail as well as advertisements for new mail routes. Publishers often disputed these awards, insisting their rivals' circulation claims were fraudulent. The publisher of the *Donaldsonville Chief* explained that his refusal to state his circulation was due to "the general exaggerations of neighboring journals; we are not willing to make it appear the *Chief* is behindhand in popularity when we know our circulation to be greatly in excess of [theirs]." Most papers supplied Rowell with circulation information but only after most certainly padding the figures. Rowell struggled through most of the rest of the century to develop effective ways to validate publishers' circulation claims.[13]

Southern circulation figures in 1870 fell below the 1860 averages for the section; although there were more newspapers, fewer people bought them. In 1871, the circulation figures for Southern metropolitan dailies fell well below the national average in every state except Louisiana; Florida, Mississippi, North Carolina, and Texas had daily circulation less than one third of the nation's average. Weekly circulation figures for all ex-Confederate states except Tennessee ranged around two-thirds of the national average. If states are ranked by the average number of copies printed yearly for each inhabitant, Southern states line up at the bottom. Whereas the national average was thirty-five copies per person per year, the tally was four in North Carolina and Arkansas; five in Mississippi and Florida; seven in Texas; eight in South Carolina; and nine in Alabama.[14] By 1871, the average circulation of a daily in the Southern states ranged from 450 in Florida to almost 4,000 in Louisiana, with most falling between 700 and 2,500. Weeklies ranged from eight to thirteen hundred. Annual subscription prices were low, usually around $2 for a weekly and $4 for a daily. Editors constantly pleaded with their subscribers to pay up and were forever threatening to cut them off if they did not. Many began to demand cash up front, but some were willing to accept payment in kind.[15]

The last source of newspaper revenue, and for numerous operations the most important, was printing patronage, which came from every level of government. The United States government selected papers in each state to publish its laws, orders, and resolutions, a practice that lasted until 1875. Although the sums paid for this service were not very substantial, editors eagerly sought the privilege so that they could be designated as official publishers for the U.S. government. In addition, state governments subsidized papers by having them publish legislative debates, laws, and legal advertisements, and judges in state judicial circuits paid newspapers to publish court notices. In every legislative session state governments identified a printer associated with an important newspaper to publish in bound volumes its journals, debates, and documents. Finally, city, town, and county governments and judicial districts arranged with local newspapers to publish their proceedings and notices. This made the county seat a prized location for a rural weekly in the South. The total income derived from these sources could be considerable, and newspapers before and after the Civil War constantly squabbled over access to this patronage. As late as 1880, according to S. D. N. North's report on the Tenth Census, the struggle for official advertising was "constant and intense" in many cities and counties.[16]

Clearly it was quite a challenge, in the nation and especially in the South, for publishers to keep their newspapers operating. Republican publishers in the South faced these same challenges, but they also confronted daunting obstacles that did not concern proprietors of Democratic papers. This was particularly true for the handful of African Americans who attempted to establish newspapers during or after the war in the South's charged racial atmosphere. These men, realizing that most white editors were either ignorant of or hostile to the concerns of the freedmen, designed their papers primarily for a black readership. Unfortunately most African Americans were illiterate, and many of these who did read could not afford to subscribe to a newspaper. Nor were there enough black business and professional people to sustain these newspapers through advertisements. Many black editors hoped for some white support and emphasized that their papers promoted racial harmony and prosperity for the whole South. In bidding for white advertising, they emphasized that former slaves were now consumers and constituted an important and growing market. Their appeals for white support went for naught, as few African American journals lasted for more than a year.[17]

Whether they were white or black, Republican editors in the South faced the reality that although freedmen overwhelmingly approved of the party and supported it with their votes, the vast majority of whites did not. They denied that the Republican Party even had a right to exist in their midst. When the United States was first established under its Constitution of 1787, Americans generally did not regard political parties as legitimate. Most deemed parties to be factions seeking only their own selfish and partisan objectives and feared that their proliferation would reduce the nation to anarchy. Nonetheless parties did develop, and eventually most citizens came not only to accept them but to regard them as essential safeguards of liberty. Party competition developed in all sections of the Union, including the South. Although this competition was heated, losers learned to acquiesce in the triumph of their opponents, for until the advent of the Republican Party in the 1850s, none of the major parties challenged the basic structure and values of American social, economic, and political life.

In the antebellum South, this willingness to accept the legitimacy of political parties was conditional. Most white Southerners expected parties to support the existence of slavery and to back constitutional doctrines allowing the states to control their own affairs without federal interference. Both Whig and Democratic parties met these conditions, but the Republican Party that appeared in the mid-1850s did not. It strenuously opposed the expansion of slavery into the western territories, and most white Southerners feared that the party would use the federal government to interfere with slavery within their states. In 1860, the Republican presidential candidate, Abraham Lincoln, was not even on the ballot in most Southern states and got only a handful of votes in that section. Rather than submit to a Republican administration, the majority of Southerners chose to secede from the Union and to fight a devastating Civil War. The policies the Republican Party implemented during and after the war solidified Southern whites' antagonism toward it, for these policies seemed to validate their worst fears. The Republicans had conducted a war against the states in the interest of national consolidation, they had overthrown slavery in the process, and they had elevated the status of freed slaves to legal equality with whites. The traditional elites of the South, which were based on ownership of land and slaves, recognized that the Republicans challenged their political hegemony, and almost all whites feared that the party would subvert the Southern racial order maintaining white supremacy. In their minds the Republicans were not at all like the antebellum Whigs and Democrats, neither of whom threatened basic Southern institutions or traditions. This new party was beyond the pale of acceptability. Regarding it as an alien force thrust into their midst by outsiders, white Southerners denied legitimacy to the Republican Party and to the state and local governments it controlled.[18]

This crisis in legitimacy posed grave problems for Republican editors hoping for a fair hearing in the South, for the ranks of Southern whites closed against them, just as Southern whites had earlier shut out other threatening influences. Before the Civil War, the press freedom that Northerners experienced had become less and less common in the South. In the North as well as in the South, antebellum journalism had been heavily partisan; most editors championed a party and many helped run one. Rivalry and debate among editors was heated, and in the South this sometimes led to violent altercations. In the North, party competition continued unabated up through the Civil War. But in the South, as sectional pressures mounted, tolerance of divergent opinions lessened, and Southern editors became more eager to fit in with the prevalent political mood in support of slavery and state rights. In 1860, an editor in Raleigh, North Carolina, complained that no one possessed less freedom than a journalist to express his own opinions: "His patrons regard him as a penny trumpet through which not a note is to be sounded, unless it accords precisely with their own music."[19]

During the secession crisis of 1860–61, a vigorous journalistic debate ensued in the South as Unionist editors challenged the fire-eaters endeavoring to lead their states out of the Union. Unionist papers attempted to take a calm approach to the heated questions of union and secession and complained that disunionist journals resorted to emotional appeals rather than to reason in advancing their cause. Once a state had made its decision to join the Confederacy, however, most Southerners expected the debate to stop. Newspaper editors who did not acquiesce in the majority's decision often faced considerable harassment. Several of the postwar South's most important Republican editors, such as Tennessee's William G. Brownlow, James Hunnicutt of Virginia, and James Newcomb of Texas, had been Unionist editors who were forced to leave their states after the war began; Ferdinand Flake chose to remain in Texas, but a mob destroyed his Galveston press. Other Unionist editors had seen their papers die from lack of subscribers and patronage.[20]

Most Southern newspapers worked hard to sustain Confederate morale during the war, but as the fighting wore on into 1863 some editors began criticizing the Richmond government, with a few even calling for peace negotiations. In

1863, an angry mob destroyed the office of one such editor, William Holden of the Raleigh, North Carolina, *Standard,* but he soon resumed publication and continued until the war ended without further interference.[21] Dissident editors like Holden appealed to many readers because they were striving to protect their states and communities from interference by the centralizing Davis administration in Richmond, and they did not challenge the sanctity of slavery. Since by the midpoint of the hostilities numerous Southern whites were growing sick of the war and increasingly resentful of Confederate measures like conscription, impressment, and taxes in kind, they could accord legitimacy to these editors who seemed to be defending, not challenging, Southern values.

In the postwar South, Republican editors failed to meet these tests of acceptability. Although white editors disagreed over what course to pursue toward the triumphant Union government, almost all of them stood fast for community self-determination and white supremacy, and like most other white Southerners they found that the Republican Party challenged these values. One Louisiana newspaper editor even proposed blocking the importation of Republican newspapers into the South, just as Southerners had attempted to ban prewar abolitionist materials from the mails. In 1866, newspaper dealers in Mobile caved in to threats and agreed not to sell *Harper's Weekly,* a New York–based Republican magazine. In 1868, only 200 people in Virginia subscribed to the *New York Tribune,* a leading Republican paper; another 117 subscribed in North Carolina, and 96 in Tennessee, both of which had large numbers of white Republican voters. Texas provided 50 subscribers to the *Tribune,* and the other seven ex-Confederate states had fewer than 20 subscribers each.[22]

As Republican journals began surfacing within the South, local newspapermen refused to recognize the new editors as members of the journalistic fraternity and sometimes excluded them from newly formed state press associations. Conservative journalists scornfully rejected offers to exchange newspapers with Republican publishers; one editor claimed he was insulted by the suggestion and would feel degraded even to read such offensive sheets. The editor of the *Star* in Panola, Mississippi, refused to exchange with the Republican *Memphis Post,* stating that he had no wish to "encourage the circulation of incendiary documents." Conservative editors derided Republican publications as "nigger papers"; in Richmond, Hunnicutt's *New Nation* was known as the *"New Nigger Nation";* the *Richmond Examiner* referred to the Republican sheet as "this stinking nuisance." In Alabama, the editor of the Democratic Tuscaloosa *Independent Monitor* referred to the Demopolis *Southern Republican* as the "Demopolis Negro Noserag," while his counterpart at the helm of a Mississippi paper characterized the *Vicksburg Weekly Republican* as a "filthy, slimy, stinking, negro-equality, negro-loving, white man-hating, hate-engendering organ of perjured scoundrels." The Mobile *News* expressed contempt for the *New Orleans Tribune*, calling it a "filthy, black republican, negrophilist journal," while the editor of the *Houston Telegraph* referred to Republican papers in his state as "the mongrel press of Texas."[23]

The editor of the *Williamsburg Gazette*, a native Southerner, complained that he and other Republicans were the targets of "the most odious and objectionable epithets" and charged with "every conceivable sin" because they stood by the United States government. A conservative Houston editor vilified his Republican counterparts in Austin as "nigger speculators," while the editor of the *Sequin Journal* called the editor of San Antonio's Republican paper a "contemptible, penniless, characterless, stealing carpetbagger." In Georgia, opposing editors referred to John Emory Bryant of the Augusta *Loyal Georgian* as "the mulatto Republican" and a "hybrid bastard." The editor of the Democratic Little Rock *Gazette* claimed that his rival at the helm of the city's Republican sheet suffered from "black vomit" resulting from "the effects of trying to swallow the moral tergiversations and nigrescent politics of that stramentous journal." Publishers of Republican sheets often complained that they and their families were treated as outcasts by local social elites. A number of editors claimed they had trouble hiring a staff because other newspapers urged prospective employees not to work for them, and those who accepted employment faced the same social ostracism their employer experienced. Jason Clarke Swayze, publisher of the Macon *American Union*, had to house his workers in his print shop because no local establishment would provide them room and board. Members of Macon's typographical union refused membership to Swayze and his printers; in Alabama Albert Griffin, editor of the Mobile *Nationalist*, complained of the same treatment.[24]

In the best of circumstances, Republican editors faced problems finding subscribers in the postwar South. Many from the party's base could not read or could not afford to buy a paper. Blacks capable of reading newspapers, Republican editors claimed, risked losing their jobs for doing so. It was also difficult to find white readers willing to brave the hostility of their friends and neighbors by subscribing to a Republican sheet. According to the editor of the *San Antonio Express*, subscribers to his newspaper tried to sneak issues out of their post offices "like thieves carrying off plunder," while the editor of the *Vicksburg Daily Times* observed that newsboys distributing his paper had to conceal copies under their coats. The editors of two New Orleans Republican newspapers reported that ruffians harassed their news dealers. Albion Tourgee of the *Greensboro Union Register* found that posters advertising his paper were torn down.

The publisher of the *Charleston Republican* complained that his city's hotels would not stock his paper.[25] Those who were willing to subscribe to Republican papers were not always sure of receiving them, for a number of editors complained that Southern postmasters and railroad workers interfered with their delivery. Hunnicutt of the Richmond *New Nation* did not have that problem, he said, thanks to the "Yankee clerks" who held positions in that city's post office.[26]

In addition to hampering the efforts of Republican publishers to build subscription lists, the South's intolerant atmosphere deprived them of other sources of income. The publisher of the *Charleston Republican* complained that anyone seeking to get job printing done at his office was "publicly and privately denounced as a traitor to his race and people." Lewis Cass Carpenter, owner of the leading Republican paper in Columbia, South Carolina, claimed that although he had property worth between $20,000 and $30,000, no bank in the city would loan him money to keep his struggling paper afloat. A Louisiana Republican editor apologized for using patent outsides, stating that a paper "ostracized as ours is, must . . . get along at the least possible expense."[27]

Across the South, merchants and professionals refused to place advertisements in Republican papers. According to the editor of the *Rutherford Star*, although the majority of his county's voters were Republicans, only one local firm advertised in his paper. The publisher of the *Louisiana State Register*, looking jealously on the advertisements published in a rival Democratic sheet, noted that "newspapers which abuse the colored people, and which utter reproaches continually against the Republican leaders in the State, are favorites with the advertising public." John Morris of the *Charleston Daily Republican* complained that Democratic editors sought to frighten potential advertisers away from his paper by claiming it had no circulation and was about to collapse. It was their political views, not their circulation figures, however, that kept business owners from advertising in Republican papers. On occasions when a Republican proprietor took over an existing newspaper, local business owners quickly switched their ads to other sheets. When Republicans acquired the *American Citizen* of Canton, Mississippi, its new editor begged businessmen to give his paper a chance before withdrawing their patronage. After Jason Clarke Swayze assumed control of the *American Union* in Griffin, Georgia, he watched with dismay as local advertisements disappeared from his paper. "Look at the advertising columns of the *Union*," he expostulated; "not a single advertisement from merchants or local traders, while the *Star* and *Herald* groan under their weight." This could also happen if an editor switched loyalties; when E. M. Pughe, proprietor of the conservative Augusta *Daily Press*, decided to support Georgia's Republican administration, he lost advertising, which he failed to regain after recanting and going back to the Democrats. He had to close his operation.[28]

Business owners who chose to advertise in Republican papers faced pressures ranging from social ostracism to the threat of economic sanction. In Georgia, the editor of the *Quitman Banner* declared he was "ashamed for every one who is so lost to the proud feelings of a white Southerner" as to advertise in the Republican *Bainbridge Weekly Sun*. Merchants in Augusta, Georgia, who advertised in the *National Republican* received letters threatening them with loss of business unless they withdrew their notices from the paper. The *Richmond Whig* published the names of the city's three merchants who advertised in the Republican *New Nation*, clearly hoping that its readers would boycott them. Whitelaw Reid, who visited the South shortly after the end of the war, claimed that "to secure [a] profitable business, a man must either sink politics altogether, or fall into the old habit of pandering to the prejudices of those with whom he traded." As an example, he cited the Unionist editor of a New Orleans newspaper who was afraid to advocate enfranchisement of the freedmen for fear of losing business. The editor informed Reid that "our only chance is to make a good *news*paper, and politically drift with the tide."[29]

Republican publishers constantly complained at how business and politics became entangled in the Reconstruction South. In the North and West, they said, people could disagree politically without these differences affecting their business relationships. The editor of the Raleigh *North Carolina Standard* warned that boycotting Republican merchants "strikes at the root of business and destroys all confidence between men of opposite parties." With so much economic uncertainty and distress already plaguing the South, he claimed, such confidence needed to be promoted, not discouraged. The editor of the Chattanooga *Daily Republican* reminded local businessmen that "radicals buy goods as well as conservatives, and that advertising is not a political transaction." Another Republican journalist insisted that "no businessman who has a thimble full of brains will make merchandise of his political opinions." Samuel Bard, a New Yorker who had arrived in the South several years before the Civil War, worked hard to convince Atlanta business owners to advertise in his Republican newspaper, the *New Era*. He distributed cards stating "No politics in business" and assured merchants that his paper's business section would be run independently of its editorial page. Except during election campaigns, Bard gave more attention to economic matters than to politics. When he did address political issues, Bard tried to define a moderate position that most whites would find acceptable. At one point in 1868, he acknowledged that he had written no political editorials for over a month, because "matters look a little foggy just now" and he was busy "sounding for the channels." Perhaps because of his political moderation, Bard was able to attract a respectable number of local advertisers.[30]

In response to the ostracism of the business community, most Republican editors pled for tolerance. "What Republican paper during a campaign," queried the *Florida Union*'s editor, "has called on its readers to injure the person or business of any Democrat?" For some journalists, however, patience ran out. The *Wilmington Post*'s carpetbagger editor initially joked that since he was "in a liberal humor" he would accept advertising from anyone who would pay for it, "even if he is a white man and a Democrat." A few months later, however, he angrily noted that most Wilmington business owners continued to advertise in the city's Democratic papers rather than his and urged his readers to patronize only those firms that advertised in the *Post*. "We have refrained from speaking of this because we are not in favor of such petty proscription," he observed, "but it is forced on us by the opposite party." A few other bitter Republican publishers also urged their readers to patronize only stores that advertised in their columns. Newspapers aimed at black readers encouraged them not to patronize racist businessmen. The editor of a Republican paper in Hampton, Virginia, in urging his black readers to buy selectively, observed that "that class of men who call colored people 'niggers' and think them fit only for slavery do not advertise in the *True Southerner*." The editor of the Mobile *Nationalist* similarly appealed to his black readers.[31]

If social ostracism and economic sanctions failed to eliminate Republican editors, their opponents sometimes resorted to violence. In a number of Southern states, whites used force to intimidate Republicans, and because of their supposed influence, journalists were favorite targets. A South Carolina publisher observed that although he held no public office, he was "regarded as more dangerous to the Ku Klux than almost any other man in the state" because he operated a Republican paper. Numbers of Republican editors reported receiving threats, and several of them were physically assaulted, often by rival editors. Such altercations among newspapermen were by no means uncommon in the antebellum South, but there were many more instances of them during Reconstruction, and the victims were almost always Republicans rather than Democrats. Occasionally someone assaulted an editor for other than political reasons. In Aberdeen, Mississippi, for instance, an actor aggrieved at the local Republican paper's review of his performance fatally shot its editor. But most of the time individuals or mobs who resorted to force were punishing Republican editors for their political views.[32]

Although E. M. Pughe had no voice in the editorial policies of his Augusta

National Republican, to his dismay this did not shield him from the wrath of a Democratic editor who took offense at an editorial in Pughe's paper and assaulted him with a whip. Two men from a rival newspaper also took a whip to the editor of the New Orleans *National Republican*. In Mississippi, after the Republican editor of the *Columbus Press* had labeled his Democratic counterpart on the *Columbus Index* a liar, the latter publicly beat him with a cane. James Sener of the *Fredericksburg Ledger* survived a beating with a bruised face and a broken arm. Pierce Burton, editor of the *Southern Republican* in Demopolis, Alabama, was brutally pistol-whipped. In Wilmington, North Carolina, several conservatives waylaid and beat the *Post*'s assistant editor, and in Louisiana a judge infuriated by remarks about him in the Opelousas *St. Landry Progress* severely caned one of its editors, Emerson Bentley. In Georgia, unknown assailants assaulted John Bryant of the *Loyal Georgian* with a club, and others shot at Joel Griffin of the *Southwest Georgian*.[33]

In a few instances, angry individuals or mobs murdered Republican editors. A few days after Bentley's caning in Opelousas, a mob swept through the town, killing a number of blacks and three whites, one of whom was another editor of the *St. Landry Progress*, C. E. Durand. In St. Francisville, Louisiana, an unidentified assailant killed D. A. Webber of the *Feliciana Republican*, and in Mississippi a Democratic editor killed Lewis Middleton, editor of the *West Point Times*.[34] Sometimes the intended victim had sufficient warning to escape his assailant, but his newspaper office might be damaged or destroyed. In Richmond, a mob threw bricks through the office windows of Hunnicutt's *New Nation* but harmed no one. A Texas mob tried unsuccessfully to burn the offices of the Jefferson *Union Intelligencer*. In 1871, a band of Ku Klux Klansmen rode into Pontotoc, Mississippi, seeking Robert Flournoy, editor of the radical *Equal Rights*, but Flournoy escaped unharmed. Several times armed mobs in Georgia chased Jason Clarke Swayze from his editorial quarters, but they never harmed him or his press. On a number of occasions, however, mobs sacked Republican newspaper offices and destroyed their presses; this happened to the *True Southerner* in Virginia, the *Rutherford Star* in North Carolina, the *Houston Union* in Texas, the *Maryville Republican* in Tennessee, the *Talladega Sun* in Alabama, and at least four Louisiana papers: the *Homer Iliad*, *St. Landry Progress*, *Attakapas Register*, and *Rapides Tribune*. In most cases the papers obtained new presses and soon reopened. On three different occasions, unknown individuals in Tennessee attempted, without success, to burn down the office of the Jonesborough *Union Flag*.[35]

This Southern white hostility toward the Republican Party and its press meant that both the organization and its newspapers would have to rely on outside support. Southern Republicans besieged Northerners with requests for aid in establishing newspapers. Since the party's basic constituents in the South were freedmen, most of whom were illiterate or could not afford a paper, some Republicans believed they should concentrate on hiring speakers to reach blacks rather than on publishing newspapers. Senator Henry Wilson, a prominent Massachusetts Republican who toured the South in 1867, returned home convinced of the wisdom of that course. Before the year was out, the Union Republican Executive Committee, which was attempting to coordinate the party's organizational activity in the South, was sponsoring over one hundred speakers there, most of them black.[36]

Southern Republicans, however, persisted in their efforts to establish newspapers, with or without Northern aid. They reached blacks by having literate freedmen read their papers at African American church gatherings or wherever else a group could be assembled. The proprietor of two Mississippi Republican newspapers later stated that if freedmen could get the papers free, they would read every word or have someone read the papers aloud. Blacks, he said, "consider every word published in a republican paper almost law, and every paper taken on a plantation is better than a dozen speakers." By 1867, Southern Republicans were already recruiting freedmen into Union Leagues, which served the party as an organizing network. Many of the party's editors had League ties and urged party members to buy their papers and read these aloud at League meetings.[37]

Republicans were especially eager to influence white attitudes in the South, and believed newspapers were necessary to achieve this goal. According to the editor of the *Charleston Free Press*, "the people who control government and shape its destinies are those who read newspapers," while his counterpart at North Carolina's *Rutherford Star* asserted that "the political opinions and sentiments of the great mass of our people [are] molded by the press." Northerners traveling in Dixie cited the important role newspapers played in a patriarchal, largely rural society where most people had few other sources of information. Thus the way editors selected and interpreted news for their readers had great potential for influencing public opinion, and Republicans were understandably alarmed that their opponents were monopolizing the press. Congressional Committee agents in the South pointed this out, as did Northern newspaper editors; John W. Forney of the Washington *Daily Morning Chronicle* warned that the Southern press "was almost entirely under the control of the enemies of the Union." Republican journalists in the former Confederacy echoed this concern that the Democratic press was still disloyal and intent on undermining the legitimacy of the new Republican regimes. John Morris of the *Charleston Republican* contended that editors, by "building up and casting down the reputations of legislators and other public officers," could determine "whether the laws under which the community lives shall be nullified or enforced."[38] Not only was most of the Southern press in unfriendly hands; Republican editors charged that unsympathetic journalists prepared the Associated Press wire service reports coming from the South.[39]

Republican editors complained that opposition newspapers in the South subjected them to a constant stream of abuse and ridicule and distorted and misrepresented their party's principles. Republican papers were necessary to get the party program before the voters, keep the record straight, and, as the editor of the *Vicksburg Weekly Republican* put it, "counter the hatred and prejudice of Democratic papers." A party press would also keep Republican voters informed about candidates and issues and remind them of dates for party conventions, primaries, and general elections. According to a North Carolina Republican editor, "nothing preserves the efficiency and promotes the power of parties so much as well conducted newspapers." The editor of the *Sumter County Republican* thus summarized the purpose of his paper: "Our object is to rally the Republicans, furnish them with weapons of intelligent controversy, post them fully in regard to the candidates and their principles, and thus secure a splendid victory for the [Republican] ticket in Tennessee."[40]

As the editor of this Tennessee paper suggested by his reference to rallying Republican voters, one of the most important tasks of a Republican journalist was to build a sense of community among party members. Republicans were bound to feel beleaguered in the South, where most white residents scorned them. By printing news of Republican activity around the state, party newspapers could make individual readers aware that they were not alone. Publishing letters from correspondents in other communities also generated a sense of shared experience and common interest among Republican newspaper readers that helped them cope with the hostile environment that many faced. The appearance of a successful party press would build self-esteem among Republicans and might also help their party gain legitimacy in the eyes of the whites who dominated Southern society.

For all of these reasons, the Republican Congressional Committee, the Republican National Committee, and the national headquarters of the Union League agreed it was important to develop a party press in the South, but none of these organizations had money to spare for funding new newspapers there. Eventually, over the course of Reconstruction, Northern Republicans helped establish some Republican newspapers in the former Confederacy, but most of them had to do without such help.[41] If a Republican press was to emerge and maintain itself in the South, the party would have to develop other means of sustaining it.

CHAPTER FOUR

Patronage Saves the Republican Press

During the Civil War, the Union Army had provided substantial assistance to Unionist and Republican newspapers. As Beaufort *Free South* editor James G. Thompson noted in 1863, "where the army goes, there goes also the newspapers, pestilential abolition journals all." During the initial phases of Reconstruction, the Republican press in the South continued to depend heavily for support on the army and on other United States government agencies. After Appomattox, a number of generals commanding U.S. troops occupying the South censored, suspended, or even closed newspapers accused of spreading rebel sentiments, and they continued the practice of placing their notices and orders in journals sympathetic to the Republican Party.

U.S. treasury officials also placed advertisements of tax sales in Republican papers. In 1866, Lyman Stickney, while still a member of the Florida tax commission, paid his brother John $670 for notices he placed in the *Florida Union*. And the U.S. War Department advertised in Southern newspapers for the ordnance and quartermaster's offices. In the early Reconstruction years, while there was still a large federal troop presence in the South, such advertising could be lucrative. By 1867, War Department offices had placed almost $2,500 in advertisements in newspapers in each of three states—Tennessee, Louisiana, and Texas—and around $2,000 in Georgia and $1,000 in Virginia. The bulk of this money went to Republican papers. In Texas, for instance, almost $2,000 went to the two San Antonio papers supporting the Republicans; in Tennessee, $1,100 went to the Nashville *Press and Times*, almost $1,000 to the *Nashville Union*, and $650 to the *Memphis Post*. In addition, many federal judges in the South posted bankruptcy notices in Republican papers.[1]

After the Reconstruction Act of 1867 placed the Southern state governments under military supervision, commanding generals kept a watchful eye on publications in their jurisdiction. Generally they refrained from interfering with newspapers, although occasionally they arrested offensive editors. In November 1867, General Edward Ord, commander of the department that included Mississippi and Arkansas, arrested the editor of the *Vicksburg Times* on the charge of interfering with the execution of the Reconstruction Acts. In Arkansas, however, he court-martialed an officer whose men had destroyed a conservative press. General John Pope, who administered the Reconstruction Acts in Georgia, Florida, and Alabama, warned that he would punish editors publishing "treasonable utterances." In 1867, he suspended the local paper in Moulton, Alabama, for six months, and during that time Republicans arranged with the paper's proprietor to use his press to issue a Republican sheet.[2]

Struggling Republican editors in the South complained that state and local printing patronage went to their conservative or Democratic rivals, many of whom denounced Congress and the Reconstruction Acts. Editors protested both to local military commanders and to Northern Republicans that such subsidies should go instead to their own papers, which supported the federal government and its policies. In response to such pleas, General Ord ordered the Arkansas government to redirect some state patronage to Republican newspapers. To the despair of Mississippi Republicans, however, he failed to take similar action in their state. In 1869, upon becoming military commander in Mississippi, General Adelbert Ames named a Republican publisher to replace the state printer elected by the legislature.[3]

The handful of Republican newspapers in Alabama, Georgia, and Florida fared well under General Pope's jurisdiction. In August 1867, he required state and local governments to place their official ads and notices in papers that did not oppose Reconstruction. By this order, Pope clearly intended to divert printing patronage from Democratic publications to these three states' few Republican papers. The general admitted that his action had precipitated a "hideous outcry" from Democratic editors, who condemned him for infringing on freedom of the press. He insisted, however, that he did not want the provisional state governments to subsidize newspapers "that try to defeat the execution of the very law by which these . . . governments have any existence." His order proved impractical, for Republican papers did not circulate widely and hence government agencies could not meet legal requirements regarding posting of notices in all parts of a state. Republican editors also claimed that state and local officials refused to comply with the order. One judge in Butler County, Alabama, issued his own paper, just large enough to contain his legal advertisements and a circus notice. Early in 1868, Pope's successor, General George Gordon Meade, revoked the newspaper order. While it lasted, however, Pope's decree redirected enough notices from sheriffs, ordinaries, bailiffs, county clerks, and bankruptcy officers to keep several Republican papers alive. In at least two Alabama cases, Republicans were able to purchase papers that were forced to close because of patronage lost under Pope's order.[4]

After the Civil War ended, the federal government resumed the practice of paying Southern newspapers to publish the U.S. laws. Congressional Republicans soon realized, however, that this patronage was not being effectively used for their party. Until 1867, Johnson's secretary of state, William Henry Seward, authorized these contracts, and they often went to conservative journals. Hence in March 1867, at the same time they passed the First Reconstruction Act, congressional Republicans revised the legislation governing the assignment of U.S. government printing contracts to newspapers. They expanded the printing covered by the legislation to include not only federal laws and treaties but also advertisements ordered by any U.S. court or executive officer. This encompassed, for instance, federal bankruptcy court notices. More importantly, the new law removed the secretary of state from the process and authorized Edward McPherson, the clerk of the House of Representatives and a dependable Republican, to identify two "loyal" papers in each Southern state to publish the U.S. laws.[5]

When the law went into effect, the secretary of the Union Republican Executive Committee, which was supervising the organization of the Republican Party in the South, claimed that only fifteen Republican papers existed there, two of them dailies. He greatly underestimated the total, which was closer to forty. Possibly the secretary was not as well informed about the South as he might have been, and he might not have been counting Unionist newspapers that by early 1867 were Republican in all but name. Hardly had the law passed when budding Republican journalists bombarded McPherson with pleas for the patronage. Some editors, apparently anticipating passage of the printing law, had hurriedly formed a press association to recommend papers to McPherson. Charles Whittlesey, an editor of the *Virginia State Journal*, chaired the association, and its secretary was John Bryant, editor of the *Loyal Georgian*. On March 4, 1867, the two men listed for McPherson twenty-one newspapers as candidates for government printing contracts.[6]

Their list included four papers from Virginia, three each from North Carolina, Georgia, Texas, and Louisiana, two from Alabama, and one each from South Carolina, Florida, and Arkansas.[7] At this point Whittlesey listed no papers from Mississippi, none having yet emerged there. He also excluded Tennessee, which was exempted from the March law. Further recommendations poured in, and during the next several weeks McPherson awarded contracts to two papers each in Virginia, North Carolina, Georgia, Alabama, Arkansas, and Texas and to three Louisiana papers. The newspaper situation in the other Southern states was still uncertain. For Mississippi, he awarded contracts to two papers, one recently opened and the other not yet being published. In South

Carolina, a fire destroyed the *New South* in the spring of 1867, and in September U.S. government printing went to the *Charleston Advocate*. McPherson had to wait for another reliable Republican paper's appearance in that state before he could award a second printing contract there. In Florida, he awarded the Jacksonville *Florida Times* patronage for the first session of the Thirty-ninth Congress but did not designate a paper for the second session.[8]

Upon receiving printing contracts, Republican editors proudly declared their publications "Official Papers" of the U.S. government. Some of them had an exaggerated notion of how much revenue these contracts would generate. John Bryant of the *Loyal Georgian*, who was trying to convince Harper and Brothers in New York to give him a loan, claimed that federal patronage would be worth at least $50,000 a year to his paper. This wildly inflated figure was probably intended to promote the Harper loan. A Northern Republican hoping to establish a party daily in Charleston, South Carolina, estimated the revenues from bankrupt notices and government advertising would amount to $10,000, a figure also much too high. In fact annual federal payments to Southern papers for the Thirty-ninth Congress averaged around $1,000. John Hayes of the *Savannah Republican* declared that the few hundred dollars he obtained for printing the laws was "too insignificant to let it influence us." Republican editors across the South, like their Northern colleagues, petitioned Congress to increase their compensation, complaining that the going rate hardly met the printing costs. Yet at least one Republican journal, the *Houston Union,* noted with pleasure that for one year its total reimbursement for publishing the U.S. laws, postal and mail matters, U.S. marshal sales, and bankrupt notices amounted to over $3,000.[9]

Such federal assistance was limited to two newspapers per state, almost always urban dailies. While patronage proved important to the papers receiving it, printing contracts alone could not sustain them. Nor was patronage available to the growing numbers of Republican country weeklies. Northern Republican editor John Forney observed that for the Southern newspapers to survive, they would have to rely on local support rather than federal patronage. *New York Tribune* editor Horace Greeley's assessment of the future of the South's Republican press was similar to Forney's. When a hopeful Republican editor from Georgia approached the dean of Republican journalists about how to finance his paper, Greeley advised "that if a newspaper could not maintain itself in Georgia, it was not worthwhile to maintain it from the North." He told another Southern editor that his paper would have to "induce people to take it and support it because of its justice, influence, and enterprise." Four years after congressional Reconstruction began, a prominent Georgia Republican warned that "unless a paper has local support, it is not worth much."[10]

It proved very difficult for Republican editors to develop this local support. Subscription lists remained hard to build, especially among African Americans. As the editor of the Alexandria *Rapides Gazette* observed, his parish's Republican Party was composed "principally of men who not only cannot read, but cannot conveniently pay for a paper." Upon closing his short-lived journal, the editor of Alabama's *Florence Republican* reflected that "there is no Radicalism in North Alabama outside of negro ranks, and as the darkies are all broke, there is no grist for the Republican mill." When an acquaintance asked a North Carolina Republican editor why he was giving up his paper, the editor replied, "Do you think I'm a d——d fool, to print a paper for a party that can't read?"[11] In any case, most white newspaper editors made little effort to appeal to the freedmen by carrying news of interest to them. It remained for the proprietors of a fledgling African American press to develop newspapers catering to blacks.

During the period from 1862, when free blacks in New Orleans established *L'Union,* until the passage of the First Reconstruction Act in March 1867, at least a dozen African American newspapers appeared in the South; of these, eight were still publishing by the latter date. Three of the more successful ones had been formed by African American cooperative efforts: the *New Orleans Tribune,* the Mobile *Nationalist,* and the Augusta *Loyal Georgian.* All three of these papers had white editors, but blacks owned and controlled them; the *Nationalist*'s proprietors assured blacks considering buying stock in the paper that they would not "be building up a white man's enterprise." Both whites and blacks owned stock in the *St. Landry Progress,* which began publication in July 1867; the paper had a biracial board of directors and its editors were white. William Scott, who moved his *Nashville Tennessean* to Maryville in 1867 and renamed it the *Maryville Republican,* also hired white editors. Although editors of these African American papers published some news of social and religious activity in their local black communities, they devoted most of their column space to political concerns. When some of his readers complained that his paper lacked information of local interest, editor John Bryant of the *Loyal Georgian* replied that "our paper is to instruct, not entertain" and advised his critics to find amusement elsewhere; Albert Griffin republished Bryant's remarks in his Mobile *Nationalist.*[12]

Black owners edited most of the other African American papers operating in 1867. These included the Raleigh *Weekly Republican;* the Norfolk *Union Republican;* and three papers in Charleston, the *Journal,* the *Advocate,* and the *South Carolina Leader,* which became the *Missionary Record* in April 1868. These papers garnered a few advertisements from local black business owners and artisans and from Northern businesses. The *New Orleans Tribune,* and for a limited time the *Charleston Advocate,* also received printing contracts from the U.S. government. Almost all of the African American papers existing in 1867 were gone by the end of 1868; the Mobile *Nationalist* disappeared in 1869 and the *New Orleans Tribune* early in 1870. The longest lasting of the African American papers appearing in the early Reconstruction years were the *Maryville Republican* and the *Missionary Record,* both of which survived until the late 1870s.[13] At least thirty more African American newspapers appeared between 1867 and 1877, but their life spans were usually brief.[14]

The vast majority of Republican newspapers were published and edited by whites and aimed at white audiences. Yet because of the postwar South's intensely partisan political atmosphere, it proved difficult to get whites to subscribe to Republican papers, and even if they did so, editors experienced problems collecting what was due them. Editor Jason Clarke Swayze of Georgia's Macon *American Union,* noting the demise of a fellow Republican's paper, said this was another example "of the littleness, the shortsightedness, and we may say the selfishness of Georgia Republicans," who would not expend a dollar for a newspaper subscription; other editors expressed similar frustrations.[15]

Republican publishers tried various stratagems to increase their newspapers' circulation. They sent agents to other towns to recruit subscribers, offered prizes for finding new readers, and provided reduced rates for group subscriptions. Some editors used their Union League ties to urge its members to buy their papers, while others sought support from members of the Grand Army of the Republic, a Union veterans' organization. In Texas, the superintendent of education for the Freedmen's Bureau asked his agents to circulate Republican papers and urged Unionists to subscribe to them. In Georgia, Swayze offered potential readers a reduced-rate subscription package that included his paper plus several leading Northern periodicals. During hard-fought election campaigns, publishers often cut subscription prices. To make it easier for subscribers to obtain their newspapers, some editors offered to accept payment in produce or other salable commodities.[16]

As we have seen, Republican publishers often experienced difficulty obtaining local advertising, but they sometimes secured ads from Northern firms like Harper Brothers and the *New York Tribune.* Two Republican papers in Virginia's Shenandoah Valley, a region with historic trade ties northward, obtained advertisements from Pennsylvania companies. Charleston's earliest Republican papers published advertisements and notices from Boston firms, partly because of the two cities' prewar trade ties and also because the editors had Boston connections.[17] Republican newspapers that were most successful in gaining local advertising were published either in cities like Atlanta, Savannah, and New Orleans, which had large numbers of Northern-born merchants, or in areas of strong Unionist sympathy, such as eastern Tennessee. Papers with large circulations garnered more local patronage than those with fewer readers. This was true, for instance, of Mississippi's two leading Republican papers, the *Vicksburg Times and Republican* and the Jackson *Pilot*, both of which ran a significant number of merchant advertisements in their columns.[18]

Almost all Republican newspaper proprietors counted heavily on obtaining patronage from state and local governments. Even Democratic papers sometimes admitted inability to sustain themselves without such patronage, and this largesse was even more essential for Republican publishers. Several Northern Republican editors predicted that if the party's publishers could secure government printing, their numbers would rise rapidly. Members of the Union Republican Executive Committee in Washington agreed. In July 1867, they concluded that their body did not have the resources to establish papers in the South and that the speediest way to do so was to give the Republican Party control of the state governments there.[19]

Most Republican editors followed the precedent set by their antebellum Whig and Democratic predecessors by combining their journalistic responsibilities with a great deal of participation in both party politics and state and local government. Several Republican editors, such as Harrison Reed of Florida, Tennessee's William Brownlow, and William Holden of North Carolina, became governors of their states. A number of Republican congressmen published newspapers during Reconstruction, including Alfred E. Buck, James T. Rapier, and Charles C. Sheats of Alabama; W. Jasper Blackburn and Michael Vidal of Louisiana; Israel Lash and Alexander H. Jones of North Carolina; James B. Sener from Virginia; Richard Whiteley of Georgia; Lewis Tillman from Tennessee; Lewis Cass Carpenter of South Carolina; John R. Lynch of Mississippi; and Josiah T. Walls of Florida. Many others served on city, county, and state Republican executive committees. Edward Cheney, editor of the *Florida Union*, chaired his state's Republican central committee during most of Reconstruction, while Valentine Dell, editor of the *Fort Smith New Era*, served for a time in the equivalent post in Arkansas.

A number of other editors also held elective or appointive offices in federal, state, or local governments, and salaries and commissions earned in these posts helped them finance newspapers. Officeholders, whether editors or not, were also expected to contribute some portion of their salaries to the party for financing political advertisements and notices published in newspapers. City policemen in Mobile, Alabama, were told to subscribe to the *Nationalist*, and in Georgia, Democrats charged that workers on the state-owned Western and

Atlantic Railroad were required to buy the Atlanta *New Era*. Assessments on officeholders sustained the *Wilmington Post* during the first three years of its existence.[20] Republican editors frequently complained, however, that Republican officeholders did not do enough to sustain their presses. The editor of the *Mississippi Pilot*, for instance, estimated that not one in ten Republican officeholders contributed any support to their party's newspapers.[21]

The most important assistance Southern governments could provide Republican newspapers was printing patronage. The first opportunity to obtain such printing came in 1867, when constitutional conventions assembled across the South. These conventions, which invariably came under Republican control, could provide considerable assistance to party editors. Delegates customarily voted to subscribe to hundreds or even thousands of copies of Republican newspapers during the weeks the conventions sat. Delegates to the Texas convention, for instance, arranged to pay approximately $172 per day for subscriptions to three Republican dailies. Most state conventions also provided for publishing their daily proceedings in several party papers and awarded to Republican publishers the contracts for final printing of the journals, debates, and constitutions. In addition, some conventions authorized a number of papers to publish their new constitutions regularly until the ratification votes took place. Often the editors receiving these printing awards were also convention delegates who participated in votes that selected printing recipients. In Arkansas, the constitutional convention designated as official printer its own secretary, John G. Price of the Little Rock *Daily Republican*.[22]

The cost of all this printing varied widely. Florida's constitutional convention appropriated $15,000 for printing costs, much of which was not expended, while its Texas counterpart approved the expenditure of $21,000 for printing and contingent expenses. In Arkansas, Price received $19,479 to print the state's convention journal and constitution. In Louisiana, payments to seven Republican papers to publish the convention's daily proceedings came to $25,000. Four Mississippi Republican publishers obtained approximately $36,000 for publishing their state convention's work.[23]

Under the terms of congressional Reconstruction, voters in each state had to approve the new constitutions drafted by these conventions and had to elect new state governments. If these new administrations were Republican, they could then direct state printing patronage to Republican newspapers. This eventually happened in every state except Virginia. There, Reconstruction ran into a number of problems that delayed a vote on the new constitution until 1869. Pierpont remained governor until April 1868, when General John Schofield replaced him with Henry H. Wells, a moderate Michigan-born Republican who had settled in Alexandria to practice law. Many Republicans hoped to run Wells for governor when elections were held under the new constitution. In the meantime, he had little state patronage to dispense, for the current legislature had named a superintendent of public printing who awarded contracts to non-Republican printers. When state elections were finally held in 1869, Wells lost his gubernatorial bid, and the new state government channeled only a trickle of printing money to the Republican *State Journal*.[24]

The process of reconstructing state governments in Mississippi and Texas also ran into delays, but by the summer of 1868 voters in the remaining seven states affected by the Reconstruction Acts had approved the new constitutions and elected new state officials. These new administrations, all Republican, identified Republican publishers to do the states' official printing. Sometimes the governor appointed the printer, subject to legislative approval. Elsewhere the legislature elected him. In Louisiana and Arkansas, lawmakers gave this power to a committee including the governor and two other elected officials. The printer selected to do the state's work also published one of the state's prominent Republican newspapers, usually a daily located in the capital. That paper became known as the "official paper" of the state as well as the administration's mouthpiece. In Tennessee, for instance, the state printing went to S. C. Mercer, editor of Nashville's leading Republican paper, the *Press and Times*. In Arkansas state printing went to John Price of the Little Rock *Daily Republican;* in Georgia to Samuel Bard of the Atlanta *Daily New Era;* in Louisiana to the proprietors of the *New Orleans Republican;* in Florida to Edward M. Cheney's Jacksonville *Florida Union;* in South Carolina to J. W. Denny, publisher of the Columbia *Daily Republican;* in Alabama to John Stokes of the Montgomery *Alabama State Journal;* in North Carolina to William Holden's *North Carolina Standard;* in Mississippi to the proprietors of the Jackson *Pilot;* and in Texas to the Austin *State Journal's* proprietors.

Since each state's official printing went to one prominent Republican publisher with facilities sufficient for producing bound volumes of debates, laws, supreme court reports, and other official documents, some administrations found ways to subsidize additional Republican papers in their states. A few governments provided for publishing laws, resolutions, announcements, and proclamations in newspapers other than the one designated by law as official. The North Carolina legislature authorized the secretary of state to select no more than one newspaper in each county to publish the state's laws. In Florida, the legislature empowered the secretary of state to designate three papers, one each in Tallahassee, Jacksonville, and Pensacola, as official papers. The amounts expended on the daily or weekly publication of these documents could exceed the payments made to the official printers for publishing bound volumes at the close of the legislative sessions. For instance, Georgia's Republican governor Rufus B. Bullock spent $50,000 in 1869 to publish proclamations and $70,000 the following year. South Carolina's legislature authorized the state's house and senate clerks to contract with various newspapers in the state to publish laws and other state advertisements at an estimated cost per session up through 1872 of $60,000. In 1868, Louisiana's Republican legislature authorized the state printing commissioners to pay fifteen newspapers scattered throughout the state for printing legislative journals, debates, and laws. In addition, each house of the legislature could identify additional papers to print these documents. Under these provisions, the government expended $1.5 million over the next three years in state warrants to cover printing expenses.[25]

Another significant source of printing patronage was city and county governments and state circuit and district courts, which also published in local newspapers ordinances, documents, and notices of court dates, bankruptcy proceedings, and tax sales. Customarily these contracts went to papers affiliated with the party controlling the local government. If the local officials were Republican, they awarded patronage to the local Republican paper. Hence some newspapers touted themselves as the official newspaper of the U.S. government, the state government, and county and city governments. The *Memphis Daily Post,* for instance, was the official United States journal, the official state journal for western Tennessee, and the official journal for both Shelby County and the Memphis city board of education. Samuel Bard, publisher of the Atlanta *New Era,* proudly boasted that his paper was the official journal for the state and national governments as well as for the city and county, which gave it a prestigious status "seldom enjoyed by one newspaper establishment, [and which suggested] advantages to newspaper readers and the business community which they will do well to heed."[26] Since in many areas Southern Republicans failed to gain control of local governments, their papers had no access to printing patronage. Instead, Republican editors complained, this patronage went to their rivals, who in numerous cases edited papers that were bitterly opposed to both the federal government and to the reconstructed state governments. Why, they asked, should such papers be rewarded, while those loyal to the state and national governments got nothing? An 1868 convention of Tennessee's Republican newspaper publishers complained to the state legislature that the "rebel" press had cornered four-fifths of the legal advertising of the state's counties. Republican papers that combated these disloyal elements, the editors averred, deserved access to such patronage. Responding to these concerns, the next session of the Tennessee legislature authorized Governor Brownlow to designate an official paper in each congressional district to publish the legal advertisements for that district's counties.[27]

Alabama enacted a similar law, and Republican legislatures in Arkansas and Texas granted their governors power to designate a paper in each judicial district of their states to handle the public printing for that district. The Florida legislature delegated first to circuit judges and then to the secretary of state the power to designate an official paper in each circuit—a paper that would do the printing for local governmental agencies and officers in that jurisdiction. South Carolina's legislature authorized the state's attorney general, comptroller general, and secretary of state to identify official papers around the state to publish state and local advertisements. Although Mississippi Republicans had adopted a state constitutional provision authorizing the legislature to designate "loyal" journals in each circuit court district, the lawmakers failed to take such action until 1874. This law authorized chancellors holding court in judicial districts to identify newspapers worthy of official advertisements.[28]

Payments from local governments could be quite lucrative. Officials in Shelby County, Tennessee, spent almost $5,000 on printing between April 1866 and July 1867. Alabama's governor designated the Demopolis *Southern Republican*, located in Marengo County, as the official paper for Marengo and also for Greene, Perry, and Choctaw counties. Democratic newspapers in Perry and Choctaw complained about probate judges' putting notices in the Demopolis sheet, but to no avail. Over a two-year span from 1869 to 1871, the Republican paper received at least $5800 in payments from the four county governments. On the other hand, a number of Republican editors complained either that local officials were refusing to obey the laws requiring them to post notices in the designated journals or that the payments they received were inconsequential.[29]

Because Louisiana conservatives controlled New Orleans and Orleans Parish, the Republican legislature authorized the state printer to publish all judicial and other notices issuing from the city and parish governments. This patronage went to the *New Orleans Republican*, which was the official organ of both the state and national governments. Accordingly that paper published state and national laws, advertisements, and bankruptcy and judicial notices, the proceedings of both state legislative houses, and the proceedings and ordinances of the New Orleans City Council. In 1870, the payments to the paper for the city's printing alone came to over $50,000. The *Republican* published an eight-page daily paper, but laws, notices, and ordinances filled most of its columns. Government printing occupied a great amount of space in many Republican papers. The editor of the *Rapides Gazette*, who had just received several numbers of the

Homer Iliad, noted that "the last with the exception of a square or two is filled up with advertisements and tax sales."[30]

Occasionally a Republican editor would criticize this dispensation of printing to the party's press, claiming that it added unduly to government expenses, alienated potential subscribers, or interfered with freedom of the press by favoring some papers over others.[31] Democratic editors unanimously condemned the partisanship involved in awarding printing contracts. The editor of the *Sumter News* condemned South Carolina's measure designating official papers to receive state printing and advertising as "the most villainous law ever enacted by the Radical Legislature." Unhappy Democratic editors claimed that their own papers possessed much larger circulations than patronage-designated Republican journals and that often the official newspapers carried reports from counties where such papers did not circulate. The editor of the Democratic *North Arkansas Times* complained that Arkansas Republicans, most of whom were "negroes and ignorant white people," had no interest in legal notices, whereas business and property owners had to buy a radical paper to access them. In response to these charges, Republican editors noted that the party in control of state or local governments had traditionally rewarded its newspaper supporters with printing patronage. Officials could not be expected to provide such contracts to publishers bent on throwing them out of office. As the Austin *Daily State Journal* observed, the uproar over the Texas printing bill was due to the fact that "Republican printers are doing the work."[32]

In addition to defending their reliance on government patronage as consistent with past political practice, Republican editors also emphasized that the political atmosphere in the Reconstruction South constituted a sharp departure from the past. Most Southern whites would not accord the Republican Party legitimacy, and Republican editors claimed that this hostility threatened the very existence of government itself. In such an environment, a government's patronage should accrue to its friends rather than to the newspapers agitating for its overthrow. The editor of the *McMinnville Enterprise* claimed that local "rebel officeholders" in Tennessee were giving printing awards to conservative papers that were "incendiary in their tendency and designs," helping thereby to weaken support for the state's Republican regime. Pierce Burton of the Demopolis, Alabama, *Southern Republican* contended that government patronage should not go to support Democratic papers that refused to recognize the legality of the existing Republican state government.[33]

Burton's comments were in defense of Alabama's 1868 law stipulating that the governor should designate no paper to publish legal advertisements "which does not in its columns sustain and advocate the maintenance" of both the U.S.

and Alabama governments. When Louisiana's constitutional convention assembled, Republican delegates justified withholding the convention's printing from Democratic newspapers because their editors, who opposed the whole Reconstruction process, would advise readers to defeat the constitution. The printing committee recommended instead that the convention publish its proceedings in six Republican papers, claiming this would "tend materially to aid the cause of reconstruction of a loyal government in this State, founded on principles of true republicanism." Republican delegates in the Mississippi convention used identical language to justify printing the convention journal in two Republican newspapers, and Samuel Bard, editor of the Atlanta *New Era,* made the same point regarding the dispensation of Georgia's convention printing. In Virginia, Republican delegates contended that printing-contract recipients should be able to take the ironclad oath and should favor the Congressional Reconstruction plan.[34]

Texas Republicans claimed that a law authorizing the governor to direct printing patronage of the state's judicial districts to party newspapers was necessary in order to reward "loyal" newspapers and to "radiate civilization into the darkest corners of the state." In 1870, when Republicans in the Mississippi legislature sought to pass a similar law, conservatives denounced it as a measure "conceived in sin, and brought forth in iniquity." To this a Republican senator retorted that he would not in any manner assist Democratic journals "which, even now, are counselling the 'shooting down of negroes' who happen to hold office." South Carolina's Republican governor, Robert K. Scott, noting that almost all papers in the state opposed the existing state government, asserted that he was "unwilling to endorse their misrepresentations, or to increase their power of mischief," by granting them public printing. In New Orleans, the publishers of the *Republican* made no apologies for receiving $50,000 of printing contracts from the city, claiming that this aid served the government's interest by enabling the paper to "combat prejudice and beat down error."[35]

Louisiana's Republican legislator W. Jasper Blackburn, who also owned the *Homer Iliad,* defended the law directing local patronage to Republican papers, claiming it contributed to press freedom by sustaining a political philosophy that would otherwise be crushed by Democratic oppression. The editor of the *Louisiana State Register* reiterated this point, noting that the Republican Party represented "the poor, the downtrodden, and the oppressed," who could not support papers by themselves. If the state's whites could only comprehend that the Republicans proposed no injustice to them, and indeed asked only "that every man be treated fairly and according to his merits, be he white or black," they would realize that the party would make the South "great, united, and free."

Republicans, however, could not transmit this philosophy to the public without government patronage for their newspapers. Both Louisiana editors admitted that Republican papers had failed to obtain what Blackburn called "voluntary advertising" from local business owners. They blamed this situation on the atmosphere of hatred and violence created and sustained by the Democratic press. In such circumstances, the legislature was justified in taking extraordinary action to keep Republican newspapers alive.[36]

Both the *Iliad* and the *Louisiana State Register* were among the many Republican sheets in Louisiana that obtained governmental advertising. In addition, the legislature granted Blackburn $6,000 to buy a new press and equipment after a mob destroyed his newspaper office. Both editors confessed that without such state patronage, their newspapers could not survive, a point other Republican editors also admitted.[37] Editors of metropolitan dailies, where costs were higher than for rural weeklies, were heavily dependent on government printing. Lucien Eaton, editor of the *Memphis Post*, told his brother that it was an "absolute impossibility for a Republican daily to live in Memphis without such political favoritism as we have had." The Austin *Daily State Journal*'s editor acknowledged the truth of Democratic charges that Texas's Republican press would die without government patronage. He contended, however, that this situation resulted from the atmosphere of proscription and intolerance that deprived the press of advertising and subscription revenues.[38]

The number of Republican newspapers in the South began to rise as Republicans, impelled by the prospect of securing government patronage, worked to gain control of the ex-Confederate states. In June 1867, John Forney, an editor of two Northern Republican papers that kept a close eye on Southern press developments, estimated that the former Confederacy had thirty-six papers he could clearly identify as Republican, with another fifty leaning in that direction. By October, he claimed there were over one hundred Republican newspapers in the South.[39] Forney's numbers were fairly accurate, and the total continued to climb. The distribution of Republican newspapers around the South, however, proved to be quite uneven.

CHAPTER FIVE

The Geographic Breadth of the Southern Republican Press

Despite the intense white-majority opposition during Reconstruction, Republicans established at least 478 newspapers in the South between 1861 and 1877. During the same period the Democrats published around 970, giving Republicans 33 percent of the South's partisan newspapers. The greatest number of Republican papers existing in a single year was 163, a figure reached in 1871. There were then around four hundred Democratic newspapers, giving the Republicans nearly 29 percent of the South's partisan sheets in that year.[1]

These figures suggest the competitiveness of the Republican press in the Reconstruction South. Figures on newspaper survivability, however, reveal that the party's newspapers were relatively short-lived. Forty-six percent of the Republican papers lasted two years or less; about a sixth of them survived only a year. Although three hundred new Democratic newspapers also disappeared within two years, they comprised 30 percent of the total number of Democratic papers, a figure two-thirds that of the failed Republican papers. At least ninety-three Republican papers, 19 percent of the party's total, lasted five years or longer, as compared to almost four hundred Southern Democratic newspapers, which represented 41 percent of that party's papers. Republicans published forty daily newspapers during the Reconstruction years, compared to the Democrats' one hundred. Only twenty-two of the Republican dailies lasted more than two years, however, compared to eighty Democratic dailies. Republican papers also had smaller circulations than their Democratic counterparts. Based on unreliable figures published in Rowell's *American Newspaper Directory*, Republican weeklies had an average circulation ranging from 450 to 750; the range for dailies was between five hundred and two thousand. Democratic weeklies had circulations averaging about one hundred more than their Republican counterparts, while figures for their dailies were often two to three times higher than those for Republican dailies.[2]

A newspaper's survival prospects depended on numerous factors, including the editor's skill and the publisher's business acumen, variables affecting Democratic newspapers as well. But because of their particular difficulty in finding advertisers and subscribers, Republican publishers were far more dependent than their Democratic counterparts on government patronage. Many of the longest-lived Republican papers were published in large towns or cities. The party established a paper in every state capital—cities where the Republicans were politically competitive. These papers attracted at least a few commercial advertisers, received printing patronage from both national and state parties, and became the official journals for the Republican state administrations. All but two were dailies, the exceptions being the weekly Tallahassee *Florida Sentinel* and the weekly Jackson *Mississippi Pilot*, which published a daily edition during Mississippi legislative sessions.

Republicans were also able to maintain dailies for various lengths of time in Charleston, Norfolk, Jacksonville, Vicksburg, New Bern, Wilmington, San Antonio, Houston, Memphis, Knoxville, and Chattanooga. Elsewhere they relied on weeklies. These papers were usually based in Republican-dominated counties and published in the county seats. Such locations facilitated publishers' quests for subscriptions, advertising, and local governmental printing contracts. Many of these counties were located in fertile agricultural areas where plantations and slaves had been common before the war and where the large Reconstruction-era black vote went overwhelmingly to the Republicans. Republican papers could also be found in some hilly and mountainous regions that had significant numbers of Unionist whites. Thus eastern Tennessee had a large number of Republican papers, as did the North Carolina Piedmont and the northwestern counties of Arkansas.[3]

The number of Republican newspapers varied widely from state to state. The least effective predictor of party newspaper strength was state population. Florida, which in 1870 was the smallest Southern state with a population of only 187,000, had twenty-two Republican papers. This figure almost equaled Virginia's total and surpassed that of Georgia, which had only seventeen, yet these two states each had almost 1.2 million inhabitants. Louisiana, which led the ex-Confederate states with seventy-three Republican papers, ranked eighth in population. Texas and Arkansas, which ranked third and fourth in their number of Republican newspapers, were seventh and tenth, respectively, in population. There was also little relationship between the total number of Republican voters in a state and the size of the party's press. The 1872 election, the most peaceful one during the Reconstruction period, saw the maximum number of Republican votes in a single election. Louisiana, Mississippi, and Texas, which ranked first, second, and third in the number of Republican newspapers, were seventh, sixth, and ninth, respectively, in the number of Republican voters in 1872.

Conversely, the three states casting the most Republican votes that year, beginning with North Carolina and followed by South Carolina and Virginia, ranked seventh, sixth, and ninth, respectively, in total Republican papers. The most important variable affecting the number of Republican papers in each state proved to be the amount of state and local printing patronage available to them. Hence, the states with the fewest Republican sheets, in addition to Florida, were Virginia and Georgia, where such patronage was limited. The states with larger numbers of Republican papers made more state and local printing available to the party press.

Although Louisiana ranked seventh among the eleven ex-Confederate states in population, it produced at least seventy-three Republican newspapers, the most in the South. This number actually exceeded the state's total of Democratic newspapers, which numbered fifty-eight during the same period. Twenty-four of the Republican papers lasted five years or more, putting that state far ahead of the others in this category; fifty of its Republican papers, or slightly more than two-thirds, lasted more than two years, putting Louisiana second only to Florida in this regard. Louisiana's large number of Republican papers was only partly attributable to the party's voting strength in the state. Louisiana Republicans won 55.8 percent of the state's vote in 1872, a figure exceeded only by North and South Carolina. The party controlled Louisiana from 1867 until 1877. The Republicans also controlled South Carolina for the same number of years, and these two states had approximately the same populations. South Carolina, however, produced only thirty-five Republican papers, far fewer than Louisiana. The chief reason for this disparity was that Louisiana adopted the most liberal program of newspaper subsidies in the Reconstruction South, a fact that also accounts for the longevity of the state's Republican sheets.

When congressional Reconstruction began in 1867, only six papers in Louisiana backed the Republicans. Three were in New Orleans: the *Tribune*, published by African Americans since midwar; the *Advocate*, a Methodist publication launched in 1866 and edited and published by Northern missionary John P. Newman, who had come to the city in 1864 to direct Northern Methodist activity there; and the *Republican*, established in the spring of 1867 by a group of Northern carpetbaggers and New Orleans Unionists that included former governor Michael Hahn. The fourth was *Blackburn's Homer Iliad*, published in Claiborne Parish by W. Jasper Blackburn. Blackburn had grown up in Arkansas, had moved to Claiborne in 1848, and was editing the *Iliad* when Louisiana seceded. A staunch Unionist, he had to hide in the woods from angry Confederates who closed his paper. At the close of hostilities he resumed publication, and he joined the Republican Party when it was formed in 1867. He would later be elected to a term in Congress. The fifth paper, the Opelousas *St. Landry Progress*, appeared in July 1867. It was published in St. Landry Parish, which had the largest population of any parish outside New Orleans. Almost a thousand free people of color lived there, and they were instrumental in founding the parish's Republican Party and in establishing the *Progress*. The sixth paper, the Monroe *Louisiana Intelligencer*, was owned and edited by Julius Ennemoser, a German Unionist.[4] By early 1868, the number of Republican sheets in Louisiana had risen to eight, with the addition of the German-language New Orleans *Deutsche Zeitung* and a new Republican paper in Plaquemine, the *Iberville Pioneer*. The Louisiana constitutional convention, which met during the winter of 1867–68, directed printing patronage to all of these papers, and the federal government gave printing contracts to the *Republican*, *Tribune*, and *Iliad*.[5]

After the Republicans gained control of Louisiana's government in the 1868 elections, the legislature established a printing commission made up of the governor, lieutenant governor, and speaker of the house to contract with a publisher to do the state's printing. This state printer's newspaper was designated as the state's official paper. He was authorized not only to publish the state's official journals and laws in bound volumes but also to publish, in his newspaper, the daily journal of both state legislative houses as well as other official materials. Since the Republicans had failed to gain control of New Orleans, the law also required the state printer to publish all judicial and other notices issuing from the city and from Orleans Parish. In addition, the law empowered the printing commission to select other Orleans Parish papers to publish state laws and/or journals. To secure the future of the Republican press outside New Orleans, the law authorized the printing commission to choose papers in parishes throughout Louisiana to publish state laws and legislative journals and to do the official printing and advertising for the parishes served by those newspapers. The state house and senate also claimed the right to identify parish papers to print legislative journals and debates, paying for this out of contingent funds.[6] Thanks to this patronage, by the end of 1868 the number of Republican papers rapidly rose, peaking in 1871 at thirty-five, a total exceeding that reached by the state's Democratic press in the same year. After that date the count gradually declined, but as late as 1877 twenty Republican papers remained in Louisiana, far more than in any other ex-Confederate state.

During Reconstruction at least a dozen Republican newspapers appeared in New Orleans, by far the largest city in the entire South with its population of 181,000. Blacks made up less than 15 percent of the city's population, however, and the Republicans were unable to carry New Orleans in the 1868 election. Although the Union Army had occupied the city for most of the war and many of its businessmen had been Unionists, local Republican papers struggled to survive and depended heavily on government patronage.[7] The *Tribune* stopped publishing in 1868, and the *Advocate* closed the following year.[8] The *Republican*, which became the state's official journal and the party's leading paper, survived until 1877. In addition, the German-language *Deutsche Zeitung* supported the Republicans, although not consistently, and the Republicans claimed two French-language papers in the city, neither of which lasted more than a year. African Americans published several papers in New Orleans in addition to the *Tribune*. In 1868, John W. Menard, an Illinois-born free black, established the *Free South*, which became the *Radical Standard* in 1870 and lasted until 1871. In that year another African American publication, the *Louisianan*, appeared in the city, and it survived into the following decade. In addition to these papers published in New Orleans, four Republican papers appeared in Jefferson Parish, which was part of the New Orleans metropolitan area and which the Republicans joined to Orleans Parish in 1869. One of these papers, the Carrollton *Louisiana State Register*, lasted from 1869 to 1874.[9]

About half the state's Republican newspapers came from the rich alluvial parishes on or near the Mississippi River. Former slaves comprised the overwhelming majority of most of these Black Belt parishes, and the Republican Party generally carried them. The longer-lived papers in this section of the state included two in St. James Parish, *Le Louisianais* and the *St. James Sentinel*, both of which lasted throughout Reconstruction. Others included the *Donaldsonville Chief*, 1871–79, the Edgard (and then Bonnet Carre) *Republican Pioneer*, 1868–75, the Houma *Terrebone Patriot*, 1868–75, the Plaquemine *Iberville Pioneer*, 1868–73, the St. Joseph *North Louisiana Journal*, 1871–77, the St. Sophie *Plaquemines Sentinel*, 1872–77, and the *Attakapas Register*, published in several places from 1869 to 1879.[10]

Ten more Republican papers came from three parishes bordering the Red River and from two so-called Florida parishes on the east bank of the Mississippi; all five of these parishes had black majorities. Natchitoches, in the parish of the same name, produced a Republican paper, the *Red River News*, from 1868 to 1874; it was succeeded by the *Weekly Republican*, which lasted until 1877. Shreveport, in Caddo Parish, had a Republican paper from 1871 to 1877, while the *Rapides Gazette* was published in Alexandria from 1869 to 1877. St. Francisville in West Feliciana Parish had three Republican papers; one of them, the St. Francisville *Feliciana Republican*, lasted from 1868 to 1875. Baton Rouge produced the *Courier*, which was succeeded by an African American paper, the *Grand Era*, published from 1870 to 1878. Its founder, J. Henri Burch, was a free black from

Connecticut who had worked on Menard's *Radical Standard* and had helped found the *Louisianan* before going on to Baton Rouge.[11]

Few Republican papers appeared far from the Mississippi or Red rivers. Several upstate Louisiana parishes had divided over secession, and some harbored Unionists during the Civil War. African Americans comprised a majority of the population in Ouachita Parish, where the Monroe *Louisiana Intelligencer* was published from 1869 to 1879. Claiborne Parish on the Arkansas border had a slight black majority, but Republicans failed to carry it during Reconstruction. Nonetheless, it was home to the staunchly Republican *Homer Iliad* from 1867 to 1875. Iberia Parish in south-central Louisiana, which also had a slight black majority, produced two Republican papers; one of them, the *New Iberia Progress*, lasted from 1872 to 1877.[12] Only two white parishes produced Republican newspapers, and none endured long. Formed in 1869 from parts of four Florida parishes, Tangipahoa had two Republican papers in Amite City, the *Tangipahoa Advocate* lasting for about three years; St. Landry Parish in south-central Louisiana was the home of the short-lived Opelousas *St. Landry Progress.*[13]

Mississippi ranked second among the ex-Confederate states with sixty-one newspapers during Reconstruction. The state's population in 1870 and the number of its Republicans voting in 1872 both ranked sixth in the South. However, the party's vote that year—63 percent—led the South. Republicans controlled Mississippi until 1875. Although the party had a relatively large number of newspapers, Democrats boasted almost twice as many, 113. Sixty-one percent of the Republican papers lasted two years or less, putting the state close to the bottom in this category.

Republicans were unable to found a paper in Mississippi until the inauguration of congressional Reconstruction in 1867. Early in March of that year, the *Vicksburg Republican* appeared, followed shortly by the *Meridian Chronicle*. Two Union Army officers, J. N. Osborn and James Dugan, owned the Vicksburg paper, with Dugan as editor. R. J. Moseley, a native Southerner, owned the *Chronicle*; its editor was J. R. Smith, a Mississippian who had opposed secession and later joined the Confederate Army. In 1867, Edward McPherson, the clerk of the U.S. House of Representatives, awarded federal printing contracts to both papers, but they continued to struggle, indicating that federal patronage alone was not sufficient to sustain Republican papers in Mississippi.[14] Early in 1868, Dugan sold his interest in the Vicksburg paper and opened the *Mississippi State Journal* in Jackson, the state capital, where the state constitutional convention called under the Reconstruction Acts was meeting. Shortly thereafter a new Republican paper appeared in Jackson, the *Mississippi Pilot*. Carpetbaggers controlled the publication; its first proprietor and editor was Edward Stafford, a Union general originally from New York and a prewar Missouri newspaper publisher. The *Pilot* soon crowded out Dugan's paper, which did not survive the year. The *Vicksburg Republican* also appeared headed for bankruptcy in 1868, but it was saved by the last-minute intervention of A. C. Fisk, a Union Army officer who bought control of it. This left the Republicans with three papers, none of them dailies. At the end of 1868, McPherson awarded government printing to the *Republican* and the *Pilot;* Smith's *Chronicle,* deprived of such assistance, soon disappeared.[15] In 1869, Republicans acquired control of the *Vicksburg Times,* and early the following year this paper merged with the *Vicksburg Republican;* the firm issued the *Times* on a daily basis and the *Times and Republican* as a weekly. In 1875, after Republicans had lost control of Vicksburg, the owners moved their paper to Jackson, where they continued publication through 1877. The *Times and Republican* and the Jackson *Mississippi Pilot,* which published weekly editions and a daily during state legislative sessions, remained Mississippi's principal Republican papers throughout Reconstruction. For several years, John Raymond was the principal owner of both the Jackson and Vicksburg papers. Both the *Pilot* and the *Times and Republican* obtained U.S. government printing contracts, and the *Pilot*'s proprietors obtained the state's printing, making it the official paper of the state government.[16]

Republicans had difficulty establishing presses outside Jackson and Vicksburg. The papers in those two cities remained the only ones to have a circulation of more than a few hundred. The new Mississippi constitution authorized the state legislature to designate loyal papers in each circuit court district to publish legal advertisements and other official notices. In anticipation of this patronage, Republican papers began to emerge in small towns. Their numbers rose to sixteen in 1869. Unfortunately for the party, Reconstruction ran into delays in Mississippi as well as in Texas, and a Republican administration was not inaugurated until 1870. At that time the legislature passed a district printing bill, but Governor James Alcorn vetoed the measure.[17] By 1872, the number of Republican papers had dwindled to ten at a time when the Democrats could count at least seventy-four. The *Pilot* was running at a loss, and the proprietors of the Vicksburg *Times and Republican* were contemplating selling their enterprise. Both papers managed to survive, and in 1874 the state legislature again passed a district printing bill. This time the new governor, Adelbert Ames, signed the measure, which encouraged a spurt of new country newspapers, but it was too late. Republican control of Mississippi was slipping away, and the 1875 legislature repealed the law.[18]

Outside Jackson and Vicksburg, the longest-running Republican newspapers in Mississippi were the Bay St. Louis *Sea Coast Republican,* 1871–76; *Columbus Press,* 1869–76; *Friar's Point Delta,* 1869–74; Natchez *New South,* 1869–74; Okolona *Prairie News,* 1870–1876; and *Woodville Republican,* 1869–77. The Columbus, Friar's Point, Natchez, and Woodville papers were published in counties with large black majorities that voted overwhelmingly Republican. The Okolona paper was published in Chickasaw County, which was almost evenly divided along racial lines; the Republicans, however, carried the county until 1875. The *Sea Coast Republican* was published in Hancock County on the Gulf Coast. Although white voters predominated in this lightly populated county, Republicans were competitive, carrying it for Grant in 1872.[19]

Texas ranked seventh among the ex-Confederate states in population and had fifty-seven Republican newspapers, placing it third in this category. The Lone Star State had 169 Democratic newspapers during Reconstruction, which placed it first in the South in this regard. The Texas Republican Party was weak, ranking ninth in the number of Republican votes in 1872 and last in terms of the percentage of the total vote that was Republican. The party did manage to control the state from 1869 to 1874 and enacted a generous system of printing patronage that was similar to Louisiana's. These provisions operated for only a little over a year, however, helping account for the fact that 44 percent of the Lone Star's papers lasted two years or less.

In the spring of 1867, when federal military authorities began implementing the congressional Reconstruction Acts in Texas, the state had four Unionist papers, all of which became Republican: the Austin *Southern Intelligencer,* the Galveston *Flake's Bulletin,* and two San Antonio papers, the *San Antonio Express* and the *Freie Presse fur Texas.* All these papers were owned and edited by white Texans. After the state's Republican Party was organized that summer, eight more party papers appeared, but half of them disappeared within a year. The short-lived Austin *Freedman's Press,* edited by African American physician Melville Keith, was established with the aid of James Newcomb, one of the Republican Party leaders in Texas and editor of two of its major newspapers. One of the new Republican papers that managed to survive, the *Austin Republican,* replaced the *Southern Intelligencer;* in Washington, Edward McPherson gave federal printing to the *Republican* and the *San Antonio Express.*[20]

In Texas, various problems delayed the election and installation of a Republican state government until 1870. At that time the newly elected Republican legislature authorized Governor Edmund J. Davis to designate a paper in each district to do official state and local printing there, a step that encouraged the emergence of more party newspapers. In 1871, when the Democrats could count sixty-seven papers, the Republicans had twenty-nine. Late that year, however, lawmakers repealed the measure, and although Governor Davis could still place executive proclamations, advertisements, and announcements in papers around the state, the Republican press began to decline.[21]

During the 1870s, the Republican Party managed to sustain six dailies in Texas, more than in any other Southern state. Four of these papers, all "scalawag"-owned and -edited, were closely associated with the Davis regime. The *San Antonio Express* remained a Republican paper until 1877, when it became an independent; its sister German-language paper, the weekly *Freie Presse fur Texas*, remained Republican throughout the decade. After 1868 federal printing patronage went to August Siemering, publisher of the two San Antonio papers, and to James G. Tracy of the daily *Houston Union*, whose paper lasted from 1868 to 1873. Tracy, who was a Confederate veteran, also became official printer for the state. In 1870, he and Siemering established the daily *Austin State Journal* in the capital, where it replaced the *Austin Republican;* the *Journal* became the official organ of the Davis administration. Its editor, James P. Newcomb, had published a Unionist paper in San Antonio before the war, but a pro-Confederate mob had destroyed his press in May 1861; Newcomb had to flee the state. After the war, he returned to Texas and settled in San Antonio, where he bought an interest in the *Express* and was one of its editors before moving on to the *Journal;* he remained with this paper until its demise in 1874. Like Tracy, he served for a time as secretary of the Republican state executive committee; he was also president of the state's Union League and secretary of state in the Davis government.[22]

The central Gulf Coast area of Texas, roughly the state's third congressional district, was the center of the state's plantation agriculture and its wealthiest section; it had traditionally dominated Texas government. Its chief cities, Galveston and Houston, were growing rapidly. The Republicans got little white support in the district but, thanks to the large black vote, carried it for Davis in 1869 and also elected a Republican congressman. Two years later, however, the Republicans lost this seat in a contested election. Republicans established at least eighteen papers in this region; despite Galveston's returning Democratic majorities during Reconstruction, nine Republican papers existed at one time or another in the city. Three of these were owned and published by African Americans. One was the state's first black-owned paper, the Galveston *Weekly Spectator,* founded and edited by Richard Nelson, who was born free in Key West and had moved to Texas before the war. His paper lasted from 1871 through the rest of the decade. Harris County, where Houston is located, produced Republican majorities until 1873; in addition to the *Union,* a Republican German-language newspaper, the *Texas Volksblatt,* was published there from 1869 to 1872. Of the remaining seven

Republican papers scattered through the third congressional district, only two lasted more than two years, the Huntsville *Union Republican,* published from 1868 to 1873, and the *Waco Register,* a Democratic newspaper that became Republican in 1873 and supported the party until the paper disappeared in 1879. Huntsville is located in Walker County, which had a large African American vote; Republicans controlled it through the 1873 elections. Waco is in McLennan County, which returned Republican majorities until 1872.[23]

East Texas, the location of the state's first congressional district, was less prosperous than the central region and home to fewer blacks. It lacked towns or cities of any significant size. Republicans narrowly carried this district for Davis in 1869, and won the congressional seat that year as well, but lost it in 1871. In 1869, Republicans earned anywhere from 10 to 29 percent of the white vote in seven counties in this district, one of which was Smith County, where the *National Index* was published in Tyler. Smith also had a large black population, and the Republicans remained competitive there throughout the 1870s, carrying the county in 1869 and again in 1871. The *National Index* proved to be one of the state's longest-lasting Republican papers, surviving from 1867 to at least 1876. The other nine Republican papers published in this district each had a life span of two years or less.[24]

The second congressional district of Texas was located in the northern part of the state, a region populated by many white Unionists. Only two counties on this district's eastern border had a population that was at least 40 percent black, and they were two of the three counties that went for Davis in 1869. Conservatives easily controlled the district's congressional seat. Despite Republicans' weakness in this area, they established twelve papers there, five of which survived for more than two years. The two longest-lived of these were the *Norton's Union Intelligencer* in Dallas, published from at least 1873 through the end of the decade, and the *McKinney Messenger,* which supported the Republicans from 1867 through at least 1872. The other three were the *Denison Cresset,* 1874–77, the *Paris Vindicator,* 1867–70, and the *Sherman Patriot,* 1871–77.[25]

The fourth congressional district of Texas lay to the west. Only Bastrop County in this region had a significant black population. A number of counties in the center of the district had a white population that was 15 percent or more German, and many of these counties had turned out a large vote against secession. Here, the Republicans showed more success in attracting white support than in the other three districts. In 1869, 50 percent or more of the whites in nine of this district's counties voted for Davis. He also received between 30 and 49 percent of the white vote in five counties, and between 10 and 29 percent in four more.[26] At one time or another during Reconstruction, seventeen Republican newspapers appeared in the fourth district, including five of its six dailies. Six of these sheets were published in Austin, the state's capital. Austin and its county of Travis had been a prewar Unionist hotbed, and Republicans were quite competitive there, carrying the county for the party's congressional candidate in 1871. Travis County's party dailies, the *Republican* and the *Journal*, were relatively long-lived, as was the German-language *Vorwarts*, published from 1871 to 1875. San Antonio, the home of two Republican dailies, had been another center of prewar Unionism; it lies in Bexar County, and 50 percent of the whites there voted for Davis in 1869. Republicans controlled the county until 1872. Davis also garnered more than 50 percent of the white vote in Nueces County, which again voted Republican in the 1873 election. The party's paper there, the Corpus Christi *Nueces Valley*, lasted from 1870 to 1874. The *Goliad Guard*, published in a county where Davis got a significant white vote, declared itself neutral but probably backed the Republicans from 1869 to 1872.[27]

Tennessee ranked first among the Southern states in population in 1870 and had fifty-one Republican newspapers during Reconstruction, making it fifth in this category. Thirty-six percent of its partisan papers were Republican. Forty-one percent of the party's newspapers lasted two years or less, while 24 percent survived for five years or more. Despite Tennessee's large population, it finished fifth in the total number of Republican votes cast in 1872 and ninth in its percentage of the total Republican vote. Republicans drew white votes from Unionist-dominated counties but could maintain control of the state administration only by disfranchising large numbers of ex-Confederates. This white Unionist support and a liberal patronage policy for party newspapers help account for Tennessee's relatively large number of Republican papers.

By 1867, Republicans were publishing thirteen papers in Tennessee. Many of them were hard pressed to survive, and Republican editors petitioned the state government for assistance. Early in 1868, Republican lawmakers obliged, authorizing Governor William G. Brownlow to identify papers to receive local printing patronage. In the wake of this law, seven new Republican papers appeared. John Ruhm and William Bailey, publishers of the Nashville *Tennessee Staats Zeitung*, controlled three of them; these papers were probably launched to take advantage of the new printing patronage. The Republicans' total of nineteen newspapers reached in 1869 was their highest for the Reconstruction years and was about half the number of Democratic sheets at the time. At least sixteen of these papers benefited from the printing law.[28]

Twenty-six of Tennessee's Republican papers, half the state party's Reconstruction-era total, came from East Tennessee, where Civil War Unionism had been strong and where the Republican Party dominated throughout the 1870s.

The longest-lived Republican sheets there were the Greeneville *New Era*, which began in 1865 and lasted into the 1880s, and Jonesborough's *Union Flag*, which survived from 1865 through 1873. In 1867, W. B. Scott removed his Nashville *Colored Tennessean* to Maryville in East Tennessee, renamed it the *Maryville Republican*, and published it until the late 1870s. The *Knoxville Daily Chronicle*, which was launched in 1870, also continued into the 1880s, and Cleveland, Tennessee, had a Republican newspaper from 1872 until 1878.[29]

Fifteen more Republican papers came from Middle Tennessee, half of them from Nashville, the state capital. Thanks to the disfranchisement of many ex-Confederates, Republicans were able to carry a number of counties in this region in 1868. With the lifting of suffrage restrictions after that date, however, Republican newspapers there began disappearing. Republicans dominated Nashville's city government from 1867 to 1869; afterward they retained the mayor's office for several years, but Democrats controlled the city council. The party lost its leading daily, the *Press and Times*, in 1869. Republicans subsequently failed to maintain a successful daily in the city but published a weekly, the *Nashville Bulletin*, from 1871 to 1875. Elsewhere in Middle Tennessee, Lewis Tillman, who in 1868 was elected to a term in Congress, kept the Shelbyville *Republican* going from 1866 through 1869, and another Republican sheet, the *Clarksville Patriot*, lasted from 1867 into 1870.[30]

In West Tennessee, Republicans established seven papers, six of them in Memphis. After Republicans lost control of the city in 1868, the *Memphis Post* disappeared; another Republican paper appeared briefly in the city during the mid-1870s, followed by the *Memphis Planet*, 1874 to 1879. The 1868 printing law did encourage the Huntington *West Tennessean*'s establishment in Carroll County. There the Republicans remained competitive, carrying the county in 1868, 1872, and 1880. In 1870, the *Tennessee Republican* replaced the *West Tennessean* and lasted until 1877.

Arkansas, which ranked tenth among the eleven ex-Confederate states in population in 1870 and also tenth in the total number of Republican votes cast in 1872, had fifty-two Republican papers, putting it slightly ahead of Tennessee. Forty-four percent of its partisan papers were Republican, ranking Arkansas third behind Louisiana and Florida in this category. Half of these papers, however, lasted two years or less. At the time congressional Reconstruction began in Arkansas, the state had only one Republican paper, Valentine Dell's *Fort Smith New Era*, which began receiving federal patronage commencing with the Fortieth Congress. In 1867, Republicans established six additional papers, including the party's only daily, the *Little Rock Republican*. When the Republicans gained control, the legislature named as state printer the *Republican*'s publisher,

John G. Price, a carpetbagger from Illinois. Additionally the *Republican* received federal patronage through the Fortieth Congress. Although the paper subsequently lost its role as an official U.S. paper, state patronage was enough to maintain it until 1876. In 1868, the legislature authorized the governor, Powell Clayton, to designate a paper in each of the state's ten judicial districts to publish legal notices, and this law remained in place until 1874. With the encouragement of such patronage, the number of Republican papers in the state swelled to twenty-two in 1869 and hovered around that figure for the next three years. This patronage also helps account for the fact that eight Arkansas papers lasted more than five years.[31]

Eight Republican papers appeared in Little Rock, the state's largest city and capital. All but the *Republican* were short-lived. Outside Little Rock, sixteen Republican papers appeared in the delta counties. Their rich soils generated large-scale cotton production, so that the delta became the historic center of the state's economic and political power. These counties had the bulk of the state's black population; freedmen were in the majority in many counties, and the Republicans carried most of them. Three delta papers lasted more than five years. The Pine Bluff *Jeffersonian Republican*, 1868–77, and the Helena *Southern Shield*, 1868–74, were both published in counties where blacks comprised about two-thirds of the population, and the Republicans carried these counties through the 1870s. The third paper, the De Vall's Bluff *White River Journal*, 1868–74, was published in Prairie County, which was about one-third black; Republicans never succeeded in carrying it.[32]

Twenty of the state's Republican newspapers appeared in the northwestern section, where the bulk of the Arkansas white population lived. This region, which was hilly or mountainous, was not suited to large-scale farming, and few blacks lived there. Numbers of this region's whites had been Unionists during the Civil War, and most of the limited white support that the Republicans obtained in Arkansas came from this region. Its three longest-lived Republican papers included Dell's *Fort Smith New Era*, the oldest Republican paper, lasting from 1863 to 1877. Fort Smith was located in Sebastian County, where the black population stood at 10 percent; the county voted Republican through the 1872 election. The *Batesville Republican* lasted almost as long, from 1867 to 1876; it was published in Independence County, which had a 6 percent black population. This paper managed to survive despite the fact that Republicans carried the county only once, in 1872. Republicans fared no better in Washington County, which they lost after 1868. The Fayetteville *Mountain Echo* was published there from 1867 through 1872. Republicans published four different papers in Pocahontas, Randolph County, between 1868 and 1874, where Republicans remained competitive through the 1872 election.[33] Six Republican newspapers appeared in the forested plains of southwestern Arkansas, which had a mixed economy and a higher percentage of blacks than the northwestern region. One of these papers, the Camden *South Arkansas Journal* in Ouachita County, lasted from 1867 to 1874. This county with a black population slightly over 40 percent had a number of white Unionists; Republicans remained competitive here throughout the 1870s.[34]

South Carolina, with a larger percentage of blacks than any other Southern state, maintained a Republican regime until the 1876 election. Nevertheless, the party faced an uphill battle trying to establish a viable press. With forty-six Republican newspapers during Reconstruction, the state ranked sixth in the South. The Democrats had fifty-two papers, which meant the Republicans could claim about 47 percent of the state's total, one of the highest figures in the South. Of the state's forty-six Republican newspapers, however, almost half died within two years. Only four papers, or 9 percent of the total, lasted at least five years, putting South Carolina last in this category. In contrast, slightly over half of the state's Democratic newspapers survived for at least five years.

In the summer of 1867, when South Carolina's Republicans met to organize their party, they had almost no newspaper support. The Darlington *New Era* had passed into conservative hands in 1866 and the *Charleston Journal* apparently disappeared sometime the following year, as did the Port Royal *New South*. Only two newspapers, both in Charleston and both church-related, backed the Republicans. By 1867, African Americans controlled one of these papers, the *South Carolina Leader;* one of its owners, Richard Harvey Cain, a minister in the African Methodist Episcopal Church, also edited it. The second paper, the *Charleston Advocate,* was founded early in 1867. Seed money for the *Advocate* came from the Clafin family of Massachusetts; its editor and publisher, Alonzo Webster, was a Methodist minister from the North. Benjamin F. Randolph, the African American Methodist minister formerly associated with the *Charleston Journal,* became the *Advocate*'s associate editor.[35]

In the spring of 1868, a third Republican paper, the *Free Press,* made a brief appearance in Charleston. Apparently it was published in order to influence the elections held that April, for it disappeared after their conclusion. By that time the *South Carolina Leader* had also disappeared, to be replaced by the *Missionary Record,* under the same ownership and editor. The *Missionary Record* continued publication for several more years but was often critical of the state's Republican leadership. In October 1868, members of the Ku Klux Klan assassinated Randolph, the *Advocate*'s associate editor, who had just been elected to the state senate. A few months later Webster transferred the *Advocate* to Atlanta.[36]

Governor Robert K. Scott's Republican administration was by then making state patronage available to party publishers. In August 1868, J. W. Denny, the state printer, established the *Daily Republican* in Columbia. Despite government patronage, the paper lasted only two months. Subsequently, state officials and Republican leaders organized the Union Printing Company, and in October 1868 it launched the *South Carolina Republican,* a Charleston weekly edited by two Northern journalists, John Morris and Myron Fox. This was the only secular paper in the state supporting the Scott administration until April 1870. That month its owners moved the paper to Columbia and began publication in Charleston of the party's first daily, the *Daily Republican,* with Morris and Fox as editors. The *Daily Republican* soon became an official paper of both the state and the U.S. governments. In the fall or winter of 1870, its owners, who probably included Governor Scott, reorganized under the name of the Carolina Printing Company. Apparently they lacked firm control of the *Republican*'s editorial policy, for Morris and Fox began criticizing the Scott administration, costing their paper state patronage. It ceased publication in September 1871. Although a handful of other Republican papers subsequently appeared in Charleston, none was successful and all were insignificant in party affairs.[37]

The Republicans fared somewhat better in establishing a press in Columbia, the state capital. In November 1870, the Carolina Printing Company began publishing the Columbia *Daily Union;* Lewis Cass Carpenter, a journalist from Connecticut and one of the company's partners, became editor. When the printing company dissolved in September 1871, Carpenter became the paper's sole owner. In January 1873, a second Republican paper appeared in Columbia, the *Daily Evening Herald.* In May, its proprietors purchased Carpenter's paper, a merger that produced the *Daily Union-Herald,* which became the leading Republican paper and the state's only party daily. It lasted until March 1877.[38]

In January 1871, the Republican legislature authorized the clerks of the state house and senate to set contracts for publishing laws and other state advertisements to newspapers around the state. The availability of this patronage helps account for the increase in Republican papers, which rose to eight in that year and reached a peak of fifteen in 1873. At least six different Republican newspapers appeared in Beaufort. Although the town was small, 90 percent of Beaufort County's inhabitants were black, and this area, in the coastal Sea Islands, had also attracted a number of Northern missionaries and investors. Although these newspapers changed titles and sometimes merged with one another, making it difficult to track their histories, the Beaufort area had at least one Republican paper throughout Reconstruction.[39]

South Carolina's Republicans had some limited success establishing newspapers in other coastal counties with large black populations that produced solid Republican majorities. Four papers appeared at different times in Orangeburg County. The longest-lived of these was the *Orangeburg News*, which became Republican in 1872; three years later it merged with a rival paper to form the *News and Times*, which remained in the Republican camp through 1877. Aiken, the seat of Aiken County, was the home of one of the party's more successful papers, the *Aiken Tribune*. Its editor, Henry Sparnick, a native South Carolinian, kept it going from 1871 to the end of 1875. Three Republican papers briefly appeared in Colleton County, one of which, the *Walterboro News*, published from 1873 to 1877. Although the publisher of a Darlington County paper, the *Darlington Southerner*, listed his paper as Democratic in Rowell's newspaper directory, he received U.S. and state government patronage for several years. Williamsburg County produced the Kingstree *Williamsburg Republican*, which survived from 1874 to 1877, and Georgetown County was home to the *Georgetown Planet*, which existed from 1873 to 1875. The latter two papers were both African American owned and edited.[40]

The only Republican papers to appear in counties dominated by whites were two in Spartanburg and one in Greenville. Spartanburg County was a Democratic party stronghold with the largest white majority of any county in the state. Nonetheless, in 1870 Kentuckian Samuel T. Poiner began publishing the *Spartanburg Republican*, but the Klan evicted him from the state the following year. His paper was succeeded by the *Carolina New Era*, which survived until 1875, in part with the aid of U.S. patronage. The third paper, the *Greenville Republican*, lasted for two years in the mid-1870s.[41]

Alabama produced thirty-six Republican newspapers during Reconstruction, putting it eighth in this category. In 1870, the state's population of just under one million ranked it fifth in the South, and in 1872 it finished fourth in the number of Republican votes cast and sixth in the Republican percentage of the total vote. Republicans published just under one fourth of the partisan papers that appeared in Reconstruction-era Alabama. Sixty-one percent of these papers lasted two years or less, ranking the state with Mississippi at the bottom in this category. Only four Republican papers lasted at least five years. Although Alabama Republicans drew support from Unionists in the northern part of the state, they were not as successful as their North Carolina counterparts in gaining white support, which helps explain why their party press was weaker. Before the advent of congressional Reconstruction, the state's only avowedly Republican paper was the Mobile *Nationalist*, established in 1865. By 1867, the strongly Unionist editor of the *Huntsville Advocate*, W. B. Figures, was ready to cooperate with the Republicans as well. After the Alabama Republicans created a state organization in 1867, the number of their newspapers rose to ten at a time when the Democrats could claim fifty-three. In 1868, Alabama's legislature authorized the governor to identify papers in each congressional district to publish local government notices. Despite this measure, few new papers appeared. By 1869, the number of Republican sheets peaked at thirteen. The printing law was repealed in 1872.[42]

About half of Alabama's newspapers came from Black Belt counties. Running through the center of the state, these counties comprised the heart of the antebellum plantation system. Here black voters heavily outnumbered whites, giving the Republicans a base that lasted throughout Reconstruction. The state's capital, Montgomery, was located in this region, and although Republicans lost control of the city in 1875, they continued to carry its county for the rest of the decade. Native white Republicans established two daily papers here: the Montgomery *State Sentinel*, launched in 1867, and the *Alabama State Journal*, which supplanted the *Sentinel* the following year. The *State Journal*'s publisher became state printer and his newspaper became the party's official paper. Federal patronage initially went to the *Nationalist* and the *Advocate*, but the *State Journal* received federal printing beginning with the third session of the Fortieth Congress and continued to benefit from it until Congress halted the subsidy. The *Journal* lasted until 1878.[43]

Republican papers appeared in four other Alabama Black Belt counties, all published in towns that were also the seats of county government. Three Republican papers appeared in Selma, Dallas County, where Republicans won majorities through the 1876 election. The longest-lived was the Selma *National Republican*, which survived from 1873 to 1876. Editor Robert A. Moseley was a Confederate Army veteran. A Freedmen's Bureau agent from Massachusetts, Pierce Burton, published the Demopolis *Southern Republican* in Marengo County from 1869 to 1871. Republicans carried Marengo through the 1870 elections and again in 1874, but no other party paper appeared there. Republicans remained competitive in Lee County through the 1872 elections, and from 1867 through 1873 four different Republican papers rose and fell there, all published in Opelika. Wetumpka, in Elmore County, was the home of the longest-lived Black Belt Republican paper outside Montgomery, the *Elmore Republican*, which lasted from 1870 to 1875. Republicans carried Elmore through the 1874 gubernatorial election and remained competitive there for the rest of the decade.[44]

In the southern part of Alabama, Republicans were able to maintain a paper in Union Springs, the seat of Bullock County, from 1870 through 1875. Bullock County bordered on the Black Belt, and African American voters outnumbered whites there also; consequently Republicans carried the county in most elections during the 1870s. Mobile, Alabama's largest city, had a black voting majority in 1867, but Republicans lost control of it in 1870. African Americans controlled the four Republican newspapers that emerged in Mobile; the longest-lived, the *Nationalist,* lasted from 1865 into 1869.[45]

Republicans were able to establish a dozen newspapers in northern Alabama, where many whites who had been Unionists during the Civil War and afterward became Republicans. Here some counties had large minorities of African American voters, and by combining their vote with that of white Unionists, Republicans were quite competitive. The most important Republican journals in this region were edited by white Unionists. In Huntsville, the Madison County seat, W. B. Figures and his *Huntsville Advocate* supported the party from 1867 until 1875, making it second only to the *Alabama State Journal* in longevity as a Republican paper. Republicans also got a strong vote in Morgan County, where Christopher Sheats, a strong secession opponent, edited the *Alabama Republican* in Decatur, the county seat. In 1872, he was elected to a term in Congress. Republicans were strong in Talladega County, carrying it in the 1868, 1872, and 1880 elections. In 1872, Robert A. Moseley, who had been elected mayor of Talladega in 1868, began publishing *Our Mountain Home;* he supported Ulysses S. Grant for president, and his paper remained in the Republican camp until 1877.[46]

Although North Carolina ranked fourth in Southern population, and the Republicans polled ninety-five thousand votes in 1872, their highest Southern total, the state published only thirty-seven Republican newspapers, putting it in seventh place among the eleven ex-Confederate states. This represented about 30 percent of the state's partisan newspapers. Almost 57 percent of these Republican papers disappeared within two years. On the other hand, over a fifth survived at least five years, putting the state second in this category, behind Louisiana. When congressional Reconstruction began in North Carolina in 1867, the state had only a handful of papers that were reliably Republican. They included William Holden's *North Carolina Standard* and the *New Bern Times,* both of which had been in existence for several years, and three papers started in 1866, the *Asheville Pioneer,* the *Rutherford Star,* and the *Greensboro Union Register.* The Asheville paper was founded by Alexander H. Jones, a native of the North Carolina mountains who had enlisted in the Union Army in 1863. He began publishing the paper in Hendersonville and moved it to Asheville in 1867. Native Carolinians also published the *Rutherford Star;* Albion Tourgee, a carpetbagger from Ohio, published the Greensboro paper. In 1867, federal patronage was awarded to the *North Carolina Standard* and the *Asheville Pioneer.*[47]

In 1867, the Republicans gained support from four new publications and also from the Salem *People's Press,* the editor of which decided to support the party.

Thus, when the Republicans took over the state in 1868, they had the backing of ten newspapers. The new state legislature made the publisher of the *North Carolina Standard* the state printer; it also authorized the secretary of state to designate newspapers in each county to publish the laws, a benefit that generally went to Republican papers. After the Republicans lost control of the legislature in 1870, this provision was repealed. Nonetheless, the number of Republican newspapers actually increased after that, reaching a peak of fifteen in 1871 during a hard-fought state election campaign. Although the Republicans never regained control of the state legislature, they remained competitive in the state, carrying North Carolina for Grant in the 1872 presidential election and electing a Republican governor as well. Most certainly the number of Republican papers in North Carolina's early stages of Reconstruction would have been larger if the legislature had directed local government printing to Republican papers. Nevertheless, Republicans controlled a number of county and city governments in North Carolina, making their patronage available to local party papers.[48]

North Carolina's eastern counties had large black populations that produced steady Republican majorities. Here carpetbaggers established three of the state's longest-lived Republican newspapers. Wilmington, a coastal city in New Hanover County, was the home of the *Wilmington Post*. In 1868, New Hanover County returned the state's largest Republican majority; Wilmington remained a Republican stronghold from the onset of congressional Reconstruction until the late 1870s. William Holden's Raleigh *North Carolina Standard* was the party's official organ until its demise in 1870 left the *Post* as the party's leading paper; it probably had the largest circulation of any Republican paper in the state. At various times it was published in daily, semiweekly, and weekly editions. Although the paper was founded by carpetbaggers, William Parker Canaday, a Confederate veteran who for a time served as Wilmington's mayor, edited the *Post* from 1872 until its demise in 1884.[49]

New Bern in Craven County, where Union soldiers established the *North Carolina Times* upon occupying the town in 1862, was the home of several Republican newspapers. The longest-lived was the *New Bern Times*, which traced its origin to the *North Carolina Times*. Ethelbert Hubbs, a Union Army veteran from the North, owned and edited the paper from 1870 until it disappeared in 1876. Hubbs obtained federal patronage for several years in the early 1870s. In the 1868 election, Craven County delivered a Republican majority second only to New Hanover's, and the party kept a grip on the county through 1896. Another long-lived paper in the eastern counties, the Elizabeth City *North Carolinian*, was published in Pasquatonk County by Palemon John, a physician and journalist from Pennsylvania; it lasted from 1869 to 1877. Pasquatonk County remained in

Republican hands into the 1870s, as did Elizabeth City. Hence all three tidewater Republican newspapers benefited from local governmental patronage.[50]

Buncombe County in the mountains of western North Carolina produced Alexander H. Jones's *Asheville Pioneer*, which lasted from 1866 to 1879, making it the state's longest-lived Republican paper after the *Wilmington Post*. The North Carolina mountains had harbored many Unionists like Jones during the war, and voters there elected him to three terms in Congress. Although Buncombe's whites far outnumbered its blacks, the county delivered majorities for the Republicans in the 1867 and 1868 elections. The party remained competitive there throughout the 1870s, and Jones's paper received federal patronage from 1867 through 1872.[51]

Most of North Carolina's Republican newspapers appeared in the state's Piedmont counties, where whites comprised about 75 percent of the population. These counties, some of which had large Quaker populations, provided a fertile field for recruiting Republican voters. Most of the region's whites were farmers who were resentful of the socioeconomic elite that dominated the state. The Civil War had brought this class conflict to the surface, since these farmers were angry at the Confederate government's stringent measures, particularly the conscription laws exempting owners of more than twenty slaves. Holden's peace movement of 1863–64 drew its main support from these counties, as did his 1865 gubernatorial campaign. In 1868, Holden carried twenty-six of the Piedmont's thirty-nine counties. During Reconstruction, Republicans probably received between a fourth and a third of eligible whites' votes in these counties, and among whites who cast ballots the Republican percentage may have ranged from 40 to 50 percent.[52]

Raleigh, the state capital, was located in the Piedmont county of Wake; here Holden published his *North Carolina Standard*, the party's official organ. After Holden was elected governor, he sold the paper to a group headed by railroad speculator Milton Littlefield; it closed in 1870. Wake County's registered voters were about evenly divided between white and black, and Republicans turned out steady majorities throughout the 1870s. The city had a Republican mayor and city council from 1868 to 1875. After Holden's paper shut down, the Raleigh *Carolina Era*, established in 1871, became the Republican party's official organ. Capably edited, it lasted until 1876. Both the *Standard* and then the *Era* received federal patronage. Outside Wake, Republicans carried Forsythe County throughout the 1870s; here the Salem *People's Press* supported the Republicans in the late 1860s, and Winston was the home of a Republican paper from 1871 through the remainder of the decade. Greensboro in Guilford County, which voted Republican through the 1872 election, produced three short-lived

Republican sheets in the early Reconstruction years; a fourth, the *New North State*, lasted from 1871 to 1879.[53]

Other Piedmont counties with Republican papers included Mecklenburg, where two short-lived sheets appeared in Charlotte, and Iredell, where the *Statesville American,* usually a Democratic paper, supported the Republicans from 1872 to 1874. Although the Democrats carried these counties, Republicans remained competitive throughout Reconstruction. Their party carried Rutherford County in the western Piedmont through the election of 1872; the *Rutherford Star,* which lasted from 1866 to 1875, was one of the leading Republican weeklies.[54]

Virginia had the second largest population among the ex-Confederate states, but during the Reconstruction era it produced a total of only twenty-four Republican papers, placing it ninth. The number of Democratic papers for the same period was at least eighty-six, almost four times as high. Although the Republican Party never controlled Virginia, its turnout was high; in 1872 the total Republican vote in Virginia ranked it second in the South. The Republican share of Virginia's total vote that year, however, was just over 50 percent, ranking it eighth in this category. At the beginning of 1867, before Virginia's freedmen gained the franchise, the state boasted six Republican newspapers. Two papers, the Alexandria *Virginia State Journal* and the Richmond *New Nation,* received printing patronage from the U.S. government. Because of delays in the state government's Reconstruction and the victory of a coalition of conservative Republicans and Democrats in the state's first election in 1869, Republican editors got almost no printing from the state and won local patronage only if their party controlled the local government. In 1868, the number of Republican papers rose to seven and hovered around that figure for the next several years. In 1869, Virginia had at least fifty-six Democratic papers, and their yearly numbers ranged between forty and fifty throughout the 1870s.[55]

None of the Republican papers circulated widely through the state. Only five lasted more than five years; 42 percent lasted two years or less, a figure that ranked Virginia fourth in this category among the ex-Confederate states. In 1870, when the Democrats had at least a half dozen dailies, the Republicans could claim only two: the Richmond *State Journal,* which had moved from Alexandria in 1868 and served as the party's official organ, and the Norfolk *Day Book,* the editor of which listed his paper as independent but used it to support the Republicans. Both papers put their daily circulation at two thousand in 1870. The *State Journal* received U.S. government patronage until Congress ended the subsidy in 1875; the paper disappeared that year. The *Day Book* continued to support the Republican Party throughout the 1870s.[56]

The location of Virginia's few Republican papers reflected the party's sources of strength in the state. A majority of Richmond's registered voters in 1867 were black, but the Republicans were never able to control the city's government. African American voters also dominated in Alexandria, Petersburg, and Norfolk, all of which sustained one or more Republican newspapers at different times. Blacks comprised a slight majority of registered voters in Campbell County, where the *Lynchburg Press* was published. Republicans there remained competitive through the 1870s. The *Press*, the other Virginia paper to receive federal patronage, survived until at least 1878 as a Republican paper. In Spotsylvania County, whites constituted a majority of registered voters, but the black vote was significant, and James B. Sener, scalawag editor of the *Fredericksburg Ledger*, won a term in Congress in 1872. His paper lasted as a Republican sheet from 1870 into 1874.[57]

A few Republican papers appeared in the Shenandoah Valley towns of Winchester, Harrisonburg, and Staunton, where whites comprised the overwhelming majority of voters. The party gathered some support there, however, and its papers lasted for several years. A Republican paper in Leesburg in Loudoun County on the Potomac River also survived for a few years, where it apparently circulated primarily among local Quakers. This county's white voters outnumbered blacks almost three to one, but a significant number of whites voted Republican; in the 1872 presidential election, the Democrats carried the county by only a single vote. A sizable minority of whites in Virginia's southwestern counties also voted for the Republican Party in the early Reconstruction years; Marion in Smythe County produced two Republican papers at different times, but neither survived for long.[58]

Virginia's total of Republican newspapers was almost matched by that of Florida, which had by far the smallest Southern population, making it difficult to sustain many newspapers of any persuasion. In 1860, Florida had twenty-two papers. It did not reach that figure again until 1870, and as late as 1877 the state total was only thirty. During most of Reconstruction, the state lacked a daily newspaper. Nevertheless, it ranked ahead of Georgia in its number of Republican papers, although the Peach State boasted a population six times as large. Even more striking, the number of Florida's Republican papers matched the total of twenty-two Democratic newspapers that appeared in the state during the same period, although the Democratic papers lasted longer. Six of Florida's Republican papers disappeared within two years; only four lasted as long as five years. Thanks to Florida's black population, which almost equaled the number of whites, Republicans were able to control the state until 1877 and during that time established newspaper subsidies that helped maintain their press.

In 1867, when congressional Reconstruction was launched in Florida, Republicans had three newspapers in the state, the Jacksonville *Florida Times,* the Jacksonville *Florida Union,* and the *Pensacola Observer.* Edward McPherson awarded a federal printing contract to the *Florida Union,* owned by Edward M. Cheney, a journalist from Massachusetts; and after Florida Republicans bought control of the *Tallahassee Sentinel* in 1868 he awarded printing to this paper as well.[59] Following the 1868 elections, Republicans gained control of the state, making its patronage available to their papers. The legislature named Cheney, who also chaired the state Republican Party, as state printer. In 1870, lawmakers transferred this privilege to the publishers of the *Tallahassee Sentinel.* In 1868, legislators had authorized Florida's secretary of state to identify three papers, one in Tallahassee, one in Jacksonville, and one in Pensacola, as official papers. At that point there were only four Republican papers in the state; the secretary granted this boon to the *Union,* the *Sentinel,* and the *Pensacola Observer.* Lacking this patronage, the fourth paper, the Tampa *True Southerner,* soon disappeared.[60]

Another law passed in 1868 authorized circuit court judges to designate one newspaper in each circuit as the official paper for publishing notices for the court and for county governments within that jurisdiction. Some of the judges proceeded to identify Democratic newspapers to receive this patronage, which probably explains why the number of Democratic papers reached nine by 1869, as compared to four Republican sheets. In 1871, the legislature replaced this law with one giving the secretary of state authority to identify papers in each judicial circuit to print legal notices. Although Jonathan Gibbs, who held this position at the time, designated some Democratic papers to receive this patronage, most went to Republican sheets, particularly under his successor Samuel McLin. As a result, the number of Republican Party papers swelled to thirteen in 1874, their largest yearly total during Reconstruction and a tally far exceeding that of Democratic rivals, which fell to five. All the Republican papers except the *Florida Union* were weeklies; that paper was occasionally published as a daily or as a triweekly.[61]

Four of the thirteen Republican papers in 1874 were published in Jacksonville. Its population of six thousand made it the state's largest city and made Duval County Florida's most populous county. The majority of voters were black, and the Republicans easily carried the county throughout Reconstruction. One of the state's two leading Republican newspapers, the *Florida Union,* was published here. The other major Republican sheet, the *Tallahassee Sentinel,* was published in Leon County, the state's second largest. Like Duval, Leon County was controlled by black voters and the Republican party.[62] Both the *Florida Union* and the *Sentinel* were published throughout Reconstruction. Republican weeklies in other parts of the state were short-lived. Most of them appeared in black-majority counties where Republicans controlled the elections. Two such papers were published at different times in Pensacola in Escambia County. Additional Republican weeklies in Gainesville, Fernandina, Lake City, and Monticello came from counties with the same characteristics. The only Republican papers published in counties clearly dominated by whites and hence by the Democrats were in Tampa, where the *True Southerner* lasted only two years, and in Key West, which had several papers, two of which were in existence in 1874. A belt of four counties south of Duval in the northeastern section of the state showed some white support for the Republicans, as did Dade County in the southeast, but no Republican papers existed in either place.[63]

During Reconstruction, Georgia had only nineteen Republican papers, the smallest total among the ex-Confederate states, despite its third-ranking population. The contemporary Democrats produced almost 130 papers. This gave the Republicans 13 percent of the total number of Georgia's partisan papers, placing the state by far the lowest in this category. Ten of the Republican journals lasted two years or less; only one survived for at least five years. These figures reflected the party's weakness in the state: Georgia ranked eighth in the number of Republican votes cast in the 1872 election and tenth in the percentage of the vote won by the Republicans.

In 1867, when congressional Reconstruction began, the future of Georgia's Republican press looked bright, for eight party papers existed. By the end of the following year, however, the number had fallen to three: the Atlanta *Daily New Era*, the Augusta *Georgia Republican*, and the Macon *American Union*. Federal patronage in 1868 went to the *New Era* and the *American Union*. The Republican administration elected in 1868 had only a limited amount of printing patronage to dispense. The legislature named as state printer Samuel Bard, publisher of the daily Atlanta *New Era*. In addition, Governor Rufus Bullock was authorized to publish official proclamations and notices in papers elsewhere in the state and used that power to direct patronage to several Republican sheets. Nothing was done, however, to ensure that Republican papers had access to the patronage of state courts and local governments. In 1870, the number of Republican papers rose to six, and it declined thereafter.[64]

Few of Georgia's Republican papers appeared outside its major cities. Republicans struggled to keep a daily newspaper alive in Atlanta, the state's capital. They never gained control of the city's government. During the brief years of Republican rule in the state, the Atlanta *Daily New Era* received both federal and state printing patronage. The paper died in 1871 and was revived in 1873, but it lasted only two more years, leaving the *Atlanta Republican* as the state's only party newspaper. When Reconstruction began, the Republicans had three newspapers in Augusta, but they all quickly folded after the party lost control of the city in December 1868. Republicans continued to show some strength in the city, however, and a party weekly appeared there from 1869 to 1871. Savannah also produced three Republican sheets, but the leading party paper there, the *Daily Republican,* turned conservative in 1867, and the other two survived only for a short time.[65]

Although Republicans polled a significant minority of white votes in northern Georgia, the region's only Republican paper outside Atlanta was the short-lived Dalton *North Georgia Republican.* The party's few papers elsewhere in the state were all in black-dominated counties or cities. Two Republican papers appeared in the cotton belt running through central Georgia. In the spring of 1868, the indefatigable editor of the Griffin *American Union,* Jason Clarke Swayze, moved his paper to Macon in Bibb County, where he kept it going until 1872, assisted by some state and federal patronage. In 1870, Swayze agreed to print another Republican journal, the Fort Valley *Southwest Georgian,* on his press. A wealthy landholder and former Confederate officer, *Southwest Georgian* editor Joel R. Griffin kept his paper alive until 1874. The only other Georgia town to boast a Reconstruction-era Republican newspaper was Bainbridge in the state's southwest corner, where black voters kept the Republican Party competitive. In 1873, Republican Congressman Richard Whiteley bought control of the local *Weekly Sun,* but this paper lasted only a short time.[66]

CHAPTER SIX

The Ideology of the Republican Press

The South's Republican editors had to balance two sometimes conflicting concerns that reflected the dilemma facing their party in the ex-Confederate states. On the one hand, they wanted to establish their party and its press as legitimate institutions entitled to share in their section's political life. At the same time, these editors hoped to build a viable political constituency among voters, both black and white. Since the bulk of Republican support came from freedmen's votes, Republican editors' efforts to rally black support made it exceedingly challenging to achieve legitimacy in the eyes of whites. Southern Democratic editors, although sometimes embarrassed by their party's identification with the antebellum secession movement, did not have to defend the Democrats' right to exist. Nor did they make more than perfunctory efforts to gain black votes. Instead, in most states they could concentrate on building a voting majority among whites by appealing to their ingrained racial prejudices, a task much easier than that facing Republicans who were trying to combat those same biases.

Although Republicans differed over various aspects of their party's program, they were unanimous in calling for freedom of speech and press in the South, for without these freedoms they could never achieve legitimacy or recruit a following. According to the editor of the *Charleston Republican*, "one of the greatest questions before the Republican party is freedom of speech." As early as 1856, when a handful of Republicans met in Wheeling, Virginia, to organize their party in that state, they called for free speech and press there. Although the editor of their leading paper, the *Wheeling Intelligencer*, did not immediately profess his political allegiance, his advocacy of free speech and press led critics to brand his paper a "Black Republican" sheet. In the middle of the Civil War, James G. Thompson of the Beaufort *Free South* hoped for "newspapers of the freest kind . . . open to discussion of every subject, and carrying light into the dark places of the land." In 1867, the Republican National Committee also hoped that free thought, speech, and press would emerge in the former Confederacy. Across the South, Republican journalists echoed these concerns. The editor of the *Dardanelle Times* claimed that of all freedoms, the most prized was the right "to know, to argue freely," and his counterpart at the *Nashville Republican* insisted that "there can be no freedom of opinion without freedom of the press."[1]

The ostracism, intimidation, and violence directed against Republicans in the South shocked and angered the party's editors. John Price of the *Little Rock Republican* stated that anyone in Arkansas who spoke out against the white establishment knew the penalty: "a short shrift and a long rope, or at best, a coat of tar and feathers, with the gracious permission afforded therewith, of leaving the state instanter, lest his respite from hanging as an appropriate penalty for his temerity be revoked." Another Republican editor thus described the spirit of intolerance in the South: "Born of ignorance, bigotry and littleness of soul, it endeavors to proscribe thought, stifle speech and bring the world to a level with its own meanness." The editorial writer for the *Walterboro News* compared the South's intolerant atmosphere to the Inquisition. Other editors echoed the theme; according to the editor of the *New Bern Daily Times,* "the denouncing of men for honest differences of opinion either in politics or religion is a species of the intolerance and persecution of the dark ages." The *Wilmington Post*'s editor claimed that "proscription may do for the dark ages . . . but it will not pass in a time like the present." Edward M. Cheney of the *Florida Union* agreed, declaring that "the time has passed, even in the South, when free speech can be suppressed by violence or when a free press can be muzzled by force."[2]

Embattled Republican journalists understood that the South's political culture needed to change if their party were to gain a foothold and their newspapers an audience there. As the Carrollton *Louisiana State Register*'s editor exclaimed, Southerners would have to "purge themselves of that unreasoning prejudice which refuses to admit that [their] political enemies can either be honest or patriotic." His Montgomery *Alabama State Journal* colleague also railed at the idea that "a man holds a through ticket to hell because he is a Radical," while John Price of the *Little Rock Republican* hoped that native Arkansans could be convinced that "a man could be a gentleman and a Republican at the same time." For the party to gain acceptance in the South, Republicans would have to challenge the political and social elites that they believed controlled the opinions of the masses of Southern whites. According to the Republican National Committee, many Southern whites had the habit of "surrendering implicit obedience to able and dextrous politicians" who were hostile to the party's principles. General John Pope, commander of occupation forces in Georgia, Alabama, and Florida, believed that lasting Reconstruction would depend upon Southerners' ability to reject their old leaders.[3]

This view that an elite dominated their section's political culture won the unanimous support of Southern Republican editors. According to the *New Bern Republican* editor, liberty of the press in the slave states had consisted of "writing and publishing whatever pleased or flattered the slave oligarchy." This atmosphere continued after the war, he charged, as Southern leaders sought to deceive the masses about the nature of the Republican Party. The editor of the *New Orleans Republican* agreed, noting that "even to this day the older papers cannot throw off the dominion of the former masters of the slave." In Richmond, the editor of the *State Journal* complained that people in his state were accustomed to "thinking *in herds*" dominated by pretentious leaders, while a journalistic colleague in Charleston claimed that every South Carolina white "is absolutely enslaved in thought and action." According to the editorial writer for the *Wilmington Post*, the condition of "mental slavery" in which most whites found themselves was "more dangerous to peace and good order than the old slavery of the Negro race." These complaints from Republican editors reverberated across the states of the former Confederacy. Editors often compared Southerners unfavorably to voters in the North, criticizing the former for their "passive minds" while hailing the latter as independent free thinkers. According to the editor of the Greensboro *New North State*, Republicans controlled the North because voters there "think and act for themselves."[4]

Republican journalists continually echoed the contention of the Austin *Weekly Republican:* "It is high time that the people should begin to think for themselves, and to question the claims of those who aspire to the direction of public affairs." In Richmond, James Hunnicutt of the *New Nation* railed against the state's clergy and politicians who would dictate to the loyal portion of the population, as did the editor of the Richmond *State Journal.* A. W. Sheldon of the *Richmond Register* weighed in with an appeal to his readers to end their "thralldom" to "an effete aristocracy." In North Carolina, the editor of the *Wilmington Post* exhorted his readers to "SCORN TO BE SLAVES," while in Mississippi W. H. Noble of the *Woodville Republican* urged whites to "throw off the yoke of demagoguism." Mississippi native Joshua R. Smith of the *Meridian Chronicle* declared that he was willing to face down the taunts and jeers of his neighbors and urged his readers to think and act for themselves as well, a plea echoed in the *Friar's Point Delta*.[5]

Some editors wondered whether Southern whites could muster the will to resist the social pressures to conform to the dominant classes' opinions. In a long column entitled "How Long, Oh Lord, How Long," John Price of the *Little Rock Republican* asked if the Southern whites would ever refuse to be "gulled and nosed about by old and incompetent self-conceited leaders." Jason Clarke Swayze of the Macon *American Union* worried that common whites had deferred to the "self-constituted respectability" for so long that it would be difficult for them to vote for the Republicans. Some were more hopeful, especially in North Carolina. The editor of the Greensboro *New North State* predicted that the only whites who would follow what he scornfully referred to as the "chivalry" were "empty-headed asses and servile miscreants, whom the aristocrats themselves despise." His counterpart at the helm of the *Asheville Pioneer,* while admitting that the fear of social ostracism among whites "has caused a degree of moral cowardice truly lamentable," also believed that many white North Carolinians would vote Republican anyway.[6]

Republican editors varied in their response to the leaders whom they accused of dictating to the mass of Southern whites. Some resorted to sarcasm in describing members of this elite, chiding them as members of "the chivalry" or the "codfish aristocracy." Pierce Burton of the Demopolis *Southern Republican* recommended that they offer lessons in how to sneer effectively. The editor of the Greensboro *New North State* predicted that a Republican victory in North Carolina would leave the "popinjays" who claimed to control society with "no other occupation than to sneer themselves to death." In the Austin *State Journal,* James Newcomb derided the Texas "chivalry" that "ignores the tooth-brush and is a stranger to soap, that protects its unclean carcass with a bowie knife, and struts in long hair and soiled linen with a breath redolent of mean whiskey."[7]

In their angry condemnation of their political opponents, a number of Republican journalists went beyond sarcasm. Editors from states or regions with bitter wartime divisions excoriated the "rebels" and strove to keep animosities alive long after 1865. Eastern Tennessee editors were especially notable in this regard, for the majority there had suffered terribly under wartime Confederate occupation. The most vindictive of all Southern Republican editors was "Parson" William G. Brownlow of Knoxville, who was Tennessee's governor from 1865 to 1869. After returning to Tennessee in 1863 to resume publishing his *Knoxville Whig and Rebel Ventilator,* he began heaping scorn on "the negro-worshipping aristocracy, the cotton and tobacco-planting lords" who had brought on the rebellion. "The *halter,*" he insisted, "should be summoned to do its appropriate work among the leaders." His hatred of those who had persecuted Union supporters during the war had no limits. "Let them be punished—let them be impoverished—let them be slain," he fulminated, "and after slain, let them be damned!"[8] In 1865, James Hood's *Chattanooga Daily Gazette* supported Brownlow's threat to retaliate if rebel mobs executed any Unionists by hanging "the most prominent amnestied gentleman" in the neighborhood where the execution had occurred. After Brownlow became governor, his son took over his paper and the editorials lost their pungency, but the son continued to hammer away at rebels, traitors, and aristocrats, as did George E. Grisham's Jonesborough *Union Flag*. Grisham, who during the war had joined the U.S. Army, claimed he was "always opposed to the *negro-ocracy class*—the class which has germinated the elements of ruin and death."[9]

Elsewhere in the South, Republican editors occasionally expressed bitterness toward their opponents; a conservative Arkansas editor remarked that the editorials in the Republican Fort Smith *Arkansas Patriot* "always read as if written with a ten-penny nail dipped in vitriol." John Emory Bryant of the Augusta *Loyal Georgian* scorned the attacks of "rebels," declaring that he was glad to be exempted from "the snare of smooth and flattering tongues." Having "suffered your manners long enough," Bryant assured his critics that he would "never stoop again to curry your favor!" One of the most abusive and perhaps the most abused of Republican editors was Jason Clarke Swayze of the Macon *American Union*. Swayze, who had come to Georgia from New York before the Civil War, had suffered much for his support of the Union. He never forgot it. He was furious at his inability to obtain local advertising and repeatedly denounced the "chivalry" that ostracized him and his family. He asserted that one could travel the world over without finding such a "nation of loafers as this pretended aristocracy of the South." Several times Swayze had to face down angry mobs, and he sent his son out of the state for schooling, but never was he physically harmed.[10]

Unlike Swayze, most Republican editors adopted a calm and objective editorial tone that they hoped would contrast favorably with the wildly emotional and hyperbolic language found in many Democratic journals. In his history of the Southern press, Carl Osthaus has observed that during Reconstruction Democratic editors fed their readers a "steady diet of distorted rhetoric and verbal abuse" with which the writers "daily inflamed political passions and racist fears and hatreds." According to the *Knoxville Daily Chronicle*'s editor, such bitter partisan feelings stirred up by conservative papers provoked distrust and jealousy, "prevent[ing] many of our best citizens from identifying with movements which under a better state of public feeling would receive their encouragement." Republican journalists lectured Democratic counterparts, urging them to shun personalities and vindictiveness and to avoid prostituting their influential positions by appealing to humanity's lowest passions. John Price of the *Little Rock Republican* drew this contrast between Republican and Democratic newspapers: "The one appeals to the moral and intellectual, the other to the baser passions of the masses; the one in fact to the man, the other to the brute." Yet Price could not avoid the temptation of responding in kind to Democratic diatribes against him and his paper. When a rival Democratic editor resumed his duties after an absence, Price observed that "the bilious, dyspeptic, and constipated chap who commonly presides over the editorial columns of the *Gazette* has apparently returned to his vomit."[11]

Most Republican editors, however, pointedly stated that unlike their Democratic rivals, they intended to cool passions by avoiding personal attacks on their political and journalistic opponents. Michael Vidal of the *St. Landry Progress* insisted that two or more papers should be able to exist in the same locality "without being at daggers with one another," and he promised to treat his opponents with courtesy, a point repeated by most Republican editors.[12] To emphasize their conciliatory approach, many Republican papers adopted as slogans quotations coined by Republican presidents Lincoln ("With malice toward none; with charity for all") and Ulysses S. Grant ("Let us have peace"). The Atlanta *New Era* put the phrase "Wisdom, Justice, Moderation" on its masthead.[13]

By stressing their moderation and civility, Republican editors hoped to win a hearing for their views, a development that clearly would serve their partisan interests and help them expose the Democrats' errors. As the editor of the *Nashville Republican* observed, "where freedom and free speech are tolerated, the crimes of the Democratic party die." Yet these editors also insisted that freedom of speech and press would advance the welfare of the South as a whole. They believed democratic values and institutions would thrive only in the presence of untrammeled debate between opposing political parties, and they claimed that intolerance and closed-mindedness had retarded Southern development. Several Republican editors claimed that had the antebellum South enjoyed a free press and free speech, slavery would not have endured and there would have been no Civil War. Unless Southerners could freely discuss social, political, and economic issues without fear of violent retribution, these editors argued, the section would stagnate, deprived of the stimulation of fresh and innovative ideas that they believed their party would present. "Societies advance through discussion, and a free interchange of opinions," stated the editor of the *New Orleans Tribune*. "Where there is no freedom," he warned, "there can also be no progress." The Southern people, the editor of the *Charleston Advocate* opined, "must have an opportunity to hear more than one side of the great questions that interest the nation."[14]

These "great questions" facing the nation, Republicans believed, were the very ones that had brought on the Civil War. The Republican Congressional Committee argued that the campaign to organize the party in the South was "but a continuation of the war . . . it is no longer the shock of armies, but the conflict of ideas." The editor of the *Charleston Free Press* echoed these views: the cause of humanity triumphed in the war, he stated, "but the war of ideas and principles still prevails."[15] In this conflict, so Republicans believed, they represented progressive values and principles identified with the North, while Southerners remained loyal to outdated and retrograde ideas. In their zeal to modernize what they regarded as a backward section, many of these Republican editors could be compared to the Northern missionaries, teachers, and Freedmen's Bureau agents who came into the postwar South. Not all of these editors, however, were Yankees; numerous Southern Republican journalists shared the same crusading spirit.

References to the progressive and even revolutionary impulses unleashed by the Civil War filled Republican editors' columns. Lucien Eaton of the *Memphis Post* rejoiced that "men and ideas are unchained." Jean-Charles Houzeau of the *New Orleans Tribune* claimed that "civilized societies" could not remain static but had to adopt progressive ideas. He and other Republican editors identified these ideas both with their party and with the best traditions of western civilization. "Republicanism," declared John Morris of the *Charleston Daily Republican*, "embodies the progressive ideas and breathes the vigorous spirit of the age." The editor of the *Livingston Messenger* saw in these ideas the spirit of "world Republicanism," while a Selma newspaper claimed that the values the party represented "move the whole of the civilized world." As Congressional Reconstruction got under way, the *Wilmington Post*'s editor was sure that "the progressive element" would shape policy in every Southern state; in Arkansas Republicans urged voters to put their shoulders to "the wheel of progress and reform."[16]

Characterizations of the South as backward and stagnant, resisting the onward march of civilization, became a common Republican editorial theme. Cheney of the *Florida Union* criticized what he called Southern "feudalism and retrogression," while Price's *Little Rock Republican* referred to his state's "semicivilization." The Republican Party, which according to the *New Orleans Republican* had lifted the South from the "quagmire" caused by slavery, should have a chance to continue its work of redemption. Albion Tourgee claimed that his newspaper would help free the South from "its slough of ignorance and prejudice." Republicans bearing the banners of "liberty and civilization," wrote the editor of the Austin *Journal*, would transform the South's old order, which he claimed was based on the "ancient quicksands of braggadocio chivalry and ostentatious wealth." The South must no longer oppose this progressive spirit, S. C. Mercer of the Nashville *Press and Times* warned; "revolutions must go forward."[17]

To implement this transformation, the editor of the *Chattanooga Daily Republican* urged white Southerners to reject "the quaint notions created by the fogy customs and precedents of bygone days." Many of his Republican colleagues also wrote of "old fogies" and appealed to the youth to throw off the "antediluvian views" and "preconceived notions" that held back Southern development. The editor of the Clarksville *Weekly Patriot* said Southerners must "travel outside the worn ruts of wont and habit," while his *Woodville Republican* counterpart urged readers to ignore the "dead past" and "grasp the living realities of the present hour." The Jacksonville *New South*'s slogan was "Wise Men Accept the Inevitable, but Strive to Shape the Future." The future belonged to the Republicans, not the Democrats, so these editors believed. John Morris of the *Charleston Republican* observed that Democrats "hug the dead, [and] give over every living principle, every inspiring idea, to the Republican party," while the *Tallahassee Sentinel*'s editor ridiculed Democrats as quaint relics whose "old saws and antediluvian maxims, however proper in an age of Roman chariots and galleys, are hardly applicable in an age [of] the locomotive and steamship."[18]

The principles and ideas espoused by the South's Republican editors had been embodied in their party's national platform since first appearing in the 1850s. Now newspaper editors intended to implement these same ideals in the South. They included fidelity to the Union, equal rights and opportunities for all, free labor, free speech, free press and free schools, and the promotion of economic development through government assistance. The Richmond *New Nation*'s masthead summed up the Republican creed: "Union, Freedom, Equal Rights, Education, and Endless Progression." These editors intended to remake the South in the Northern image. William Figures, scalawag editor of the *Huntsville Advocate,* voiced the aspirations of many of his journalistic colleagues when he predicted that Republicans would bring canals, railroads, factories, schools, churches, colleges, villages, towns, markets, and capital investment to the former Confederacy.[19]

Firm denunciations of secession and its associated state rights doctrine and affirmations of the Union's sanctity became Republican mainstays. Some editors put United States flags on their mastheads, and occasionally a paper would feature a quotation from President Andrew Jackson, "The Federal Union—It Must and Shall Be Preserved," or from Daniel Webster, "Liberty and Union—Now and Forever—One and Inseparable." Others emblazoned such phrases as "Freedom and Nationality" or "One Country—One Constitution—One Destiny" at the tops of their papers. The editor of the *Charleston Republican* declared that in his paper, "the Nation will be deemed greater than the State." State rights, these editors averred, were inconsistent with nationalism and liberty. The South had used state rights doctrine to defend slavery and to justify secession, whereas the Republicans had used national power to save the Union and to emancipate the slaves. The war had not settled these issues, however. Congress had passed laws to protect the civil and political rights of all citizens, and Southerners were now resisting these federal policies, once again in the name of state rights. Republican editors insisted that the supremacy of U.S. laws and constitutional amendments must be maintained and enforced.[20]

The most important principles incorporated into these Reconstruction laws and amendments involved equal civil and political rights for the South's freedmen. Since the war's end, African American editors had worked for that goal and saw its achievement as an act of justice toward the former slaves. A few white editors, fearful of a white blacklist, chose to downplay these principles, but most agreed with James Newcomb of the *San Antonio Express,* who asserted his determination to defend "a people assailed in a hundred newspapers in the state as unfit to exercise equal rights." John Price of the *Little Rock Republican* put the slogan "The Union of Our Fathers, and the Equality of All Men before the Law" at his paper's masthead, and declared that giving the freedmen equal political rights was "good old democratic doctrine." Price was a Northerner, but many of the most outspoken black suffrage advocates were native white Southerners like Newcomb. A. B. Norton of the Austin *Southern Intelligencer* claimed that equal civil and political rights were "in harmony with the genius of republican government, and founded alike on justice and sound policy." S. C. Mercer, editor of the Nashville *Press and Times* and one of Tennessee's first Unionists to call for enfranchising blacks, claimed voting was "an inherent right" of citizens of a free government. He also repeatedly contended that the Republican commitment to equal rights accorded with the Golden Rule. Several other editors saw the achievement of equal rights as God's work.[21]

It was the Republicans' record on freedom and equal rights that won them the support of most African American voters. Republican editors constantly reminded the freedmen of their party's record, especially during the first elections under the Reconstruction Acts. The former slaves faced heavy pressure from their white employers not to vote or to vote against the Republicans. Thus editors reminded people of the abuses they had suffered as slaves and warned them that if the Republicans did not win control of their states, the freedmen could lose their newly won rights. The papers emphasized such benefits as civil rights legislation and public schools that the party could provide and warned black voters not to be lured away by the Democrats' false promises.

Although white Republican editors defended and advanced black rights, especially at election time, their papers clearly were aimed at members of their own race. Most of them had little to say about black religious, social, and cultural activities, and they crafted most of their political editorials with whites in mind. Several factors explain this lack of attention to developing a larger black readership. White Republican editors simply had less interest than did their black colleagues in writing for the black community. They surely recognized that most freedmen were either illiterate or unable to buy papers. They also thought the mass of freedmen had no choice but to vote for their party. Most importantly, white Republican editors were more concerned about addressing whites than blacks because they believed that the key to gaining legitimacy for the party and building a reliable political constituency was to attract such support. The problem lay in identifying potential white Republican voters and convincing them to cross the color line, without simultaneously sacrificing the interests of the party's black adherents.

A significant number of white editors chose to challenge racial prejudice head-on, and several of them were Southern natives. The editor of the *Asheville Pioneer*, which served white readers of the western North Carolina mountains, expressed the hope that "the bitter prejudice against this long oppressed race" would soon pass away and that whites would learn that "negroes are as competent to take care of themselves as we are." The editor of the *Louisiana State Register* declared that "prejudice is the foe we fight." W. E. Kendrick of the *Chattanooga Republican* urged his party not to conceal its equalitarian principles but instead to confront and eradicate the prejudice that endangered people. According to Texas editor James Newcomb, "the spirit of complexional caste" had produced "a one sided, selfish, barbarous civilization." Nothing, he said, was more opposed to the principles and spirit of republican institutions, which were designed to benefit all citizens. Several Republican editors claimed that prejudice was the result not of race differences but of slavery, which had given whites a feeling of superiority and blacks a sense of degradation. Henry Sparnick of the *Aiken Tribune* denied that there was "an incurable antagonism between the races" and declared that the best way to restore good race relations was for whites to recognize the rights of blacks.[22]

On occasion a Republican editor would challenge the widely held assumption that the white race was superior to nonwhite races. Kendrick of the *Chattanooga Republican* ridiculed the idea that "the life, liberty, and property of men will receive protection in the ratio, as they approximate or recede from the Anglo-Saxon in color and physiognomy." Another editor contended that neither Jesus Christ nor the apostles had been "of the present white race." James Newcomb pointed to a number of black spokesmen and politicians, including Frederick Douglass, Henry McNeal Turner, John Langston, and George Ruby of Texas, as evidence of African American intellectual capability. *St. Landry Progress* editor Michael Vidal, who was of French descent, quoted the Marquis de Lafayette and other Frenchmen who endorsed the intellectual equality of the races. J. C. Mann published a long essay in the *Wilmington Post* disputing the contention that African Americans were inferior, stating that their post-emancipation progress proved otherwise.[23]

Most Republican editors did not try to convince their readers that blacks and whites were inherently equal, but they did devote considerable column space to calming white fears and suspicions regarding black behavior. They insisted that contrary to the contention of many whites, the former slaves were not indolent and would become productive workers provided their labor was fairly compensated. Houzeau of the *New Orleans Republican* did point out, however, that "the negro has as much right to be lazy . . . as his white-skinned neighbor." Several editors remarked that they saw much more evidence of indolence among whites than among blacks. They also published information about black property owners and pointed out that blacks were paying their share of taxes.[24] When white planters complained that blacks would no longer work on their land and proposed importing Chinese laborers, most Republican editors condemned the idea. They protested that the Chinese would displace blacks who had earned the right to labor as free workers. According to James Newcomb, planters proposed the idea to provide themselves with a new form of slave labor so that they could "perpetuate their feudal system."[25]

Republican editors praised African Americans for their eagerness to obtain an education and defended them against charges of disorderly and disruptive behavior, claiming that stories of black crime consisted of unsubstantiated rumors.[26] Several Republican journalists accused Democratic editors of employing a double racial standard in discussing crime. According to George Nason of the *New Bern Daily Republican,* if a black man was killed by an ex-rebel, "they say the scoundrel was not fit to live," whereas if a black murdered a white, "it is proof they are all unfit to govern themselves." J. C. Mann of the *Wilmington Post* insisted that his fellow journalists must learn that "white lives are not more sacred than lives of colored men," a point repeated by the editor of the *Louisiana State Register.* In Georgia, Republican editors John Emory Bryant and Jason Clark Swayze both complained that while white officers were quick to arrest blacks for suspected criminal behavior, repeated white violence against blacks went unpunished.[27]

Whites received repeated editorial assurances that they need not fear that newly enfranchised freedmen would "Africanize" the South. In states where blacks were in a numerical minority, editors were quick to emphasize it.[28] Several stressed that although blacks were now voting, whites would still dominate because they owned most of the South's property and enjoyed the advantages of superior education, social influence, political experience, and what William Scruggs of the *Atlanta Daily Opinion* referred to as "that prestige which ever attaches to the Anglo-Saxon race." Another Georgia editor also revealed his racial bias when he assured his readers that "the minority, composed of an inferior race," could not dominate the state.[29]

Republican journalists were constantly refuting Democratic charges that their party's black-rights advocacy would encourage the freedmen to take revenge against their former oppressors, inaugurating a race war. Whites, these editors insisted, need not fear violent retribution from angry ex-slaves. Freedmen were peaceably inclined and had no aggressive designs on whites. The *Austin Republican*'s white editor revealed his own racist stereotypes when he assured readers that slavery had trained the African American to be docile and submissive: "Two hundred years of industrious servitude have softened his wild passions, and have taught him to curb his untamed will and to obey." Other editors also stressed what G. K. Gilmer of the Harrisonburg *American Union* described as the "amiable, docile and imitative" nature of African Americans. Gilmer acknowledged, however, that all men were equal before God and possessed natural, inalienable rights.[30]

The real threat of race war, Republican editors averred, came from Southern white propagandists and editors who were stirring up prejudice against blacks for political advantage by advocating a "white man's government." Such a divisive course, they predicted, was certain to inflame racial hostility. Whites, not blacks, were guilty of initiating acts of racial violence that were occurring all over the South. Whites had nothing to fear from blacks' gaining political power, for they would not abuse it as whites had. The editor of the Montgomery *Daily State Sentinel* claimed the new voters "will not tar and feather men for advocating unpopular opinions. They will not shoot or hang men for teaching that the Constitution be obeyed."[31] A few writers warned whites, however, that the freedmen would defend themselves if provoked beyond endurance.[32]

The best guarantee against continuing Southern racial turmoil, Republican editors agreed, was for whites to respect the rights of former slaves. "A war between the races cannot take place," claimed the editor of the *New Bern Republican*, "if they live under similar circumstances, have the same requirements and the same rights." The editor of the *Alabama State Journal* agreed, stating that the only way for the South to rid itself of "the Negro question" was to acknowledge blacks' humanity and to recognize their rights. He assured his white readers that such action "does not deprive the white man of any right or privilege, and certainly does not depress his condition."[33]

Trying to convince white voters that the freedmen's elevation would not deprive them of any rights or privileges proved a difficult editorial task. At the onset of Reconstruction, Congress had coupled blacks' enfranchisement with that of ex-Confederates; many of the latter were also barred from office under terms of the Fourteenth Amendment. Once constitutional conventions had convened in each of the ex-Confederate states, however, Congress left it to them to decide whether to continue disfranchisement. Southern Republicans could not reach agreement on this issue. Eventually Virginia, Mississippi, Louisiana, Arkansas, and Alabama provided for some sort of political disability for ex-Confederates; the others did not. By 1872, only Arkansas continued to deprive whites of the vote.[34]

Southern whites feared that the Republican Party would confiscate their property as well as take away their vote, but such a program never materialized. A handful of Republicans did indeed call for such measures, and others threatened to confiscate property if Southerners resisted the implementation of the Reconstruction Acts. Yet most of the party's leaders and spokesmen, including its editors, opposed the idea. The other issue that caused consternation among Southern whites was the fear that Republicans would force "social equality" of the races, depriving whites of the right to select their own company. In particular, Democrats charged that Republicans would compel white and black children to attend school together. They also claimed that civil rights laws barring the segregation of African Americans on streetcars and railroads deprived whites of their right of free association. The result of such measures, Democrats warned, would be racial assimilation or amalgamation.

The refutation of such Democratic allegations was a constant editorial challenge for Republicans. Branding the charges for what they were—appeals to race prejudice—editors insisted that no one had any intention of forcing whites to admit blacks into the parlor. They ridiculed white fears of amalgamation by noting that the South was already full of light-skinned African Americans who were products of interracial unions. Only a few black editors, and on rare occasions a white one, endorsed integrated schools. Most would have agreed with Edward Stafford of the Jackson *Mississippi Pilot,* who in accepting the establishment of separate colleges for blacks and whites observed that "we have to take mankind as we find it, and what we would like to have, and what we can obtain, may be two [different] things." Black editors all called for equal accommodation laws; white editors differed more over this than over the "mixed school" question, but most defended such measures as a legitimate extension of the party's commitment to equal rights.[35]

Republican editors clearly spent much of their time on the defensive, fending off exaggerated charges leveled by their opponents. They were able, however, to devise a series of arguments appealing to whites to overcome racial prejudices and to vote alongside blacks for Republican candidates. They made a particular appeal to whites who had supported the Union during the war, warning that unless Unionist whites stood with the freedmen, former Confederates would regain control of state governments. These Southern Republican editors waved the bloody shirt as much as did their Northern Republican counterparts in this effort to exploit wartime animosities. Across the South, they identified their Democratic opponents with secession and blamed Democrats for suffering and death produced by the Civil War. During the war, they reminded readers, Confederate leaders had saddled everyone with conscription, impressment, and heavy taxes; the same men would control the postwar South if others did not intervene and vote Republican, warned the editors.

In Virginia, William B. Downey, who eventually edited the *Loudon Republican,* assured Thaddeus Stevens that "there is no Union man who does not infinitely more fear and dread the combination of the recent rebels than that of the recent slaves." Republican editors in Tennessee, Arkansas, and Texas—states with significant numbers of wartime Unionists—constantly reminded readers of their oppression at the hands of the Confederates. During the war, eastern Tennessee Unionists had suffered more from Confederate rule than their counterparts in any other part of the South, and Republican editors were not about to let them forget it. For several years after the war, these Republican papers referred to their opponents as rebels. They kept the memories of wartime atrocities alive, resurrecting the massacre of black Union soldiers at Fort Pillow and the deplorable Confederate prison conditions at Andersonville and Belle Isle. The same men who had hunted down and killed Unionists or forced them into Confederate armies, and who were still harassing loyalists even though the war was over, were, Republican editors claimed, attempting to gain control of the state.[36] To prevent this, white Unionist editors argued, their readers should unite with blacks, many of whom had fought and died for the cause. Governor William G. Brownlow, who had once advocated black colonization, proclaimed in 1868 that "the colored man has vindicated his right to freedom and the vote by his loyalty during the war."[37]

During the latter stages of the war, Valentine Dell used his *Fort Smith New Era* to castigate traitors and secessionists who had abused Arkansas Unionists. The war had hardly ended before Dell was calling for enfranchising blacks so that they could join loyal whites in preventing the rebels' return to power. John Price also devoted a number of *Little Rock Republican* editorials to attacking secessionists and rebels and reminding Unionists how they had suffered and continued to suffer from reprisals.[38] In Texas, the editor of the Austin *Southern*

Intelligencer told his readers that only a fool would entrust the state government "to the narrow, selfish, treasonable men" who had led the state into the Civil War. James Newcomb filled the *San Antonio Express* with provocative references to Fort Pillow, the military despotism of Jefferson Davis, treason, and condemnation of rebels. He warned Union men that "the fires of rebellion are simply smothered not quenched" and urged them to vote Republican.[39]

In other parts of the South, where overt wartime Unionism had been less evident, Republicans appealed to those who had initially opposed secession but who had later supported the Confederacy. This was particularly the case in Alabama and North Carolina, where editors identified secession with the Democrats who had voted for Breckinridge in 1860. Repeatedly they urged old Union men to abandon the treasonous Democrats and join the Republican Party. Scalawags William Figures of the *Huntsville Advocate* and Arthur Bingham of the Montgomery *Alabama State Journal* were the most prominent advocates of this course, seeking support from those who had voted for Stephen A. Douglas or John Bell, both of whom had run against Breckinridge in 1860.[40] In North Carolina, a number of editors appealed to "Old Line Democrats," "Jackson and Jefferson Democrats," and "Henry Clay Whigs" to oppose the ex-Confederate leaders they claimed had gained control of the state government.[41] Occasionally editors in other states made the same pleas.[42]

Republicans had to realize, however, that in most states only a minority of Southern whites had actively campaigned against secession, and an even smaller number had remained loyal to the Union during the war. They had to find ways to appeal to whites other than exploiting antebellum and wartime animosities. Indeed, such tactics could backfire by alienating former Confederates otherwise attracted to the party. Many Republican editors hoped to convince whites that the Republican Party championed not only the rights of blacks but also those of all Southern citizens. It was "wicked" for Democrats to call upon white men to control the South, claimed the editor of the *Charleston Daily Republican;* "it is not a matter of race but of citizenship." Republicans, they insisted, believed in a color-blind society. Several publishers placed on their mastheads a quotation from Horace Maynard, a scalawag Tennessee congressman: "Let our laws and our institutions speak not of white men, and not of red men, not of black men, not of men of any complexion; but like the laws of God—the Ten Commandments and the Lord's Prayer—let them speak of the people."[43] The *Nashville Republican*'s editor claimed that "it is not for the rights of the Negro that we are contending, but for the rights of human nature." In Florida, the editor of the Jacksonville *Union* asserted that the party stood for the proposition "that honest labor shall reap the reward of its own industry and every man white or black shall have an equal chance in the race of life."[44]

The fact that numerous Republican editors supported women's rights, and particularly suffrage for women at a time when that reform had limited Northern support and almost none in the South, indicates that they believed in the comprehensive nature of the equal rights doctrine.[45] They also believed this approach would get them votes. Appealing to immigrants, especially Germans, they stressed that the party recognized no divisions based on race, color, religion, or nationality. The editor of the *Nashville Republican,* which was published by a German American, contended that "a German Democrat is an absurdity"; his counterpart at the helm of the Atlanta *German Gazette* warned readers that the same men who formerly sold slaves would "not be very fastidious about selling a 'dutchman.'"[46] During Reconstruction a number of the South's German-language papers and several French papers in Louisiana supported the party.[47] Republican editors spent most of their time, however, trying to convince native white Southerners that a party based on equal rights had much to offer them.

Almost all carpetbag editors and many scalawags believed that Southern whites could be divided into two distinct socioeconomic classes. The smaller of the two was made up of privileged, wealthy Southerners who had long dominated the section's politics. This group they identified as "aristocrats," the "chivalry," or the "kid-glove gentry." The other class, the vast majority, they characterized as mechanics, laborers, yeoman farmers, and "poor whites," or men with "dirty shirts." The latter group of whites, Republican editors asserted, shared common interests with the masses of freedmen. Workers of both races should support the Republicans, they urged, for the party stood for a society based on equal opportunity with special privileges for none and equal rights for all. Class as well as racial inequities had to give way. The Republican Party alone, they claimed, stood ready to resist the wealthy aristocrats who would maintain their own prerogatives and would exploit workers both black and white. Although only a few outspoken editors consistently employed this sort of class appeal, there was not a Republican paper in the South that did not resort to it, especially prior to elections. It was by far the major arguing point that Republicans used in soliciting white support during the early phases of Reconstruction. When whites failed to flock to the Republican Party in response to these arguments, editors began appealing to them in other ways. Even in the last stages of Reconstruction, however, some editors, possibly out of frustration, sought to exploit what they believed was the South's latent class antagonism.

On October 30, 1867, during a heated campaign for ratifying the new state constitution and electing state officials, William Holden's *North Carolina Stan-*

dard published a lengthy appeal to the state's white workers. This editorial, which was republished in several Republican papers, touched on many of the themes developed by other Republican editors. "Southern aristocrats and secession oligarchs," Holden told his white readers, had stigmatized them as "mean whites, poor white trash, and greasy mechanics." Before the war these aristocrats had passed laws benefiting slaveholders while discriminating against white workers. Once the war began, these same oligarchs had forced white farmers into the army to fight for slavery while the oligarchs remained safely at home. After the war, the government taxed them to pay for its cost, leaving them poor and in debt. At long last, however, a party had appeared in the South that honored working people and advocated their interests. The Republican Party opposed both the enslavement of the black worker and the exploitation of the white; it would elevate the laborers of both races. Whites should resist divisive appeals to racial prejudice and unite with blacks to oust the aristocrats from power. "Now is the golden hour of reformation," Holden exhorted his readers. "Let your voices be heard, like the sound of mighty waters, demanding free schools, free learning, and equal rights with other men."[48]

Republican newspapers across the South carried variations on or additions to these themes. Everywhere Republican editors stressed that slavery, through its oppression of black workers, had simultaneously devalued the labor of whites. In Wilmington, the *Post*'s editor warned workers of both races that the conservative party believed "*poverty is a crime and labor is a disgrace.*" The editor of a Corpus Christi Republican paper assured his readers that "those who would enslave a black man, would make a white man a slave if they had the power." In Georgia, John Emory Bryant of the *Loyal Georgian* insisted that the blows the slave owners administered to the backs of their slaves "were aimed at all actual producers of wealth," while the editor of the *Columbus Press* warned that although slavery was gone, aristocratic Democrats still "consider it their right to *crack the whip*" over whites as well as blacks.[49]

The key issue in the South, many Republican editors insisted, was not the rights of blacks but the rights of labor against capital. In Tennessee, the editor of the *Nashville Republican* claimed that the rebellion was launched "for the right of capital to own labor . . . no matter what the color of either the capitalist or the laborer." According to John Bryant, now that slavery was gone, the issue was not what to do with the freedmen but "what shall we do with the *laborer?*" The editor of the Charleston *Southern Celt* urged black and white workers in that city to unite, for "the interests of labor are identical all over the world." In Virginia, A. M. Crane of the *Winchester Journal* contended that capital arrogantly sought "exactions of labor which it has no right to ask." As an example, he pointed to a Virginia law that punished people for enticing workers from their employers. Although this legislation was targeted at black workers, it threatened the rights of whites as well. By limiting workers' opportunity to seek higher wages, the law would "give to monopoly another sinecure, and take from competition another aid." G. K. Gilmer of the Harrisonburg *American Union* denied the conservative contention that a surplus of labor in Virginia created a rivalry between the races for jobs. The labor of all the state's people, he said, was necessary to develop its resources.[50]

A *Little Rock Republican* correspondent claimed that "no one class [is] entitled to a monopoly of rights to the prejudice of those of other classes." Editors of the Republican newspapers across the South took up this theme. Sometimes they emphasized their concern for equal political rights, calling for the elimination of property requirements for holding office and urging that governmental posts be filled by election rather than appointment. In North Carolina, Republicans sought to tap a strong current of democratic reformism by calling for the election rather than appointment of county officials and judges, for more frequent elections, and for annual sessions of the state legislature. Some editors talked about reforming legal codes and practices to eliminate class favoritism. Robert J. Alcorn, editor of the *Friar's Point Delta,* promised Mississippi whites that if they voted Republican, "your courts will no longer be deaf to the cry of the poor." Equal rights, asserted Houzeau of the *New Orleans Republican,* meant that courts in criminal trials would treat rich and poor alike, rather than protecting villains "because they come from good families." He even proposed that the state provide lawyers for the poor of both races. Some editors called for abolishing imprisonment for debt.[51]

For Republicans, equal rights also required repealing laws discriminating against workers and enacting measures protecting them. Before the war, many states had laws permitting creditors to place liens on mechanics' tools and farmers' lands. Republicans promised to repeal such laws and pledged to authorize farm workers to secure crop liens so that they would be paid before the landowner settled any other obligations.[52] For the editor of the *Woodville Republican,* securing equal rights for all meant passing legislation "that will protect the poor man in his humble cottage equally as well as the rich one in his castle." Many Republicans recognized the appeal of such an idea and proposed granting relief for debtors and exempting homesteads from seizure. In Georgia, in particular, Republicans emphasized these measures in bidding for white votes. Even there, however, debtor relief proved controversial. Some editors thought such innovations endangered property rights, and others argued that their beneficiaries would be wealthy business owners who had borrowed money rather than mechanics and farm workers.[53] Homestead exemptions protecting the property of poor and rich alike proved more popular, and Republican editors across the South pushed for such legislation.[54]

Numerous Republican journalists claimed that the South's tax structure discriminated against poor people and workers. Several editors drew attention to laws disfranchising voters unable to pay poll taxes and called for reducing or eliminating the levy.[55] Many of them stressed how state tax codes favored wealthy planters by shifting the tax burden from land to other revenue sources. For example, states assessed taxes against dogs, rifles, mechanics' and farmers' tools, hacks, wagons, drays, carts, and household items. They required many tradesmen and businessmen to obtain licenses and taxed their earnings. In Mississippi, Republican journalists condemned what one called the "barbarous tax laws" enacted by the state's Democratic legislature from 1865 to 1867. According to the editor of the *Vicksburg Daily Times,* the state's poor paid two and one half times as much tax on their trades as the rich paid on their land. The editor of the *Woodville Republican* estimated that in his county, landowners paid $3500 in taxes on four hundred thousand acres of land, while thirty businessmen paid $3600. H. B. Whitfield of the *Columbus Press* claimed that the owner of a confectionary shop and restaurant paid $72 in taxes in 1866, while a landowner with twenty-two bales of cotton and twenty head of cattle paid only $27.40. The author of an article in the *Friar's Point Delta* concluded that "the wealthier a man is the less taxes he has to pay," so that the tax burden fell on poor people who were unable to change the system because they lacked "a rich man's influence or a rich man's money."[56]

Protecting large, uncultivated tracts from taxation, the editor of the *Walterboro News* observed, allowed planters to perpetuate "that most dangerous of all oligarchies—a landed aristocracy." Republicans proposed shifting the tax burden back to real estate by exempting such items as pets, household furnishings, and tools from taxation and reducing or wiping out license fees. They claimed that land was not taxed at its full value and proposed to alter this by appointing assessors to evaluate property rather than having the landowners do it. If the large landholder objected to such measures, wrote the editor of the Jackson *Pilot,* "let him squirm." Never again, the editor added, would Mississippi return to "the happy condition it experienced in the good old Democratic days, when the 'mudsills' and 'poor white trash' staggered under the burdens of taxation so that the ruling class might wallow in inglorious ease and increase in unearned wealth." In Arkansas, John Price proposed taxing bankers, brokers, insurance companies, and other corporations: "If a poor farmer is taxed on his sheep and hogs, why should not a rich capitalist be taxed on the money he has locked up in his safe?"[57]

In their bidding for white working-class support, all Republican papers emphasized the importance of establishing public schools. Not only the freedmen but also poverty-stricken whites deserved educational opportunity, they claimed. In Virginia, Republican editors pointed out that the state appropriated funds for ten colleges while refusing to establish common schools. This system, James Hunnicutt claimed, benefited the sons of "Negro-oligarchs and landed lords" at poor families' expense. Everywhere Republican editors emphasized that the wealthy classes' monopoly on education helped maintain their grip on power and deprived white masses of an important opportunity to improve themselves. Samuel Bard of the Atlanta *New Era* argued that opposition to homestead and school proposals revealed a determination to "depress the poor man for the benefit of the rich." The state, William Scruggs of the Atlanta *Daily Opinion* insisted, must educate children of the "mechanic, the day laborer, [and] the poor man."[58]

Employing such class rhetoric to court the votes of white yeoman farmers and mechanics created a dilemma, for most editors also wanted to garner the support of the South's business and professional classes. Sometimes they categorized these groups with the working class and argued that "aristocrats" exploited them all. Even this approach was divisive, however, threatening to drive away large landowners who might be convinced to join the party. Searching for a more inclusive appeal, Republicans began emphasizing the importance of stimulating the South's economic growth, a development that would benefit everyone. According to historian Mark Summers, Republicans preached the "gospel of prosperity," hoping to convince Southern whites of all classes that voting for the Republican Party was the best way to promote economic recovery and growth. In 1867, Republicans emphasized that as long as the South remained out of the Union, political uncertainty would result in business stagnation. Since Republicans controlled the United States Congress, the quickest way to restore the ex-Confederate states was for Southern whites to cooperate with the Reconstruction Acts and vote for Republican regimes. Then Northern capital and immigration would pour into the section, and the new Republican governments would enact programs stimulating economic growth.[59]

These new governments, Republican editors contended, would promote a diversified economy with a thriving agriculture based on small farms, a growing industrial base, and new mines to extract the region's rich mineral resources, all tied together by an expanding railroad network. With slavery gone, the free labor system that replaced it, with its incentives for self-improvement and hard work, would transform the South. Public schools would contribute to economic growth by educating the working class. Believing the Southern economy was underdeveloped, they enthusiastically courted Northerners and European immigrants. They were also eager to promote the southward march of capital. Every Republican editor became a local booster, touting the attributes of a particular city, town, or county that would lure workers and investors.

Realizing that its soil and climate were some of the South's most valuable resources, these editors eagerly promoted agricultural development. All of them hoped that with the demise of slavery, the great plantations it had sustained would pass away as well, leaving the South dotted with farms tilled by independent white and black yeomen. Repeatedly these editors called for the breakup of large landholdings. They were sure that heavily mortgaged Southern planters would have to sell off much of their land, and when this did not happen, some editors recommended raising taxes on idle acres to force sales. To make farms more productive, they filled their papers with information about new scientific farming techniques.[60]

The Republican plan for Southern economic growth relied heavily on government assistance. To encourage industrial development, Alabama editors recommended exempting workshops and factories from taxation and promised their owners tariff protection. Mississippi and Louisiana editors called for state and federal aid for levee rebuilding. In Virginia, Republicans hoped for federal aid to enlarge the James River and Kanawha Canal, to dredge the James, and to build more lighthouses. The editor of the Corpus Christi *Nueces Valley* urged his state government to dredge a ship channel to the Gulf. The editor of the *Tallahassee Sentinel* called on Florida to drain overflow lands and improve navigation by opening canals.[61]

Of all Republican proposals for government assistance to business, however, the most popular and ultimately the most controversial proved to be aid for railroad construction. After the war many Southerners hoped to build a New South based not only on thriving agriculture but also on mines, mills, and factories. To effect such economic transformation, the South required a dependable transportation system. Before the war Southern governments had promoted railroads, and the conservative governments elected in 1865 had continued these antebellum policies, but few railroads were actually built. Hence there was ample precedent for Republicans to identify railroad development as a key element in their program of revitalizing and modernizing the Southern economy. The issue had immense political potential. Planters would benefit from rising land values generated by increased railroad access. Railroads would enable merchants and industrialists to expand their markets and would open up the South's plentiful coal, iron, and timber resources. Laying the rails would provide employment for workers of both races. No wonder, then, that Republican editors linked the steam engine with the printing press as forces that would transform their region.[62]

The body of ideas, issues, and appeals that Republican editors ultimately amassed to attract Southern voters incorporated many internal conflicts and inconsistencies. The most obvious centered on race: the Republicans stood for equal rights for African Americans, a goal that most Southern whites opposed. Another touched on class. Some Republicans hoped to break down planter domination in the South and establish governments based on the poor of both races, while others hoped to pull these planters, along with business and professional classes, into the party. Republicans also disagreed about how to treat ex-Confederates, some wanting to disfranchise them, others hoping to bring them into the party. As some of these differences diminished in significance, others replaced them; intraparty strife would haunt the South's Republican Party throughout Reconstruction.

CHAPTER SEVEN

Differences in Approach

Southern Republican editors generally agreed on their party's commitment to the Union, to equal rights, and to the promotion of a free labor economy. Despite this common ground, however, intraparty factions quickly spawned divisions in the party's press, leading the *Alabama State Journal*'s editor to complain that "Republican journals and party members generally are more given to fault finding within than without their party." On the other hand, he noted, Democratic editors defended one another: "Their guns are always turned on the hated Republicans alone." Echoing these comments, a Texas Republican publisher admitted to a colleague that "we hate each other worse than we do the Democrats."[1]

Divisions within the Republican journalistic fraternity reflected tactical and philosophical differences that plagued the Southern Republican Party as a whole throughout Reconstruction. These differences initially surfaced in debates over concrete issues, such as confiscation or disfranchisement. The debates frequently centered on racial fault lines in the party. Republicans argued about which groups of whites to solicit for support and how to balance such efforts against the need to maintain the backing of African Americans. The latter concern led to debates over the wisdom of equal accommodation laws and running black candidates for office. These issues were all interrelated, and Republican editors came down on all sides of them, making categorization difficult. One can, however, define some marked differences within their ranks, particularly early in Reconstruction.

By 1868, one group of Republican newspapers could be labeled as radical on the basis for their support for one or more of four propositions: confiscation, disfranchisement, the rights and interests of freedmen, and building a party on an alliance of white and black workers. The few papers advocating confiscation appeared early in Reconstruction, and they were led by the earliest and most radical of all, the *New Orleans Tribune,* the South's leading African American publication. During and immediately after the war, the *Tribune*'s editors urged federal confiscation of plantation land and its redistribution to the freedmen.

When that did not happen, they suggested other ways to shift this property into laborers' hands, such as taxing uncultivated lands to force their sale or leasing state lands. After becoming chief editor, Jean-Charles Houzeau advanced several schemes for financing producer-run cooperatives that would enable the freedmen to buy land and share the income derived from farming it.[2]

Michael Vidal, an editor of the Opelousas *St. Landry Progress*, which was owned by both blacks and whites, had served on the *Tribune* staff and shared Houzeau's interest in land redistribution. By 1867, however, he knew there was no chance of federal land confiscation, a conclusion also accepted by the *Tribune*. Vidal speculated that perhaps Louisiana's Republican government could take land from some of the former slaveholders if they were fairly compensated, but that also was highly improbable. Recognizing the unlikelihood of these proposals being implemented, Vidal and other Republican editors finally embraced a measure Congress had passed in 1866 that opened Southern federal lands to freedmen and loyal whites for homesteading.[3]

Only a few of the South's white-owned Republican papers advocated confiscation. In Arkansas, scalawag Valentine Dell of the *Fort Smith New Era* called for "the destruction of the landed aristocracy . . . by confiscating the lands of leading rebels." Several Tennessee papers edited by native white Unionists, including Brownlow's *Knoxville Whig*, Mercer's Nashville *Press and Times*, and Grisham's Jonesborough *Union Flag*, proposed confiscating ex-Confederates' property and using the proceeds to pay the war debt or to compensate Unionists for their wartime losses. John Hardy, editor of the Montgomery *Alabama State Sentinel*, called for confiscating lands of planters who discharged workers for voting.[4] In Virginia, the black editor of the Hampton *True Southerner* recommended seizing abandoned lands, while several papers threatened confiscation for Southerners who resisted the Reconstruction Acts. Conservative Republicans charged James Hunnicutt of the Richmond *New Nation* with supporting confiscation, but he denied the charge.[5]

Although most Republican editors did not endorse outright confiscation, many discussed other ways to redistribute Southern land. Almost all Republican papers hoped the plantation system would collapse, and several proposed dismantling it by taxing unused acreage.[6] Albion Tourgee of the *Greensboro Union Register* suggested that the federal government help freedmen purchase land. No paper other than the *Tribune* considered producer cooperatives, although the editor of the Mobile *Nationalist* did recommend consumer cooperatives.[7] In South Carolina, several Republican editors urged planters to sell some of their land to those who worked it and appealed to Northerners to purchase Southern plantations and sell or lease them in small lots to the freedmen. Eventually South Carolina's new Republican regime created a state land commission to buy tracts of land for resale to the freedmen, a program welcomed by John Morris, the editor of both the *South Carolina Republican* and the *Daily Republican*.[8]

A larger number of editors took what contemporaries agreed was a radical position in favor of imposing political disabilities on ex-Confederates. John Emory Bryant of the Augusta *Loyal Georgian,* William Holden of the Raleigh *North Carolina Standard,* Alexander H. Jones of the *Asheville Pioneer,* and John Hardy of the Montgomery *State Sentinel* all wanted to bar ex-Confederate leaders from holding office. The following favored disfranchising them: A. M. Crane of the *Winchester Journal* and Hunnicutt of the Richmond *New Nation* in Virginia, John Price of the *Little Rock Republican* and Valentine Dell of the *Fort Smith New Era* in Arkansas, John Silsby and Albert Griffin of the Mobile *Nationalist* in Alabama, James Newcomb of the *San Antonio Express* in Texas, Jason Clarke Swayze of the Macon *American Union* in Georgia, and Albion Tourgee of the *Greensboro Union Register* in North Carolina.[9] In Tennessee, almost all Republican papers backed Brownlow's *Knoxville Whig* in supporting state laws disfranchising most of the state's ex-Confederates.[10] In Mississippi, where Republicans were badly divided over the wisdom of disfranchisement, editors J. R. Smith of the *Meridian Chronicle* and Frederick Speed of the *Vicksburg Republican* opposed it.[11]

Jean-Charles Houzeau of the New Orleans *Tribune* supported the Fourteenth Amendment provision barring a certain class of ex-Confederates from office. He opposed disfranchisement, however, claiming it would be impossible to administer and could only create contention. Furthermore, he warned his black readers, "If we refuse the franchise to any class, it can as well be withheld from us." Also opposing disfranchisement was the editor of the New Orleans *Louisianan,* which became the South's most outspoken African American paper following the *Tribune*'s demise. On the other hand, carpetbagger Emerson Bentley, who became editor of the *St. Landry Progress* in 1868, supported disfranchising ex-Confederates until they demonstrated their acceptance of the Reconstruction Acts.[12]

Even more Republican editors strongly supported equal rights for the freedmen. Here, too, the *New Orleans Tribune* took the most advanced or radical position. Houzeau early insisted that African Americans deserved the full panoply of civil rights, including jury service, and the paper was the first in the South to advocate enfranchising the freedmen. African Americans could not wait patiently for Christian teaching and education to weaken racism, Houzeau believed; "prejudice," he claimed, "can only be destroyed by the strong arm of power." Scarcely had the war ended when the paper began calling for abandoning separate streetcars for blacks, and it was soon pushing equal accommodations laws, integrated schools, and elimination of the ban on racial intermarriage. Houzeau also insisted that blacks play a leading role in the Republican Party and demanded their fair share of elective and appointive offices. At a time when the specter of a race war terrified whites, the *Tribune* insisted that blacks had a right to arm themselves for protection against white violence.[13]

The *Tribune's* equal rights proposals were too comprehensive for most Southern Republican newspapers, but many papers—particularly other black-owned ones—supported at least some of the *Tribune's* positions. New Orleans was the only Southern city to experiment with integrated schools, and the black-owned *Louisianan* backed the effort. Its editor William G. Brown also supported equal accommodations laws, as did two African American editors in Texas, Melville Keith of the Austin *Freedman's Press* and Frank Webb of the *Galveston Republican,* and white editor Albert Griffin of the Mobile *Nationalist.* In Georgia, James M. Simms of the *Freemen's Standard* called on the legislature to sanction interracial marriages. Brown, Webb, Tabbs Gross of the *Arkansas Freeman,* and William Scott of the *Maryville Republican* also called on the Republicans to give their black constituents a larger share of political offices.[14]

A significant number of white editors closely monitored issues of concern to blacks and expressed enthusiastic support for civil and political rights for the freedmen. Occasionally they covered African Americans' social and political meetings and discussed the activities of their churches. This group included Bryant of the *Loyal Georgian* and Swayze of the *American Union* in Georgia; Griffin of the Mobile *Nationalist* in Alabama; Lucien Eaton of the *Memphis Post* and S. C. Mercer of the Nashville *Press and Times* in Tennessee; Tourgee of the *Greensboro Union Register* and the editors of the *Wilmington Post* in North Carolina; D. B. White's Hampton *True Southerner,* Hunnicutt's *New Nation,* Charles Whittlesey's Richmond *State Journal,* and the *Petersburg Times* in Virginia; and a number of Republican papers in South Carolina and Mississippi, states where blacks either had a voting majority or were close to it.

Although the white editors of these Republican papers were emphatic in their endorsement of black rights, they either ignored or opposed the school integration issue. In western North Carolina, where few blacks lived and whites adamantly opposed mixed schools, the editor of the *Rutherford Star* firmly declared that "such a policy *will not be tolerated."* Samuel Ashley, who helped establish the *Wilmington Post,* took a stand against segregated schools when he was a constitutional convention delegate, but his paper did not echo these views. Even in South Carolina, where blacks cast more ballots than whites, John Morris of the Charleston *Republican* supported separate schools, claiming that any integration effort was doomed to fail and would only delay the establishment of a public school system. In Mississippi, where blacks also outvoted whites, Robert W. Flournoy of the Pontotoc *Equal Rights* advocated integrating both public schools and the state university, but the state's other editors opposed such ideas. A. C. Fisk of the *Vicksburg Republican* made it clear that the Republican Party should adopt a system of free schools "for each of the two great separate races of our people." In Little Rock, John Price of the *Republican* denounced as "nonsense and twaddle" Democratic charges that the Republicans would compel black and white children to attend the same schools.[15]

Several white editors in this group who shied away from mixed schools did endorse state public accommodations laws. In Charleston, Alonzo Webster of the *Advocate* was hesitant to push for blacks' equal access to the city's streetcars, urging that readers "patiently wait" for the state to pass laws protecting such rights. Morris of the *Republican* insisted, however, that African Americans must have the right to ride in cars, visit theaters, and marry freely. In Little Rock, Price defended a state law guaranteeing blacks equal access to railroad cars, and in Tennessee Mercer of the *Press and Times* condemned efforts to deprive freedmen of this right as "a remnant of an old prejudice." In Virginia, both Crane of the *Winchester Journal* and Hunnicutt of the *New Nation* criticized whites who did not want blacks riding with them on railroad cars. Before the war, Crane noted sarcastically, masters and slaves riding together on trains caused no controversy. In Mississippi, both the leading Republican papers endorsed a state civil rights law guaranteeing blacks equal access to public accommodations.[16]

Only a few white editors favored blacks' arming themselves for protection against white violence. In Alabama, U.S. Army officers briefly shut down Albert Griffin's Mobile *Nationalist* after he published an editorial telling blacks that firing weapons into the air was a waste of ammunition and that if attacked they should fire directly at their assailants. In Georgia, Jason Clark Swayze of the *American Union*, probably the most outspoken white Republican editor in the South, told blacks that if the Ku Klux Klan murdered any of their number, they should "lay every house in ashes within miles of the spot where such blood was spilled." He also exhorted them to "shoot down [anyone who] opposes you." Conservative newspapers denounced Swayze's remarks, and a mob threatened to run him out of town.[17] In Richmond, James Hunnicutt defended blacks' right to form military organizations, and during the early Reconstruction years several other Republican papers endorsed recruiting blacks into state militias to help control violent whites.[18]

Only a few white Republican editors, led by Hunnicutt of the *New Nation*, endorsed the right of blacks to run for office. John Stokes, editor of the *Alabama State Journal*, contended that African Americans should get a representative share of his state's federal appointments, and in Tennessee S. C. Mercer hoped African Americans would play an important role in Nashville politics. Republican editors in Georgia did protest when whites expelled black members of the first state legislature assembled under the Reconstruction Acts, but they remained cool toward the idea of freedmen running for office. Swayze, who was so insistent on blacks' right to arm themselves, complained that they were voting for candidates of their own color rather than for better qualified whites. In Louisiana, Michael Vidal of the *St. Landry Progress* urged blacks not to become candidates, while in Charleston, Mobile, and Little Rock, Republican editors Morris, Griffin, and Price warned freedmen not to draw the "color line" by voting solely for candidates of their own race.[19]

During the initial stages of Reconstruction, numerous Republican editors took a radical position in favor of building a political alliance of black and white workers and farmers. A handful of Republican papers in two major Southern cities, New Orleans and Charleston, earnestly advocated the rights of urban workers of both races. During the war, the Republican Party in New Orleans had championed equitable pay and an eight-hour day for workers, and both the *Tribune* and the *St. Landry Progress* supported these recommendations.[20] In Charleston, several papers took up the workers' cause. As early as October 1865, the carpetbagger editor of the *South Carolina Leader* applauded efforts of the city's white workers to organize, and in November 1868, the editor of the *Charleston Advocate* addressed a particular appeal to white working men, urging votes for the Republican mayoral candidate if they wanted lower rents and higher wages.[21]

In the fall of 1869, John Morris enthusiastically backed a strike of Charleston's black longshoremen, contending that "their cause is the cause of every workingman in this city, of every trade, whether white or colored." Noting that white workers opposed these efforts, he warned them that their wages would not rise until blacks' wages did and urged them as well as blacks to organize unions. Morris added that "if we cannot get over these race prejudices we can get around them" by organizing blacks and whites separately. He also advocated a statewide farm workers' organization to agree on uniform contracts and wage rates, and he urged passage of legislation authorizing workers' liens on crops and land to secure their wages. When a state workingmen's convention did assemble in Charleston, Morris allotted it front-page coverage and spoke to its delegates. Another editor who addressed the convention, L. C. Northrop, a native white, also began using the columns of his Irish-American publication, the *Southern Celt*, to champion the cause of both white and black workers.[22] Outside South Carolina, however, only a few papers expressed interest in labor reform.[23]

Most Republican editors proposed no specific plans for redistributing property or organizing workers into unions. Many, however, tried appealing to white yeoman farmers and workers by stimulating their antagonism toward the wealthier and more influential whites, whom they identified as "aristocrats." These efforts began during the war, which had brought latent class divisions to the surface, especially in areas where Unionist sympathy was already strong. Numerous whites resented conscription laws exempting planters and were driven to desperation by Confederate tax and impressment policies. Some Union army-camp journals tried to exploit such resentment. In 1862, the editor of the Memphis *Union Appeal* urged "working men, mechanics, and laborers" to rally against the Southern aristocrats who had precipitated the rebellion and who regarded all labor as disgraceful. In January 1865, the editor of the Norfolk *New Regime* printed a long excerpt from the *Philadelphia Press* contending that the South's "governing class" had exploited the "producing class" by denying it education and crushing its loyalty to the Union. The writer urged laboring men in the South to end the war and seize power from the planters who had precipitated it.[24]

Southern white Unionist editors also picked up this class rhetoric during the war. In 1863, William G. Brownlow of Tennessee claimed that "the 'low flung', aye, the 'mudsills' of society, the hard-fisted yeomanry of this country are going to govern it, and the *respectability* of the land may prepare to meet their humiliation." S. C. Mercer railed in his Nashville *Daily Times and True Union* at "the rapacious slaveocracy"; in one 1864 issue, a correspondent reminded nonslaveholders of their suffering at the planters' hands and admonished them to cease being "the base slaves of these cold-hearted aristocratic few." In Arkansas, Valentine Dell used his *Fort Smith New Era* to denounce Southern aristocrats for subverting "the rights of the great mass of the laboring white population" and warned them that "the poor have forsaken you, and they will be your masters."[25]

The Civil War also exacerbated class consciousness in North Carolina. The state's Unionist and Republican editors sought to exploit it by urging poor white workers to unite with the freedmen under the Republican banner. Albion Tourgee, who began publishing his *Greensboro Union Register* in November 1866, helped organize a Loyal Reconstruction League to rally poor whites and blacks to "wrest power from the rich as such." J. B. Carpenter used the columns of his *Rutherford Star* to condemn the aristocrats' "selfishness, Toryism and Tyranny" and urged North Carolinians, "whether they be white or black," to vote "as interest might dictate, not as the would be aristocrats might wish." William Holden made similar appeals in his *North Carolina Standard,* as did Alexander H. Jones's *Asheville Pioneer* and several *Wilmington Post* editors. As late as 1875, a letter in the *Post* signed "mechanic" bemoaned the Democrats' using "the poor white man to hold the negro down."[26]

A number of editors in other states also resorted to class-oriented appeals to white yeomen to join with blacks in support of the Republican Party. They included John Bryant of the *Loyal Georgian* and Jason Clarke Swayze of the Macon *American Union* in Georgia; John Price of the *Little Rock Republican* in Arkansas; Albert Griffin of the Mobile *Nationalist* and John Hardy of the Montgomery *State Sentinel* in Alabama; and James Newcomb of the *San Antonio Express* and Austin *State Journal* in Texas. Virginia produced a number of radical journals espousing an interracial workers' alliance, including A. M. Crane's *Winchester Journal,* Hunnicutt's Richmond *New Nation,* A. W. Sheldon's *Richmond Register,* and John P. Wright's *Lynchburg Press.* Several Mississippi editors also urged such a laborers' coalition, including J. R. Smith of the *Meridian Chronicle,* several editors on the staff of the *Vicksburg Republican,* and Robert J. Alcorn of the *Friar's Point Delta.* All these journalists urged white readers to abandon their racial prejudices and cooperate with blacks against their common persecutors.

Historian Michael Perman has labeled as "radical" those Republicans who sought a coalition of African Americans and poor whites. He has also identified their political approach as "expressive," aimed at maximizing support from the party's initial constituency by sticking closely to its original principles.[27] Although most editors in this group did not support what they considered more extreme proposals for confiscation, integrated schools, and black access to political office, they were nonetheless stronger advocates of black civil and political rights than were other Republican journalists. They wanted to secure their party's base among black voters and white Unionists and hoped to enlarge this coalition by appealing to white workers and yeoman farmers.

Many of these editors were scornful of other Republicans' proposals to reach out for support to wealthier, more educated, more "respectable" classes of white Southerners. In Louisiana, where a number of white Republicans were pleased when ex-Confederate General James Longstreet joined their party, Houzeau of the *New Orleans Tribune* warned: "Accession is not always strength." The party, he said, must not compromise its principles by weakening its platform to appeal to "the spirit of prejudice and timidity." In Georgia, Jason Clarke Swayze urged Republicans not to court the support of the state's landed class, insisting that the party should rely on the "bone and sinew" of blacks and laboring whites. He would rather be surrounded by "a corporal's guard of honest men, with crusts and water on which to subsist," than "revel amid luxuries in a den of thieves." In states with a significant number of white Unionists, such as Tennessee, Arkansas, and Texas, many editors also opposed any concessions to former Confederates. Price of the *Little Rock Republican* urged the party not to court their votes unless they "have recanted their errors." In Texas, James Newcomb denounced proposals to woo "some conservative place-hunter or tool." In North Carolina, J. B. Carpenter of the *Rutherford Star* opposed any courting of Democrats, stating that his paper would stand for the Republican Party "in its purest form."[28]

Opposed to such radicals stood a group of Republican journalists Michael Perman has described as "centrists." These editors eagerly sought the support of white Southerners from the landed, business, and professional classes. Hence they favored programs to promote economic development and "modernize" the South, particularly state aid for railroads. Hoping for conciliation, they opposed the imposition of political liabilities on ex-Confederates. Although they were usually willing to defend the equal rights of blacks, they concentrated on attracting white support to the party. Perman has defined the centrist strategy as "competitive" rather than "expressive," for these editors were ready to moderate their party's principles in order to expand its constituency.[29]

This group of centrist editors had much in common with their more radical counterparts. They all endorsed the Union and a strong central government, advocated civil and political equality for the freedmen, and recommended many common economic proposals. Numerous radicals, for instance, supported railroad aid, and almost all editors promoted public schools, mechanics' lien laws, and homesteads. The difference between the radicals and the centrists can be seen partly in the issues each group chose to emphasize. It also surfaced in the tone and style of editorials. In courting white yeoman and worker support, the radicals, or "expressives," to use Perman's term, employed more divisive rhetoric than did the centrists, or "competitives," who were eager to build the broadest possible support base in the white community. Jean Folkerts, on the other hand, has argued that radical Republican editors were trying to build a sense of community among the party's core elements, while the moderates sought to legitimize the party in the eyes of the South's more influential white elements. Some editors' attempts to accomplish both goals proved difficult, for efforts to gain the first could well endanger achievement of the second and vice versa.[30]

The most conservative of the centrist editors stood ready to downplay almost all aspects of their party's program in order to attract upper-class white support. Several Georgia editors belonged to this group, including John E. Hayes of the

Savannah *Republican,* E. H. Pughe of the *Augusta Press,* William L. Scruggs of the *Atlanta Daily Opinion,* and Samuel Bard of the Atlanta *New Era.* All four men gave lukewarm support to civil rights for blacks and accepted their enfranchisement only because Congress required it. Scruggs even claimed that after the state returned to the Union, its legislature could disfranchise the freedmen. By the summer of 1868, their conservative racial views prompted Hayes and Pughe to leave the Georgia Republican Party.[31]

Samuel Bard, whose journalistic career spanned Reconstruction and placed him at the helm of newspapers in several states, better exemplifies a centrist Republican editor. Originally from New York, Bard had moved to Louisiana around 1848 and by 1860 was publishing newspapers in Caddo and Shreveport. Bard joined the Louisiana Democratic Party and became an ardent secessionist. In 1866, he moved to Georgia to take over the Atlanta *New Era.* Upon his arrival in Atlanta, whites welcomed him as a "State Rights Democrat of the old school." He then disappointed them by joining the Republicans, although he was slow to admit his new loyalty publicly. Bard edited the *Era* until 1869, when Ulysses S. Grant appointed him Idaho's territorial governor. Instead of going there, however, Bard ended up in Arkansas, where he served in the state legislature and owned and edited the Fayetteville *Mountain Echo.* In the summer of 1870, he returned to Atlanta to take command of a new paper, the *True Georgian,* which lasted about a year. In 1872, Bard popped up in Tennessee as editor of the Chattanooga *Herald,* but the next year he was back in Georgia to revive the defunct Atlanta *Era.* This paper also soon failed, and Grant then appointed him city postmaster. As late as 1875, Samuel Bard was still active in Republican newspaper publishing, serving on the staff of the Montgomery *Alabama State Journal.*[32]

As editor of the Atlanta *New Era* from 1866 until 1869, Bard staked out a centrist position on Reconstruction issues. He became an ally of ex-governor Joseph Brown, who joined the Republican Party at the same time. Both men courted business support for the party and objected to imposing political disabilities on ex-Confederates. Bard urged Georgia Republicans to seek the support of all those willing to forsake the past and develop the state's material resources, build industry, and organize public schools. During the 1868 elections to ratify Georgia's new constitution and elect its first state government, Bard did appeal for working-class support, contending that Democrats' opposition to homesteads and schools revealed their determination to depress the poor and benefit the rich. He said little about black rights, however, and, like William Scruggs, suggested that once the new constitution was in place, white Georgians could amend it to disfranchise blacks.[33]

After the election, Bard set out to make the *Era* a "live Conservative Republican paper." Declaring his intention to attract men "from the best material of the white population," Bard abandoned his class-oriented appeals to white workers and devoted most of his attention to noncontroversial business and social matters. He promised to use the *Era* to "improve and elevate our colored friends as far as can be," especially by supporting public schools, but assured his readers that "this is, and always will be a white man's government." He warned radical advocates of black rights that "High church Republicanism will do very well for the Northern states, but we [believe] . . . that the low church policy is the best for the party in the South at this particular time." Bard eventually broke with Rufus Bullock, Georgia's Republican governor, when Bullock sought to restore military rule after the legislature expelled its newly elected black members. In December 1870, disgust with Bullock led Bard to announce his abandonment of the Republicans to rejoin the Democratic party. He did not follow through on his threat, although many party papers questioned his commitment to the Republicans. Despite his inconsistent record on state issues, Bard loyally supported the Grant administration in Washington, which rewarded him with patronage. As late as February 1876, Bard was denouncing the Democratic Party.[34]

In Texas, Ferdinand Flake, owner of the Galveston *Flake's Bulletin,* followed a course similar to Bard's. He too was reluctant to avow himself a Republican. Although he eventually supported congressional Reconstruction and agreed that freedmen must have civil rights, he was a reluctant convert to black enfranchisement. He feared that with the ballot blacks would become militant and warned that their participation in the Republican Party would drive away whites. He especially opposed the Union League's efforts to organize black voters, calling its leaders demagogues who would inspire black hostility toward whites. Like Bard, Flake was eager to court middle- and upper-class whites and devoted considerable attention to promoting the economic development of Texas. Also like Bard, he criticized his own state's Republican governor for being too radical, hoping that by taking a more conservative stance the party would attract Democratic support. He flirted with third-party movements, and although he remained a Republican, some editors regarded him as an apostate before his death in 1872.[35]

Numerous other Republican editors eventually came to share Bard's and Flake's interest in expanding the party's ranks beyond its initial constituency of freedmen and Unionist whites. At the outset of congressional Reconstruction, however, radical Republican editors dominated the party press in Arkansas, Tennessee, North and South Carolina, Virginia, and Mississippi. At this time many of the party's centrist papers came from Alabama, but Florida, Georgia, Texas, and Louisiana also had prominent examples. As time went on, editors advocating more radical approaches to party organization fell by the wayside, and the centrist press grew stronger across the South. While they lasted, however, the radical papers in several states carried on a heated contest with centrists for the soul of the Republican Party.[36]

During the initial stages of Reconstruction, debates over disfranchisement and which groups of whites to court caused the most dissension among Republican editors. In most ex-Confederate states, Republicans were just beginning to organize their party and mobilize a constituency. The decisions they made at this time about policy and programs could well determine the party's destiny. As Republicans struggled with these matters, they faced white hostility and intimidation at every turn, conditions that helped the radicals make the case for their particular approach. Nonetheless, moderate or centrist editors appeared in most states to vie for control of their party's direction. In a few states, national party leaders played a crucial role in the outcome of this struggle among Southern journalists. Moderate Republicans dominated key national committees, and—most important for the South's struggling newspapers—they controlled the dispensation of federal printing contracts. Several radical papers that failed to obtain or subsequently lost this federal patronage quickly disappeared.[37]

In March 1867, when Congress authorized Edward McPherson to dispense printing patronage in the South, Florida's newspaper situation was uncertain. The Jacksonville *Florida Union* was turning conservative, so McPherson awarded printing to W. H. Christy, a Floridian who had opposed secession and was now editing the Jacksonville *Florida Times*. In May, Edward M. Cheney, a Boston journalist, bought control of the *Florida Union*. The two Jacksonville editors became journalistic spokesmen for Florida's rival Republican factions. A group of centrist Republicans led by Harrison Reed hoped to build a coalition of business-oriented conservatives that would restore the state to the Union and promote its economic development. Although these men supported civil and political equality for the state's freedmen, they downplayed that commitment in order to attract white support. Radicals who were mobilizing freedmen through the Union Leagues opposed the Reed Republicans. Radicals were more outspoken in their support of black rights, hoped to maximize freedmen's involvement in state politics, and recommended disfranchising leading Florida ex-Confederates and barring others from holding office. In this contest, Cheney backed Reed while Christy supported the radicals. Although a number of congressional radicals backed Christy's paper, McPherson switched patronage from the *Times* to the *Union*, a decision that undoubtedly contributed to the *Times*'s subsequent demise, leaving the radicals without a journal. The editor of

Florida's other leading Republican paper, the *Tallahassee Sentinel*, also espoused centrist views, as did the *Pensacola Observer*.[38]

In Louisiana, several claimants for federal patronage petitioned McPherson. These included the editors of the *Homer Iliad*, a northern Louisiana Unionist paper, and two New Orleans journals, the *Tribune*, which had been in existence since midwar, and the newly founded *Republican*. McPherson initially awarded printing to the *Iliad* and *Republican*, but under pressure from Benjamin Butler and other congressional radicals, he also agreed to subsidize the *Tribune*. By 1867, the *Tribune* was already unpopular among centrist Louisiana Republicans, who feared its editors were trying to give party control to African Americans. After the *Tribune* called for appointing a black man as mayor of New Orleans, John P. Newman, the Methodist missionary who edited the *New Orleans Advocate*, warned the freedmen that they were "ingrates" for forgetting their Northern benefactors. In turn, the *Tribune*'s editor accused Newman of courting "Confederate chieftains" and other whites whose loyalty to Republican principles was dubious. The editor of the German-language New Orleans *Deutsche Zeitung*, who claimed he would never become a "Black Republican," likewise opposed the radicals.[39]

A rift also quickly developed between Houzeau's *Tribune* and the *Republican*. Editors of the latter paper defended black rights and interests but questioned the *Tribune*'s more radical positions. Houzeau ridiculed the *Republican*'s editors for courting the support of ex-Confederates like General James Longstreet and criticized the paper's owners, some of whom were carpetbaggers. In 1868, after the *Tribune* refused to support carpetbagger Republican gubernatorial nominee Henry Clay Warmoth, one of Warmoth's backers convinced McPherson to withdraw federal printing from the black-owned paper, thus halting its publication shortly thereafter. The career of Louisiana's other leading radical paper, the Opelousas *St. Landry Progress*, also came to an end in 1868 after a mob trashed its offices, killed one of its editors, and chased the other out of town.[40]

When North Carolina's Reconstruction began, radicals ran most of the handful of Republican newspapers, including the Raleigh *North Carolina Standard*, *Wilmington Post*, *Asheville Pioneer*, *Rutherford Star*, and *Greensboro Union Register*. All these papers courted the support of freedmen and white laborers and chastised secessionists and ex-Confederates. The *New Bern Republican*'s scalawag editors also emphatically endorsed black rights but showed a greater interest than the other papers in winning support of the business community by emphasizing the party's commitment to railroad construction. They hoped to recruit "Old Line Democrats" and "Henry Clay Whigs" to the party. The scalawag editor of the Salem *American Advocate* was similarly inclusive and was even willing to accept secessionists, provided they recanted their earlier views.⁴¹ The most outspoken radical editor, Albion Tourgee, had been the first to endorse suffrage for African Americans and was actively involved in organizing them into Union Leagues. Tourgee distrusted Holden and his followers for having submitted to Confederate authority during the war; he wanted to build the party on a base of blacks and Unionists of the "straitest sect" who had been consistently loyal to the United States. Such views alarmed Northern Republicans, who looked to Holden to lead their party in North Carolina. Although Tourgee secured leading Northern Republican radicals' endorsements, McPherson refused to award him a federal printing contract, instead granting the privilege to Holden and to Alexander H. Jones of the *Asheville Pioneer*. Tourgee's paper soon disappeared.⁴²

Virginia was home to a number of radical newspapers, but not all survived through 1868. In 1866, a mob had destroyed D. B. White's Norfolk *True Southerner;* its African American editor Joseph Wilson launched the *Union Republican* in Norfolk, but it soon disappeared. In January 1868, the radical *Richmond Register* appeared but lasted only two months. That summer local radicals established the *Petersburg Times,* and it joined Hunnicutt's *New Nation,* the *Winchester Journal,* and the Alexandria *State Journal* in supporting black rights and the disfranchisement of ex-Confederates. The three papers opposed efforts of moderate Republicans like editor G. K. Gilmer of the *American Union* to attract ex-Whig support.⁴³

The most controversial of Virginia's radical editors was James W. Hunnicutt of the *New Nation*. Hunnicutt's radical views, his popularity among black voters, and his volatile temperament cost him support among Virginia's white Republicans. The Alexandria *State Journal,* which had received wartime federal assistance, continued to publish the U.S. laws during Reconstruction. In 1867, Hunnicutt complained that by monopolizing the printing, the *Journal*'s proprietors "are growing rich while I am being starved out," and McPherson awarded Hunnicutt the second Virginia printing contract. In 1868, moderate Republicans controlling the party convention refused to nominate Hunnicutt for governor and attempted to buy control of his paper. The *State Journal*'s publishers moved it from Alexandria to Richmond, and the *New Nation* lost its federal printing contract. By the end of the year Hunnicutt's paper was gone, although the *State Journal, Petersburg Times,* and *Winchester Journal* continued to espouse radical views.⁴⁴

The handful of Republican papers in Georgia waged a bitter struggle for survival, leading their editors to slash at each other as well as at the Democrats. In

1867, six Georgia publishers vied for the privilege of printing the U.S. laws; Jason Clarke Swayze of the *American Union* complained that several of his editorial rivals supported Reconstruction only to obtain government patronage. McPherson had difficulty sorting out these competing claimants, especially since several had been reluctant to identify publicly with the Republican Party. When a group of Augusta Republicans headed by future governor Rufus Bullock asked McPherson to grant a contract to the Augusta *Daily Press*, John Bryant of the *Loyal Georgian* complained that until very recently the *Press* had been a "contemptible Rebel sheet." In turn, E. H. Pughe, publisher of the *Press*, advised McPherson that not one Augusta merchant advertised in Bryant's paper, which he claimed circulated only among the freedmen. "White people," Pughe asserted, "should have a chance to see the laws."[45]

McPherson awarded contracts to John Hayes's *Savannah Republican* and to Bryant's *Loyal Georgian*, but that did not end the bickering. Former Georgia governor Joseph Brown, a recent Republican convert, urged McPherson to switch support from Bryant to Samuel Bard's Atlanta *New Era*, insisting that the *Loyal Georgian* "had nothing of the confidence of the people that the *Era* has." Other state Republicans attacked the editor of the *Savannah Republican*, claiming—correctly, as it turned out—that Hayes was turning against the Republican Party. McPherson agreed to transfer patronage from Hayes's paper to the *New Era*, eliciting a howl from William Scruggs of the Atlanta *Daily Opinion*, who complained that he had been a loyal congressional supporter for some time, whereas the *New Era* was "a very recent convert to the cause." In April 1868, Scruggs lost control of his paper, and its new proprietors endorsed the state Democratic ticket. By year's end, only two Republican papers remained alive in Georgia, the conservative *New Era* and Swayze's radical *American Union*, both recipients of federal patronage.[46]

In 1868, the only radical editors among Alabama's handful of Republican papers were Albert Griffin of the Mobile *Nationalist* and John Hardy of Montgomery's *Alabama State Sentinel*. Both men favored political disabilities for ex-Confederates, took a strong stand for black rights, and urged white yeomn to join the party. Hardy, however, criticized Northern radicals like Charles Sumner and Thaddeus Stevens and also shot barbs at his colleague Griffin. He joined centrist editors William Figures of the *Huntsville Advocate*, Christopher C. Sheats of the Decatur *Alabama Republican*, and J. W. Phillips of Opelika's *East Alabama Monitor* in urging Republican support by Alabama Unionists. These editors emphasized that the Republican Party would help restore the state's economy, develop its resources, and draw in railroads and factories. At the time McPherson was dispensing U.S. printing contracts, the *Nationalist* and *Advocate* were Alabama's only Republican papers and hence received the awards.[47]

In Texas, the three leading Republican papers in 1868, Galveston's *Flake's Bulletin*, the *San Antonio Express*, and the *Austin Republican*, were all scalawag edited. The only radical was James Newcomb of the *San Antonio Express*, who favored disfranchising ex-Confederates and hoped to build the party on a coalition of freedmen and Unionist whites from the yeoman and working classes. While A. B. Longley of the *Austin Republican* supported the Republican stand on equal civil and political rights, he shared Flake's concern that the party was becoming overly identified with blacks' interests. He was also suspicious of appeals to small farmers and poor whites, believing that they were "too much governed by the vote yourself a farm sentiment." He sought support from so-called "moderate Southerners" who, "humbugged by the old aristocracy," had gone along with secession. While Longley endorsed the Republican commitment to universal education and uniform taxation, he also advocated developing the state's economy by building railroads and attracting immigrants and capital. Of these three papers, Flake's was the least committed to the Republicans, and McPherson awarded printing contracts to the other two.[48]

In Mississippi, the only two Republican papers in existence early in 1868, the *Meridian Chronicle* and the *Vicksburg Republican*, received the federal printing. Both could be considered radical. Later in the year, carpetbagger Edward Stafford opened the Jackson *Pilot*, and his editors walked a careful line between radical and centrist positions. The paper endorsed black rights but also courted white support for the party, particularly among ex-Whigs, and it promoted a variety of schemes for diversifying the state's economy.[49] In South Carolina, the three Republican papers existing in Charleston in 1868—the *Advocate, Free Press,* and *Missionary Record*—all defended African Americans' rights. The first two papers, however, disappeared before the year's end, and the *Missionary Record* pursued an increasingly conservative course. This left the Charleston *South Carolina Republican*, which appeared in October 1868, as the state's only reliable Republican paper. Under John Morris, it adopted a radical philosophy. U.S. printing went first to the *Advocate* and then to the *South Carolina Republican*.[50] In Arkansas and Tennessee, almost all Republican editors took radical positions in favor of disfranchising ex-Confederates and of civil and political rights for African Americans, and they promoted a biracial coalition of farmers and workers to keep their governments out of aristocratic hands.

Despite some significant losses, including Bryant's *Loyal Georgian*, Tourgee's *Union Register,* the *New Orleans Tribune,* and the *St. Landry Progress,* by late 1868 radical editors dominated the fledgling Republican press in most of the South. They had the upper hand in Arkansas, Tennessee, Virginia, both Carolinas, and Mississippi. Editorial influence in Georgia and Texas appeared split between the two camps. Only in Louisiana, Alabama, and Florida did moderates control the Republican press. Beginning in 1869, however, this balance would rapidly shift away from the radicals and toward the moderates all across the South.

As that year began, Republicans controlled all the ex-Confederate state governments except for Mississippi, Texas, and Virginia, which had not yet completed the reorganization stipulated by the Reconstruction Acts. Republicans anticipated dominating those reorganized governments as well. The party had elected Ulysses S. Grant as president, and Republicans North and South now hoped to resolve the sectional issues that had divided the nation for so long. Southern Republicans particularly yearned for resolution, for as long as partisan debate focused on these issues, their party would continue to founder. Edward M. Cheney, editor of the Jacksonville *Florida Union,* claimed that Grant's election represented a victory for centrists like himself who stood between radical Republicans calling for disfranchisement and radical Democrats desiring a white man's government. Now, he said, Republicans could hope for unity among all classes of people.[51]

Numerous other Republican editors asserted that the election had settled Reconstruction, and now the party should be generous in victory, attempt to win over its former opponents, and emphasize economic development. Alabama centrist editors, already in control of the state's Republican press, found evidence in the state balloting that old Union men were crossing over to their party. The editor of Opelika's *East Alabama Monitor* hoped Republicans would encourage more white support by adopting a "generous and kind" policy toward their political opponents, claiming that these people would help "build our railroads, improve our rivers, and cultivate our lands." Now that the election was over, the editor of the *Selma Press* insisted, it was time to push education programs and develop the state's industrial potential. Even radical editor Albert Griffin now agreed that with Reconstruction concluded, issues like specie resumption, banks, and tariffs would come to the fore, leading former Whigs to join the Republicans. Griffin's increasingly conservative course soon triggered his ouster by the blacks who controlled his paper, and it closed soon afterward.[52]

In North Carolina, several Republican editors expressed similar convictions that Grant's election had inaugurated a new era for the South. George W. Nason of the *New Bern Daily Republican* stated that with the election over, the party's leaders had to concentrate on attracting capital and immigration to the state, a point echoed by J. C. Mann of the *Wilmington Post.* The editors of the radical

Rutherford Star now called upon the legislature to appropriate funds for public schools and to aid "every railroad asking for it."[53] In Georgia, William Scruggs of the Atlanta *New Era* declared that with the great issues of Union and freedom settled, the state's "solid men," including Old Line Whigs and "even wiser Democrats," should join the Republicans in support of railroads, schools, and factories. In Virginia, James Sener of the *Fredericksburg Ledger* championed issues like schools, railroads, and river-navigation improvements. The Richmond *State Journal* also took on a more moderate tone. Charles Whittlesey, editor since its 1862 appearance in Alexandria, left the paper, and Robert W. Hughes, a native Virginian and centrist Republican, began writing for it. Edward Daniels, Whittlesey's successor, announced a "new career" for the paper, as it would be promoting public schools, home industry, and free banking. The paper also appealed to poorer whites by stressing debt relief and equitable taxes as well as public schools. In Texas, editors James Newcomb and James G. Tracy now debated which issues the party should emphasize; Newcomb wanted to promote public schools, while Tracy favored railroads and internal improvements.[54]

The conviction that new, less controversial questions must come to the fore of the South's political agenda helps explain why the influence of radical Republican newspapers in most Southern states began to decline precipitously after 1868. After that year's elections, several radical editors admitted the failure of their efforts to convert white yeoman farmers and workers to the Republican cause. John Hardy of the *Alabama State Sentinel* estimated that of his state's twenty thousand Union men, only seven thousand had voted for the constitution. He complained that the others, while sympathizing with the Republicans, had been unable "to exhibit the independence and manhood of the Negroes" and had not voted. Those whites, Hardy concluded, were "as completely under the rebel lash" as they had been in 1861. Jason Clarke Swayze of the *American Union* was equally frustrated with the lack of white support for Georgia's Republicans. When, he asked, "will the voters of the South cast their votes for their own interest, instead of the interest of the man whom they revere because of his wealth, and whose first interest is to keep the poor man poor, that he may remain rich?" Radical editor Joel Griffin of the *Southwest Georgian* echoed these complaints, noting that despite the benefits Republicans offered the state's poor whites, they remained the aristocrats' "subservient tools" and voted Democratic. In Arkansas, where Republicans barely carried the constitution, John Price contended that conservative intimidation had reduced the Republicans' white support: "many quiet persons wanted to vote but were afraid." He hoped that this class, "though timid and hesitating now," would eventually join the party.[55]

Within a year after the election, the Richmond *New Nation,* Raleigh *North Carolina Standard, Meridian Chronicle,* Mobile *Nationalist,* Montgomery *Alabama State Sentinel, Petersburg Times, Winchester Journal,* and many of Tennessee's radical papers had disappeared. In ensuing years, those Republican editors who still employed class-conscious rhetoric in appealing to white farmers and workers continued to express frustration at the atmosphere of intolerance and prejudice that discouraged these groups from crossing over to the Republicans. In 1872, Lewis Cass Carpenter of the *Columbia Daily Union* observed that it would take years for the South's masses to free themselves from the "tyranny of their political, religious, [and] social leaders" and to think for themselves. During a heated municipal election in 1874, the *Vicksburg Times* editor bemoaned the ease with which Democrats influenced or coerced whites into voting for their candidates. Were white voters, he queried, "so lost to every sense of independent, upright manhood, as to bow [their] necks to the yoke" and allow political demagogues to use them "as serfs and bondsmen to do their bidding?"

During Florida's 1876 campaign, even the centrist *Florida Union* published a number of articles entitled "Democracy versus the Poor Man," but the series had hardly ended before the paper's editors were complaining that the state's "honest yeomanry" still admired the aristocratic leaders of the Bourbon Democrats.[56] The course of Jason Clarke Swayze of the Macon *American Union* provides a vivid illustration of an editor who wavered between radical and centrist approaches. When Georgia's Reconstruction began, Swayze was an outspoken radical, calling for disfranchisement and repeatedly publishing editorials calling on white workers and yeoman farmers to overcome their racial prejudices and join African Americans in the Republican Party. By the end of 1869, however, Swayze was expressing disappointment with the Republicans' white turnout, had abandoned class-oriented appeals, and was avidly courting the votes of ex-Whig planters and businessmen, emphasizing that the Republican economic program was exactly what Whigs had once championed. Then, as state elections neared in December 1870, he again resorted to class issues, seeking to unite poor voters of both races against the aristocratic opposition. Once again these appeals went for naught; Georgian voters delivered a crushing defeat for the Republicans, who lost control of both houses of the state legislature. Now the frustrated Swayze returned to his moderate appeals to upper-class whites, even seeking the support of previously scorned Southern Democrats. When his pleas for political and racial harmony were answered by a race riot that struck Macon in 1872, the frustrated editor gave up his paper and left the state.[57]

The Republicans' failure to win white working-class votes undoubtedly encouraged their editors to seek the South's wealthier, more educated, and more influential whites. If this group exercised so much sway over poorer, less educated whites, then perhaps Republicans had been courting the wrong group. If they could gather the South's so-called "natural leaders" into their party, they should gain the white yeomanry as well. To achieve this goal, however, Republicans would have to abandon not only their class appeals but also their proscriptive policies toward ex-Confederates. Then they might be able to attract support from Democrats, many of whom also saw the need to move beyond Civil War and Reconstruction issues and claimed they were ready to accept citizenship and suffrage for the freedmen.[58]

Republicans in six Southern states had inserted some sort of disfranchisement provisions into their state constitutions. Soon after Republicans gained control of state governments in Alabama and Louisiana, they removed these provisions; in Arkansas the provisions remained for several years.[59] In 1869, the other three states, Virginia, Tennessee, and Mississippi, all held elections in which the amnesty question played a key role. Voters in Virginia were to cast ballots on the proposed constitution that disfranchised a number of ex-Confederates and launched a new state government. Republicans supporting disfranchisement chose Henry H. Wells as their gubernatorial candidate; a group of centrists calling themselves "True Republicans" nominated Gilbert C. Walker on a platform supporting suffrage for blacks and amnesty for whites. Rather than running their own candidate, Virginia Democrats endorsed Walker. To their immense satisfaction, the newly elected President Grant ordered a separate vote on the disqualifying sections of the Virginia constitution. During the campaign, Walker drew support from only a few Republican editors, led by George K. Gilmer, formerly of the Harrisonburg *American Union*. James W. Hunnicutt, possibly angry because the Republicans had not run him for governor, abandoned his earlier radical views and appeared on the Walker ticket as a congressional candidate. He also edited a campaign paper, the Richmond *Independent Republican*, on Walker's behalf. The state's remaining handful of Republican papers supported Wells, among them the Richmond *Virginia State Journal, Petersburg Times,* and *Winchester Journal,* as did the previously conservative editor of the Williamsburg *Virginia Gazette*. In the ensuing election, which was delayed until July 1869, voters approved the constitution while rejecting its disqualifying clauses; handed Walker a convincing victory over Wells; and gave the antiradical coalition control of the state legislature. A few months later, two radical papers—the *Petersburg Times* and the *Winchester Journal*—closed, and the *Virginia State Journal* took on a more moderate tone.[60]

By 1869, some Tennessee Republican editors were also ready to abandon disfranchisement. Lewis Tillman, proprietor of the Shelbyville *Republican,* had always opposed proscription, and he was joined by the editors of the *Nashville Republican,* its German-language counterpart the *Staats Zeitung,* and the *McMinnville Enterprise.* Other divisions beset the party as well, caused by disagreements over railroad policy and Governor Brownlow's use of martial law and the state militia to deal with the Ku Klux Klan and by growing friction between scalawags and carpetbaggers competing for patronage. In the summer of 1869, a state election for governor and state legislators brought these intraparty divisions to a head. DeWitt Senter, who had become governor after Brownlow's appointment to the U.S. Senate, hoped to be elected to a term of his own but was opposed by another Republican, William B. Stokes. After Senter announced his opposition to all disfranchising requirements, Tennessee's Democrats decided to support his candidacy.[61]

The ensuing contest between Senter and Stokes divided the Republican journalistic fraternity. Fearing that party division would allow conservatives to seize control of the state, the *Memphis Post* refrained from supporting either candidate. Other Republican editors, however, began to take sides; the *Greeneville New Era,* Jonesborough *Union Flag,* Huntington *West Tennessean, Chattanooga Republican,* and *Athens Republican* endorsed Stokes, while the Philadelphia *Union Pilot,* Clarksville *Weekly Patriot,* and *Lebanon Record* came out for Senter.[62] The new editor of the *Knoxville Whig,* who had recently purchased that paper from former Governor Brownlow, threw his paper's support behind Senter. The state's other leading Republican paper, the Nashville *Press and Times,* initially supported Stokes, but during the summer Senter backers bought control of the paper and forced the retirement of its editor, S. C. Mercer. The Stokes camp launched a new publication in Nashville, the *Daily Republican State Journal,* but it soon failed. Although John Ruhm's Nashville *Staats Zeitung* switched its support from Senter to Stokes, this did not compensate for Stokes's loss of the *Press and Times.* In the ensuing election, Senter won the governorship and the Democrats secured control of the legislature.[63]

The Tennessee Republicans' defeat in 1869 forced a number of the party's radical journals to close. The campaign had also cost them the support of the state's only African American paper, the *Maryville Republican.* Publisher and part owner William B. Scott had initially backed Stokes, but the other proprietors discharged the paper's white editor, M. L. McConnell, put Scott's son in his place, and raised the banner for Senter in place of Stokes. The new editor advocated reconciliation with former Confederates and denounced the Stokes forces with such vigor that a leading conservative paper, the Nashville *Republican Banner*, urged its readers to subscribe to Scott's paper and give it to their black employees. By 1876, the *Maryville Republican* was openly backing the Democratic Party.[64]

In the summer of 1868, Mississippi Republicans had suffered a bitter defeat when voters rejected the new state constitution. Democrats had used force and intimidation to reduce the black vote, and almost no whites had opted for the Republicans, possibly because of the constitution's disfranchisement provisions. Republican editors J. R. Smith of the *Meridian Chronicle*, Frederick Speed of the *Vicksburg Republican*, and Jefferson Wofford of the *Corinth News*, all of whom had made spirited overtures to white yeomen and workers, had opposed disfranchisement and contended that the issue had cost them the election. Although Edward Stafford of the Jackson *Pilot* appealed to President Grant to impose the rejected constitution on Mississippi, Wofford and Archie C. Fisk, who took over editorship of the *Vicksburg Republican* in the fall of 1868, urged Grant to order a new election on the constitution that would allow a separate vote on its disfranchisement provisions. Grant complied with this request, duplicating the arrangements he had made in Virginia.[65]

In the ensuing campaign, Mississippi Republicans split along lines similar to the party's schisms in Virginia and Tennessee. Republicans opposed to disfranchisement, led by editors Wofford and Speed, organized the National Union Party and nominated Grant's brother-in-law, Lewis Dent, for governor; the state Democratic Party also endorsed Dent. Not to be outdone, centrists in the regular Republican Party got their organization to reject proscription as well. They named an ex-Whig, James Lusk Alcorn, as their gubernatorial candidate. Stafford now brought the influence of his Jackson *Pilot* to bear for Alcorn and wrote editorial after editorial appealing for ex-Whigs' support. The Alcorn forces gained another ally when African American minister and politician James Lynch, who believed that proscriptive policies had alienated Mississippi's whites, began publishing the Jackson *Colored Citizen* on behalf of moderate Republicanism. That summer President Grant, after reviewing the results of conservative Republican movements in Virginia and Tennessee, concluded that both had turned their states over to foes of Reconstruction. Therefore he used his influence against the Dent movement and in favor of Alcorn in Mississippi. When the election was held, Alcorn won a convincing triumph, heralding the victory of centrist Republicanism in the state. The radical *Meridian Chronicle* soon stopped publishing, and Mississippi's other major party papers in Vicksburg and Jackson espoused centrist views.[66]

Reconstruction also ran into delays in Texas, which held an election for state officials and a new constitution at about the same time as Mississippi and Virginia. In the Lone Star State, bitter divisions within Republican ranks had tied the constitutional convention in knots. The largest Republican block consisted of centrists from central Texas led by A. J. Hamilton and the current provisional governor, E. M. Pease. Opposing them were radicals from east and west who resented their domination of the state. Leading the radicals were A. J. Hamilton's brother Morgan Hamilton, constitutional convention president Edmund Davis, and James P. Newcomb of the *San Antonio Express*. These men favored the doctrine of *ab initio*, which called for the nullification of all post-secession state laws and resolutions; advocated dividing the state into three new states corresponding to east, central, and west Texas; expressed stronger support for black rights than did the moderates; and favored some measure of disfranchisement.[67]

The editors of the *San Antonio Express* and *Austin Republican* played leading roles in the Republican factional rivalry, and both criticized Ferdinand Flake, who was reluctant to endorse either faction and even opposed organizing the Republican Party in 1867. Eventually, to Newcomb's disgust, Flake sided with the Pease forces and joined them in attacking the Union Leagues.[68] The *Republican*'s editor, A. B. Longley, tried to play down differences over *ab initio* and division of the state, defended the Union Leagues, and endorsed some limited disfranchisement, but the *San Antonio Express* constantly attacked him and the "Austin ring" that Newcomb contended was trying to dominate the party.[69] Ultimately centrists won most of the convention battles. Delegates rejected the *ab initio* doctrine, stalled the effort to partition the state, and defeated radical disfranchisement proposals.[70]

After the convention adjourned, the Republican factions solidified into two parties, each with its own executive committee and state organization. Some Republicans, concerned because A. J. Hamilton was making overtures to the Democrats, worked to heal the party's breach. Flake and James G. Tracy of the recently founded *Houston Union* supported those efforts but leaned toward Hamilton. Ultimately the conciliation efforts failed, and the centrists nominated Hamilton for governor while the radicals ran Davis. The Democratic press commented favorably on Hamilton, and the party decided not to run a candidate in the gubernatorial election. Newcomb compared Hamilton's candidacy with Gilbert C. Walker's in Virginia, warning that Democrats would swallow the Texan Republican if he were elected. Hamilton got the support of the *Austin Republican* and Flake's paper, while the rest of the state's Republican press backed Davis, including San Antonio's *Express* and *Freie Presse*, the *Houston Union*, and the *Tyler Index*. President Grant, agreeing with Newcomb about the parallels between the Hamilton and Walker candidacies, eventually used federal patronage to support Davis's Republicans. In the ensuing election, held in December, Davis won a very narrow victory.[71]

The results of these 1869 state elections were mixed. Through their coalition tactics, Democrats had won control of Virginia and Tennessee, but centrist Republicans had headed them off in Mississippi, while more radical pro-Davis Republicans barely clung to power in Texas. Elsewhere members of both parties closely watched events in these states, particularly in Virginia and Tennessee. In South Carolina, some Democrats and at least one centrist Republican editor, T. C. Andrews of the *Orangeburg News,* toyed with the idea of organizing a coalition along the lines of Walker's in Virginia. John Morris of the *Charleston Republican* was certain that such a movement would fail. He noted that South Carolina's Republicans had never supported disfranchisement, thereby nullifying the issue that had figured in third-party movements elsewhere. Additionally Walker, since his Virginia election, had backtracked on pledges to protect black rights. Morris insisted that South Carolina's freedmen, who comprised a majority of voters in the state, would never abandon the Republicans. In 1870, the state's Democrats ran a disaffected Republican for governor on a Union Reform Party ticket, but Republican governor Scott easily defeated him. In Alabama, the editor of the *Selma Press* also predicted that any effort by Democrats to try the "Walker-Senter" style in that state would fail, since Republicans were already removing disabilities imposed on ex-Confederates. John Stokes of the *Alabama State Journal* agreed that third-party movements like Virginia's would not work and that voters would have to choose between the Republicans and Democrats. In North Carolina, Republican journalists made the same comments.[72]

In Georgia, Samuel Bard was overjoyed at Virginia's results and also applauded Dent's candidacy in Mississippi: "Go it Dent, Go it Moderation." Bard hoped that Tennessee would follow Virginia's example, and he anticipated employing it in Georgia. By the summer of 1869, Georgia was in turmoil. The previous September Democrats in the state legislature, along with a handful of white Republicans, had expelled black members of both houses. In response Governor Bullock had asked Congress to restore Georgia to military rule and reseat the ousted blacks. His proposal split the Georgia Republican Party as well as the editors of Georgia's only two Republican papers. Bard and his *New Era*, along with John Emory Bryant, formerly of the *Loyal Georgian,* backed the efforts of former governor Joseph Brown, who urged Republicans unhappy with Bullock to unite with moderate Democrats to throw the governor out.[73] Jason Clarke Swayze used his *American Union* to defend the governor and attack Bard's wing of the party. Bryant, he charged, had "turned traitor to his party and gone over to the Rebels . . . hoping to be pampered by the 'respectability,'"

Differences in Approach 141

and he contemptuously dismissed Bard as "an unprincipled hermaphrodite bastard." Not to be outdone, Bard declared that "J. Skunk Swayze" was "a man without character, without talents and so entirely ignorant of the proprieties of life as to make his presence disgusting and offensive to all gentlemen where he is best known."[74]

Although Bullock eventually got his way, the Republican split continued. In January 1870, Bullock's supporters bought control of the *New Era*, but Bard, with Bryant's aid, then established the *True Georgian* in order to continue his attacks on the governor. Bryant also opened a new paper, the Augusta *Georgia Republican*, and turned its editorial barrels on Bullock. Both editors continued to seek an alliance with Democrats. They refused to defend the state administration against Democratic corruption charges, and Bryant accepted Democratic support in a losing bid to become speaker of the Georgia House of Representatives. The Democrats, however, did not need Bard's and Bryant's help to dislodge Bullock. In state elections held in December 1870, they won an overwhelming majority in the state legislature, and late the following year the governor fled Georgia to avoid impeachment.[75]

In Arkansas, a number of Republicans unhappy with Governor Powell Clayton's administration organized a "Liberal Republican" party to attract Old Line Whigs and Republicans who wanted to follow a middle course between "old fogy Democrats" on the one hand and "mad, reckless unbridled Radicalism on the other." Like the Walker movement in Virginia, they declared their support of the Grant administration, opposed any curtailment of freedmen's rights, and advocated amnesty for ex-Confederates. They launched their own newspaper, the *Liberal*, and also picked up newspaper support from an unexpected source, the *Arkansas Freedman*, edited by Tabbs Gross. A former slave who had purchased his freedom and had lived in Cincinnati before the war, Gross arrived in Arkansas in 1867 and in July opened his paper, pledging to work for both universal suffrage and universal amnesty. In October 1869, Gross served as a vice president of the Liberal Republican state convention at Little Rock, where delegates laid plans to win control of the legislature in the upcoming state election of 1870.[76]

John Price of the *Little Rock Republican* was quick to denounce the Liberals. He drew comparisons between them and the Senter movement in Tennessee, where "weakened Republicans" hoped to advance their party's cause by restoring the ballot to disfranchised whites. The result in that state, claimed Price, was "revolution": the overthrow of Republican rule and exercise of mob violence against blacks. He warned his readers to avoid the path of Tennessee and Virginia voters and promised to "open the war to the knife and the knife to the hilt" against the Arkansas Liberals. In the ensuing elections in 1870, Clayton forces kept control of the legislature, although intraparty strife continued.[77]

By the end of 1870, Republicans had lost Tennessee and Georgia and had failed to win control of Virginia. In the remaining eight ex-Confederate states still controlled by the party, radicals everywhere except in Arkansas had lost the disfranchisement battle to centrists. Radical editors were well represented in that state, as in South Carolina and Texas, but elsewhere centrists controlled the party press. Few editors any longer showed interest in promoting a coalition of white and black workers. Instead they courted the support of "respectable" whites. Editors still disagreed, but now they argued over how to respond to the Ku Klux Klan, whether to annul the ban in the Fourteenth Amendment against former Confederate leaders holding office, how to respond to blacks' demands for access to office and for public accommodation laws, and how hard to push economic issues like assistance to railroads.

CHAPTER EIGHT

Continuing Factionalism

Although centrists quickly came to dominate the Southern Republican press, stifling discussions of confiscation, disfranchisement, and potential black and white workers' alliances, editors continued to disagree over policy matters. Michael Perman has suggested that as radicals faded out of the picture, a new faction, which he calls the regulars, emerged to replace them. The regulars saw the need for white support, but they were more concerned than the centrists about protecting their party's black voter base. Hence centrists and regulars differed over how to respond to the Ku Klux Klan and how to deal with African American demands for additional civil rights laws and for a greater share of political patronage. Most of the regulars were carpetbaggers who controlled federal patronage posts in the South and who wanted to use those positions to reward the party faithful rather than to court new sources of support. The centrists, on the other hand, were more often than not scalawags who hoped to use patronage to draw other Southern whites into the party.[1]

After 1872, centrists began defecting to the political opposition, leaving the regulars in control of the dwindling number of states still under Republican rule. Democrats continued to place these regimes on the defensive, charging them with reckless extravagance, corruption, raising taxes, and undermining state credit. Those attacks, and the failure of state railroad aid to advance Southern prosperity, forced the party to reevaluate its commitment to such subsidies. By 1874, Republican editors everywhere were calling for retrenchment and reform, and governors in the four states still under the party's control began working toward those ends. But by then it was too late. Within two years, Southern whites had overthrown the South's last Republican regimes.

One of the issues creating continued Republican dissension was the question of how best to respond to the emergence of the Ku Klux Klan. Between 1868 and 1871, Democrats resorted to a wave of terror, primarily Klan-organized, to sweep the Republicans from the South. The Klan and other white supremacist groups assassinated black and white Republican leaders and drove freedmen from the polls. This violent campaign waged by determined whites graphically underscored the Republican Party's failure to win legitimacy in the states of the former Confederacy. Although Whigs and Democrats had waged heated contests in the prewar South, neither had relied on force, intimidation, or murder to carry elections. Despite the hopes, pleas, and exhortations of Republican newspaper editors, many Southern whites still regarded the party as an illegitimate institution undeserving of recognition and acceptance, let alone of support. These whites regarded the new state constitutions, and the Republican governments elected under them, in the same light; they would not accord legitimacy to either.

Republican editors did unite in condemning the Klan. They gave full and detailed coverage of its activity and sought to implicate rival Democratic editors in its actions by charging that the hyperbolic fulminations against the Republicans in the Democratic press encouraged the violence. At first Democratic papers tended to deny the Klan's very existence. When evidence of its activity became too obvious to deny, Democrats claimed that Klansmen were merely defending whites from black terrorists.[2] They also accused Republican editors of exaggerating Klan activity for partisan purposes and warned that such unsubstantiated charges of violence kept capital and labor from entering the South, harming the region's economy. Republican journalists insisted that Klan violence was pervasive and could not be ignored. It was this violence, they pointed out, and not reports about it that kept capitalists from investing in the South and workers from migrating there. A. B. Chapin of the *Greensboro Register* argued the Democrats could never lure immigrants as long as they brandished "the whip, the revolver, the cane, and the brand!"[3]

Aware of the challenge that the Klan posed to the legitimacy both of their party and of the state governments their party controlled, Republican editors developed rhetorical counterattacks. Some characterized Klan activity as treasonous. In Alabama, after angry whites pistol-whipped Demopolis *Southern Republican* editor Pierce Burton, he claimed that "young Confederates believe they are fighting the Civil War again in killing Republicans." Pinckney Rollins of the *Asheville Pioneer* called Klansmen "disloyal to the bone."[4] A number of Republican editors asserted that the fundamental issue in the contemporary South was not the civil and political equality of blacks but the rule of law. Lucien Eaton of the *Memphis Post* claimed that the antagonism toward Tennessee's Republican administration was not simply political; "it involves the very existence of a republican form of government." Palemon John, editor of the Elizabeth City *North Carolinian*, insisted that governments must have the power of self-preservation. In Raleigh, the editor of the *Carolina Era* warned that the "red arm of lawlessness" was threatening to defeat the will of the people. Pierce Burton labeled Klan violence in Alabama a threat to free government, a point echoed by his colleague at the helm of the *Alabama State Journal,* who claimed that the Klan challenged the basic purpose of government, which was to protect the rights and security of citizens.[5]

Republican journalists recognized that if the new state regimes could not maintain law and order and protect their citizens, they were surely doomed, for even their own supporters would desert them. "We must have protection," said the editor of the *Rutherford Star,* "or no Republican can remain." Republican editors could not agree, however, on how to provide that protection. Occasionally a radical editor called on Republicans to form their own organization "to Ku Klux the KKK." In 1869, A. B. Chapin's *Greensboro Register* published a letter signed "Retribution," which urged retaliation against the Klan: "Assassination must be met by lynching, and midnight murder by midnight execution. A dozen hangings will save a hundred murders." The editor of the *Columbia Union* advised Republicans to organize vigilance committees to "shoot down on sight the first disguised man who is seen prowling about." In Georgia, Jason Clarke Swayze called on blacks to defend themselves against the Klan, urging them to "shoot down every rebel who opposes you." Most Republican editors, however, avoided such exhortations or condemned them. Samuel Bard declared that he had never seen anything "so evil in its nature" as Swayze's remarks and called the Macon editor "this child of the devil."[6]

In several Upper South states, where Republican governors could draw on the numerous native whites who had joined their party, deploying the state militia against the Klan remained a possibility. But use of military force aroused internal party dissension. Regular Republican editors supported strong measures to defend their party's voters, while centrist editors feared such tactics would drive away potential white voters. When news of Klan depredations first spread in Tennessee early in 1868, a furious Governor Brownlow called on Unionists to break up Klan organizations, "and if need requires this in dispersing them, exterminate them." In July, he asked the legislature to pass a new militia act enabling him to deal with the Klan, and the proposal led to considerable debate. The Shelbyville *Republican*'s centrist editor opposed the use of any military force in the state, whether it be state militia or U.S. regulars, but other papers came to the governor's support, insisting that law and order must be maintained.[7]

Tennessee's leading Republican paper, S. C. Mercer's Nashville *Press and Times,* deserted Brownlow on the militia issue. Early in 1868, Mercer had condemned the Klan, but by the summer he was opposing Brownlow's efforts to use state forces to cope with the violence. Once he had supported the formation of black militia units, but in August he warned that armed freedmen might endanger the community. He even claimed that Brownlow would recruit blacks from Kentucky to join the militia, a charge that Democratic editors eagerly reprinted. Mercer and John Ruhm, editor of Nashville's German-language Republican paper and also of the *Nashville Republican*, had already taken opposing sides in the city's Republican factionalism, and now the two men hammered at each other over the advisability of calling out the militia. Mercer castigated Ruhm as an "apostate," a "renegade," a "lying scoundrel," a "worthless carcass," and a "dirty dog." Ruhm, for his part, calmly replied that "it may not be pleasant to be assailed by a fisherwoman, but it is not very dangerous." Ultimately Brownlow obtained his legislation, although a number of Republicans voted against it. Early in 1869, Brownlow called out the militia, but he soon disbanded it, much to the relief of the editor of the *Athens Republican*, who complained that the force had been a great expense and had not hauled any criminals to justice.[8]

When Klan violence appeared in Arkansas in 1868, John Price of the *Little Rock Republican* urged the state government to arm the militia and deploy it against the terrorists. If the rebels wanted war, he contended, "let us be prepared to give it to them at once, and all along the line." When centrist Republicans urged a more cautious approach, Price denounced "the pernicious delusion that a policy of conciliation should be adopted towards the malignant and unreconstructed adherents of the 'lost cause.'" That fall, however, his paper generated a serious uproar in the Arkansas Republican Party when it published editorials criticizing Governor Powell Clayton for suspending the writ of habeas corpus and using the state militia to arrest Klansmen. Price was out of town at this time, and an associate editor, T. C. Peek, wrote these editorials. Several Arkansas congressmen complained that the Little Rock paper was an embarrassment to them in Washington, for it seemingly validated Democratic attacks on the Powell administration. Republicans attending a Little Rock meeting declared that the paper could no longer be regarded as an exponent of Republican principles. A number of state legislators signed a resolution reading Price and his paper out of the party, and in January 1869 the house deposed him as speaker. Price quickly moved to head off these challenges. Peek accepted responsibility for the recent editorial positions of the *Republican* and resigned. Price, noting that the state legislature had passed resolutions endorsing Clayton's actions and realizing that these actions had effectively destroyed the Klan in Arkansas, now claimed that Clayton's martial-law declaration had "been productive of much good." He avowed firm support for the state administration and pled for party harmony.[9]

In North Carolina, several Republican papers condemned the Ku Klux Klan and supported Governor William Holden's strongly worded warnings to the organization. The governor, however, did not take any firm steps against the Klan until the summer of 1870, when he suspended the writ in two counties and sent the militia to arrest and try Klansmen before a military commission. In the ensuing uproar, a federal court ordered the men released, and Democrats had a field day charging the governor with civil-liberties violations. Holden's son Joseph, now editor of the *North Carolina Standard*, defended his father's actions, but the *Rutherford Star*'s editors, who had become bitter opponents of Holden, did not, although they condemned Klan violence. After Republicans lost control of the state legislature that fall, Palemon John of the Elizabeth City *North Carolinian* speculated that the outcome might have been different had Holden used military force earlier.[10]

In Alabama, centrist governor William H. Smith refused to activate the militia to deal with the Klan, fearing that this would alienate the native whites he hoped would eventually join his party. A number of Republicans condemned Smith's caution, but the editor of the *Selma Press* defended him, claiming "an ill-disciplined militia is an instrument which may do more harm than good." In April 1870, John Stokes, editor of the party's leading paper, the *Alabama State Journal*, criticized Smith for his forbearance, but after watching Democrats win in North Carolina following Holden's use of the militia there, he changed his mind. Declaring martial law in Alabama, he warned, would "do harm to the innocent and ruin the Republican party and the state." If Klan violence persisted, Stokes hoped that U.S. troops, not the state militia, would be employed. Demopolis *Southern Republican* editor Pierce Burton published a number of articles detailing Klan outrages and criticized Smith for not employing the state militia against it. In the summer of 1870, with a new state election coming up, Burton hoped the Republicans would nominate someone who would "enforce the laws." The party convention, however, renominated Smith and then chose Burton as his running mate, leading the editor grudgingly to endorse Smith's "mild and conciliatory policy" toward the Klan and to agree with him that the state should rely on federal troops instead of militia to cope with violence. In the disputed election that followed, Democrats carried Alabama. Crucial to their success was the decline in the Republican vote in four counties where the Klan had been active.[11]

In Mississippi, another centrist governor, James Lusk Alcorn, was also reluctant to take strong measures against the Klan. In Georgia, the Republican regime refused even to organize a militia. Increasingly aware that state governments seemed unwilling or unable to deal with the waves of violence threatening to engulf them, Republicans turned to the federal government for relief. In 1870 and 1871, Congress enacted a series of Enforcement Acts to deal with the Klan. The most stringent, the Ku Klux Klan Act of April 1871, allowed federal officials to bring Klansmen to trial for violating the civil and political rights of others and authorized the president to suspend the writ and, if necessary, use federal troops to restore order. Such centralization of power in Washington elicited immediate condemnation from Democrats, who warned that the process would destroy local self-government. Some congressional Republicans even drew back from this expansion of federal power over the states.[12]

In the South, Republican editors divided over the advisability of using federal troops to deal with the Klan. A few took a radical position in affirming national supremacy over the states. Some months before the passage of the first Enforcement Act, John Morris of the *Charleston Republican* declared that the federal government must protect the civil and political rights of all its citizens; if this was centralization, he said, it "should have been accomplished long ago." A month before Congress passed the first Enforcement Act, the *Alabama State Journal*'s editor declared it was time for the federal government to "stop tinkering" with state rights: "States exist now only as geographical divisions of territory, for the more convenient administration of national law." Everything of a strictly political character, he claimed, "whether of right, duty, or privilege, must be the subject of national legislation." He called on Congress to provide a "broad and catholic definition" of the rights of citizens and to give the federal government ample power to protect those rights throughout the nation. Both Morris and the *State Journal*'s editor endorsed the Enforcement Acts. In North Carolina, Palemon John declared that the doctrine of state rights was inconsistent with nationalism and liberty and pronounced Democratic warnings about centralization of power "a snare and a delusion." Lewis Cass Carpenter of the Columbia *Daily Union* also ridiculed Democratic fears of centralization, claiming that Republicans had actually decentralized power by wresting it from a small minority of slaveholders and enfranchising over a million citizens.[13]

In Alabama, Pierce Burton and the editors of the *Mobile Herald* and *Selma Press* also supported the enforcement measures, but the Opelika *Weekly Era and Whig* editor John Fowler denounced the Ku Klux Klan Act, claiming it would destroy liberty. In New Orleans, both Michael Hahn's *New Orleans Republican* and the black-owned *Louisianan* urged the federal government to employ the new laws. The editor of the *Louisiana State Register* in nearby Carrollton, however, called the Ku Klux Klan Act "a war measure adopted in time of peace" and warned that it gave the president almost dictatorial power. The editor of the Alexandria *Rapides Gazette*, which bore the motto "Let Us Have Peace," fretted that the federal troops' presence in the state could only inspire more violence.[14]

Early in 1871, the editor of the Jackson *Mississippi Pilot* saw no need for new Klan legislation. But an increase in racial violence, especially a riot in Meridian, soon persuaded him otherwise, and he backed the use of troops at the polls. The editor of the *Vicksburg Times* also supported the Ku Klux Klan Act, as did Virginia's leading Republican paper, the Richmond *State Journal*. The Atlanta *New Era*, which was the Bullock administration's mouthpiece, defended the Enforcement Acts passed in 1870, but after Republicans lost the Georgia elections that fall, the governor changed course. Frantically courting white support, Bullock opposed any further enforcement legislation, claiming that the state could handle any violence without federal intervention. The editor of the *New Era*, William Scruggs, repudiated the 1871 Ku Klux Klan Act. Bryant and his *Georgia Republican* supported it, as did Swayze of the Macon *American Union;* he even secured an appointment as a federal commissioner to help enforce the law. In South Carolina, after President Grant suspended the writ of habeas corpus in several counties and sent in troops to stop the Klan, James G. Thompson of the Columbia *Union-Herald* called for their removal, prompting the state legislature to condemn him as an "enemy to Republicanism."[15]

In December 1871, James B. Sener of the *Fredericksburg Ledger* suggested that granting amnesty to ex-Confederates barred from office by the Fourteenth Amendment would "do more to quiet the South than a dozen Ku Klux laws." By that time, congressional sentiment to remove the disability was growing, and in the South most Republican editors, not all of them centrists, supported the move, especially after Grant endorsed amnesty in 1872. Several African American newspapers recommended amnesty, including the New Orleans *Louisianan*, New Orleans *Republican Standard*, *Arkansas Freeman*, and *Mobile Herald*.[16] In North Carolina, the editors of the Wilmington *Post* and *North Carolina Standard* had called for amnesty as early as 1869, followed later by the Raleigh *Carolina Era*, *New Bern Times*, and Greensboro *New North State*. On the other hand, Pinckney Rollins of the *Asheville Pioneer* and J. B. Carpenter of the *Rutherford Star* favored keeping ex-Confederates from office; Carpenter even went to Washington in 1871 to lobby against an amnesty bill.[17]

The only remaining Republican papers of any significance in Georgia divided over amnesty, the centrist Atlanta *New Era* in favor and Swayze's more radical *American Union* opposed. Of Alabama's leading Republican papers, only the *Selma Press* hesitated to endorse removing political disabilities, asking that Klan violence stop first.[18] In Louisiana, besides the New Orleans *Louisianan*, the *New Orleans Republican*, New Orleans *National Republican*, and *Louisiana*

State Register all recommended amnesty. In Texas, the Corpus Christi *Nueces Valley* and the Austin *Journal,* the Davis administration's organ, both called for amnesty, as did South Carolina's *Columbia Daily Union*.[19] In Arkansas, papers favoring the elimination of disfranchisement in the state also supported removing the Fourteenth Amendment's political disabilities, while those favoring continued disfranchisement, most notably the *Little Rock Republican,* wanted to continue the amendment.[20]

By 1872, a number of Republicans in the Northern and border states who dubbed themselves Liberals were pushing a reform agenda that included an amnesty offer to the South. These men were disgusted with the rampant corruption in Washington and disappointed with Grant's failure to push their goals of civil service reform and tariff reduction. They favored less government, not more, and were becoming increasingly critical of Grant's reliance on military intervention in the South to sustain corruption-tainted governments. Increasingly they accepted the dominant Southern white view that ignorant blacks and unscrupulous carpetbaggers dominated these governments at the expense of propertied and educated white Southerners. Through civil service reform in Washington and amnesty in the South, they hoped to bring more respectable men into government and into the party as well. Their desire to put Reconstruction issues behind them meshed with the Democratic Party's proclamation of a "New Departure" that accepted the permanence of the Reconstruction amendments. When the Liberals decided to run their own candidate, Horace Greeley, against Grant in the 1872 presidential contest, the Democrats endorsed Greeley. The regular Republicans then rushed to pass an amnesty act eliminating the Fourteenth Amendment disability for most Southerners affected.[21]

Although amnesty thus ceased to be an issue, the Greeley candidacy nevertheless gained support from centrist Republicans in several Southern states. Regular Republicans, on the other hand, supported Grant's reelection. In Arkansas, scalawag Republicans resentful of carpetbag domination of the government had helped create the Liberal Republican movement there in 1869. Like the Northern Liberals, they hoped to curb the powers of the state government, reduce its expense, and eliminate corruption. They too wanted to attract the support of respectable native whites and urged an end to disfranchisement and to the Fourteenth Amendment's ban on officeholding. By 1870, the Arkansas Liberals were publishing the *Arkansas State Journal* in Little Rock, and although its motto advocated "charity to all and malice toward none," editor Joseph Brooks condemned supporters of carpetbag governor Powell Clayton as "copperhead thieves" and "buzzard-roost corruptionists." Not to be outdone, John Price of the *Little Rock Republican* accused Brooks of "gangrenous slander," claiming he had "traduced and defamed" every officer in the state in response to the "cravings of his own inordinate ambition."[22]

Although Price made several efforts to effect a reconciliation between his paper and the rival *Journal*, the Republican factions hardened; Brooks and his followers became known as the "Brindletails," while the Clayton regulars were dubbed "Minstrels" because Price had once appeared in a Little Rock minstrel show. In 1872, the Brindletails endorsed Greeley and ran Brooks for governor. The Minstrels, who stood by Grant, made a bid for white support by pitting native white Southerner Elisha Baxter against Brooks. Most of the state's Republican papers supported Grant and Baxter, while most Democrats backed Brooks. Baxter won a narrow victory, but once in office he disappointed his Republican backers by pushing for amnesty and soliciting Democratic support. Desperate to dislodge Baxter, Republicans attempted to place their former opponent Brooks in the governor's mansion, claiming that he had been cheated from victory in 1872. In the meantime Brooks's former Democratic supporters endorsed Baxter. The state appeared to be on the verge of civil war; ultimately the federal government sustained Baxter, bringing an end to Republican rule in Arkansas.[23]

The Liberal movement also helped shape Louisiana's internal party strife. In 1868, Republicans had elected as governor Henry Clay Warmoth, who adopted centrist policies to build the party. By 1870, Warmoth faced considerable Republican opposition led by James F. Casey, the New Orleans customs collector. The customs-house faction struck an alliance with Warmoth's lieutenant governor, Oscar Dunn, an African American who, like many other Louisiana blacks, was displeased with Warmoth for not backing an equal accommodations law. Upon Dunn's death late in 1871, Warmoth engineered the election of another African American, P. B. S. Pinchback, to take his place, but the intraparty division persisted. By 1872, it threatened to cost Republicans control of the state.[24]

The split divided the state's Republican press, including its African American newspapers. J. Henri Burch, an African American member of the lower house, owned the Baton Rouge *Grand Era* and through it attacked Warmoth, as did J. Willis Menard, editor of the New Orleans *Republican Standard*. Pinchback, who owned the New Orleans *Louisianan*, backed the governor. Pinchback's jousting with Menard led the editor of the Baton Rouge *State Journal* to observe that since both papers were controlled by blacks, they should not be bickering. The editor of the *Louisianan* retorted that the *Standard*, "which has borne as many names as a sing-sing convict," was not "inspired by colored men's talents nor by colored men's money." He boasted that the *Louisianan* had never published a single line written by a white, whereas the *Standard*'s editorials "always involved white men's utterances under a black man's name." The *Louisianan* made the same charge against the *Citizen's Guard*, which replaced the *Standard* in June 1871. This paper, also anti-Warmoth, survived only a few months.²⁵

Warmoth did not run again for governor in 1872. He and his followers backed the Liberal Republican presidential candidate, Horace Greeley, and in the state election joined Democrats to support a fusion ticket featuring John McEnery for governor. A coalition of Republicans led by the customs-house faction backed Grant for president and ran William Pitt Kellogg against McEnery. Some of the state's most prominent Republican newspapers, including Blackburn's *Homer Iliad*, Warmoth's *New Orleans Republican*, the Carrollton *Louisiana State Register*, the German-language *Deutsche Zeitung*, and Pinchback's *Louisianan*, leaned toward Greeley. Few, however, could swallow McEnery, who was an outspoken Democrat. The *New Orleans Republican* claimed that the McEnery ticket represented "the negro-hating, schoolhouse burning, fire-eating Bourbonists. . . . Good these last ditchers cannot learn, and bad they cannot forget." Grant easily carried the state. An ensuing dispute over the gubernatorial winner was eventually settled in Kellogg's favor.²⁶

By 1872, Texas Republicans were dividing along roughly the same lines as the Arkansas and Louisiana factions. Centrist Republicans led by Senator Morgan Hamilton accused the Davis administration of corruption and excessive expenditures and complained that the Texas laws creating a state police force and militia overly concentrated power in the governor's hands. *Houston Union* editor James G. Tracy urged Davis to repudiate the militia laws and reduce expenditures but did not break with the administration. In 1872, some dissident Republicans including Ferdinand Flake endorsed Horace Greeley, and even August Siemering, publisher of the two San Antonio Republican papers, was tempted to back the Liberal candidate. Most of the state's Republican papers eventually supported Grant, including Siemering's *San Antonio Express*. Greeley carried Texas that fall, however, and Republicans lost control of the legislature, presaging the party's final collapse a year later.²⁷

In 1872, editors of at least four Florida Republican newspapers endorsed Greeley: the Jacksonville *Florida Republican, Fernandina Observer, Lake City Herald,* and Pensacola *Express*. Resentful of carpetbagger influence in Tallahassee and concerned about excessive state spending and corruption, the Liberals urged their readers to vote for the state Democratic ticket. The party's two leading newspapers, the Jacksonville *Florida Union* and the *Tallahassee Sentinel*, backed Grant, and the regular Republicans ran a Florida native for governor, defusing the carpetbagger issue. In the ensuing election, regular Republicans carried

Florida for Grant and their state ticket but barely maintained control of the legislature. In Georgia, where the Republican press was almost nonexistent, Macon *American Union* editor Jason Clark Swayze, who had once been an outspoken radical, endorsed Greeley. In Alabama, Greeley gained the support of one of the state's leading Republican papers, William Figures's *Huntsville Advocate;* the more influential *Alabama State Journal* ultimately endorsed Grant. Elsewhere in the South, the Liberal candidate drew little Republican support, editorial or otherwise.[28]

Greeley's overwhelming defeat in 1872 was a disastrous blow to the centrists, for it left regulars in control of the party machinery and governments of most Southern states still in Republican hands: Arkansas, Louisiana, South Carolina, Florida, and Mississippi. Despite the centrists' decline, dissension continued to plague the Republicans. Some of the issues disrupting the party had been present since the onset of Reconstruction. A major internal conflict involved blacks' increasing resentment at the party's failure to push for more effective public accommodations laws or to elevate more of their race to political office. The public accommodations issue had first appeared in the South on the state level early in Reconstruction. In 1868, the Tennessee legislature approved a measure guaranteeing blacks equal access to common carriers. Similar bills in Alabama and North Carolina failed to pass; Georgia and Arkansas enacted measures allowing each race equal but separate accommodations. Beginning in 1869, South Carolina's legislature passed a series of laws requiring equal treatment in public accommodations and licensed businesses. Legislatures in Mississippi, Florida, and Louisiana also approved equal accommodations laws, but in each case centrist governors vetoed them. By 1873, however, these three states as well as Texas forbade common carriers to discriminate.[29]

Most Republican editors defended these state laws. The editor of the Jackson *Pilot* asserted that with the help of such measures, "ancient prejudices" standing in the way of equal rights would be removed one by one, "gently if they can, forcibly if they must."[30] There was considerable disagreement among Southern Republicans, however, about the wisdom of federal legislation guaranteeing African Americans equal access to public accommodations. Charles Sumner had introduced such a measure in the U.S. Senate in 1870; in 1872 he had tried to add it as an amendment to the amnesty measure passed that year. As late as 1874, it was still mired in congressional debate. In 1875, after removing its most controversial provision requiring school integration, Congress finally approved the measure.[31]

Reaction to Sumner's bill varied across the South. In Georgia, Jason Clarke Swayze of the Macon *American Union* ridiculed the measure, stating that while blacks were entitled to certain constitutional rights, "we have yet to learn that those rights include the unnatural one of social equality." The black-owned New Orleans *Louisianan* endorsed Sumner's original proposal, but the editor of the *Mobile Herald,* also owned by African Americans, advised against it, warning that whites would shut down schools rather than integrate them. In Alabama, the scalawag editor of the Talladega *Our Mountain Home* contended that white Republicans would desert the party if it endorsed mixed schools. After Congress removed the bill's integrated school provisions, several editors in states with large black populations supported it, viewing it as necessary to secure their party's voting base. The editor of the *Vicksburg Times* commented that "where all are common citizens, all must enjoy common rights." H. B. Whitfield of the *Columbus Press* in Mississippi endorsed the bill's "great principles," although warning that Democrats would use it to stir up white prejudice against blacks. The editor of South Carolina's *Walterboro News* declared the civil rights bill to be "perfectly just and proper"; in Florida, J. S. Adams of the Jacksonville *New South* ridiculed Democratic charges that the measure would force race mixing.[32]

In states with significant numbers of white Republicans, editors were more critical of the civil rights law, noting that white opinion overwhelmingly opposed it and warning that Democrats would exploit the issue. In Alabama, Arthur Bingham of the *State Journal* ridiculed Democratic charges that the measure would allow Congress to take over schools, churches, colleges, and railroads, but the new editor of the *Huntsville Advocate* predicted that the law would polarize races in the state and lead to violence and bloodshed across the South. In Tennessee, the editor of the *Knoxville Chronicle* opposed passage of the Civil Rights Act but also censured Democrats for using it to exploit white racial fears. North Carolina's Republican papers opposed the law as well. Virginia congressman James B. Sener, owner of the *Fredericksburg Ledger,* voted against the civil rights bill, but his fellow Georgia legislator Richard Whiteley, who edited the *Bainbridge Sun,* voted for it, assuring his constituents that the measure only guaranteed "public rights" and would not force social equality. Republicans fearful of the political consequences of supporting the federal civil rights law believed their predictions were confirmed when the 1874 elections crushed their party's hopes for a revival in North Carolina, Tennessee, and Alabama and gave Democrats control of the United States House of Representatives for the first time since 1860.[33]

If some white Republican editors were ambivalent about public accommodations laws for blacks, many more were opposed to elevating African Americans to political office. Reconstruction had scarcely begun before some white Republican editors had tried to discourage black political ambitions. The editor of the

Wilmington Post, angry at freedmen seeking office "a generation ahead of [their] time," had thus contrasted the party's Northern and Southern wings: "*There* all the intellect, the virtue, and religion are within its folds—here all the contrary elements cling to us and we have *an awful weight to lift.*" Jason Clarke Swayze had also worried about blacks' "forcing themselves into positions for which they are yet unfitted," a point echoed by his Republican rival Samuel Bard of the Atlanta *New Era.*[34] Even in Louisiana, where the majority of the voters were black, white Republican editors had expressed these concerns. The *New Orleans Tribune* had alarmed white Republicans by insisting that African Americans get a fair share of elective and appointive positions. Governor Henry Clay Warmoth had accused the *Tribune* of trying to "Africanize" the state, and New Orleans papers like the *Advocate, Deutsche Zeitung,* and *Republican* had expressed similar concerns. Even Michael Vidal, editor of the radical *St. Landry Progress,* had hoped blacks would not become candidates. Although the *Tribune* disappeared in 1869, its African American successor, the New Orleans *Louisianan,* continued to denounce the doctrine "that negroes shall do all the voting and white men hold all the positions." In 1870, the *Republican*'s Michael Hahn, claiming that blacks lacked education and political experience, had warned them not to "plunge madly and blindly into politics." Rural Louisiana papers had expressed similar concerns. The editor of the *Rapides Gazette* had urged blacks to "eschew politics and public matters generally," while editors of other parish papers had contended that men should be elevated to office because of their integrity and intelligence, not their color.[35]

In other states where Republicans were heavily dependent on the support of black voting majorities, white editors were not so opposed to African Americans' running for office. In Florida, the editor of the Jacksonville *New South* contended that an African American should fill one of the state's two congressional seats but not both. The editors of the *Charleston Republican* and Jackson *Pilot* contended that Republicans should field black candidates in counties with heavy black majorities, and both of Mississippi's leading Republican papers endorsed the election of two African Americans to the state's U.S. Senate seats. The *Pilot*'s editor also contended that blacks in the state legislature were equal in intelligence and education to many of its white members.[36]

On several occasions, African Americans who believed that their states' white Republican editors were not sufficiently supportive of black political aspirations established their own papers. Several such journals appeared in Alabama. When African American James T. Rapier first ran for Congress in 1870, no white paper printed any of his speeches, and several refused even to acknowledge his candidacy. In response, Rapier founded his own paper in Montgomery, the

Republican Sentinel, and used it to promote his renewed run for a congressional seat in 1872. Arthur Bingham, editor of the *Alabama State Journal,* calling black Republicans "poor deluded creatures," urged voters not to support Rapier. Despite such opposition, Rapier won the election and then discontinued the paper. Two other African American papers, both published in Mobile, also disappeared following the 1872 campaign. The next year Philip Joseph, a black Republican leader who had helped found the *Mobile Herald,* established the short-lived *Montgomery Watchman* to provide newspaper support for black candidates in Alabama's Black Belt. In Florida, African American congressman Josiah T. Walls bought the white-owned Gainesville *New Era* in 1873 and used it for several years to promote his career. In South Carolina, black congressman Robert Smalls employed his *Beaufort Standard* for the same purpose. In Arkansas, Tabbs Gross of the *Arkansas Freeman* accused the *Little Rock Republican*'s John Price and his carpetbagger friends of monopolizing state offices at the expense of African American Republicans.[37]

At the outset of congressional Reconstruction, blacks had been willing to stand aside in favor of white candidates, but by the early 1870s, as the freedmen gained in political sophistication, they became increasingly resentful of white monopolization of power and place. As the African American editor of the *Vicksburg Plain Dealer* put it, the idea that whites could hold the offices while blacks did the voting "had played out." By 1873, the number of black officeholders in the states still under Republican control began to grow. Alarmed white editors started accusing African Americans of drawing a political color line by voting only for fellow blacks. The editor of the Richmond *Daily State Journal* asserted that blacks must demonstrate their ability to hold office and "not claim it as a matter of right," a point echoed by the editor of the Alexandria *Rapides Gazette,* who warned that blacks must "drop the question of color as a political open sesame to advancement for which [they] may be unfit." In Mississippi, the editor of the *Columbus Press* warned that the policy of running only colored men for office "has finally brought the Republican Party, not only of the south but of the nation, up to the very verge of destruction," a point repeated by his *Natchez Post* colleague. The editor of the *Vicksburg Times,* while grudgingly allowing that blacks deserved their fair share of offices, did ask the freedmen to back candidates "who speak English that is not half jargon" and who were taxpayers.[38]

The concerns expressed by many white editors about limiting blacks' role in the Republican Party went hand in hand with their growing willingness to allow ex-Confederates to vote and hold office. In Alabama, Albert Griffin of the Mobile *Nationalist,* who was critical of black aspirations for office, had recommended amnesty in order to "enlarge the pool of good men" from which Republicans could choose political candidates. J. W. Phillips, editor of the *East Alabama Monitor*, had also urged an end to disfranchisement in order to recruit Republicans "from the best material of the native white population"; and the editor of the *Louisiana State Register* favored amnesty so that the party could court "men of stature." In Mississippi, the *Vicksburg Times* editor hoped "capitalists, merchants and businessmen" would start attending Republican conventions, instead of the "shiftless classes," people he claimed were manipulated by the Union Leagues. The editor of the New Orleans *National Republican,* fearing that the freedmen would vote for corrupt Republicans rather than for conservatives, urged the party to attract the support of "old and respectable" Louisiana whites who could provide honest leadership.[39]

Such references to "men of stature" and "old and respectable" whites revealed that the Southern Republicans were increasingly divided along the lines of nativity as well as race, pitting scalawags against carpetbaggers. Scalawag jealousy of carpetbag influence in the party emerged shortly after Reconstruction began, exacerbated by Democratic attacks on "outsiders" who, they claimed, controlled Republican policy. Hence Republican editors had to devote considerable column space to defending carpetbaggers against criticism from both inside and outside the party, emphasizing that Northerners brought capital, enterprise, and new ideas into the South and were often instrumental in establishing public school systems. They warned that hostility to newcomers threatened to retard Southern economic, social, and political development. According to John Morris of the *Charleston Republican,* carpetbaggery, rather than being a term of reproach, was "the symbol of live and intelligent enterprise in the midst of a . . . large class slow to learn anything beyond the traditional ways of their ancestors." He equated carpetbaggers with deep plowing, clean cultivation, machinery, water power, manufacturers and mechanic arts, mines, and schoolhouses.[40]

Scalawag hostility to carpetbaggers was especially marked in Louisiana, where Northerners controlled the state Republican organization. The editor of the *Rapides Gazette* wanted candidates who were longtime Louisiana residents rather than "six-months men," a point repeated by the editor of the New Orleans *National Republican.* By 1874, W. Jasper Blackburn, one of the earliest white Southerners to join the Louisiana party, was complaining that it was dominated by Northerners and "Negro bummers."[41] This animosity toward carpetbaggers also appeared in states that had a significant number of wartime Unionists, such as Texas, Arkansas, Tennessee, and Alabama. In Texas, editors of the Galveston *Flake's Bulletin,* the *Austin Republican,* and the *Houston Union* all complained about carpetbaggers' crowding Southern Unionists out of office. In Arkansas,

Valentine Dell's *Fort Smith New Era* echoed the same concerns, as did the editor of the *Magnolia Flower*, who warned that carpetbag governor Powell Clayton "has too much ignored the *native* element" in the party. Scalawags organized the Liberal movement that opposed Clayton and the *Little Rock Republican*'s carpetbag editor, John Price. Price lashed out in return, claiming that such attacks on carpetbaggers usually came from "self-imposed representatives of a defunct and rotten aristocracy . . . supposed to dine on derringers and Arkansas toothpicks." He was proud to be a carpetbagger, for men like him were bringing Northern values of patriotism and freedom and a commitment to free schools and free speech to a land that lacked these advantages. "We will not admit," he declared, "that a land which did not know of a public school is productive of superior intelligence."[42]

In Tennessee, a number of scalawags complained that carpetbaggers controlled too many offices. In the fall of 1868, Nashville *Press and Times* editor S. C. Mercer ran as a native against the regular Republican congressional nominee, who was from the North. Such tensions led the *Knoxville Whig*'s editor to publish a list of state officials showing that only one came from outside the state and that all the state's congressmen save one were from the South. In 1869, the editor of the *Alabama State Journal* published a similar list proving that most of that state's offices went to native white Alabamians. Three years later, however, the paper had a new editor, scalawag Arthur Bingham, and both he and William Figures of the *Huntsville Advocate* complained that a clique of Northerners controlled the state party and that federal appointments went to them rather than to native-born Republicans. Figures was so angry at President Grant for making these appointments that he deserted the party in 1872, backing Liberal Republican Greeley for president and the Democratic Party's gubernatorial candidate.[43]

Similar resentment at supposed carpetbagger domination of state organizations appeared elsewhere in the South. In Georgia, Jason Clark Swayze, who had not come to Georgia until shortly before the war, was so angry at Grant for appointing "hungry, never-satisfied carpetbaggers" to office that he too declared his intention of supporting Greeley. In Virginia, James B. Sener of the *Fredericksburg Ledger* complained that the state's Republican Party suffered from "uneducated and unfit white men and colored men [who] thrust themselves forward and control the party," and he urged Republicans to recruit more respectable support from native Virginians, an appeal echoed by John R. Hathaway of the *Norfolk Day Book*. In North Carolina, the editor of the *Rutherford Star* complained that Governor Holden was appointing too many carpetbaggers to office. Several Florida Republican papers backed an 1872 movement to draft

Ossian B. Hart to run for governor, hoping his candidacy would increase the influence of "Southern loyalists" in the party.[44]

Southern Republican editors eager to recruit native white support for their party sometimes looked to Unionist Democrats who had voted for Stephen A. Douglas in 1860. Results were disappointing. In 1874, Robert Moseley, editor of the Talladega *Our Mountain Home,* complained about the "meekness" with which the old union element of Alabama's Democratic Party submitted "to the sneers and snubs and insults . . . of their arrogant and haughty secession brethren."[45] Most editors looked to ex-Whigs rather than Democrats for support, particularly if they had once been Whigs themselves. They contended that since the Civil War had settled the divisive slavery issue, both Republicans and ex-Whigs stood together in support of the Union, protective tariffs, a national banking system, and aid to internal improvements. Sometimes editors expressed the same disappointment at the former Whigs' unwillingness to brave social ostracism and cross over to the Republicans that Moseley expressed about the Democrats. The editor of the *Mobile Herald* complained that such men lacked "moral courage."[46]

Although many Republican editors enthusiastically endorsed aid to railroads as the best way to promote Southern prosperity and thereby attract support from well-to-do whites, including ex-Whigs, some dissented from this approach. In Texas, Republican journalists debated whether the state should aid railroads or schools. As early as 1867, the editor of the Austin *Weekly Intelligencer* had declared that public schools were more important, a point repeated in 1869 by James Newcomb of the *San Antonio Express.* Newcomb warned in 1870 against "indiscriminate subsidizing" of railroads, and that year Governor Davis vetoed two railroad aid bills, while at the same time securing money for public schools. The ensuing outrage over his vetoes threatened to divide the party, but in 1872 the Republican convention managed to patch over the differences, endorsing free public schools "at the smallest cost possible" and calling for "reasonable state aid" for internal improvements.[47]

As Republican administrations began granting aid to railroads, Democrats claimed that such policies increased states' debts and endangered their credit. These Democratic attacks forced Republican editors onto the defensive. By 1869, evidence of waste and corruption in railroad projects in Tennessee, North Carolina, and Alabama prompted a number of Republican journalists in those states to call for an end to subsidies. In Tennessee's gubernatorial campaign that year, Stokes's supporters contended that he would end railroad aid but that Senter would not.[48] In North Carolina, the *Rutherford Star* editor asserted that Governor Holden's policy of granting roads liberal assistance was ruining the state's credit. Even the editor of the Raleigh *Standard* admitted that state aid under Holden was excessive and involved bribery and payoffs, as did his counterpart at the Elizabeth City *North Carolinian.*[49]

In 1869, the editor of the *Alabama State Journal* advised the state legislature not to approve a bill granting generous assistance to railroads. He invoked the Tennessee and North Carolina examples as proof that such a measure could destroy the state's credit. Demopolis *Southern Republican* editor Pierce Burton, who voted against the proposal, claimed the state would be wiser to use its credit to establish mills and furnaces rather than railroads, a position the *State Journal* endorsed. Despite such opposition, the measure passed, and even the editor of the *Mobile Herald* later admitted that its implementation during Governor William H. Smith's administration involved corruption. He and the editors of the *Selma Press* and *Huntsville Advocate* all opposed further aid to railroads. In Arkansas, the *Little Rock Republican* editor also opposed embarking on any ambitious railroad programs, warning that they would endanger the state's credit. His opposition notwithstanding, the state did aid railroads, but Governor Clayton limited assistance to just a handful of the railroads seeking it and made sure that the companies completed the construction for which they received subsidies. Nonetheless, in 1872 Valentine Dell's *Fort Smith New Era* opposed any further state railroad assistance.[50]

Editors supporting railroad development pointed out that governments secured railroad loans by obtaining prior liens on the companies' property.[51] North Carolina and Alabama editors emphasized that Democrats as well as Republicans had voted for railroad bills and that Democrats operated most of the roads benefiting from the aid.[52] They also observed that antebellum Democratic regimes had loaned money to railroads, thereby increasing the states' debts. In Louisiana, the *New Orleans Republican*'s editor reminded readers of the debt accumulated by Democrats who ran the government immediately after the war.[53] After Democrats gained control of Alabama in 1871, Republicans accused the ensuing administration of corruption in implementing its railroad policies, leading to an unnecessary increase in that state's debt.[54]

Democrats contended that Republican regimes wasted money not only on railroads but on other projects as well, thereby driving up taxes and endangering economic growth. They also claimed that many Republican officials were incompetent and dishonest. Republican editors scrambled to answer such charges, realizing that they raised serious questions about the legitimacy of the state regimes. Some defended increased state expenditures by pointing out that governments were now providing services such as public schools that either had not existed before or were poorly funded. The editor of the *South Carolina*

Republican recited a long list of what he regarded as Republican accomplishments in his state, including achieving equal rights, equitable taxes, abolition of property qualifications for officeholding, free public schools, homestead laws, public works, and funding of the old state debt. The Democrats, he noted, objected to the cost of this "magnificent record." Was money, he asked, "to be put against human rights; against fair play; against evenhanded justice; against the elevation and education of all men?" In Texas, the editor of the *San Antonio Express* admitted that the Davis government's expenses were high, but he noted that the outlay provided law and order on the frontier, paid for schools, and promoted immigration.[55]

In Arkansas, John Price of the *Little Rock Republican* pointed out that whereas antebellum taxes had been lower, back then the state had enjoyed no railroads or public schools. He reminded his readers that during the war, the Confederate government had assessed a 10 percent tax in kind on Arkansas farmers. Now that the war was over, he commented, the state would have to generate increased revenue to stimulate internal improvements and construct schools. The benefits of these programs would far outweigh their costs. He also emphasized that Republicans enacted a new assessment law in order to equalize taxes, not raise them. The editor of the *Columbia Daily Union* compared South Carolina tax rates to those in the North that relied on income generated by land rather than on land value. On this basis, he concluded, whereas a Wisconsin dairy farmer paid $5 in taxes for every $100 of income, a South Carolina cotton farmer paid forty-five cents. He also contended that Democratic landowners were undermining the state's credit by delaying payment of their taxes.[56]

Many Republican editors admitted that corruption tainted their states' regimes and called for its elimination. In North Carolina, Palemon John of the Elizabeth City *North Carolinian* blamed the party's 1870 defeat on the "foolish, extravagant, impractical legislation" of the previous two years, and George W. Nason of the New Bern *Republican and Courier* stated that the party could regain power only by "advocating honest men and measures." Arthur Bingham, editor of the *Alabama State Journal*, blamed his state's corruption on carpetbaggers and called upon scalawags to clean up the Republican Party. John Price, editor of the party's leading paper in Arkansas, called on its governmental leaders to institute rigid economies that would lead to tax reductions, a plea echoed in Valentine Dell's *Fort Smith New Era*.[57]

These attempts to end railroad subsidies, lower taxes, and clean up corruption did not stave off Republican defeat in Texas and Arkansas; after 1874, only Louisiana, South Carolina, Mississippi, and Florida remained in Republican hands. Party members in all four states now struggled to forestall defeat by making concessions to reformers. By then it was clear that rather than progressing rapidly under the stimulus of railroad development, the Southern economy was stagnating. Although there were many reasons for this situation, including a nationwide panic and depression commencing in 1873, Southern voters were sure to blame the Republicans, who had promised to usher in a new era of prosperity upon taking office. Now Republican editors claimed that their states would prosper as their governments halted subsidies, cut taxes, and embarked upon retrenchment and reform.[58]

In Louisiana, corruption seemed endemic throughout Reconstruction. Even Republican editors in other states expressed shock at conditions there.[59] By January 1871, noting what he called extravagant legislative expenditures, the editor of the *Louisiana State Register* warned that if the party did not institute reforms, it would lose control of the state: "We cannot afford to be robbed in the name of republicanism any more than we can afford to be beaten and shot in the name of democracy." The *Louisianan* editor called for curbing party corruption, as did his counterpart on the Alexandria *Rapides Gazette*. By November 1873, even the editor of the *New Orleans Republican,* the party's official organ, was warning that Northern Republicans would abandon Southern brethren who failed to bring corruption under control. Republican governor William Pitt Kellogg, having assumed power after a bitterly contested 1872 election, moved the state toward fiscal responsibility. Invalidating some debts and funding others, he reduced Louisiana's overall bonded indebtedness, cut back on overall expenditures, and reduced tax rates.[60]

Florida also experienced increased demand for reform coming from within the Republican Party. In 1872, Republicans elected Ossian B. Hart as governor on a platform that the Jacksonville *Florida Union*'s editor pledged would commit the party to retrenchment, efficiency, tax reduction, schools, and improved credit for the state. Hart died in office, but by 1874 his successor, Marcellus Stearns, had reordered Florida's finances, stopped the use of state credit to aid corporations, and improved tax collections.[61] In South Carolina, John Morris of the *Charleston Republican* was condemning corruption in Governor Robert K. Scott's administration as early as 1870 and calling on Republican legislators to purge their chambers of unfit members. By 1872, Lewis Cass Carpenter of the *Columbia Daily Union* was making the same comments. James G. Thompson, editor of the *Beaufort Republican,* also denounced the "villainous ring" in the state house; in 1872 he supported a reform ticket that failed to prevent the election of Scott's successor, Robert K. Moses. If anything, the new governor proved to be more corrupt than Scott, leading the party's chief newspaper, the Columbia *Union-Herald,* to call for "honest, earnest, and complete reform."

Scalawag Henry Sparnick, editor of the *Aiken Tribune*, also called upon the party to eliminate "waste, corruption, and incompetence." By 1874, Republican editors were all backing reformer Daniel H. Chamberlain for governor. Once in office, Chamberlain, like Kellogg in Louisiana, worked to consolidate and fund the debt, reduce costs, and cut taxes, and the editors of the *Union-Herald* loyally supported his efforts.[62]

By November 1871, both of Mississippi's major Republican papers, the *Vicksburg Times* and the Jackson *Pilot*, were calling for retrenchment and reform in state government. Governor Ridgley Powers, however, proved unable to deliver on his pledge to achieve those goals. In the 1873 gubernatorial campaign, the *Pilot* backed Adelbert Ames, while the *Times* supported former governor James Lusk Alcorn, who was running for the post again. Both candidates promised reform; Ames won the election but soon discovered that the Republican legislature was not interested in reducing expenses. Nor was he able to contain corruption, which became especially rampant on the county level. Disappointed, the editors of the *Times* began to criticize Ames, leading their counterparts at the *Pilot*, who stood by him, to condemn the Vicksburg paper as "bolting" and "anti-Republican." The editor of the *Columbus Press* also expressed disappointment with the legislature's failure to reduce expenditures.[63]

In the end, it mattered not whether the South's remaining Republican governors reformed their state administrations. Many years ago W. E. B. DuBois observed that what white Southern Democrats feared most was honest, efficient, competent Republican governments, for these the Democrats could not condemn.[64] Whether state governments were honest or dishonest, expensive or economical, the majority of Southern whites were determined to eliminate those regimes. In 1875, Democrats unleashed a tidal wave of violence and intimidation that drove the Republicans from power in Mississippi. The following year they applied the same methods in Florida, Louisiana, and South Carolina. The outcome of elections in those three states remained in dispute for months; when the disputes were finally resolved in 1877, Democrats emerged in control of all three of them.

CHAPTER NINE

The Two-Edged Sword of Patronage

Everywhere in the Reconstruction South, the newly formed Republican Party faced a set of interrelated problems. Its leaders had to struggle to build a constituency through which they could gain and keep political power. Simultaneously, they tried to convince hostile white Southerners to accept their party as a legitimate institution entitled to compete for this political power. These goals, however, proved to be mutually exclusive. In their quest for political legitimacy, for instance, Republican governors often sought out moderate Southern whites by offering them offices and opposing equal accommodations laws. Such steps risked alienating their core constituents, most of whom were African American. After gaining power, governors in some states sought to consolidate and maintain that control by disfranchising whites, postponing elections, or establishing state returning boards that could overturn elections Democrats might have carried through fraud or intimidation. Such undemocratic measures undermined Republican efforts to prove that their state regimes were legitimate and deserving of recognition, if not support.[1]

Similar contradictions confounded Republican efforts to establish a party press in the South. Republican publishers believed that such a press was absolutely necessary if the party was to recruit and maintain a reliable constituency. It could also be an important means of gaining the party recognition and even acceptance from the mass of Southern whites. But editors composing their columns faced the same dilemma that confronted Republican officeholders and other spokespersons. Their efforts to recruit and sustain a loyal following among blacks and yeoman whites heightened the difficulty of convincing wealthier and more prestigious Southern whites to accept the party as legitimate, let alone to join it. And they found that lavish dispensation of government printing patronage, which was the lifeblood of the Republican press, also undermined their quest for legitimacy.

The fact that in the face of considerable white hostility during Reconstruction, Republican publishers were able to establish over four hundred papers in the ex-Confederate states testifies to the importance they attached to having a party press. Numerous Republican publishers operated their papers at a loss rather than close them.[2] A great many of the papers that managed to survive did so by means of government printing patronage, but this same patronage also contributed to the downfall of the party and the press. Since most Republican publishers were desperate for government printing, they often competed against one another for it. Groups fighting for control of state Republican organizations tried to channel this printing to their own papers and deny it to their opponents. Hence patronage became one of many issues contributing to the factionalism that plagued the Republican Party in state after state across the South. In some states, the heavy reliance of the Republican press on this patronage also drove printing expenses to embarrassing heights, lending ammunition to their Democratic opponents, who criticized Republican administrations for wasteful spending. Some Republican governors tried to preempt such criticism and gain support from erstwhile opponents by subsidizing Democratic as well as Republican sheets, but to little avail. Republican publishers faced a difficult dilemma: without patronage most of them could not exist, yet relying on it weakened their party both within and without.

Most of the newspaper competition for U.S. government printing patronage occurred in 1867 and 1868, when Edward McPherson, clerk of the House of Representatives, awarded the initial contracts. Occasionally Republican squabbles over federal patronage broke out in subsequent years, and they did not end until 1875 when the federal government terminated the printing subsidy. Sometimes publishers quarreled over who was to inherit the printing contract of a suspended paper. In other instances, publishers complained that McPherson was ignoring their region of a state when he dispensed contracts. Such disputes emerged in Virginia and North Carolina, where state-government patronage was feeble or nonexistent, leaving Republican publishers to rely on Washington for support. In North Carolina, protests from the eastern part of the state convinced McPherson to transfer printing from the *Asheville Pioneer,* located in the western mountains, to the *New Bern Times.* Other disputes reflected differences in party strategy. In 1870, Louisiana Republicans convinced John Menard to transfer the printing contract for his *New Orleans Standard* to the German-language New Orleans *Deutsche Zeitung,* but Menard was soon asking for the contract's return, claiming that the recent election had found "precious few" Germans voting Republican. Factionalism played a role two years later in a dispute over federal printing patronage in Texas. Several Republicans led by James Newcomb, claiming that the *San Antonio Express* had "fallen from grace" and had a "very limited circulation," unsuccessfully sought to transfer federal printing from the *Express* to Newcomb's Austin *State Journal.*[3]

After the Republican Party gained control of Southern governments, most publishers shifted their attention from Washington to patronage available at the state and local levels. In most states Republicans avoided haggling over printing for their state constitutional conventions. In some cases there was only one Republican paper capable of undertaking this work. If multiple papers existed, convention delegates usually spread printing among as many as they could. In Louisiana and Texas, however, controversies over convention printing reflected significant policy differences within the Republican Party.

Louisiana delegates were deeply divided over which of the major New Orleans papers, the *Tribune* or the *Republican*, should get the convention's official printing. Two African American delegates nominated the radical *Tribune*, while a pair of white delegates proposed the more centrist *Republican*. After an angry debate, the delegates voted 46 to 45 to grant the printing to the *Tribune*. Undeterred, the *Republican*'s backers sought to undermine the rival newspaper, especially when they found out that the *Tribune* had farmed out some of its printing to the conservative *New Orleans Times*. As the convention ended, carpetbaggers proposed allowing the *Republican* to print the journal in pamphlet form, but white radicals and freedmen voted this down.[4]

In Texas, similar rivalry broke out between backers of the *Austin Republican*, the centrist Republican paper that was the official organ of provisional governor E. M. Pease, and the more radical *San Antonio Express*, which backed Edmund J. Davis. When delegates proposed to subscribe for two thousand copies of the *Austin Republican* and authorized it to publish the convention journal each day, the *San Antonio Express* editor complained. Davis, the presiding officer, induced the convention to purchase five hundred copies of the *Express* and four hundred copies of its sister paper, the *Freie Presse*, and to publish the journal in them as well. Ferdinand Flake, whose Galveston newspaper was ignored, condemned "this plundering of the public treasury for the benefit of party newspapers—for which the authors ought to blush." When the convention finished its work, debate arose over which paper should be allowed to publish the bound volumes of the journal and the new constitution. The Davis faction, rather than grant this privilege to the *Austin Republican*, prevented a vote on the question. In 1870, after Davis had become governor, the legislature awarded this printing to J. G. Tracy and August Siemering, who published San Antonio and Houston papers supporting the administration.[5]

The Mississippi convention also experienced some bickering over its printing contracts, but this was apparently unrelated to any factional disputes. The delegates initially named as official printer James Dugan, publisher of the newly founded *Mississippi State Journal* in Jackson. They also arranged to publish their daily proceedings in Dugan's paper and in the two other current Republican journals. A few months later, while the convention was still in session, a new Republican paper, the *Mississippi Pilot,* appeared in Jackson. Its first proprietor and editor was Edward Stafford, a Union general originally from New York, who had been a Missouri journalist prior to the war. Moved either by the manipulations of Stafford, who was himself a member of the convention, or by a concern that Dugan would be unable to execute the terms of his printing contract, convention delegates allowed Stafford to take over much of the work. Dugan was furious. He reminded the delegates that he had come to the state a year before "as a pioneer" and had established a Republican paper "at a time when none other had the moral courage" to undertake such a project. Loss of the convention patronage would force his paper to close, "and that would be a poor reciprocation for the personal sacrifice I have made in advancing the interests of the Republican party." Ultimately the state paid Dugan more than $26,000 for convention printing, and Stafford only $4,000; but even then Dugan was unable to keep his paper going.[6]

Once Republicans gained control of the new governments established by these constitutions, they were able to designate newspaper publishers as their states' official printers. In many states, governors became part owners of these official papers. Some state legislatures gave their governors the power to publish proclamations, orders, and other official pronouncements in additional newspapers; in a number of instances, legislatures also authorized governors to designate papers to do the official printing for state courts and county governments. These laws fulfilled their purpose of subsidizing a party press, but they also exacerbated party infighting by giving governors a powerful tool for obtaining press support for their policies and for disciplining dissenting editors. In some states such laws also led to excessive expenditures on printing.

Southern Republican regimes were quite vulnerable to Democratic charges that they were wasteful and extravagant, running up large state debts. As evidence, Democratic editors were fond of pointing to increased expenditures on printing. In every state these costs exceeded prewar levels. Some of this increase was due to the rapid postwar escalation of newsprint prices. Labor costs rose as well. These pressures affected both Democratic and Republican printers. In 1866, when Florida's secretary of state complained to Charles Dyke, Democratic editor of the *Tallahassee Floridian,* that his bid for printing state laws was extravagant, Dyke defended his figures by pointing out that paper and labor costs had soared since 1860.[7] Printing costs also rose because the Republican legislatures met for longer periods and enacted more laws and generated more reports than did their predecessors. In several states, however, printing costs were clearly excessive. In most cases, reform governors eventually began paring them back, but by then it was too late to stem the tide of conservative opposition that was sweeping Republicans out of office.

In Virginia, North Carolina, Tennessee, Alabama, and Florida, printing expenditures rose during Reconstruction but not as significantly as they did in other states. Virginia's legislature, which never fell under Republican control, appropriated $10,000 per year for printing from 1866 to 1869; in the fiscal year 1869–70 expenditures rose to $24,000, and they climbed to almost $40,000 during the first year of Gilbert C. Walker's administration, 1870–71. The following year, however, expenditures dropped to around $25,000. Since the Republicans had little access to state printing, patronage figured little in their papers' positions during the 1869 election race between Henry H. Wells and Walker. Throughout the 1870s, the Republican press struggled to survive without government patronage. The party's flagship paper, the Richmond *State Journal*, disappeared in 1875, to be succeeded by the Richmond *State*, which lasted only a couple of years. By 1880, Virginia had only two Republican papers, the *Norfolk Day Book* and the Staunton *Valley Virginian*.[8]

In North Carolina, the Republican legislature provided little state aid to party newspapers other than to make the Raleigh *North Carolina Standard* the official printer and to allow the secretary of state to designate certain newspapers to publish state laws. This meant that Governor Holden exercised little leverage over Republican newspapers that criticized his administration. It also meant that printing expenses did not reach the levels they did in other states. In 1866, the state legislature spent $8,732 on printing. After Republicans gained control of the state, printing costs rose to $28,000 for 1868–69 and $34,000 the following year. In 1870, after conservatives won control, the new state legislature, protesting what it called "exorbitant rates" expended during the previous two years for public printing, reduced the next fiscal year's expenditures to $22,292, and they continued to decline afterward. The Democrats also repealed the law allowing the secretary of state to publish laws in various state newspapers. Unlike in Virginia, however, North Carolina Republicans had drawn a significant minority of white votes, and hence, although the party's papers declined from their peak of fifteen in 1871, the state still had six Republican sheets as late as 1880. Two of these, the Elizabeth City *North Carolinian* and the *Wilmington Post*, had emerged early in Reconstruction in the eastern part of the state. Three more were found in the Piedmont and one in the mountainous west.[9]

Tennessee's Brownlow administration awarded the state's printing to the publishers of the Nashville *Press and Times*. Brownlow also designated other papers to publish the state laws. In addition he was authorized to identify newspapers in each congressional district to publish legal advertisements from local governments. In at least one case, his choice of a newspaper for these responsibilities determined the outcome of a heated local contest between rival editors and the Republican factions they represented. In Memphis, two Republican factions battled to control the city's government and the local congressional seat. The *Memphis Post* supported the more radical faction, which counted heavily on African American voters, while its rival the *Bulletin* backed the more moderate group. Brownlow directed printing to the *Post*, helping to sustain it while its rival succumbed.

After Senter and the Democrats gained control of the state in 1869, state printing costs, which had risen to slightly over $30,000 a year under Brownlow, dropped just below $20,000 and stayed at or below that amount for a number of years. One of the first acts of the new Democratic legislature was to pass "an act to restore justice to the press of Tennessee" by repealing the law governing the placement of legal advertisements. This action had an immediate impact on the Republican press. In 1869, the *Memphis Post* gave up its daily edition, its editor stating the paper would exist only as a weekly "until such time as it may be possible to revive Republicanism properly." A few months later, the paper closed its doors. The party's other daily, the Nashville *Press and Times*, also disappeared in 1869. Thanks to the Republican Party's strength among East Tennessee's former Unionists, however, the Volunteer State boasted sixteen Republican papers when Reconstruction ended in 1877, a total exceeded only by Louisiana's twenty. In 1880, Tennessee still had twelve Republican papers, twice as many as Louisiana, which came next. Of these twelve papers, eleven were in East Tennessee.[10]

Alabama spent $15,559 for printing for the fiscal year ending September 30, 1867, plus another $16,158 for printing the revised code; disbursements for the succeeding fiscal year came to $20,103. When the Republicans gained control of the state, they awarded official printing to the publishers of the Montgomery *Alabama State Journal*, which kept it until the party lost control of the state in the 1870 elections. The victorious Democrats then transferred the printing contract to W. W. Screws, proprietor of the *Montgomery Advertiser*. In 1871, Screws's paper began calling for enforcing state laws against the Klan, prompting Pierce Burton of the Demopolis *Southern Republican* to observe that if the Montgomery paper's new editorial position was the result of "obtaining 'pap' from the state," he hoped the *Advertiser* received a wet nurse. Under Republican rule, printing expenditures rose to $29,000 the first year and $44,048 the following year. In the next two years under a Democratic governor, spending dropped to $32,800 and then $25,302. The legislature also began dismantling the system Republicans had established for directing local patronage to their party newspapers. Although the Republicans regained the governorship in 1872 and restored printing to the *Journal*, expenditures rose only slightly, to $26,835 in 1873. In 1874, Republicans lost Alabama for good. The number of the state's Republican papers, which had reached a dozen in 1869, fell to five in 1875 and to two in 1877. That year saw the folding of the longest-lived of the Republican sheets, the Montgomery *Alabama State Journal*. By 1880, Alabama had only three Republican papers, all in the northern part of the state.[11]

In Florida, as in other states, printing costs rose even before the Republicans took office, doubling between 1860 and 1866. During the fiscal year 1866–67, the state spent $17,093 on printing, and when the Republicans took control of the state in 1868, Governor Harrison Reed, noting that printing costs had totaled $1,000 for the first four days of the new legislature, urged its members to "save the state from exorbitant demands in this direction." The governor's concerns may have stemmed from the fact that since the new legislature had not yet elected a new printer, this money was going to Charles Dyke, a Democrat. Eventually Edward M. Cheney, publisher of the Jacksonville *Florida Union*, became state printer. Reed, who was eager to court business-minded conservatives, appointed Democrat Robert H. Gamble as state comptroller, and in November 1868, Gamble complained that since the Republicans had taken office they had spent $16,790 on printing. In 1869, the state's printing expenditure stood at $17,205, again eliciting a protest from the comptroller, who compared this figure to the $4,500 expended in 1860. Printing charges in 1870 rose to $26,790 and totaled $23,170 the following year. By that time the publisher of the *Tallahassee Sentinel* had replaced Cheney as printer. After 1871, expenditures fell, totaling about $17,000 by 1874.[12]

Throughout Reconstruction Florida's subsidies to newspapers remained controversial. Democrats continually grumbled about excessive payments made to the state printer. They also objected to the law permitting the secretary of state to designate a newspaper in each judicial circuit to publish official notices from local governments and state courts at the same rate the state paid for its printing. Even though the Florida secretary of state Jonathan Gibbs made many of these awards to Democratic newspapers, Democrats in the legislature pushed through a repeal of this law in 1873. The repealing act's text apparently was stolen, however, and the old law remained in effect. Gibbs died in 1874 and was succeeded by Samuel McLin. McLin was also an editor of the *Tallahassee Sentinel* and designated his paper to do the printing for the second judicial district. Printing for the fourth district he awarded to the Jacksonville *Florida Union*. The Republican editor of the Jacksonville *New South*, possibly miffed because his paper was ignored, criticized the advertising law for not allowing papers to compete for publishing legal notices. As a consequence, he claimed, printing costs were 30 percent higher than they should be, thereby imposing an "exorbitant tax" on business. He noted that the publisher of the *Union* was the state printer and that the governor, Marcellus Stearns, was one of its owners. Two years later the editor of another of Jacksonville's Republican papers, the *Sun*, also denounced the law.[13]

In 1875, Governor Stearns sought to reduce the compensation rates under the advertising law, but instead the legislature pushed through a measure repealing it. Stearns then vetoed the repealing resolution, and the legislature failed to override his action. Stearns also lectured the legislature about the extravagant cost of printing its own journals. His concern might have been due to the fact that the lower house was controlled by Democrats who awarded their printing to Charles Dyke. Dyke defended his charges, and in so doing actually provided cover for Republican printers as well, by stating that for the last two or three years Florida's printing expenditures had been lower than those of any other state and far less remunerative to printers than before the war. He noted that the state printer was paid in depreciated state scrip but had to cover expenses in cash. In any case, by 1875 state printing costs had fallen to $11,740. When Democrats gained control of the state in 1877, they nullified the advertising law. The number of Republican papers had by then plummeted from a high of thirteen to six, which included the Jacksonville *Florida Union*. By 1880 that paper had become Democratic, however, leaving the Republicans with only two Florida newspapers, one in Ocala and one in Tampa.[14]

In the remaining ex-Confederate states, printing costs of Republican regimes rose more steeply, fueling Democratic charges of extravagance and corruption. Patronage also played a greater role in Republican infighting there. In Georgia, Republicans took over the state government in mid-1868 and spent only about $15,000 for printing the rest of the year, an amount consistent with that spent by previous administrations. In 1869, the legislature appropriated $28,000 for printing and then doubled this to over $57,000 the following year. The party's official newspaper, Samuel Bard's Atlanta *New Era*, received most of this money. In 1869, after Bard came out in opposition to Bullock's plan to submit the state to another reconstruction under U.S. military rule, the governor cut off his printing patronage, forcing Bard to recant. Shortly thereafter the disgruntled editor left the state, and two Atlanta businessmen acting in Bullock's interest bought control of the paper, which then ardently sustained the administration and received liberal doses of patronage.[15]

In addition to the amounts allocated for state printing, Bullock expended a considerable sum to publish proclamations in newspapers around the state. Before the war, the annual cost of publishing such proclamations had ranged from $500 to $3,000. In 1869, Bullock expended over $45,000 for this purpose. Samuel Bard, who by then had lost Bullock's support, attacked the governor for these expenditures, as did the state treasury secretary Nedom Angier, who had likewise fallen out with Bullock. Angier charged the governor with misusing state funds and resisted paying warrants issued for publishing the proclamations. In 1869 and again in 1870, the legislature inquired into these expenditures, and Angier delivered testimony damaging to Bullock. No charges developed from the investigations, however, probably because Bullock, hoping to broaden the base of his support, had paid much of this money to Democratic newspapers. In retrospect, the money Bullock spent wooing the Democratic press did not save his administration. Instead, the escalating expenditures only augmented the state debt, angered taxpayers, and frustrated Republican editors who wanted a larger share of the spoils. After Bullock fled the state in 1871, a legislative committee accused him of spending a total of $140,397 on printing, exclusive of the amounts paid to the public printer. The legislature repealed the law authorizing the publication of gubernatorial proclamations and named a Democrat as state printer. The number of Georgia's Republican newspapers was never high, peaking at six in 1871; by 1877, the party was down to one. In 1880, there were two Republican papers in Georgia, both published in Atlanta by the same firm.[16]

Bitter factionalism also beset the Arkansas Republican party and often it found expression in squabbles among newspapers over patronage. Members of the first Republican legislature engaged in heated debate over whether to name the *Little Rock Republican*'s proprietor as state printer. Opponents including *Fort Smith New Era* editor Valentine Dell complained that the *Republican*'s editor, John Price, was not from Arkansas. Native Arkansans attempted to direct the state printing to a new paper they established in Little Rock, the *True Republican*. Price responded that the Republican legislature should give the printing to its leading organ, not one designed to break it down. He railed against supporters of the *True Republican* who thought the "inestimable privilege" of having been born or raised in Arkansas gave them the right to control party patronage. Price's *Little Rock Republican* got the printing, and the *True Republican* disappeared.[17]

In Arkansas, printing expenditures in the early 1850s had ranged from $7,000 to $18,000; during the last two years of the Civil War printing costs totaled $17,637. When Republicans took control of the state in 1868, the legislature appropriated "a sufficient sum" rather than a specific amount for state printing.

State legislator Valentine Dell began attacking Price and his "Little Rock clique," claiming that Price was overcharging for his work. Price in turn accused Dell of using "his feeble and cross-grained intellect" to sow seeds of dissension in Republican ranks. When Price and his paper got into trouble late in 1868 for editorials criticizing Governor Powell Clayton, the Little Rock city government moved to withdraw its printing from the paper, and in the lower house, Dell and his followers instituted an investigation aimed at depriving Price of the state's printing as well. Another of Price's legislative critics, Joseph Brooks, helped found a new Little Rock paper, the *Liberal,* hoping to obtain for it the state printing these critics were trying to wrest from Price.[18]

Although Price lost his federal printing contract at this time, apparently because his editorial policy also disturbed the state's congressional delegation, he was able to retain the state's printing, and the *Liberal* went under. Its backers, however, replaced the *Liberal* with the *Arkansas State Journal,* which briefly received U.S. patronage. The *Journal's* editors, one of whom was Brooks, continued to criticize the state over the amount of money paid to Price for his work. In 1870, Price admitted that "there has been an extraordinary amount of public printing done," but he claimed he was only undertaking what the legislature had ordered. This printing included the journals for both houses for 1868 and 1869, the constitutional convention proceedings for 1864, and legislative journals for 1864 to 1867. According to the *Little Rock Gazette,* from July 1868 to March 1871 the state paid $209,213 in printing charges. In 1871, after Price had finished publishing these back journals, Governor Powell Clayton called for reducing public printing expenditures. "In no department," he argued, "is there greater call for a judicious economy than this," and he cited the scores of useless documents that were produced every year. The legislature then agreed to limit printing expenses to $50,000 per annum.[19]

During the 1872 gubernatorial contest between the Minstrels backing Elisha Baxter and the Brindletails supporting Brooks, most of the state's Republican papers supported Baxter, no doubt influenced by the Minstrels' utilization of the law allowing the governor to designate official newspapers around the state. Baxter, the winner, then disappointed his backers by granting this patronage to Democratic newspapers and naming the *Little Rock Gazette* official printer for the state. Deprived of sustenance, the daily *Little Rock Republican* shrank to a weekly and soon disappeared. In November 1874, after their party secured control of the state, Democratic legislators agreed to contract state printing to the lowest bidder; appropriations for printing averaged $32,000 a year for the next two years, about half of what the Republicans had expended in 1873. The number of Republican newspapers fell from a high of twenty-six in 1872 to six in

1877. By 1880, the total had dwindled to four, including the South's longest-lived Republican paper, Valentine Dell's *Fort Smith New Era*.[20]

Most of the Republican papers in Texas backed Governor Edmund J. Davis in 1870, including the *Express* and the *Freie Presse fur Texas* in San Antonio, the *Houston Union*, and the *Austin State Journal*. The *Journal* became the administration's official organ, the San Antonio and Houston papers obtained U.S. patronage, and the *Union*'s publisher became state printer. The legislature also authorized Davis to designate an official paper in each judicial district to do its public printing, a measure that greatly assisted his efforts to build newspaper support elsewhere in the state. Conservative papers quickly denounced the measure; one sarcastically observed that "we expect Radical papers will appear under this law as thick as little frogs after a summer shower, and when the legal patronage is withdrawn, they will disappear as suddenly, and be as little missed." Condemnation came from Republicans as well. Frank Webb, publisher of an African American paper, the *Galveston Republican*, objected that whites monopolized this printing. The editor of the *Austin Republican* scornfully referred to papers Davis designated for the various judicial districts as "chicken-pie organs" and "pap papers." James Newcomb of the *Daily State Journal* dismissed these attacks, claiming that "all the squealing of those outside the pen goes for nought." In November 1870, however, a leading Texas Republican, U.S. Senator Morgan Hamilton, called for repealing the district printing law. The measure was "a monstrous wrong," he contended, inflicting great inconvenience on business owners and local officials "for the benefit only of the proprietors of newspapers." No party, he insisted, "can bear up under such legislation as this." A year later the bill repealing it became law without Davis's signature.[21]

Texas Democrats also grumbled, as did their party throughout the South, about the escalating cost of state printing, contending that it exceeded the entire cost of prewar state government. In the legislature they denounced the state printers as "swindlers, thieves, cormorants, and vultures." Republicans alienated from the Davis regime picked up the cry; according to the editor of the *Austin Republican*, in the first six months of 1870 the state paid the printers $80,000, twice what the preceding government had paid for two years of printing. Senator Morgan Hamilton and newspaper editor Ferdinand Flake also condemned the expenditures; in 1871, Flake claimed that over the preceding year the state had paid out more than $100,000 for printing.[22]

Critics of the state's printing expenditures were on the mark. For the fiscal year 1869–70, the legislature appropriated $30,000 for printing; two years later, printing expenditures had risen to slightly more than $100,000. The state printers defended themselves by claiming that printing expenses were much higher in neighboring Louisiana. They also pointed out that they paid in gold for paper, labor, and binding, while the state reimbursed them in depreciated warrants. The last Republican legislature reduced printing expenditures to around $20,000 for fiscal 1872–73; although Democrats controlled the state legislature thereafter, expenditures rose to around $46,000 for fiscal 1873–74 before falling to $14,000 the following year. Republican papers in Texas declined from a high of twenty-six in 1870 to seven in 1877. In that year, the *San Antonio Express*, which had long been a leader among state Republican journals, declared itself independent in politics. By 1880, only five Republican papers remained in the state, including the long-lived San Antonio *Freie Presse fur Texas*.[23]

Mississippi's scalawag governor, James Lusk Alcorn, who had been elected to that post in 1869, found himself engaged in intraparty controversies that were partly related to state printing patronage. In 1870, the legislature authorized itself to name "loyal" newspapers in each of the state's judicial districts to publish the official advertising of local governments. A convention of Democratic newspapers passed resolutions denouncing the enactment; the Jackson *Clarion* condemned it as an "iniquitous measure to impose a tax on widows and orphans for the support of Radical newspapers." Claiming that the law deprived local authorities of the right to place such advertising, Alcorn vetoed it. He admitted that the bill would help subsidize the Republican press but argued that "a party which cannot move forward without the crutches of public wrong, ought not to be kept upon its feet." The state's few Republican papers condemned the governor's action. The *Vicksburg Daily Times* denounced the governor's "cowardly treachery" and predicted that his veto, which the paper claimed was copied from the Democratic press convention's resolutions, would be the "death knell of the party" if the legislature failed to override it. The veto stood, however, shattering Republican hopes for a strong state press.[24]

Alcorn also complained that the state's printers, Kimball, Raymond and Company, were overcharging the state. During the five years preceding Alcorn's 1870 inauguration, Mississippi governments spent about $12,000 a year on printing. In the first year under Republican rule, expenditures rose to almost $53,000, and in 1871 they soared to $127,848. In the summer of 1871, while the legislature was not in session, Alcorn canceled the state's contract with Kimball and Raymond, ostensibly because of these excesses, and awarded the printing to his cousin Robert J. Alcorn and Hiram Fisher. This pair immediately established the Jackson *State Leader*, which supported Governor Alcorn. According to the *Vicksburg Times*, the *State Leader* was printed in the office of the Democratic Jackson *Clarion*.[25]

Kimball, Raymond and Company also published the Jackson *Pilot,* and Alcorn's action probably had less to do with printing expenses than with his anger at the *Pilot* for criticizing his administration. Nonetheless, the *Pilot*'s editor, A. W. Webber, had to fend off attacks from the *Clarion* focused on escalating printing costs. Webber complained that Alcorn had furnished statistics to the *Clarion* which it then published, demonstrating that over a thirteen-month period the state had spent $160,000 on printing. The *Pilot* editor did not contest the figure. But he said it reflected eighteen months of printing, not thirteen, and noted that the most recent legislative session had lasted almost a year. He reminded the *Clarion* that in 1858 the state had paid it $23,000 for printing for a legislative session lasting thirty days and said, at that rate, the *Pilot* should have received $268,954 for its work. Webber further countered that Alcorn had approved the compensation rate for the state's printing and explained that about a third of the state's payment to the *Pilot*'s owners was in depreciated currency.[26]

Late in 1871, Alcorn resigned the governorship to take a U.S. Senate seat, and Lieutenant Governor Ridgely Powers succeeded him. When the legislature met in 1872, it returned the printing to the *Pilot,* and the *State Leader* disappeared. The new contract did not end the *Pilot*'s difficulties, however. During its attacks on the *Pilot*'s owners, the *Clarion* demonstrated that the state had paid them $41,000 for publishing a six-hundred-page volume of documents and an additional $31,000 for producing department reports. Three times in 1872, Governor Powers recommended that the legislature drastically reduce state printing rates and curtail the excessive printing of documents, claiming that such extravagance "subordinates the general interest to that of private individuals." Finally, just before the legislators adjourned, they approved a measure cutting rates back to 1857 levels, making it impossible for the printers to reap a profit.[27]

This was quite a blow not only to the *Pilot* but also to the *Vicksburg Times,* the state's only party daily. Three years earlier, J. B. Raymond, the *Pilot*'s principal owner, had purchased a controlling interest in the Vicksburg paper to keep it afloat, and by 1872 he was spending several thousand dollars of his own money to keep both sheets going. Both papers also received federal government printing contracts, but this was not enough to sustain the *Times* without state revenue, and Raymond had to put the Vicksburg paper up for sale. A group of Republicans bought it, and the new editors adopted a stance more conservative than that of its previous owners, which perhaps explains how it survived without state patronage. When the new legislature met in 1873, it debated proposals to restore printing rates and also considered passing a district printing bill similar to the one Alcorn had vetoed three years earlier. The Vicksburg paper, which ran a significant amount of local advertising from merchants in this

Republican stronghold, was critical of both measures. The legislature did raise printing rates (although not to 1870 levels) but failed to enact a district printing bill. Because a gubernatorial campaign was under way that year pitting Alcorn against the other United States senator, Adelbert Ames, Powers threatened to veto the printing hike unless the *Pilot* supported Alcorn. The paper agreed to strike a neutral stance, but once the bill became law, the *Pilot* came out for Ames while the *Vicksburg Times* leaned toward Alcorn.[28]

During the campaign, Alcorn made quite an issue of the *Pilot*'s allegedly excessive reimbursements for public printing, a charge that Democratic papers eagerly repeated. After winning the election, Ames recommended reducing state expenses, and several reform Republicans urged cutting printing costs. The 1874 legislature, however, rejected Ames's proposal and instead enacted a district printing bill similar to the one Alcorn had vetoed four years earlier. With such encouragement, the number of Republican papers increased, reaching a peak of thirty that year. Nevertheless at least one district judge believed the measure caused more harm than good: "If there is a judicial district or county in the state in which [the party's true interest] has been promoted by this law, we have yet to be informed of the fact." Competition for the printing had caused dissension among Republicans and brought odium on the courts. Such public legislation for partisan purposes was unjust, he warned, and "apt to defeat the object for which it is designed."[29]

Printing costs for the state declined to about $71,000 in 1872 but remained slightly above that figure for the following year. In the first year of Governor Adelbert Ames's administration, the printing bill climbed to almost $79,000. The *Vicksburg Times* editor, who had opposed the 1874 printing bill and also the hike in printing rates, complained that a large portion of the state's tax revenues went to pay the *Pilot*'s exorbitantly high charges. When the *Pilot* characterized the *Times* as "anti-Republican," the latter retorted that the *Pilot*'s editor was so "blinded by the $100,000 for printing" that he could not see the need for retrenchment. The *Times* urged Ames to repudiate the *Pilot* and withdraw public printing from it. In the spring of 1875, the owners of the *Times* moved the paper from Vicksburg to Jackson, ostensibly in order to provide the capital with a daily Republican paper but also to counter the *Pilot* more effectively. The *Times* criticized the Ames administration, calling for additional retrenchment and reform, while the *Pilot* castigated such Republican critics as "miserable, malignant mongrels who snarl and snap at everybody and everything."[30]

Although in 1875 Mississippi's printing expenditures fell to $50,000, the two newspapers continued to battle each other more than their common opponents. That summer evidence mounted that Democrats were planning to use force to control the fall state elections. When the *Pilot* asserted that the only way to treat White League ruffians was "to take them by the throat and choke them to the ground," and added that "the free use of the double-barrelled shotgun, properly pointed, would do some good just now," the *Times* denounced the remarks as incendiary. That fall conservatives swept the Republicans from power in a tidal wave of violence, and the *Pilot* closed down. Even then the *Times* could not resist taking a final shot at its rival, contending that the *Pilot*, by its "ill advised, vindictive course," had substantially contributed to the Republican defeat. "We have no tears to shed," the *Times* editor admitted, "over the sad fate of the *Pilot*." In 1876, its first year of Democratic or "Redeemer" rule, Mississippi slashed state printing expenses to $22,000. The following year, the *Jackson Times* disappeared. By 1877, the party was down to six papers, and in 1880 it had only one.[31]

South Carolina's Republican governors also employed printing patronage to reward papers supporting their administrations and to punish those opposed. In 1870, the Carolina Printing Company, formed by a group of state officials including Governor Robert K. Scott, controlled two papers, the *Charleston Daily Republican* and the *Columbia Daily Union*. The administration then contracted with the company to do the state's printing. After the *Republican*'s editors began charging the administration with corruption, Scott withdrew its patronage, forcing the paper to close. The *Daily Union* supported Scott's successor, Franklin Moses. In 1873, Moses bought control of the paper, which by then had become the *Daily Union-Herald*. The following year, under new owners, the paper backed Daniel H. Chamberlain for governor. Once elected, Chamberlain did much to rebuild the party's fortunes in the wake of the corruption associated with the Moses regime.[32]

In 1871, the clerks of the state house and senate, A. O. Jones and Josephus Woodruff, bought control of Governor Scott's publishing firm, renaming it the Republican Printing Company. The state legislature then authorized the two men to let contracts for the public printing, which they proceeded to assign to their own company. Their responsibility also included awarding contracts to papers around the state to publish laws and other state advertisements. Both Scott and Moses made sure to distribute these contracts among Democratic as well as Republican newspapers. According to Woodruff, Scott hoped that sharing patronage with opposition papers would "temper the tone of the press and insure a quiet, peaceable administration of the laws." In 1874, of twenty-five papers receiving state aid, only eight were Republican. Possibly this money helped to moderate the stance of the state's leading conservative paper, the Charleston *News and Courier*, but otherwise the opposition party press's criticism of the Republicans was unrestrained.[33]

Scott and Moses both employed printing patronage to keep Republican papers in line. In 1873, for instance, suspension of state aid to the Colleton *Gazette*, which was attacking Moses, caused it to close. Scott's control of patronage, however, did not sway James G. Thompson, editor of the *Beaufort Republican*, who denounced the governor and his "villainous ring." In 1872, Thompson's paper supported Greeley for president and in the gubernatorial race backed a Republican reform candidate who ran against Moses. After Moses won, Republicans resentful of Thompson's defection opened a rival newspaper in Beaufort, the *Southern Standard*, owned by Robert Smalls, the leading black politician in the Sea Islands. Smalls chaired the state senate printing committee and secured state printing for his paper. The rival sheets carried on a bitter editorial war in which Thompson accused the *Standard*'s owner of robbing the state by charging it exorbitant printing amounts. After Thompson left Beaufort to edit the Columbia *Union-Herald*, he continued the offensive against the whole system of state printing.[34]

South Carolina's printing expenditures were extremely high and accompanied by much corruption. To keep the state money flowing, Jones and Woodruff shamelessly bribed state legislators and other officials, including the strategically placed Robert Smalls. After Republicans had lost control of South Carolina, a Democratic investigating committee alleged that for several years the annual printing expenditure was sufficient to provide every voter in the state a bound copy of the laws. Over a two-year period, the state paid over $150,000 to three administration dailies and another $86,000 to weeklies for publishing various state laws and documents; in addition, over $42,000 went to five opposition dailies and almost $64,000 to twenty-nine opposition weeklies.[35]

According to the state comptroller, South Carolina's printing expenses from November 1871 to October 1872 reached almost $430,000, leaving a deficiency of $325,000. In its 1872–73 session, the legislature appropriated $450,000; $250,000 of this amount was designated to pay for printing ordered by the previous two legislatures, which included legislative journals, six volumes of state statistics, thirty-five hundred copies of revised statutes, five thousand extra copies of records of Ku Klux Klan trials held in the state, five thousand extra copies of reports of a joint legislative investigating committee, two volumes of supreme court decisions, and one thousand extra copies of general assembly reports and resolutions. Payments to newspapers around the state for publishing laws for the previous two legislatures came to $75,000; the lawmakers earmarked $100,000 for state printing for 1872–73 and $25,000 for newspaper advertising of laws passed in that session. Republican editor Henry Sparnick of the *Aiken Tribune* claimed that Democrats had exaggerated this expenditure, "large as we admit it to have been under any circumstances." He observed that the appropriation for fiscal 1872–73 was much less than amounts from previous years, which had totaled as much as $125,000. Much of the money for publishing laws in newspapers had gone to Democratic sheets; Sparnick contended that a rival paper in his own town had received more from the state than he had. He also noted that the state treasurer had made partial payments to him in depreciated notes while reporting that the state had paid the whole amount.[36]

In 1874, the Republicans elected Daniel H. Chamberlain governor on a reform platform. In his inaugural address, Chamberlain condemned the existing system of public printing as "utterly incapable of defense or excuse." For the past three years, he charged, the house and senate clerks had contracted for public printing and made drafts for payment "out of any moneys in the treasury not otherwise appropriated," with no limit fixed for such expenditures. He put the cost of public printing under this system at $843,073 from 1868 to 1874. The state had spent another $261,496 on advertising in local newspapers, bringing the total to $1,104,569. Most of this amount, $918,629, had been spent over the preceding three years. During the fiscal year 1874–75, the state spent another $160,000 on printing. At Chamberlain's urging, the legislature reduced printing appropriations for the 1875–76 fiscal year to $50,000, but it had to designate additional funds to meet deficiencies in previous years' printing allocations. By 1877, the year Democrats regained control of South Carolina, the state was down to five Republican newspapers; in 1880, there were none.[37]

Republican printing excesses peaked in Louisiana. The state's pre–Civil War printing costs had been much higher than elsewhere, reaching $60,000 one year, apparently because state documents were printed in both English and French. Louisiana's postwar government expended $50,000 on printing in both 1866 and 1867. In the first three years of Republican rule, however, Louisiana paid out $1.5 million in state warrants for printing. The New Orleans *Picayune* estimated that as much as $625,000 of this largesse went to the state printers who were owners of the *New Orleans Republican*. Printing the 1871 house journals alone cost $68,000. The *Picayune* observed that Governor Warmoth, who owned one fourth of the *Republican*'s stock, benefited directly from these payments. Much of the rest went to newspapers around the state designated by the administration to print state laws and official notices or to papers that published journals of both legislative houses in their columns. In 1871, the state paid $180,000 to New Orleans papers other than the *Republican* for such work. The legislature also required the Orleans Parish to publish its official material in the *Republican* at a cost that reached $50,000 in 1870.[38]

Inevitably this expenditure triggered criticism. Even though the state paid for printing in warrants worth half their face value, the amounts were clearly excessive. Democrats insisted that the state printing rate was in some cases six times higher than prewar averages. Texas state printers used such Louisiana figures to argue that their own charges were not excessive. The New Orleans mayor, who was a Republican, complained that if his city were allowed to make its own printing arrangements, it could save $37,000 a year.[39]

Printing patronage became an important weapon in the struggle between Governor Henry Clay Warmoth and a Republican faction led by the New Orleans customs collector, James F. Casey. In November 1871, Casey's forces established the *National Republican,* edited by George Carter, speaker of the house. Warmoth's paper, the *New Orleans Republican,* claimed the new sheet was supported primarily by contributions from federal officeholders. In turn, the *National Republican* charged that Warmoth was profiting personally from state patronage directed to the *Republican.* Both sides struggled for control of printing patronage directed to parish newspapers. In 1868, the legislature had empowered the governor, lieutenant governor, and house speaker to select journals in the parishes to do both state and parochial printing. In July 1871, members of the customs-house faction assembled a press convention where delegates from several dozen Republican newspapers heard Speaker Carter pledge that he and his ally, Lieutenant Governor Oscar Dunn, would direct this patronage to parish papers opposing the governor. Warmoth then criticized Dunn's and Carter's printing awards, claiming that legislative journals had been published in "fifteen obscure newspapers, some of which have never existed, while some of those that did exist never did the work they were employed to do." Later that year Dunn died, and Warmoth engineered the election of another African American politician, P. B. S. Pinchback, to the lieutenant governorship. Warmoth and Pinchback proceeded to cancel almost fifty printing contracts previously awarded by Dunn and Carter. Warmoth justified this as a reduction of unnecessary state expenditures, but most of his targets were newspapers opposing him.[40]

Before leaving office, Warmoth urged the legislature to reduce the prices paid for printing laws and journals in country papers, claiming this could save the state $150,000 a year. Warmoth's successor, William Pitt Kellogg, revoked a number of printing contracts, saving the state approximately $100,000. In 1872, the legislature reduced printing appropriations to around $155,000, and to $125,000 the following year, which still left Louisiana's printing budget much higher than that in other states. In 1875, the legislature restricted publication of statutes and journals to the official newspaper, and in 1876 it further reduced printing appropriations. After Republicans lost control of the state, the first Redeemer legislature limited the printing appropriation to $30,000. Liberal patronage policies had given Louisiana the largest number of Republican newspapers in the South, and it still had twenty in 1877, by far the largest number of any Southern state for that year. In 1880, however, it was down to six, three of them in New Orleans.[41]

After climbing rapidly as Reconstruction began, the number of Republican newspapers in the South declined swiftly as Democrats returned to power. During the years from 1865 to 1877, Republicans published about 31 percent of the region's partisan papers. The Reconstruction year with the highest number of Republican papers was 1871, with 163 in operation, or about 29 percent of the section's total. By 1877, the year the last Republican regimes disappeared in the South, the number of Republican papers had shrunk to seventy-six, 40 percent of which were in Tennessee and Louisiana. By 1880, the Republican total had fallen to forty-three, of which twelve were in Tennessee. In that year Republicans published only 10 percent of the partisan papers in the South.

Southern Republican editors responded in various ways to the collapse of their party's fortunes. Some tried to reconcile themselves to the new order of things. In Georgia, Jason Clarke Swayze, choleric editor of the Macon *American Union*, kept his paper going for about a year after Republicans lost control of the state in 1871. Chastened by defeat, he declared himself willing to "make friends of former rebels—Ku Klux, if you please," and claimed that he could detect "the gradual but certain emancipation of the Southern people from their deep prejudice." Infuriated after a Macon race riot in October 1872, however, he exclaimed that "a large class of people of the South were still uncivilized." The day after the riot, he advertised his paper for sale. He insisted he was not selling for financial reasons but observed that "when we have a choice of Heaven or Hell" he would certainly choose the former.[42]

In Alabama, where Republicans had regained state control in the 1872 election, a Northerner, G. M. Johnson, became owner of the longtime Republican paper, the *Huntsville Advocate*. In 1873, he adopted a stance similar to the one Swayze had taken the year before, favoring "malice toward none and charity toward all" and promising to promote northern Alabama's economic development. After Democrats won the 1874 election, however, he relinquished control of the paper. The *Advocate*'s new editor took an independent stance in politics. Robert A. Moseley also used the columns of his Talladega *Our Mountain Home* to promote charity and good feeling among Alabama's races and parties, but he did not back off in his advocacy of equal civil and political rights for blacks. In the spring of 1876, he sold his paper to a Democratic proprietor. During that year's presidential campaign in Alabama, Samuel Bard, the peripatetic editor who was now with the *Alabama State Journal*, also emphasized the Republican principles of equality before the law, free speech, free press, and free schools. His paper disappeared the following year.[43]

Other Republicans who faced defeat and elimination in their states similarly emphasized the values of free speech and open discussion and pled for a reduction in party animosity and abuse. They also continued to concede that their party needed to cleanse itself of corruption. As a crucial Mississippi election neared in 1875, several of the state's Republican editors warned that their party would lose unless it reformed itself. After Democrats won control of the state in a violence-ridden election, the editor of the Jackson *Daily Times* confessed that sundry Republican laws and measures were "inexcusable" and that many of the party's candidates had deserved to lose. He hoped that the party would reorganize under men of better character and work to end the internal bickering that had contributed to its defeat.[44]

By 1876, Republican regimes survived only in Florida, Louisiana, and South Carolina. In the aftermath of that year's contested presidential election, the editor of the *New Orleans Republican* urged the Republican candidate, Rutherford B. Hayes, not to secure the White House by turning those states over to the Democrats. The few Republican editors left in the other two states, however, were more resigned to defeat. In South Carolina, the editor of the *Beaufort Republican* had concluded before the election that the Republicans would lose and that "honesty and worth would reassert itself." The editor of the Columbia *Union-Herald* asserted that South Carolina's Democrats put the welfare of their state foremost, and he supported their quest for home rule, stating that it would bring stability and prosperity to South Carolina. When Democrats gained control of Florida, the editor of the Jacksonville *Florida Union* congratulated them on their restraint, convinced that the new state government would be headed by young and progressive men who would not seek revenge on the defeated Republicans. His paper's sole current aim, he claimed, was "to satisfy the business public and to subserve the best interests of the whole people [of the state] without regard to party." The *Florida Union* continued to endorse the national Republican party until 1880, when it fell under Democratic control.[45]

As the lights of the Republican Party winked out across the South, its editors looked back across its brief history in their section. *Asheville Pioneer* editor Pinckney Rollins, on commemorating the close of the paper's sixth year in 1872, noted that from its first issue the *Pioneer* had had to "combat the worst prejudices and passions of . . . that class of men in our State who deemed it an hereditary prerogative to hold the sceptre and rule the humble class just as their selfishness or caprice prompted." The paper's efforts had not been in vain, he concluded. The future was full of hope "for those worthy men in the South whose stumbling block in the road to political and social advancement was their poverty and whose stigma, in the eyes of their opulent neighbors, consisted in earning their bread by the sweat of the brow." Two years later Valentine Dell, who had edited the *Fort Smith New Era* since its inception in 1863, watched his party lose control of Arkansas and compared the Republicans' performance favorably to that of the Democrats, whom he charged with resisting emancipation and Reconstruction, fanning sectional strife, and fomenting race hatred. In Dell's eyes, the Republicans, by contrast, had sought to protect the rights of the humblest citizens of whatever race or class. In 1876, Edward M. Cheney, who had been associated with the Jacksonville *Florida Union* since 1867, contended that although Republican regimes in states like South Carolina, Mississippi, and Louisiana had been plagued with poor leadership and corruption, on the whole the results of Republican influence had been good for the South, bringing much needed reforms, creating prosperity, and "laying the foundation for future happiness."[46]

Whatever the Republicans had been able to achieve in the South owed much to their editors. In the face of constant ostracism and threats to their papers and even to their lives, they had kept a party press alive. Some of those editors were probably corrupt. John Hardy of the Montgomery *State Sentinel* supposedly took bribes while serving as an Alabama legislator, and John McClure of the *Little Rock Republican* was accused of bribing Arkansas lawmakers. In Florida, Edward Cheney of the *Florida Union* was involved in possibly illegal railroad and land speculations.[47] In some states, most notably South Carolina and Louisiana, certain Republican publishers benefited handsomely from the large subsidies the state governments lavished on them. But most Republican editors made little or no profit from their enterprises and often ran them at a loss, keeping newspapers operating with money from their own pockets. And through their efforts, they not only helped keep their party alive but also maintained its most idealistic principles.

Republican editors on the whole were convinced that the South would not develop without a free exchange of ideas, and they worked to combat social and sectional prejudices that limited or denied freedom of speech, thought, and press. Beginning with their opposition to the Black Codes in 1865–66, Republican editors fought for equal rights for African Americans and sought to counter Democratic appeals to white racism. Many editors hoped to uplift white farmers and laborers, whom they considered as oppressed as the freedmen. Most editors joined in the crusade to bring railroads to the South, hoping thereby to regenerate and modernize the Southern economy, and they later struggled to cleanse Republican administrations of corruption and inefficiency. Again and again they met with frustration. Radical editors failed to convince many white yeomen to join them in challenging the South's entrenched elites, while the efforts of more centrist editors to appeal to these same elites were similarly rebuffed. Railroads did not prove to be the panacea for Southern economic ills that Republicans had hoped. Instead, corruption and failed railroad schemes helped to bring their party down.

Nor did the Republican editors make much headway in their campaign to combat white racism, but as long as their papers endured, they kept the cause of civil and political equality alive. As Hiram W. Lewis, former sheriff of Lowndes County and one of the editors and publishers of the *Columbus Press*, announced that he was closing the paper and leaving Mississippi in November 1875, he praised the Republican Party for its commitment to the civil and political rights of all men and to the belief in the brotherhood of man. The blacks of the South, he declared, were part of the country, with the full rights of citizens, and should be treated as such. A year later, the editor of the *Jackson Daily Times*, whose paper was also about to go under, declared that "when the white people of Mississippi are entirely free, and not until then, will the colored people enjoy all the blessings which American citizenship should secure."[48] As long as white Mississippians followed the teachings of intolerant and proscriptive leaders, he predicted, "we can contemplate nothing but strife and insecurity, paralyzing industry, crippling enterprise, and inviting poverty and desolation." During the next ninety years, the history not only of Mississippi but of most of the South would prove the accuracy of his prediction.

Appendix: Republican Newspapers by State, 1865–1877

This list of Republican newspapers, organized by state, gives their titles, followed by frequency of issue (d = daily, t = triweekly, sw = semiweekly, w = weekly). The first set of dates refers to the years the paper was published. If the paper changed from Republican to Democratic, or vice versa, I have listed only the dates during which it appeared as a Republican journal. In making these determinations I relied heavily on George P. Rowell's *American Newspaper Directory*, which gives the date of the newspaper's establishment, its frequency of issue, its political affiliation, and its editor and publisher, as well as the size and number of its pages and its subscription cost.

Rowell, however, did not begin publishing his directory until 1869, and occasionally after that date an existing newspaper did not make his list. In some instances, publishers did not reveal their paper's political affiliation to Rowell, or identified it as neutral when it was not. Occasionally a paper identified in Rowell as Democratic turned out to be Republican. To do an inventory of Republican papers in the Reconstruction South prior to 1869, I relied on the newspapers themselves, which often clipped from one another, and also a variety of secondary sources. I used the newspapers to correct for Rowell's failure to identify some of them published after 1869 as Republican.

The second set of dates indicates what issues of each newspaper are still available for the years during which it appeared as a Republican publication. My main source for this undertaking was the Online Computer Library Center (OCLC) national bibliographic database, which I supplemented with the publications or lists produced by various state newspaper projects, some of which are still ongoing. Dates in brackets indicate that the run for that year or those years is not complete. I have used the abbreviations "nr" for no record and "is" for issue.

Tracing the trajectory and genealogy of individual newspapers is often complicated by the frequency with which newspapers changed their titles, a characteristic common to nineteenth-century American journalism. In an extreme example, one 1877 South Carolina newspaper had eight identities and antecedents in eight years: the *Beaufort Republican and Sea Island Chronicle* (1869–71) became the *Beaufort Republican* (1871–73). This newpaper then merged with the *Port Royal Commercial* in 1873 to become the *Port Royal Commercial and Beaufort Co. Republican*, which merged in 1874 with the Beaufort *Southern Standard* (1872–74) to constitute the *Port Royal Standard and Commercial*, and this in turn merged in 1877 with the Beaufort *Tribune* to form the *Beaufort Tribune and Port Royal Commercial* (1877–79). As a result of such frequent changes, the names of papers in this appendix may not always be consistent with those given in the main text.

No doubt, despite my efforts, some Republican newspapers may have eluded me, and some papers may exist that I have not been able to locate. Readers wishing to find which libraries, archives, or other depositories have issues or files of the newspapers listed should consult the OCLC.

ALABAMA (36)

Asheville *St. Clair Eagle*	w	1868–69	[1868–69]
Attala *Republican Union*	w	1871–72	nr
(prev. Gadsden *Republican Union*)			
Centreville *Apprentice*	w	1869–70	nr
Cullman *Southern Emigrant*	w	1876–77	nr
Dadeville *Tallapoosa News*	w	1868–69	nr
Dadeville *Tallapoosian*	?	1867	nr
Decatur *Alabama Republican*	w	1867–72	nr
Demopolis *Southern Republican*	w	1869–71	1869–71
Florence *Republican*	w	1874	[1874]
Gadsden *Republican Union*	w	1869–70	nr
(cont. as *Attala Republican Union*)			
Herald and Times	w	1871–73	[1871–73]
(prev. *Union Springs Times*; cont. as *Union Springs Herald*)			
Huntsville Advocate	t,w	1865–74	[1865–68], 1869–74
Lebanon *Republican Union*	w	1868–69	nr
Livingston *Messenger*	w	1867	[1867], 1 is
Mobile *Herald*	w	1871–72	[1871–72]
Mobile *Nationalist*	w	1865–69	1865–69
Mobile *Republican*	d,w	1870–72	[1870–72]
Mobile *Watchman*	w	1873–74	[1874], 1 is
(apparently also Montgomery *Watchman*, same years)			
Montgomery *Alabama State Journal*	d,w	1868–77	1868–76
Montgomery *Alabama State Sentinel*	d	1867–68	1867–68
Montgomery *Republican*	w	1874	[1874]
Montgomery *Republican Sentinel*	w	1872	[1872], 1 is
Moulton *Union*	w	1867–68	[1867–68]
Opelika *East Alabama Monitor*	w	1868–69	[1868–69]
(cont. as Opelika *Union Republican*)			
Opelika *East Alabama Signal*	w	1872–73	nr
Opelika *Union Republican*	w	1869	[1869]
(prev. Opelika *East Alabama Monitor*)			
Selma *National Republican*	t,w	1873–76	[1876], 1 is
Selma *Press*	w	1869–71	[1869–71]
Selma *Republican Union Advocate*	w	1867	[1867], 1 is
Talladega *Our Mountain Home*	w	1872–76	[1872–76]
Talladega *Sun*	w	1869–71	[1869–71]
Tuscaloosa *Reconstructionist*	w	1867–68	[1867, 1868]
Union Springs Herald	w	1873–75	1873–75
(prev. *Herald and Times*)			
Union Springs Times	w	1870–71	[1870–71]
(cont. as *Herald and Times*)			

Wetumpka *Elmore Republican*	w	1870–75	[1870–74]
Wetumpka *Elmore Standard*	w	1867	[1867]

ARKANSAS (52)

Arkadelphia *South Western Republican*	w	1872	nr
Arkansas City *Post*	w	1875–76	[1876], 2 is
Augusta *Sentinel*	w	1873–74	[1873], 1 is
Batesville *Republican*	w	1867–76	[1868], 1873–76
Camden *South Arkansas Journal*	w	1867–74	[1868], 1 is [1873], 1 is
Clarksville *Arkansas Standard* (prev. Fort Smith *Standard*)	w	1868–69	[1868], 1 is
Dardanelle *Eye of the West*	w	1872–73	[1873], 1 is
Dardanelle *Times*	w	1869–70	[1869], 2 is
De Vall's Bluff *White River Journal*	w	1868–74	[1868], 2 is [1873], 1 is
Dewitt *Indicator*	w	1877	nr
Dewitt Sentinel	w	1869–71	[1869], 1 is
DeWitt *The Elector*	w	1866–68	[1867], 1 is
El Dorado *Herald*	?	1871	nr
Fayetteville *Mountain Echo* (prev. Fayetteville *Radical*)	w	1867–72	[1867, 1868, 1871]
Fayetteville *News*	w	1871–74	[1873], 1 is [1874], 2 is
Fayetteville *Radical* (cont. as Fayetteville *Mountain Echo*)	?	1867	nr
Forrest City *Free Press* (prev. *Madison Free Press*)	w	1868–71	[1870–71]
Fort Smith *Arkansas Patriot*	w	1871–73	[1871, 1872, 1873]
Fort Smith *New Era*	w	1863–77	[1863–67, 1869–77]
Fort Smith *Standard* (cont. as Clarksville *Arkansas Standard*)	w	1867–68	[1867–68]
Harrisburg *Republican*	?	1870	nr
Harrison *Boone County Advocate*	w	1870–72	[1870], 1 is
Helena *Clarion*	d,w	1871–74	[1871, 1873]
Helena *Southern Shield*	w	1868–74	[1870]
Helena *Tribune*	w	1877	nr
Hot Springs Courier	w	1869–70	[1869–70]
Hot Springs *Visitor*	w	1877	[1877], 2 is
Jacksonport *Arkansas Statesman*	w	1869–73	[1873]
Lewisburg *Western Empire*	w	1872–74	[1873], 1 is
Lewisville *Red River Post* (prev. *Washington Post*)	w	1871	nr
Little Rock *Arkansas Freeman*	w	1869–71	[1869–70]

Little Rock *Arkansas State Journal* (prev. Little Rock *Liberal*)	d	1869–73	[1871–73]
Little Rock *Dispatch* (cont. as Little Rock *Republican*)	d	1866–67	nr
Little Rock *Evening Star*	d	1877	1877
Little Rock *Liberal* (cont. as Little Rock *Arkansas State Journal*)	?	1869	nr
Little Rock *Republican* (prev. Little Rock *Dispatch*)	d,w	1867–75	1867–75
Little Rock *True Republican*	d	1869	nr
Little Rock *Unconditional Union*	w	1864–66	[1864–66]
Madison Free Press (cont. as *Forrest City Free Press*)	w	1868–69	[1868], 1 is
Magnolia *Flower*	w	1869–73	nr
Monticello *Sage of Monticello*	?	1870	nr
Ozark *Tablet*	w	1870–71	nr
Pine Bluff *Jefferson Republican*	w	1868–77	[1870, 1873, 1875–76]
Pocahontas *Courier and Express* (prev. Pocahontas *Randolph Express*)	w	1873	nr
Pocahontas *Randolph County Courier*	w	1870–72	[1871], 1 is
Pocahontas *Randolph Express* (cont. as Pocahontas *Courier and Express*)	w	1868–72	nr
Pocahontas *Randolph Republican*	w	1874	nr
Russellville *National Tribune*	w	1871–74	[1871, 1873]
Searcy *Arkansas Tribune*	w	1870–76	nr
Washington *Carpetbag*	?	1868	nr
Washington *Post* (cont. as Lewisville *Red River Post*)	w	1868–70	nr
Wittsburg *Gazette*	w	1871–74	[1873], 1 is?

FLORIDA (22)

Fernandina Observer	w	1871–74	[1872, 1873, 1874]
Fernandina *Peninsula*	w	1863–64	[1863–64]
Gainesville *Florida Independent*	w	1870–73	[1870], 1 is [1873], 2 is
Gainesville *New Era*	w	1873–74	[1873], 1 is
Jacksonville *Florida Agriculturist*	w	1874–77	[1874–75]
Jacksonville *Florida Republican*	w	1871–73	[1873], 1 is
Jacksonville *Florida Sun*	w	1872–77	[1876, 1877]
Jacksonville *Florida Times*	w	1865–68	[1865–66]
Jacksonville *Florida Union*	d,w	1867–77	[1867–77]
Jacksonville *Herald*	w	1865	[1865], 1 is
Jacksonville *New South*	w	1874–75	1874–75

Appendix

Key West Dispatch	w	1872–77	[1872], 1 is
			[1873], 1 is
			[1876], 1 is
Key West *El Republicano*	w	1876	nr
Key West *Guardian*	w	1870–74	[1873], 1 is
Key West *Key of the Gulf*	w	1875–77	[1876–77]
Lake City *Herald*	w	1872–75	[1871–72]
Monticello *Advertiser*	w	1872–75	[1873], 1 is
Pensacola *Florida Express*	w	1872–75	[1871, 1872, 1875]
Pensacola *Observer*	t,w	1866–70	[1866, 1868]
Pensacola *Republican*	w	1872–74	[1872], 1 is
			[1874], 1 is
Tallahassee *Sentinel*	w	1868–77	[1868–76]
Tampa *True Southerner*	w	1868–69	[1868]

GEORGIA (19)

Atlanta *Daily Opinion*	d,w	1866–68	1867–68
Atlanta *Deutsche Zeitung*	w	1870–72	nr
Atlanta *Gate City*	w	1874–75	nr
(cont. as Atlanta *Republican*)			
Atlanta *New Era*	d,w	1867–71, 1874–75	nr
Atlanta *Republican*	w	1876–77	[1876], 1 is
(prev. Atlanta *Gate City*)			
Atlanta *True Georgian*	d	1870–71	[1870], 1 is
Atlanta *Whig*	w	1872	[1872], 1 is
Augusta *Colored American*	w	1865–66	[1865–66]
(cont. as Augusta *Loyal Georgian*)			
Augusta *Daily Press*	w	1866–67, 1869	1866–67, 1869
Augusta *Georgia Republican*	w	1869–71	[1870, 1871]
Augusta *Loyal Georgian*	d,w	1866–68	[1866–68]
(prev. Augusta *Colored American*)			
Augusta *National Republican*	d,w	1867–68	[1868]
Bainbridge *Weekly Sun*	w	1873–74	[1873–74]
Dalton *North Georgia Republican*	w	1867–68	[1867], 1 is
Fort Valley *Southwest Georgian*	w	1870–74	[1873], 1 is
Griffin/Macon *American Union*	w	1867–73	1867–73
Savannah *Daily Republican*	d	1865–67	1865–67
Savannah *Freemen's Standard*	w	1868	[1868]
Savannah *Journal*	w	1872–73	[1872]

LOUISIANA (73)

Alexandria *Rapides Gazette*	w	1869–77	1871–73, 1876, 1877
Amite City *Independent*	w	1874–76	[1874]

Amite City *Tangipahoa Advocate*	w	1869–72	[1869–71]
Baton Rouge *Courier*	w	1869–70	[1869–70]
(cont. as Baton Rouge *Grand Era*)			
Baton Rouge *Grand Era*	w	1870–77	[1873, 1874, 1875, 1877]
(prev. Baton Rouge *Courier*)			
Baton Rouge *State Journal*	w	1871–72	[1872], 1 is
Bellevue *Bossier Sentinel*	w	1876–77	[1876], 1 is
Brashear *Attakapas Register*	w	1868–78	[1870, 1875, 1876–77]
(pub. in Franklin, 1871–74; Morgan City 1876–77)			
Carrollton *Louisiana State Register*	w	1869–74	1870–72, 1873
Carrollton *Radical Standard*	w	1868–69	[1868, 1869]
(cont. as New Orleans *Republican Standard*)			
Carrollton *Sentinel*	w	1873–75	nr
(also pub. as Gretna *Jefferson Sentinel*)			
Clinton *Herald*	?	1868–70	[1870], 1 is?
Convent *Le Louisianais*	w	1865–83	[1865–81]
Convent *St. James Sentinel*	w	1869–77	1873–75
Delta *Madison Mail*	w	1868–70	nr
Donaldsonville *Ascension Republican*	w	1870–71	nr
Donaldsonville *Chief*	w	1871–78	1871–78
Edgard *Republican Pioneer*	?	1868–75	[1868, 1873]
(also pub. in Bonnet Carre)			
Elton *Eagle*	w	1868–69	nr
Feliciana *Ledger*	w	1876–77	nr
(prev. St. Francisville *Dunn Leader*)			
Gretna *Jefferson Sentinel*	w	1873–77	1873–76
(also pub. as Carrollton *Sentinel*)			
Homer *Blackburn's Homer Iliad*	w	1867–75	[1867–68, 1875]
Houma *Terrabone Banner*	w	1873–75	nr
Houma *Terrabone Patriot*	w	1868–73	[1870, 1873]
Houma *Terrabone Republican*	w	1871–77	[1871, 1875]
Lafourche *Reformer*	?	1871–72	nr
(also pub. as Thibodaux *LaFourche Republican*)			
Lake Providence *Carroll Republican*	?	1874	nr
(also pub. as Providence *Carroll Republican*)			
Lake Providence *True Republican*	w	1875–76	[1876]
Marksville *Avoyelles Republican*	w	1873–77	[1873, 1876]
Marksville *Weekly Register*	w	1868–72	[1868–69]
Monroe *Louisiana Intelligencer*	w	1865–77	[1868, 1873, 1874, 1876]
Napoleonville *Assumption Advocate*	w	1867–69	[1869], 1 is
Napoleonville *Assumption Chronicle*	w	1868–72	[1871], 1 is?

Natchitoches *Red River News*	w	1868–78	[1868, 1871, 1873, 1876]
Natchitoches *Weekly Republican*	w	1874–77	[1875, 1876]
New Iberia *Iberia Statesman*	w	1871–73	nr
New Iberia *Progress*	w	1872–77	nr
New Orleans *Advocate*	w	1866–69	[1866–67]
New Orleans *Black Republican*	w	1865	[1865]
New Orleans *Christian Republican*	w	1870–71	nr
New Orleans *Citizen's Guard*	w	1871	nr
New Orleans *Deutsche Zeitung*	d	1867–77	1869–77
New Orleans *Free South*	w	1868	[1868], 1 is
New Orleans *Le Sud*	w	1873–74	[1873], 1 is
New Orleans *Louisianan*	sw,w	1870–82	1870–82
New Orleans *Mitrailleuse*	w	1871–72	[1871–72]
New Orleans *National Republican*	d,w	1871–72	1871–72
New Orleans *Republican*	d,w	1867–77	1867–68, 1871–76
New Orleans *Republican Standard* (prev. Carrollton *Radical Standard*)	w	1868–71	1869–70
New Orleans *Tribune*	d,t,w	1864–69	1864–67, 1869
Opelousas *St. Landry Progress*	w	1867–68	1867–68
Plaquemine *Iberville News*	w	1871–73	[1873], 1 is
Plaquemine *Iberville Pioneer* (cont. as Plaquemine *Pioneer and News*)	w	1868–74	[1869, 1870, 1871]
Plaquemine *Iberville Republican*	w	1874–77	[1875, 1876]
Plaquemine *Pioneer and News* (prev. Plaquemine *Iberville Pioneer*)	w	1874	nr
Point Coupee *Echo*	w	1869–71	[1869–71]
Pointe A La Hache *Empire Parish*	w	1868–71	nr
Pointe A La Hache *Plaquemine Republican*	w	1872–74	nr
Pointe Coupee *Republican*	w	1871–77	[1872, 1873, 1874, 1877]
Ponchatoula *Livingston Herald*	w	1868–69	[1869], 1 is?
Providence *Carroll Republican* (also pub. as Lake Providence *Carroll Republican*)	w	1871–73	[1873]
Providence *Lake Republican*	w	1873–75	[1873, 1874]
Shreveport *Republican*	w	1871–72	nr
Shreveport *South-Western Telegram*	w	1873–77	[1873, 1874]
Starlight *Sparta Times*	w	1870–71	1870–71
St. Francisville *Dunn Leader* (cont. as *Feliciana Ledger*)	w	1872–75	[1873–75]
St. Francisville *Feliciana Republican*	sw,w	1869–74	[1869–73]
St. Joseph *North Louisiana Journal*	w	1871–77	1872–74
St. Martinsville *Echo*	w	1872–78	[1873], 1 is
St. Martinsville *Times*	w	1871–72	nr

St. Sophie *Plaquemines Sentinel*	w	1872–77	[1873, 1876]
Thibodaux *LaFourche Republican*	w	1869–71	[1868, 1870]
(also pub. as *Lafourche Reformer*)	1874–76	[1876]	
Thibodaux *LaFourche Union*	w	1876	nr

MISSISSIPPI (61)

Aberdeen *True Republican*	w	1874–76	[1875], 1 is
Ashland *Benton County Argus*	w	1873–77	[1873, 1876]
Austin *Cotton Plant*	w	1871–77	[1873, 1876]
Austin *Republican*	w	1872–74	[1873], 1 is
Brandon *Eastern Argus*	w	1874–75	nr
Canton *American Citizen*	w	1874–75	1874–75
Canton *Canton Citizen*	w	1869	nr
Columbus *Lowndes County Republican*	w	1869–70	[1869], 1 is
(cont. as *Columbus Press*)			
Columbus Press	w	1870–76	1873–76
(prev. Columbus *Lowndes County Republican*)			
Corinth Courier	w	1872–73	nr
Corinth *New Era*	w	1870–71	[1870], 1 is
Corinth News	w	1868	[1868]
Corinth Republican	w	1871	nr
Corinth Union	?	1867	nr
Fayette Vindicator	w	1874–75	nr
Floreyville Star	?	1874	nr
Friar's Point Delta	w	1869–74	[1869–71]
Friar's Point Signal	w	1868–70	nr
Greenville Republican	w	1873–75	nr
Grenada Republican	w	1874–76	[1876], 1 is
Hernando *North Mississippian*	w	1870–71	nr
Holly Springs *Mississippi Tribune*	w	1874–75	nr
Holly Springs *North Mississippian*	w	1871–72	[1871], 1 is
Holly Springs *Star*	w	1870	[1870], 1 is
Jackson *Colored Citizen*	?	1869–71	nr
Jackson *Daily State Register*	?	1870	nr
Jackson Daily Times	d	1875–78	[1875–76]
(prev. *Vicksburg Times and Republican*)			
Jackson *Mississippi Pilot*	d,w	1868–76	[1869–76]
Jackson *Mississippi State Journal*	w	1868	[1868], 1 is
Jackson *People's Journal*	?	1870	nr
Jackson *State Leader*	d,sw,w	1871–72	[1872]
Jackson *Tribune*	?	1871	nr
Kosciusko *Central Republican*	w	1872–74	[1873], 1 is

Appendix

Kosciusko Chronicle	w	1871–72	[1871–72]
Lexington Advertiser	w	1871–72	[1872]
Lexington Holmes County Republican	w	1874–75	[1874], 1 is?
Macon Free Opinion	?	1874–75	[1874], 1 is?
Meridian Chronicle	sw,w	1867–68	1868
Meridian Daily Gazette	?	1873–74	nr
Natchez New South	w	1869–74	[1873], 1 is?
(cont. as New South and Post)			
Natchez Post	?	1873–74	nr
(cont. as New South and Post)			
New South and Post	?	1874–76	[1874], 1 is?
(merger of Natchez New South and Natchez Post)			
Okolona Prairie News	w	1870–76	[1873, 1874]
Oxford Oxonian	w	1869–70	nr
Oxford Richochet	w	1874–75	nr
Pontotoc Equal Rights	w	1870–71	nr
Sea Coast Republican	?	1873–77	[1873, 1876]
(prev. Shieldsboro Bay St. Louis Gazette)			
Senatobia Signet	w	1873–75	[1874]
Shieldsboro Bay St. Louis Gazette	w	1871–72	
(cont. as Sea Coast Republican)			
Starkville Whig	w	1875	nr
Summit Times	w	1873–75	[1873] ?
Vicksburg Colored Citizen	?	1867	nr
Vicksburg Monitor	w	1875–76	[1875], 1 is
Vicksburg Plain Dealer	w	1874–75	[1875], 1 is
Vicksburg Republican	?	1867–69	[1867], 1868
Vicksburg Times and Republican	d,w	1870–75	1870–75
(cont. as Jackson Daily Times)			
West Point Times	w	1873–74	[1873], 1 is
			[1874], 1 is
Winona Republican	?	1871	nr
Woodville Republican	w	1869–77	[1869–70, 1872]
Yazoo City Herald	w	1872–77	[1875]
Yazoo City Republican	w	1869–71	nr

NORTH CAROLINA (37)

Asheville Pioneer	w	1867–77	[1867–75]
(prev. Henderson Pioneer)			
Bakersville Roan Mountain Republican	w	1876–77	[1876, 1877]
Beaufort Old North State	sw,w	1864–65	1865
Charlotte North Carolina Guardian	d	1866–67	[1867]

Charlotte *Union Republican*	w	1867–69	[1868]
Elizabeth City *North Carolinian*	w	1869–77	1869–77
Greensboro *New North State*	w	1871–77	1871–77
Greensboro *Republican*	w	1870–71	[1870]
Greensboro *Republican Gazette*	w	1869–70	[1869]
Greensboro *Topic* (prev. Greensboro *Union Register*)	?	1869	[1869], 1 is
Greensboro *Union Register* (cont. briefly as Greensboro *Topic*)	w	1866–69	[1869]
Henderson *Pioneer* (cont. as *Asheville Pioneer*)	w	1866–67	[1866–67]
Jefferson *Weekly Times*	w	1870–71	nr
Lexington *Central*	w	1875–76	[1876]
Mount Airy *Surry Visitor*	w	1872–77	[1872, 1874, 1876]
New Bern *Republican* (combined with *New Bern Times*, 1869)	d,t,w	1867–68	1867–68
New Bern *Republic and Courier* (cont. as *New Bern Times and Republic-Courier*)	w	1871–74	[1871–74]
New Bern *Times* (combined with *New Bern Republican*, 1869)	d	1865–76	1865–74
New Bern Times and Republic-Courier (prev. New Bern *Republic and Courier*)	?	1874–76	[1874, 1876]
Raleigh *Carolina Era* (cont. as Raleigh *Era and Examiner* and Raleigh *Era*)	w	1871–73	1871–73
Raleigh *Daily Examiner* (cont. as Raleigh *Era and Examiner*)	d	1874	[1874]
Raleigh *Daily Telegram*	d,w	1871	[1871]
Raleigh *Era* (prev. Raleigh *Carolina Era*)	?	1875–76	[1875–76]
Raleigh *Era and Examiner* (prev. Raleigh *Carolina Era* and Raleigh *Daily Examiner*)	w	1874	[1874]
Raleigh *Gazette*	w	1870–71	[1871], 1 is
Raleigh *Journal of Freedom*	?	1865	[1865]
Raleigh *North Carolina Standard*	d,w	1865–70	1865–70
Raleigh *Weekly Republican*	w	1867, 1874	[1867, 1874]
Rutherfordton *Rutherford Star*	w	1866–75	[1866–75]
Salem *American Advocate*	w	1870–71	[1870]
Salem *People's Press*	w	1869–70	[1870]
Statesville American	w	1872–74	1872–74
Washington Index	w	1867	[1867]

Appendix

Wilmington Post	d,sw,w	1867–77	1867–77
Wilmington *Union and Republican*	w	1871–72	nr
Winston *National Republican*	w	1871–73	[1872], 1 is
(cont. as Winston *Union Republican*)			
Winston *Union Republican*	w	1873–77	[1874–77]
(prev. Winston *National Republican*)			

SOUTH CAROLINA (46)

Abbeville *Republican*	w	1873	nr
Abbeville *True American*	w	1873	nr
Aiken *Tribune*	w	1871–76	[1876]
Beaufort County Times	w	1871–74	[1871, 1872]
(cont. as Blackwell *Barnwell County Times*)			
Beaufort *Free South*	w	1863–64	[1863–64]
Beaufort *Republican*	w	1871–73	[1871–73]
(prev. *Beaufort Republican and Sea Island Chronicle*; cont. as *Port Royal Commercial and Beaufort County Republican*)			
Beaufort Republican and Sea Island Chronicle	?	1869–71	[1869, 1870]
(cont. as *Beaufort Republican*)			
Beaufort *Southern Standard*	w	1872–74	[1872–73]
(cont. as *Port Royal Standard and Commercial*)			
Beaufort *Tribune*	w	1874–76	1874–76
(cont. as *Beaufort Tribune and Port Royal Commercial*)			
Beaufort Tribune and Port Royal Commercial	w	1877–79	[1877]
(merger of *Beaufort Tribune* and *Port Royal Standard and Commercial*)			
Blackwell *Barnwell County Times*	?	1874–75	nr
(prev. *Beaufort County Times*)			
Blackwell *Sun*	w	1875	nr
Carolina New Era	w	1869–74	nr
(prev. *Spartanburg Republican*)			
Charleston *Advocate*	w	1867–69	[1867–68]
Charleston *Daily Evening Bulletin*	d	1873	[1873]
(cont. as *Charleston Daily Express*)			
Charleston Daily Express	d	1875	[1875], 1 is
(prev. Charleston *Daily Evening Bulletin*)			

Charleston *Daily Republican* (cont. as *Charleston Republican*)	d,w	1869–72	1869–71, 1872
Charleston *Free Press*	w	1868	[1868]
Charleston *Independent*	w	1875–76	[1876], 1 is
Charleston *Journal*	w	1866–67	[1866], 2 is
Charleston *Missionary Record*	w	1868–77	[1871, 1873, 1876]
Charleston *Nationalist*	d	1871–72	nr
Charleston *Republican* (prev. Charleston *Daily Republican*)	d	1876–77	[1876]
Charleston *South Carolina Leader*	w	1865–66	[1865–66]
Charleston *South Carolina Republican* (moved to Columbia 1869–70)	w	1868–70	[1868–70]
Charleston *The Southern Celt*	w	1869–73	[1872–73]
Colleton Gazette (cont. as *Colleton Republican*)	w	1872–73	nr
Colleton Republican (prev. *Colleton Gazette*)	w	1874–75	nr
Columbia *Daily Evening Herald*	d,w	1873	[1873]
Columbia *Daily Republican* (cont. as *South Carolina Republican*)	d	1868	[1868]
Columbia *Daily Union* (briefly Columbia *Union-Herald*)	d	1870–75	[1871, 1872–74]
Columbia *Union-Herald* (merger of Columbia *Daily Union* and *Herald*)	nr	1873–74	nr
Darlington *New Era*	w	1865–66	[1865–66]
Georgetown *Planet*	w	1873–75	[1873, 1874]
Greenville *Republican*	w	1873–75	[1873]
Kingstree *Williamsburg Republican*	w	1873–77	[1874, 1876]
Orangeburg *Carolina Times*	w	1865–67	[1866–67]
Orangeburg *Free Citizen*	w	1874–76	[1875]
Orangeburg News	w	1872–75	1872–75
Orangeburg News and Times	w	1875–77	1875–77
Port Royal *Commercial and Beaufort County Republican* (merger of *Beaufort Republican* and *Port Royal Commercial*; cont. as *Port Royal Standard and Commercial*)	nr	1873–74	[1873–74]
Port Royal *New South*	w	1862–66	[1862–65]
Port Royal *Standard and Commercial* (merger of *Beaufort Southern Standard* and *Port Royal Commercial and Beaufort County Republican*; cont. as *Beaufort Tribune and Port Royal Commercial*)	?	1874–76	[1874–76]

Appendix

South Carolina Republican	?	1869–70	[1870]
(prev. Columbia *Daily Republican*)			
Spartanburg Republican	w	1870–71	[1871], 1 is
(cont. as *Carolina New Era*)			
Walterboro News	w	1873–77	[1873–75]

TENNESSEE (51)

Athens News	?	1874–77	nr
Athens Republican	w	1867–69	[1867–69]
Chattanooga Citizen	w	1870–71	[1870], 1 is
Chattanooga Commercial	?	1877–88	[1877–88]
Chattanooga Daily Republican	d,w	1867–69	1867–69
Chattanooga Herald	d,w	1872–73	nr
Chattanooga *Tennessee Weekly Journal*	w	1876	[1876], 1 is
Clarksville Patriot	w	1867–70	[1867, 1869]
Cleveland *Commercial Republican*	w	1872–74	[1873–74]
(cont. as Cleveland *Weekly Herald*)			
Cleveland *Weekly Herald*	w	1874–76	1875–76
(prev. Cleveland *Commercial Republican*)			
Clinton *Union Pilot*	w	1868–69	[1869], 1 is
Columbia Times	?	1876	nr
Cookeville News	w	1870–73	[1873], 1 is
Dandridge *Watchman*	?	1877–80	[1877–80]
Elizabethton Republican	w	1876	[1876], 1 is
Gallatin *Sumter County Republican*	w	1868	[1868]
Greeneville *New Era*	w	1865–86	[1865–86]
Harrison *Unconditional*	w	1866–67	[1867], 1 is
Huntington *Tennessee Republican*	w	1870–77	[1871], 2 is [1873], 1 is
Huntington *West Tennessean*	w	1868–70	[1868–69]
Jonesborough *Herald and Tribune*	w	1869–77	[1869–76]
Jonesborough Times	?	1877–78	[1877–78]
Jonesborough *Union Flag*	w	1865–73	[1865–73]
Kingston *Roane County Herald*	?	1877–78	[1877–78]
Kingston *Valley News*	w	1873–74	[1873–74]
Knoxville Daily Chronicle	d,w	1870–74	[1870–73]
(cont. as *Knoxville Whig and Chronicle*)			
Knoxville *Daily True Republican*	d	1871	[1871]
Knoxville Whig	w	1864–69	1866–69
Knoxville *Whig and Chronicle*	?	1870–82	[1870–82]
(prev. *Knoxville Daily Chronicle*)			
Lebanon Record	w	1868–69	[1868–69]

Maryville *Independent*	?	1873–76	[1873–76]
Maryville *Republican*	w	1867–77	[1867–77]
Maryville *Soldier's Gazette*	w	1870–71	[1870], 1 is
McMinnville *Enterprise*	w	1866–70	[1866–70]
Memphis *Bulletin*	d	1855–68	[1867]
Memphis *Die Neue Zeit*	?	1862–67?	nr
Memphis *Planet*	?	1872–77	[1872–77]
Memphis *Post*	d,t,w	1866–69	1868–69
Memphis *Republican*	?	1872–73	nr
Memphis *Weekly Republican*	w	1866	[1866]
Murfreesboro *Freedom's Watchman*	w	1867–68	[1867–68]
Nashville *Bulletin*	w	1871–76	[1873], 1 is
Nashville *Colored Tennessean*	w	1865–66	[1865–66]
Nashville *Daily Republican*	d,w	1868	[1868]
Nashville *National True Republican*	w	1874–75	nr
Nashville *Press and Times*	d,w	1863–69	1866–69
Nashville *Tennessee Staatszeitung*	d,w	1866–70	[1866], 1 is
Nashville *Tennessee Tribune*	w	1870–72	[1870–72]
Nashville *Union*	d	1862–66	1862–66
Philadelphia *Union Pilot*	w	1868–69	nr
Shelbyville *Republican*	w	1866–69	[1866, 1868, 1869]

TEXAS (57)

Austin *Daily State Journal*	d,w	1870–74	1870–74
Austin *Freedman's Press*	w	1868	[1868]
Austin *Republican*	d,w	1867–71	1868–71
Austin *Southern Intelligencer*	w	1865–67	1865–67
Austin *Texas Staats Zeitung*	t,w	1873–74	[1873], 1 is
Austin *Vorwarts*	d,w	1871–75	[1871–73]
Bastrop *Deutsche Zeitung* (cont. as Brenham *Texas Volksbote*)	w	1873–74	nr
Blanco City *West Texas Republican*	w	1872–73	nr
Bosque *Beacon*	w	1867–68	[1867–68]
Brenham *Texas Volksbote* (prev. Bastrop *Deutsche Zeitung*)	w	1874–77	1874–77
Brownsville *Ranchero*	d,w	1871–75	nr
Brownsville *Republican*	sw	1867–68	[1867]
Bryan *Brazos Eagle*	w	1870–71	nr
Calvert *Tribune*	sw	1870–72	[1871, 1872]
Canton *Weekly News*	w	1872–74	[1873], 1 is
Corpus Christi *Nueces Valley*	w	1869–74	1870–74
Corsicana *Progressive Age*	w	1873–74	nr
Crockett *Central Journal*	?	1869–70	nr
Crockett *East Texas Herald*	w	1872–73	nr

Dallas *Norton's Union Intelligencer*	w	1871–76	1871–73, 1874–76
Denison *Cresset*	d,w	1874–76	nr
Denison *New South*	w	1873–74	nr
Fort Worth *Northern Texas Epitomist*	w	1873–74	nr
Galveston *Argus*	w	1875–76	nr
Galveston *Flake's Bulletin*	d,sw,w	1865–72	1865–72
Galveston *Free Man's Press*	w	1868	[1868]
Galveston *Mercury*	w	1874–75	[1874–75]
Galveston *Republican*	w	1868, 1871	[1868, 1871]
Galveston *Standard*	sw	1872–73	[1872, 1873]
Galveston *Unabhangige*	w	1873–75	nr
Galveston *Union*	t,w	1868–72	1868–69
Galveston *Weekly Spectator*	w	1871–76	[1873]
Georgetown *Watchman*	w	1867–71	[1867, 1869, 1870, 1871]
Goliad *Guard*	w	1869–72	[1869–72]
Hamilton *West Texas Herald*	?	1871	nr
Houston *Texas Volksblatt*	w	1867–72	1869–71
Houston *Union*	d,t,w	1868–73	1868–70
Huntsville *Union Republican*	w	1867–73	[1869, 1871]
Jasper *Jasper County Radical*	w	1870–71	nr
Jefferson *Radical*	w	1869–71	[1869–70]
Jefferson *Texas Mail*	w	1873–74	nr
Liberty *Observer*	w	1870	[1871]
Livingston *Republican*	?	1867	nr
Lockhart *Texas Digest*	w	1870–71	nr
Marshall *Weekly*	w	1870–72	nr
McKinney *Messenger*	w	1867–74	[1867–72]
New Braunfels *Vorwarts*	?	1869	nr
Paris *Texas Vindicator*	w	1867–71	[1867–68, 1871]
Quitman *Clipper*	?	1867–68	nr
Sabine Pass *Sabine City Union*	w	1868–71	nr
San Antonio *Express*	d,w	1866–76	1867–76
San Antonio *Freie Presse fur Texas*	w	1865–80	1865–80
Sherman *Patriot*	w	1871–77	[1873, 1876, 1877]
Starr's Academy *Intelligencer*	w	1869	nr
Tyler *National Index*	w	1866–76	[1869, 1870, 1873, 1876]
Tyler *Weekly Newsletter*	w	1872	nr
Waco *Register*	sw,w	1870–79	[1875, 1876]

VIRGINIA (24)

Alexandria *Daily State Journal* (cont. as Richmond *State Journal*)	d	1862–68	[1864, 1865, 1866, 1868]
Alexandria *Liberal Citizen*	w	1871–72	[1871], 1 is
Fredericksburg *Ledger*	sw	1870–74	1870–74

Hampton *True Southerner*	w	1865–66	1865–66
Harrisonburg *American Union*	w	1866–68	1866–68
Leesburg *Loudon Republican*	w	1869–72	[1870, 1871, 1872]
Lynchburg *Press*	sw,t,w	1869–76	[1869–71, 1873, 1876]
(cont. as *Weekly Press and Record*)			
Lynchburg *Radical Record*	w	1867	[1867], 1 is
Marion *Record*	w	1866–70	[1867], 2 is
(cont. as *Weekly Press and Record*)			
Marion *Southwestern Chronicle*	w	1873	nr
Norfolk *Day Book*	d	1870	nr
Norfolk *Old Dominion*	d	1863–66	[1863–64, 1865–66]
Norfolk *Union Republican*	w	1866–67	[1867], 1 is
Petersburg *Daily Times*	d	1868–69	1868–69
Richmond *Independent Republican*	w	1869	[1869]
Richmond *National Virginian*	sw,w	1870–72	[1871]
Richmond *New Nation*	d,w	1865–68	[1865, 1866, 1867, 1868]
Richmond *Register*	d,sw,w	1868	[1868]
Richmond *State*	d	1876–77	[1876, 1877]
Richmond *State Journal*	d,w	1868–76	[1868–74]
(prev. Alexandria *Daily State Journal*)			
Staunton *Valley Virginian*	w	1871–77	[1873, 1876, 1877]
Weekly Press and Record	?	1870–76	[1870–76]
(merger [1870] of *Lynchburg Press* and *Marion Record*)			
Winchester *Journal*	w	1865–69	1865–69
Williamsburg *Virginia Gazette*	w	1869–71	[1869]

Notes

Introduction

1. Frank Luther Mott, *American Journalism, A History: 1690–1960*, 3rd ed. (New York, 1962), 167–92, 253–81, 368–70; Culver H. Smith, *The Press, Politics, and Patronage: The American Government's Use of Newspapers, 1789–1875* (Athens, Ga., 1977), xi, 12–13, 19, 22, 42, 60, 70; Hazel Dicken-Garcia, *Journalistic Standards in Nineteenth-Century America* (Madison, 1989), 29–62; Gerald J. Baldasty, *The Commercialization of News in the Nineteenth Century* (Madison, 1992), 14–35; William E. Gienapp, " 'Politics Seem to Enter into Everything': Political Culture in the North, 1840–1860," in *Essays on American Antebellum Politics, 1840–1860*, ed. William E. Gienapp et al. (College Station, Tex., 1982), 41–42; Carl R. Osthaus, *Partisans of the Southern Press: Editorial Spokesmen of the Nineteenth Century* (Lexington, Ky., 1994), 1–4.

2. Dicken-Garcia, *Journalistic Standards*, 47–48, 52, 161–62; Baldasty, *Commercialization of News*, 25; Thomas D. Clark, *The Southern Country Editor* (Indianapolis, 1948), 23; Charles Francis Ritter, "The Press in Florida, Louisiana, and South Carolina and the End of Reconstruction, 1865–1877: Southern Men with Northern Interests" (Ph.D. diss., Catholic University of America, 1976), 12–15, 26–30, 32–34.

3. Michael Perman, *Reunion without Compromise: The South and Reconstruction, 1865–1868* (Cambridge, Mass., 1973), 352–53; Clark, *Southern Country Editor*, 23; Donald E. Reynolds, *Editors Make War: Southern Newspapers in the Secession Crisis* (Nashville, 1966), vii, 5, 9–10.

4. Osthaus, *Partisans of the Southern Press*, 10.

5. Richard H. Abbott, *The Republican Party and the South, 1855–1877: The First Southern Strategy* (Chapel Hill, 1986), 3–41.

6. Reynolds, *Editors Make War*, 214–17; Sidney Andrews, *The South since the War* (Boston, 1866), 389; E. Merton Coulter, *The South during Reconstruction, 1865–1877* (Baton Rouge, 1947), 289; *Laurensville Herald* quoted in Jeanette M. Bergeron, "Reconstruction Journalism in South Carolina" (master's thesis, University of South Carolina, 1974), 8, 39; Clark, *Southern Country Editor*, 22.

7. For a stimulating discussion of the Republicans and the problem of legitimacy, see Lawrence N. Powell, "Southern Republicanism during Reconstruction: The Contradictions of State and Party Formation" (paper presented at the annual meeting of the Organization of American Historians, 1984).

8. Jean Folkerts, "Functions of the Reform Press," *Journalism History* 12 (1985): 22–25. See also Theodore R. Mitchell, *Political Education in the Southern Farmers' Alliance, 1887–1900* (Madison, 1987), 96–107; Lawrence Goodwyn, *Democratic Promise: The Populist Moment in America* (New York, 1976), 354–81. In the late 1820s, Northern Antimasons organized a third party to combat the allegedly insidious influence of Freemasonry. Convinced that the existing political press would not give them a fair hearing, they established papers of their own, arguing that a "free press" was necessary to "enlighten and stimulate public opinion." See Baldasty, *Commercialization of News*, 15, 17, 29.

9. Robert H. Woody, *Republican Newspapers of South Carolina* (Charlottesville, Va., 1936).

10. Coulter, *The South during Reconstruction*, 287; Hodding Carter, *Their Words Were Bullets: The Southern Press in War, Reconstruction, and Peace* (Athens, Ga., 1969), 45–46. The two papers Carter cites with approval are the *Savannah Republican* and the Atlanta *New Era*, both of which were quite conservative. Eric Foner, *Reconstruction: America's Unfinished Revolution, 1863–1877* (New York, 1988); Mark Wahlgren Summers, *The Press Gang: Newspapers and Politics, 1865–1877* (Chapel Hill, 1994), 213. Present-day historians continue to use the Reconstruction-era epithets "carpetbagger" (a Northern-born politician or businessperson living in the post–Civil War South) and "scalawag" (a white Southern Republican) without endorsing their pejorative implications. Foner, *Reconstruction*, 295.

1. Origins of the Southern Republican Press

1. Richard Lowe, "Republican Newspapers in Antebellum Virginia," *West Virginia History* 28 (1967): 282–84; Richard Lowe, *Republicans and Reconstruction in Virginia, 1856–1870* (Charlottesville, 1991), 8–10; Donovan H. Bond, "How the Wheeling *Intelligencer* Became a Republican Organ," *West Virginia History* 11 (1950): 160–84.

2. Stephen V. Ash, *When the Yankees Came: Conflict and Chaos in the Occupied South, 1861–1865* (Chapel Hill, 1995), 44, 58.

3. James Marten, "For the Army, the People, and Abraham Lincoln: A Yankee Newspaper in Occupied Texas," *Civil War History* 39 (1993): 130; Lester J. Cappon, "The Yankee Press in Virginia, 1861–1865," *William and Mary Quarterly* 2nd series, 15 (1935): 81–88; Robert H. Woody, *Republican Newspapers of South Carolina* (Charlottesville, 1936), 3–10.

4. The editor of one Unionist paper admitted that he had only one hundred subscribers and "a few transient ads" and that the only means of maintaining his paper was through job work contracted with the War Department. See *Fort Smith New Era*, March 18, 1865.

5. On the history of government printing patronage, see Culver H. Smith, *The Press, Politics, and Patronage: The American Government's Use of Newspapers, 1789–1875* (Athens, Ga., 1977). For Seward's action in awarding printing contracts during the war, see "Miscellaneous Letters Received Regarding Publication of the Laws, 1784–1875," E-151 in Record Group 59, General Records of the Department of State, National Archives,

Notes to Chapter One

Washington, D.C. (hereafter cited as R.G. 59). For a list of papers receiving U.S. patronage, see E-154, "Lists of Publishers of Laws, 1850–1974," R.G. 59, National Archives.

6. Carrol H. Quenzel, *Edgar Snowden, Sr., Virginia Journalist* (Charlottesville, 1954), 41–44.

7. Francis H. Pierpont to William Henry Seward, December 24, 1863; D. Turner to Seward, December 30, 1863; and Cowing and Gillis to Seward, December 13, 1865, R.G. 59, National Archives. *Journal of the Constitutional Convention . . . at Alexandria convened February 13, 1864* (Alexandria, 1865), 6, 47; Lowe, *Republicans and Reconstruction*, 10–24, 208 n.38; Smith, *The Press, Politics, and Patronage*, 237.

8. Lenoir Chambers and Joseph E. Shank, *Salt Water and Printer's Ink: Norfolk and Its Newspapers, 1865–1965* (Chapel Hill, 1967), 5–6; Cappon, "Yankee Press in Virginia," 85–86; Spencer Wilson, "Experiment in Reunion: The Union Army in Civil War Norfolk and Portsmouth, Virginia" (Ph.D. diss., University of Maryland, 1973), 97, 100, 162, 188, 210–11, 221. Francis H. Pierpont to William Henry Seward, December 24, 1863; R. E. Gassett and others to Seward, January 2, 13, 1864; Benjamin Butler to Seward, December 20, 1864; L. A. Hagans to Seward, January 2, 1865; E. M. Brown to Seward, January 11, March 5, 1865; A. Watson Atwood to Seward, January 25, 1865; W. J. Cowing to Seward, January 25, February 28, 1865; Charles Botts and others to Seward, April 5, 1865, R.G. 59, National Archives.

In June 1862, federal troops seized the press and materials of the Williamsburg *Virginia Gazette* and began publication of the *Cavalier*, using its columns to promote loyalty to the Union, opposition to slavery, and support for the Lincoln administration. The editors published a few issues in 1862; the press and type were moved from Williamsburg to Yorktown, where they printed a few more issues in 1863. These materials eventually ended up at Fortress Monroe in dilapidated condition. After the war, the *Gazette*'s publisher, R. A. Lively, found them and returned them to Williamsburg, where he resumed publication of his paper.

9. Woody, *Republican Newspapers*, 3–6.

10. Ibid., 6–9; Willie Lee Rose, *Rehearsal for Reconstruction: The Port Royal Experiment* (Indianapolis, 1964), 78, 277–78, 317; James G. Thompson to William Henry Seward, August 15, 1864, R.G. 59, National Archives; *Florida Union*, March 25, 1865; Woody, *Republican Newspapers*, 9–10; W. L. King, *The Newspaper Press of Charleston* (Charleston, 1872), 124–25.

11. Norman D. Brown, *Edward Stanly: Whiggery's "Tarheel Conqueror"* (University, Ala., 1974), 242–45; Alan D. Watson, *A History of New Bern and Craven County* (New Bern, N.C., 1987), 381, 412; New Bern *North Carolina Times*, January 9, 16, May 25, June 22, 1864; George Mills Joy to William Henry Seward, March 27, April 9, December 10, 1864, January 1, 2, 1865, R.G. 59, National Archives.

12. W. McKee Evans, *Ballots and Fence Rails: Reconstruction on the Lower Cape Fear* (New York, 1966), 41, 47–48, 216; Munson and Cook to William Henry Seward, March 18, 1865, R.G. 59, National Archives. The *Herald of the Union* shortly began to appear as the *Herald*; it lasted until early 1866.

13. Horace Gibbs Davis Jr., "Newspapers of Pensacola, 1821–1900," *Florida Historical Quarterly* 37 (1959): 433, and "Florida Journalism during the Civil War" (master's thesis, University of Florida, 1952), 31, 83, 85, 87; John Allen Meador, "Florida Political Parties, 1865–1877" (Ph.D. diss., University of Florida, 1974), 11–12.

14. Davis, "Florida Journalism during the Civil War," 94–97; Meador, "Florida Political Parties," 14–16; John E. Johns, *Florida during the Civil War* (Gainesville, 1963), 192–93.

15. Johns, *Florida during the Civil War*, 200; Davis, "Florida Journalism during the Civil War," 98, 99–102, 191–92; Morrill and Stickney to William Henry Seward, November 26, 1864, January 5, 1865, R.G. 59, National Archives.

16. Richard H. Abbott, "The Republican Party Press in Reconstruction Georgia, 1867–1874," *Journal of Southern History* 61 (1995): 726–27; Savannah *National Republican*, December 29, 1865; *Savannah Daily Herald*, January 11, 1865.

17. Fayette Copeland, "The New Orleans Press and Reconstruction," *Louisiana Historical Quarterly* 30 (1947): 301–2; Peyton McCrary, *Abraham Lincoln and Reconstruction: The Louisiana Experiment* (Princeton, 1978), 166–67.

18. McCrary, *Abraham Lincoln and Reconstruction*, 166–67.

19. Ibid., 186–236; Ted Tunnell, *Crucible of Reconstruction: War, Radicalism and Race in Louisiana* (Baton Rouge, 1984), 26–50.

20. N. P. Banks to William Henry Seward, January 11, 1864; Hill and Hill to Seward, February 4, 1864; W. R. Fish to Seward, March 21, 1864, R.G. 59, National Archives. Copeland, "New Orleans Press," 306; McCrary, *Abraham Lincoln and Reconstruction*, 213, 221–25, 268, 272; Tunnell, *Crucible of Reconstruction*, 58, 60.

21. Thomas J. Davis, "Louisiana," in *The Black Press in the South, 1865–1979*, ed. Henry Lewis Suggs (Westport, Conn., 1983), 151–56; William P. Connor, "Reconstruction Rebels: The *New Orleans Tribune* in Post-War Louisiana," *Louisiana History*, 21 (1980): 161–63; Jean-Charles Houzeau, *My Passage at the New Orleans Tribune: A Memoir of the Civil War Era*, ed. and with an introduction by David C. Rankin, trans. Gerard F. Denault (Baton Rouge, 1984), 19–23, 34–35; McCrary, *Abraham Lincoln and Reconstruction*, 181, 199, 229; Joseph Logsdon and Caryn Cosse Bell, "The Americanization of Black New Orleans, 1850–1900," in *Creole New Orleans: Race and Americanization*, ed. Arnold R. Hirsch and Joseph Logsdon (Baton Rouge, 1992), 221–29. For a careful analysis of *L'Union*, see Caryn Cosse Bell, *Revolution, Romanticism, and the Afro-Creole Protest Tradition in Louisiana, 1718–1868* (Baton Rouge, 1998), 223–52.

22. Connor, "Reconstruction Rebels," 163–70; Houzeau, *My Passage at the New Orleans Tribune*, 23–38; Davis, "Louisiana," 156, 159; Bell, *Revolution, Romanticism*, 252–55.

23. Tunnell, *Crucible of Reconstruction*, 85; Howard J. Jones, "Biographical Sketches of Members of the 1868 Louisiana State Senate," *Louisiana History* 19 (1978): 71–73; Davis, "Louisiana," 156–59; *Black Republican*, May 13, 1865; Logsdon and Bell, "Americanization of Black New Orleans," 229–30, 238–39.

24. John S. Kendall, "The Foreign Language Press of New Orleans," *Louisiana Historical Quarterly* 12 (1929): 374; Tunnell, *Crucible of Reconstruction*, 162–63; Robert T. Clark Jr., "Reconstruction and the New Orleans German Colony," *Louisiana Historical Quarterly* 23 (1940): 502.

25. Copeland, "New Orleans Press," 308 (quote); McCrary, *Lincoln and Reconstruction*, 249, 310; John Rose Ficklin, *History of Reconstruction in Louisiana through 1868* (Baltimore, 1910), 76.

26. William C. Harris, *With Charity for All: Lincoln and the Restoration of the Union* (Lexington, Ky., 1997), 58–72, 149–53.

27. Richard N. Current, *Lincoln's Loyalists: Union Soldiers from the Confederacy* (Boston, 1992), 218; Gordon McKinney, *Southern Mountain Republicans, 1865–1900: Politics and the Appalachian Community* (Chapel Hill, 1978), 12, 16–27.

28. Guy Harry Stewart, "History and Bibliography of Middle Tennessee Newspapers, 1799–1876" (Ph.D. diss., University of Illinois, 1957), 43–45, 155–57; Peter Mazlowski, *Treason Must Be Made Odious: Military Occupation and Wartime Reconstruction in Nashville, Tennessee, 1862–1865* (Millwood, N.Y., 1978), 55; Walter T. Durman, *Reluctant Partners: Nashville and the Union, July 1, 1863–June 30, 1865* (Nashville, 1987), 65–72. S. C. Mercer to William Henry Seward, May 10, 1862; William Cameron to Seward, July 16, 1863; Andrew Johnson to Seward, March 5, 1864, R.G. 59, National Archives.

29. Joseph H. Parks, "Memphis under Military Rule, 1862–1865," *East Tennessee Historical Society Publications* 14 (1942): 34–35; Ernest Walter Hooper, "Memphis, Tennessee: Federal Occupation and Reconstruction, 1862–1870" (Ph.D. diss., University of North Carolina, 1957), 32, 41, 48; Karl J. R. Arndt and May Olsen, *German-American Newspapers and Periodicals, 1732–1955: History and Bibliography*, 2nd ed. (New York, 1965), 613; U.S. Congress, *House Select Committee on the Memphis Riots* (Washington, D.C., 1866; repr. N.Y., 1969), 212–15.

30. For a recent treatment of East Tennessee's tortured history during the Civil War, see Noel C. Fisher, *War at Every Door: Partisan Politics and Guerrilla Violence in East Tennessee, 1860–1869* (Chapel Hill, 1998).

31. E. Merton Coulter, *William G. Brownlow, Fighting Parson of the Southern Highlands* (Chapel Hill, 1937), 179–205, 250–51; W. G. Brownlow to William Henry Seward, April 2, 1864, R.G. 59, National Archives; Gilbert E. Govan and James W. Livingood, "Chattanooga under Military Occupation, 1863–1865," *Journal of Southern History* 17 (1951): 28, 37.

32. Vernon M. Queener, "The Origin of the Republican Party in East Tennessee," *East Tennessee Historical Society Publications* 13 (1941): 78–80; Durman, *Reluctant Partners*, 72–73, 155, 182, 184.

33. James Welch Patton, *Unionism and Reconstruction in Tennessee, 1860–1869* (Chapel Hill, 1934), 86–87, 98–104, 114, 119; *Daily Nashville Union*, June 10, 1864, January 17, 1865; *Chattanooga Daily Gazette*, March 5, June 10, 1864; *Memphis Daily Bulletin*, May 8, June 15, 1864, January 21, 1865. In 1865, the Nashville *Press* merged with the *Daily Times and True Union*; S. C. Mercer, who controlled the new paper, called the *Press and Times*, strongly supported the Brownlow government and eventually the Republican Party.

34. Carl H. Moneyhon, *The Impact of the Civil War and Reconstruction on Arkansas* (Baton Rouge, 1994), 96, 102, 110, 121–22, 130–32.

35. Ibid., 157; Ed Bearss and Arrell M. Gibson, *Fort Smith: Little Gibraltar on the Arkansas* (Norman, Okla., 1969), 239, 263, 271; Fred W. Allsopp, *History of the Arkansas*

Press for a Hundred Years and More (Little Rock, 1922), 417–18, 565–66; *Fort Smith New Era*, October 8, November 10, 1863, February 6, May 21, 1864.

36. Allsopp, *History of the Arkansas Press*, 355; Moneyhon, *Impact of the Civil War*, 157–58. The *Western Clarion* issued a prospectus in March 1864 and published an unnumbered issue on May 2; it did not appear on a regular basis until April 1, 1865, and that issue is numbered vol. 1, no. 1.

37. Moneyhon, *Impact of the Civil War*, 160–62; *Fort Smith New Era*, December 26, 1863, April 2, May 21, June 18, 1864; *Daily National Democrat*, November 9, December 5, 1864; *Western Clarion*, April 1, 1865; William Burnett to Seward, April 14, May 10, 1864, January 28, 1865, and C. C. Bliss to Seward, April 25, 1864, R.G. 59, National Archives.

38. John G. Barrett, *The Civil War in North Carolina* (Chapel Hill, 1963), 174, 181–97; William T. Auman and David D. Scarboro, "The Heroes of America in Civil War North Carolina," *North Carolina Historical Review* 58 (1981): 340; Mark W. Kruman, "Dissent in the Confederacy: The North Carolina Experience," *Civil War History* 27 (1989): 295–313.

39. J. G. de Roulhac Hamilton, *Reconstruction in North Carolina* (New York, 1914), 50; Sidney Andrews, *The South since the War* (Boston, 1866), 158; Whitelaw Reid, *After the War: A Tour of the Southern States, 1865–1866*, ed. with an introduction by C. Vann Woodward (New York, 1965), 42–44; William C. Harris, *William Woods Holden: Firebrand of North Carolina Politics* (Baton Rouge, 1987), 89–159.

40. T. Conn Bryan, *Confederate Georgia* (Athens, Ga., 1953), 9–10, 139–52.

41. Malcolm C. McMillan, *The Disintegration of a Confederate State: Three Governors and Alabama's Wartime Home Front, 1861–1865* (Macon, Ga., 1986), 1–4, 22, 41, 58–62, 128–31; Walter Lynwood Fleming, *Civil War and Reconstruction in Alabama* (New York, 1905), 218–20.

42. James W. Garner, *Reconstruction in Mississippi* (New York, 1901), 126–27; John K. Bettersworth, *Confederate Mississippi: The People and Policies of a Cotton State in Wartime* (Baton Rouge, 1943), 205–44. Ira A. Batterton to William Henry Seward, November 4, 1864, January 9, 1865; N. P. Banks to Seward, December 27, 1864, R.G. 59, National Archives.

43. Current, *Lincoln's Loyalists*, 93–103; Carl H. Moneyhon, *Republicanism in Reconstruction Texas* (Austin, 1980), 9–16; James Marten, *Texas Divided: Loyalty and Dissent in the Lone Star State, 1856–1874* (Lexington, Ky., 1990), 22–35.

44. John L. Waller, *Colossal Hamilton of Texas* (El Paso, 1968), 34–55; N. P. Banks to William Henry Seward, December 27, 1864, R.G. 59, National Archives.

45. Raleigh *North Carolina Standard*, New Bern *North Carolina Times* (soon renamed the *New Bern Times*), Pensacola *Observer*, *Savannah Republican*, *Fort Smith New Era*, New Orleans *Deutsche Zeitung*, Memphis *Bulletin*, Memphis *Die Neue Zeit*, Nashville *Daily Press and Times*, *Brownlow's Knoxville Whig*.

46. *Wilmington Herald*, Beaufort *Old North State*, *Chattanooga Daily Gazette*, Helena *Western Clarion*, Little Rock *Unconditional Union*, Little Rock *National Democrat*.

47. In 1866, conservative proprietors controlled all four papers.

2. Limited Expansion

1. Joe Gray Taylor, *Louisiana Reconstructed, 1863–1877* (Baton Rouge, 1974), 58–77.

2. Richard Lowe, *Republicans and Reconstruction in Virginia, 1856–1870* (Charlottesville, 1991), 17–37; Henry T. Shanks, "Disloyalty to the Confederacy in Southwestern Virginia, 1861–1865," *North Carolina Historical Review* 21 (1944): 118–35; Alexandria *Virginia State Journal*, August 17, September 4, 1865.

3. Thomas B. Alexander, *Political Reconstruction in Tennessee* (Nashville, 1950), 101–9; Thomas S. Staples, *Reconstruction in Arkansas, 1862–1874* (New York, 1923), 101–9; Carl H. Moneyhon, *The Impact of the Civil War and Reconstruction on Arkansas* (Baton Rouge, 1994), 199.

4. Dan T. Carter, *When the War Was Over: The Failure of Self-Reconstruction in the South, 1865–1867* (Baton Rouge, 1985), 27, 32; Eric Foner, *Reconstruction: America's Unfinished Revolution, 1863–1877* (New York, 1988), 187.

5. John L. Bell Jr., "Andrew Johnson, National Politics, and Presidential Reconstruction in South Carolina," *South Carolina Historical Magazine* 83 (1981): 354–66; Francis Butler Simkins and Robert H. Woody, *South Carolina during Reconstruction* (Chapel Hill, 1932), 43–44; Jerrell H. Shofner, *Nor Is It Over Yet: Florida in the Era of Reconstruction, 1863–1877* (Gainesville, 1974), 32–46; Elizabeth Studley Nathans, *Losing the Peace: Georgia Republicans and Reconstruction, 1865–1871* (Baton Rouge, 1968), 11–14; William C. Harris, *Presidential Reconstruction in Mississippi* (Baton Rouge, 1967), 11–13, 228–30; James M. Swords to William Henry Seward, September 27, 1865, R.G. 59, National Archives; Dan T. Carter, *When the War Was Over: The Failure of Self-Reconstruction in the South, 1865–1867* (Baton Rouge, 1985), 40–45.

6. Thomas M. Owen, *History of Alabama and Dictionary of Alabama Biography*, 4 vols. (Chicago, 1921), 3:575; *Southern Advocate*, July 18, 1860; Sarah Woolfolk Wiggins, "Unionist Efforts to Control Alabama Reconstruction, 1865–1867," *Alabama Historical Quarterly* (1968): 51; Sarah Woolfolk Wiggins, *The Scalawag in Alabama Politics, 1865–1881* (University, Ala., 1977), 8.

7. Wiggins, *Scalawag*, 8, and "Unionist Efforts to Control Alabama Reconstruction," 52–54, 57–58; Carter, *When the War Was Over*, 45–46.

8. Carter, *When the War Was Over*, 47–54; William C. Harris, *William Woods Holden: Firebrand of North Carolina Politics* (Baton Rouge, 1987), 159–95. The Salisbury *Union Banner* and the *Wilmington Herald* disappeared shortly after the election. The Charlotte *Western Democrat*, while continuing to speak well of Holden, never became a Republican paper. See Harris, *William Woods Holden*, 192, 243.

9. J. G. de Roulhac Hamilton, *Reconstruction in North Carolina* (New York, 1914), 138, 140; James Lawrence Lancaster, "The Scalawags of North Carolina, 1850–1868" (Ph.D. diss., Princeton University, 1974), 89–90; New Bern *Weekly Times*, September 25, 1866; *Rutherford Star*, May 30, September 26, 1866; Harris, *William Woods Holden*, 205–6. Pennington moved to Alabama, where he was elected as a Republican to the state senate in 1868. See Raleigh *North Carolina Standard*, February 19, 1868.

10. James Marten, *Texas Divided: Loyalty and Dissent in the Lone Star State, 1856–1874* (Lexington, Ky., 1990), 130–32; Carl H. Moneyhon, *Republicanism in Reconstruction Texas* (Austin, 1980), 17–22, 22–44.

11. Walter L. Buenger, "Secession and the Texas German Community: Editor Lindheimer vs. Editor Flake," *Southwestern Historical Quarterly* 82 (1978–79): 382–89, 394–97; Moneyhon, *Republicanism in Reconstruction Texas*, 20. A. J. Hamilton to William Henry Seward, October 6, 1865; Ferdinand Flake to Seward, July 25, 1865; George W. Paschal to James Harlan, October 10, 1865, R.G. 59, National Archives.

12. Selma M. Raunick, "A Survey of German Literature in Texas," *Southwest Historical Quarterly* 33 (1929): 145–46; James Alex Baggett, "Origins of Early Texas Republican Party Leadership," *Journal of Southern History* 40 (1974): 446–47; Marilyn McAdams Sibley, *Lone Stars and State Gazettes* (College Station, Tex., 1983), 280–81, 294, 296, 298; A. B. Norton to William Hunter, June 27, 1865, R.G. 59, National Archives.

13. John L. Waller, *Colossal Hamilton of Texas* (El Paso, 1968), 63; Marten, *Texas Divided*, 146–47; Charles W. Ramsdell, *Reconstruction in Texas* (New York, 1910), 109, 123; Moneyhon, *Republicanism in Reconstruction Texas*, 46–50; *Weekly Southern Intelligencer*, April 5, 12, May 24, June 7, 1866. On the *McKinney Messenger*, see Albert H. Latimer to William Henry Seward, February 22, 1866, R.G. 59, National Archives, and *Weekly Southern Intelligencer*, June 23, 1866.

14. Foner, *Reconstruction*, 196–97, 239–41.

15. Charles H. Ambler, *Francis H. Pierpont: Union War Governor of Virginia and Father of West Virginia* (Chapel Hill, 1937), 315; New Bern *North Carolina Times*, January 9, 1864; *Rutherford Star*, May 30, 1866; Raleigh *Weekly North Carolina Standard*, March 28, 1866; Jonesborough *Union Flag*, April 13, 1866.

16. *Chattanooga Daily Gazette*, March 5, 1864; *Fort Smith New Era*, October 8, November 10, 1863; see also *Memphis Morning Post*, January 15, 1866; *Nashville Daily Union*, December 19, 1863, March 3, 1864; *Brownlow's Knoxville Whig and Rebel Ventilator*, February 20, 1864 (hereafter cited as *Knoxville Whig*); New Bern *North Carolina Times*, January 9, March 23, 1864; Helena *Western Clarion*, April 1, 8, 1865; Richmond *Republic*, August 31, 1865.

17. *Brownlow's Knoxville Whig and Rebel Ventilator*, November 11, 1863, April 30, 1864, April 19, 1865; Jonesborough *Union Flag*, February 16, April 13, 1866; Greeneville *New Era*, September 9, 1865; John Richard Dennett, *The South as It Is: 1865–1866* (Repr., New York, 1965), 133; Joe A. Mobley, *James City: A Black Community in North Carolina, 1863–1900* (Raleigh, 1981), 52, 55; *Florida Union*, September 30, October 28, December 9, 1865.

18. *Memphis Morning Post*, January 16, 23, 26, 27, 1866; Nashville *Daily Press and Times*, September 4, 12, 1865, Feb. 11, 1866; *Weekly North Carolina Standard*, March 21, August 8, October 10, 1866; *Huntsville Advocate*, November 17, 1871; Wiggins, *Scalawag*, 8; Austin *Weekly Southern Intelligencer*, October 4, 11 (quote), 1866; Alrutheus A. Taylor, *The Negro in Tennessee, 1865–1880* (Washington, D.C., 1941), 14–17, 276 n.66; *Flake's Bulletin* quoted in *Weekly Southern Intelligencer*, February 8, 1866; *Fort Smith New Era*, July 23, September 10, 1864, April 29, May 6, 13, 27, 1865; Shelbyville *American Union*, August

5, 1865; *McMinnville Enterprise,* May 19, 1866; Alexandria *Virginia State Journal,* August 18, October 12, 24, 26, 1865; Richmond *Republic,* January 7, 13, 28, February 24, 1866; Harrisonburg *American Union,* April 28, September 22, 1866.

19. Fort Smith *New Era,* April 29, 1865; Richard H. Abbott, *The Republican Party and the South, 1855–1877: The First Southern Strategy* (Chapel Hill, 1986), 61–71.

20. Horace Gibbs Davis Jr., "Florida Journalism during the Civil War" (master's thesis, University of Florida, 1952), 192–95; Leonard Henderson Sims, "A Study of the Florida Press during the Reconstruction Years, 1865–1870" (master's thesis, University of Florida, 1958), 22, 23, 30–31, 48, 49; *Florida Union,* June 17, 24, July 29, 1865, May 5, 1866; John Allen Meador, "Florida Political Parties, 1865–1877" (Ph.D. diss., University of Florida, 1974), 38, 54–55; Canter Brown Jr., *Ossian Bingley Hart: Florida's Loyalist Reconstruction Governor* (Baton Rouge, 1997), 161, 175.

21. John Hayes to John Andrew, May 24, 1865, Andrew Papers, Massachusetts Historical Society, Boston, Mass.; *Savannah Republican,* April 25, September 4, October 4, November 20, 1865; Carter, *When the War Was Over,* 239; *Savannah Daily Herald,* September 8, 9, 1865.

22. Ruth Currie-McDaniel, *Carpetbagger of Conscience: A Biography of John Emory Bryant* (Athens, Ga., 1987), 56–65; John R. DeTreville, "Reconstruction in Augusta, Georgia, 1865–1868" (master's thesis, University of North Carolina, 1979), 29, 43, 50; Augusta *Colored American,* December 30, 1865, January 13, 1866; I. Garland Penn, *The Afro-American Press and Its Editors* (Springfield, Mass., 1891; repr., New York, 1969), 100–104; Martin E. Dann, ed., *The Black Press, 1827–1890: The Quest for National Identity* (New York, 1971), 29, 90, 140–46. There is no evidence of Shuften's antebellum status. After the Republican Party was organized in Georgia, he urged blacks to join it. See Edmund L. Drago, *Black Politicians and Reconstruction in Georgia: A Splendid Failure* (Baton Rouge, 1982), 33.

23. Simkins and Woody, *South Carolina during Reconstruction,* 41, 55.

24. Darlington *New Era,* July 18, 25, 1865; *South Carolina Leader,* October 7, 21, 1865, March 31, May 12, 1866; Robert H. Woody, *Republican Newspapers of South Carolina* (Charlottesville, 1936), 11–13. See references to the *South Carolina Leader* in Mobile *Nationalist,* July 5, 1866, noting that earlier in the summer the paper had "turned traitor" but that by July it had changed hands and was again a "loyal colored man's paper." The *Leader* called for enfranchising the freedmen and supported the Republican Party. See Mobile *Nationalist,* July 26, August 23, 1866.

25. Moneyhon, *Republicanism in Reconstruction Texas,* 52–58; Marten, *Texas Divided,* 147; *Weekly Southern Intelligencer,* November 25, 1865, June 28, August 30, October 11, 1866; *Flake's Bulletin* quoted in *Weekly Southern Intelligencer,* January 17, 1867; Henry Lewis Suggs and Bernadine Moses Duncan, "North Carolina," in *The Black Press in the South,* ed. Henry Lewis Suggs, 258; Edward P. Brooks to James Harlan, September 25, 1865, R.G. 59, National Archives; Raleigh *Journal of Freedom,* September 30, 1865; Otto Olsen, *Carpetbagger's Crusade: The Life of Albion Winegar Tourgee* (Baltimore, 1965), 34–35, 61, 63; Raleigh *Daily Progress,* May 27, 1865; *North Carolina Standard,* September 26, 1866;

Rutherford Star, October 10, 1866; Alan D. Watson, *A History of New Bern and Craven County* (New Bern, N.C., 1987), 429.

According to excerpts published in his newspaper, Edward P. Brooks served four years in the Union Army. He was captured at one point and escaped from a Confederate prison. In 1865, he was the North Carolina correspondent for the *New York Times* and also served as an editor of the Raleigh *Progress* until he established his own paper. See Raleigh *Journal of Freedom,* October 14, 1865.

26. *Huntsville Advocate,* November 17, 1871; Wiggins, *Scalawag,* 8; Mobile *Nationalist,* July 19, 1866; Michael W. Fitzgerald, *The Union League Movement in the Deep South: Politics and Agricultural Change during Reconstruction* (Baton Rouge, 1989), 34–36; Allen Woodrow Jones, "Alabama," in *The Black Press in the South,* ed. Henry Lewis Suggs, 23–24; Maxine D. Jones, "Edward Chalmers Silsby and Talladega College," *Alabama Review* 41 (1988): 271–73; Dennett, *The South as It Is,* 300–302.

27. *Fort Smith New Era,* April 29, 1865; Philip D. Uzee, "The Beginnings of the Louisiana Republican Party," *Louisiana History* 12 (1971): 204–6; *New Orleans Tribune,* September 28, 1865; Ralph Morrow, *Northern Methodism and Reconstruction* (East Lansing, 1956), 221.

28. Lowe, *Republicans and Reconstruction in Virginia,* 41, 48; Richmond *Republic,* May 17, 27, July 25, 1865, February 10, 14, 1866 (quote from March 1, 1866); Lester J. Cappon, *Virginia Newspapers, 1821–1935: A Bibliography with Historical Introduction and Notes* (New York, 1936), 25–26, 140; *Norfolk Post* quoted in Nashville *Weekly Press and Times,* March 11, 1866.

29. Lowe, *Republicans and Reconstruction in Virginia,* 40–41, 57–58; Alfred H. Terry to John Underwood, September 30, October 7, 1865, Underwood Papers, Library of Congress, Washington, D.C. (hereafter cited as LC); Philip S. Foner, ed., *The Life and Writings of Frederick Douglass,* 4 vols. (New York, 1950–1955), 4:54–55; John C. Underwood to John Andrew, October 4, 1865, Andrew Papers, Massachusetts Historical Society, Boston, Mass.; Richmond *New Nation,* March 22, May 24, June 21, November 29, 1866, February 7, 28, 1867, December 18, 1868.

30. Robert Francis Engs, *Freedom's First Generation: Black Hampton, Virginia, 1861–1890* (Philadelphia, 1979), 93–94; *True Southerner,* December 14, 1865, January 18, 25, March 8, 29, November 24, 1866; Thomas C. Parramore, *Norfolk: The First Four Centuries* (Charlottesville, 1994), 227, 236.

31. Frederick Morton, *The Story of Winchester in Virginia* (Strasburg, Va., 1925), 146–48, 184, 187; John W. Wayland, *A History of Rockingham County, Virginia* (Dayton, Va., 1912), 115–16, 132–22, 156–57; *Winchester Journal,* October 22, 1865; Harrisonburg *American Union,* May 26, September 29, 1866 (quote), October 27, 1866; Lowe, *Republicans and Reconstruction in Virginia,* 59–60.

32. *Memphis Bulletin,* March 1, June 11, 1865; Greeneville *New Era,* December 23, 1865, July 7, September 9, 1866; Greeneville *National Union,* March 14, 1867, clipping in David Patterson to William Henry Seward, March 18, 1867, R.G. 59, National Archives; Mitzi V. Bible, ed., *Community in Transition: Greene County, Tennessee, 1865–1900* (Greeneville,

Notes to Chapter Three 213

Tenn., 1986), 15–16; *Colored Tennessean*, October 7, 1865; Jonesborough *Union Flag*, December 8, 1865. On Scott, see Charles W. Cansler, *Three Generations: The Story of a Colored Family of East Tennessee* (Kingsport, Tenn., 1939), 14, 26–28, 32–34, and Samuel Shannon, "Black Newspapers in Tennessee," in *The Black Press in the South*, ed. Henry Lewis Suggs, 313–15.

33. *Chattanooga Daily Gazette*, June 19, 1864, January 18, 1865; Nashville *Daily Press and Times*, August 18, September 8, 1865, January 28, 1866; *Brownlow's Knoxville Whig*, October 11, 1865, April 4, 1866; Alexander, *Political Reconstruction in Tennessee*, 47; Greeneville *New Era*, September 15, 1866; Memphis *Weekly Republican*, March 1, 1866; *Memphis Morning Post*, May 2, 1866; Frank B. Williams, "John Eaton, Jr., Editor, Politician, and School Administrator, 1865–1870," *Tennessee Historical Quarterly* 10 (1951): 291–92; Walter J. Fraser Jr., "Lucien Bonaparte Eaton: Politics and the Memphis *Post*, 1867–1869," *West Tennessee Historical Society Papers* 20 (1966): 20 n.3; Shelbyville *Republican*, October 19, 1866.

34. New Bern *Weekly Times*, October 9, 1866; Nashville *Daily Press and Times*, June 24, 1866; Memphis *Weekly Republican*, August 5, 1866; *Weekly North Carolina Standard*, September 26, 1866; *Rutherford Star*, October 10, 1866; *Memphis Morning Post*, May 2, 1866; Patton, *Unionism and Reconstruction in Tennessee*, 124–32.

35. *Florida Union*, July 14, 28, 1866; Greeneville *New Era*, September 15, 1866; *Memphis Post*, June 30, 1866; *Savannah Herald*, September 9, 1865, Feb. 23, 1866; New Bern *Weekly Times*, August 21, September 25, 1866; *Savannah Daily Republican*, July 12, August 14, October 1, 1866; *Weekly Southern Intelligencer*, October 11, 1866.

36. Culver H. Smith, *The Press, Politics, and Patronage: The American Government's Use of Newspapers, 1789–1875* (Athens, Ga., 1977), 237–38.

37. Henry Wilson to William Henry Seward, December 20, 1865; George Cahoon to Seward, December 21, 1865; John Stryker and others to Seward, May 22, 1866, R.G. 59, National Archives. Hampton *True Southerner*, April 12, 1866; *Fort Smith New Era*, June 3, 1872; Moneyhon, *Republicanism in Reconstruction Texas*, 51. For a list of newspapers Seward selected for this printing patronage, see E-154, "Lists of Publishers of Laws, 1850–1874," R.G. 59, National Archives.

38. Abbott, *Republican Party and the South*, 66–72.

39. Alexander, *Political Reconstruction in Tennessee* 118–19; E. Merton Coulter, *William G. Brownlow, Fighting Parson of the Southern Highlands* (Chapel Hill, 1937), 328–29; Nashville *Daily Press and Times*, March 11, 19, 1866; Abbott, *Republican Party and the South*, 67–71, 73; Lancaster, "Scalawags of North Carolina," 436 n.30, 439 n.71.

40. Foner, *Reconstruction*, 271–77.

3. The White South Confronts the Republican Press

1. *Great Republic*, January 10, 1867.

2. Donald E. Reynolds, *Editors Make War: Southern Newspapers in the Secession Crisis* (Nashville, 1966), 3–4.

3. Lester J. Cappon, *Virginia Newspapers, 1821–1935: A Bibliography with Historical Introduction and Notes* (New York, 1936), 22–23; T. Conn Bryan, *Confederate Georgia* (Athens, Ga., 1953), 204–5, 207; Carl R. Osthaus, *Partisans of the Southern Press: Editorial Spokesmen of the Nineteenth Century* (Lexington, Ky., 1994), 103–4; Horace Gibbs Davis Jr., "Florida Journalism during the Civil War" (master's thesis, University of Florida, 1952), 17; John K. Bettersworth, *Confederate Mississippi: The People and Policies of a Cotton State in Wartime* (Baton Rouge, 1943), 329–31, 336, 340; J. Cutler Andrews, "The Confederate Press and Public Morale," *Journal of Southern History* 32 (1966): 464; Thomas D. Clark, *The Southern Country Editor* (Indianapolis, 1948), 20.

4. Frederick Hudson, *Journalism in the United States from 1690 to 1872* (New York, 1873), 771; Simon Newton Dexter North, *History and Present Condition of the Newspaper and Periodical Press of the United States*, Vol. 8 of 10th Census (Washington, D.C., 1884), 59, 182.

5. Clark, *Southern Country Editor*, 35; Frank Allen Dennis, "West Tennessee Newspapers during the Civil War, 1860–1865" (Ph.D. diss., Mississippi State University, 1970), xvi–xvii; John Calhoun Ellen Jr., "Political Newspapers of the Piedmont Carolinas in the 1850's" (Ph.D. diss., University of South Carolina, 1958), 26; Emma Lou Thornbrough, "American Negro Newspapers, 1880–1914," *Business History Review* 40 (1966): 473; Fred W. Allsopp, *History of the Arkansas Press for a Hundred Years and More* (Little Rock, 1922), 19; North, *History and Present Condition*, 180.

6. Ellen, "Political Newspapers of the Piedmont Carolinas," 20; Edward E. Cheney to Charles Forbush, May 10, 1867, in New England Emigrant Aid Company Records, Kansas State Historical Society, Topeka; Elizabeth City *North Carolinian*, August 31, 1871; Macon *American Union*, October 10, 1872; Robert H. Woody, *Republican Newspapers of South Carolina* (Charlottesville, 1936), 35; J. M. Tomeny to William E. Chandler, April 4, 1868, and Martin Ryder to William Claflin, October 3, 1868, both in William E. Chandler Papers, LC.

7. Allsopp, *History of the Arkansas Press*, 35; Woody, *Republican Newspapers*, 19n; Thornbrough, "American Negro Newspapers," 473.

8. Dennis, "West Tennessee Newspapers," x; Alfred McClung Lee, *The Daily Newspaper in America* (New York, 1937), 743; Knoxville *Whig*, December 27, 1865.

9. Osthaus, *Partisans of the Southern Press*, 144; Austin *Daily State Journal*, May 10, 1870; *Daily Austin Republican*, January 31, 1871; *Savannah Daily Herald*, May 22, 1867; Atlanta *Daily New Era*, October 20, 1868; James Dugan to Edward McPherson, October 29, 1867, Edward McPherson Papers, LC; *Louisiana State Register*, April 27, 1870; O. S. Lee and Company to W. E. Chandler, August 18, 1872, William E. Chandler Papers; Loren Schenwinger, *James T. Rapier and Reconstruction* (Chicago, 1978), 112. Ruby's letter can be found in James A. Padgett, ed., "Reconstruction Letters from North Carolina, Part V," *North Carolina Historical Review* 19 (1942): 74–75 (Padgett incorrectly identified Ruby's paper and placed it in North Carolina).

10. North, *History and Present Condition*, 58, 94–95, 114; Lee, *Daily Newspaper*, 349; Allsopp, *History of the Arkansas Press*, 37; Clark, *Southern Country Editor*, 51–54; Frank Presbrey, *The History and Development of Advertising* (Repr., New York, 1968), 273–74.

Notes to Chapter Three

11. North, *History and Present Condition*, 53, 79; Lee, *Daily Newspaper*, 172; *Columbus Press*, January 23, 1875; *Louisiana State Register*, April 27, 1870; Clark, *Southern Country Editor*, 37.

12. Presbrey, *History and Development of Advertising*, 266–69; Lee, *Daily Newspaper*, 339, 348–51.

13. *Rowell's American Newspaper Directory, 1874* (New York, 1874), 75; Nashville *Weekly Press and Times*, January 7, 10, 1866; Nashville *Union and Dispatch*, January 12, 1867; Presbrey, *History and Development of Advertising*, 275; Lee, *Daily Newspaper*, 341–42; North, *History and Present Condition*, 75; Carolyn Stewart Dyer, "Census Manuscripts and Circulation Data for Mid-19th Century Newspapers," *Journalism History* 7 (1980): 47. Occasionally a publisher's correspondence would refer to his paper's circulation, making it possible to compare his private estimation with the figures he gave to Rowell. In 1869, for instance, the publisher of the *Memphis Post* told his brother that the paper had around 250 subscribers, but he reported 1,500 to Rowell. The proprietor of the *Advertiser* in Lexington, Mississippi, told William E. Chandler that he had fewer than 150 subscribers but informed Rowell he had 350. On the figures for the *Memphis Post*, see *Rowell's American Newspaper Directory, 1870* (New York, 1870), 744, and Walter J. Fraser Jr., "Lucien Bonaparte Eaton: Politics and the Memphis *Post*, 1867–1869," *West Tennessee Historical Society Papers* 20 (1966): 22 n.; for the *Advertiser*, see *Rowell's American Newspaper Directory, 1872* (New York, 1872), 90, and O. S. Lee and Co. to William E. Chandler, August 18, 1872, William E. Chandler Papers.

14. *Compendium of the Ninth Census* (Washington, D.C., 1872), 511; *Rowell's American Newspaper Directory, 1871* (New York, 1871), 6–7.

15. *Rowell's American Newspaper Directory, 1871*, 6; Clark, *Southern Country Editor*, 48.

16. Culver H. Smith, *The Press, Politics, and Patronage: The American Government's Use of Newspapers, 1789–1875* (Athens, Ga., 1977), passim; John C. Ellen Jr., "Newspaper Finance in North Carolina's Piedmont and Mountain Sections During the 1850's," *North Carolina Historical Review* 37 (1960): 499–501; North, *History and Present Condition*, 65, 87 (quote). One historian who studied Wisconsin's pre–Civil War press concluded that local government patronage comprised as much as half the income of the state's newspapers. See Carolyn Stewart Dyer, "Political Patronage of the Wisconsin Press, 1849–1861: New Perspectives on the Economics of Patronage," *Journalism Monographs* 109 (February 1989), cited in Gerald J. Baldasty, *The Commercialization of News in the Nineteenth Century* (Madison, 1992), 19, 22.

17. See the articles on the several ex-Confederate states in Henry Lewis Suggs, ed., *The Black Press in the South, 1865–1979*, ed. Henry Lewis Suggs (Westport, Conn., 1983); Thornbrough, "American Negro Newspapers," 467–69, 472–77; Howard N. Rabinowitz, *Race Relations in the Urban South* (New York, 1978), 231–32, 237; Vernon Lane Wharton, *The Negro in Mississippi, 1865–1890* (Chapel Hill, 1947), 272; Nashville *Colored Tennessean*, October 7, 1865, July 18, 1866; Savannah *Freemen's Standard*, March 7, 1868; Mobile *Nationalist*, February 8, 1866; *New Orleans Tribune* advertisement published in the *Nationalist*, December 27, 1866.

18. Eric Foner, *Reconstruction: America's Unfinished Revolution, 1863–1877* (New York, 1988), 346; Otto Olsen, "North Carolina: An Incongruous Presence," in *Reconstruction and Redemption in the South*, ed. Otto Olsen (Baton Rouge, 1980), 156–97; Ted Tunnell, *Crucible of Reconstruction: War, Radicalism and Race in Louisiana* (Baton Rouge, 1984), 5–6, 153–70; Lawrence N. Powell, "Southern Republicanism during Reconstruction: The Contradictions of State and Party Formation" (paper presented at the annual meeting of the Organization of American Historians, 1984), passim.

19. Osthaus, *Partisans of the Southern Press*, 1–11; Virginius Dabney, *Pistols and Pointed Pens: The Dueling Editors of Old Virginia* (Chapel Hill, 1987), passim; quotation from Reynolds, *Editors Make War*, 10.

20. Reynolds, *Editors Make War*, 210–17, 171–73; *Fredericksburg Ledger*, August 6, 1869.

21. Andrews, "Confederate Press and Public Morale," 445–65; Osthaus, *Partisans of the Southern Press*, 102–16; William C. Harris, *William Woods Holden: Firebrand of North Carolina Politics* (Baton Rouge, 1987), 138–39.

22. Joe Gray Taylor, *Louisiana Reconstructed, 1863–1877* (Baton Rouge, 1974), 120; Mobile *Nationalist*, August 30, 1866; *New York Tribune*, January 4, 1868.

23. E. Merton Coulter, *The South during Reconstruction, 1865–1877* (Baton Rouge, 1947), 291 n.40; Jeanette M. Bergeron, "Reconstruction Journalism in South Carolina" (master's thesis, University of South Carolina, 1974), 87–88; Montgomery *Alabama State Journal*, June 21, 1872; Talladega *Our Mountain Home*, May 20, June 3, 1874; Augusta *National Republican*, February 19, 1868; Griffin *American Union*, August 18, 1867; Frank B. Williams, "John Eaton, Jr., Editor, Politician, and School Administrator, 1865–1870," *Tennessee Historical Quarterly* 10 (1951): 293; *Selma Press*, January 30, 1869; Richmond *New Nation*, August 16, 1866; *Richmond Examiner* quoted in *Memphis Morning Post*, April 18, 1866; Leslie Winston Smith, "Richmond during Presidential Reconstruction, 1865–1867" (Ph.D. diss., University of Virginia, 1974), 123; Demopolis *Southern Republican*, October 18, 20, 1869; *Vicksburg Weekly Republican*, March 3, 1868; *New Orleans Tribune*, September 9, 1865; *Weekly Austin Republican*, November 6, 1867.

24. *Williamsburg Gazette*, July 1, 1869; *San Antonio Express*, September 25, 1867, April 7, 1868; Augusta *Weekly Loyal Georgian*, August 24, 1867; John E. Bryant to J. F. Long, [draft, 1868], John E. Bryant Papers, Duke University, Durham, N.C.; Little Rock *Evening Republican*, December 9, 1867; Demopolis *Southern Republican*, October 26, 1870; Macon *American Union*, December 5, 1872; Mobile *Nationalist*, December 27, 1866.

25. Mobile *Nationalist*, June 7, 1866; Richmond *Republic*, January 29, 1866; *Columbus Press*, August 22, 1874; Richmond *New Nation*, March 24, 1867; *San Antonio Express*, March 13, 1868; *Vicksburg Daily Times*, October 28, 1871; *New Orleans Tribune*, September 5, 1866; *New Orleans Republican*, September 24, 1870; Otto Olsen, *Carpetbagger's Crusade: The Life of Albion Winegar Tourgee* (Baltimore, 1965), 67; *Charleston Republican*, May 26, 1870.

26. Mobile *Nationalist*, February 1, 1866, March 7, 1867; Griffin *American Union*, September 13, 1867; Harrisonburg *American Union*, May 11, 1867; Jackson *Daily Mississippi Pilot*, January 13, 17, 1871; Atlanta *Daily Opinion*, November 23, December 10,

1867; Atlanta *New Era,* February 10, 1869; *Knoxville Whig,* March 18, 1868; Jacksonville *Florida Union,* October 24, 1868; *Vicksburg Weekly Republican,* March 10, September 13, 1868; Richmond *New Nation,* October 4, 1866

27. *Charleston Republican,* October 4, 1869; L. Cass Carpenter to W. E. Chandler, September 21, 1872, William E. Chandler Papers; Alexandria *Rapides Gazette,* February 1, 1873.

28. Mobile *Nationalist,* December 27, 1866; *Rutherford Star,* August 29, 1868; *Louisiana State Journal,* April 4, 1870; *Charleston Daily Republican,* September 27, 1869; Canton *American Citizen,* July 25, 1874; Griffin *American Union,* November 1, 1867; *Woodville Republican,* October 9, 1869; Augusta *Daily Press,* April 18, 1869; Mark Wahlgren Summers, *The Press Gang: Newspapers and Politics, 1865–1877* (Chapel Hill, 1994), 209–10.

29. *Bainbridge Weekly Sun,* October 22, 1873; Richmond *Daily State Journal,* April 21, 1871; *Columbus Press,* August 22, 1874; Augusta *National Republican* quoted in Griffin *American Union,* November 8, 1867; John R. DeTreville, "Reconstruction in Augusta, Georgia, 1865–1868" (master's thesis, University of North Carolina, 1979), 64; Richmond *New Nation,* November 8, 1866; Whitelaw Reid, *After the War: A Tour of the Southern States, 1865–1866,* ed. with an introduction by C. Vann Woodward (New York, 1965), 235.

30. *Knoxville Daily Chronicle,* May 3, 1870; Alexandria *Rapides Gazette,* December 28, 1872; Demopolis *Southern Republican,* May 26, 1869, August 31, 1871; Raleigh *Carolina Era,* October 26, 1871; Raleigh *North Carolina Standard,* May 5, 1868; *Chattanooga Daily Republican,* April 23, 1868; *Nashville Republican,* August 15, 1868; Atlanta *Daily New Era,* April 21, 24, May 30, 1868, January 3, 1869; first quote, August 22, 1868; second quote, May 31, 1868. In 1872, when Bard began publishing a paper in Chattanooga, he declared that "our business motto is no politics in business"; *Daily Chattanooga Herald,* February 20, 1872. A growing belief that affiliation with a political party harmed a paper's financial prospects was one of the factors contributing to a decline in partisan journalism during the late nineteenth century. See Baldasty, *Commercialization of News,* 128–29.

31. Jacksonville *Florida Union,* December 14, 1876; *Wilmington Post,* October 30, 1867, April 4, 1868 (first quote), June 18, 1868 (second quote); *Vicksburg Weekly Republican,* November 1, 1868; Augusta *Weekly Loyal Georgian,* August 24, 1867; Harrisonburg *American Union,* August 3, 1867; Charlotte *Union Republican,* April 1, 1868; *North Carolina Standard,* May 5, June 17, 1868; Richard H. Abbott, "Jason Clarke Swayze, Republican Editor in Reconstruction Georgia, 1867–1873," *Georgia Historical Quarterly* 79 (1992): 343; Hampton *True Southerner,* March 29, 1866; Mobile *Nationalist,* November 29, 1866.

32. L. Cass Carpenter to W. E. Chandler, October 6, 1872, William E. Chandler Papers; *Memphis Morning Post,* March 25, 1868; John Hayes to Nathaniel Banks, February 5, 1867, Nathaniel Banks Papers, LC; Atlanta *Daily New Era,* April 10, 1868, February 24, 1870; Woody, *Republican Newspapers,* 27n.; *New Bern Daily Republican,* November 29, December 1, 1868; James W. Garner, *Reconstruction in Mississippi* (New York, 1901), 349; Jerrell H. Shofner, *Nor Is It Over Yet: Florida in the Era of Reconstruction, 1863–1877* (Gainesville, 1974), 192; William C. Harris, *The Day of the Carpetbagger: Republican Reconstruction in Mississippi* (Baton Rouge, 1979), 599; Summers, *Press Gang,* 217.

Later in the nineteenth century, Populist editors in the South who challenged traditional beliefs and institutions also struggled to gain subscribers and advertising. Like their Republican predecessors, they sometimes received threats. A few lost their printing establishments to mob violence, and at least one Populist editor was killed. According to Lawrence Goodwyn, coping with this violence gave Populist editors "a sense of driving moral purpose," a comment that could also be made about Republican editors during Reconstruction. See Lawrence Goodwyn, *Democratic Promise: The Populist Moment in America* (New York, 1976), 356.

33. Earl L. Bell and Kenneth C. Crabbe, *The Augusta Chronicle: Indomitable Voice of Dixie, 1785–1960* (Athens, Ga., 1960), 74–75; New Orleans *National Republican*, August 13, 1872; *Columbus Press*, June 6, 1874, April 9, 1875; *Fredericksburg Ledger*, October 30, 1874; Demopolis *Southern Republican*, December 7, 21, 1870; W. McKee Evans, *Ballots and Fence Rails: Reconstruction on the Lower Cape Fear* (New York, 1966), 222; Carolyn DeLatte, "The St. Landry Riot: A Forgotten Incident of Reconstruction Violence," *Louisiana History* 67 (1976): 45; Taylor, *Louisiana Reconstructed*, 168; Ruth Currie-McDaniel, *Carpetbagger of Conscience: A Biography of John Emory Bryant* (Athens, Ga., 1987), 67; Atlanta *New Era*, February 24, 1870. For attacks on Republican editors in Texas, see *San Antonio Express*, June 4, July 15, 1868, May 13, July 2, 1871.

34. C. E. Harper, "The Country Press of Louisiana, 1860–1910" (master's thesis, Louisiana State University, 1929), 34–35; Geraldine Mary McTigue, "Forms of Racial Interaction in Louisiana, 1860–1880" (Ph.D. diss., Yale University, 1975), 178, 257, 294–97; Harris, *Day of the Carpetbagger*, 599.

35. Raleigh *North Carolina Standard*, November 13, 1867, for the account of the attack on the Richmond *New Nation;* Carl H. Moneyhon, *Republicanism in Reconstruction Texas* (Austin, 1980), 95; Allen W. Trelease, *White Terror: The Ku Klux Klan Conspiracy and Southern Reconstruction* (New York, 1971), 95, 96, 98, 129, 130, 295, 304, 338, 344; Garner, *Reconstruction in Mississippi*, 349; Abbott, "Jason Clarke Swayze," 349; *San Antonio Express*, July 16, 24, 1869; *Chattanooga Daily Republican*, January 22, 1868, on the *Maryville Republican; Rutherford Star*, June 24, 1871; Rhoda Coleman Ellison, *History and Bibliography of Alabama Newspapers in the Nineteenth Century* (University, Ala., 1954), 174; Washington *Daily Morning Chronicle*, July 13, 1868, on the *Homer Iliad;* Howard A. White, *The Freedmen's Bureau in Louisiana* (Baton Rouge, 1970), 150; Taylor, *Louisiana Reconstructed*, 168; Harper, "Country Press of Louisiana," 39; on Jonesborough *Union Flag*, see Nashville *Daily Press and Times*, October 24, 1866.

Sometimes newspaper offices burned, but arson could not be proved. This happened to two newspapers in Arkansas, the Russellville *National Tribune* and the Pocahontas *Randolph Republican;* see Allsopp, *History of the Arkansas Press*, 652, and *Batesville Republican*, April 30, 1871. Despite South Carolina's volatile atmosphere, only one Republican editor, Samuel Poiner, felt it necessary to leave the state; see Bergeron, "Reconstruction Journalism in South Carolina," 62, 68.

36. R. R. Butler to James Edmunds, May 23, 1867, in Marcus Ward Papers, New Jersey Historical Society Collections, Newark, N.J.; T. H. Davis to Benjamin Butler, March

17, 1867, Butler Papers, LC. Joseph E. Brown to Thomas Tullock, June 29, 1868; James H. Clements to William E. Chandler, August 12, 1868; A. B. Jones to Chairman, July 9, 1872; O. S. Lee and Co. to W. E. Chandler, August 18, 1872, William E. Chandler Papers. F. R. Cape to John Covode, August 28, 1867, John Covode Papers, LC; W. E. Chandler to William Claflin, December 19, 1868, Claflin Family Papers, Rutherford B. Hayes Presidential Library, Fremont, Ohio; John Robinson to Thaddeus Stevens, February 22, 1866, and Joseph McMurry to Stevens, April 20, 1866, both quoted in Padgett, "Reconstruction Letters from North Carolina, Part I," *North Carolina Historical Review* 18 (1941): 181–83; William McKinley Cash, "Alabama Republicans during Reconstruction: Personal Characteristics, Motivations, and Political Activity of Party Activists, 1867–1880" (Ph.D. diss., University of Alabama, 1973), 99; *Boston Advertiser*, May 23, 1867; Richard H. Abbott, *The Republican Party and the South, 1855–1877: The First Southern Strategy* (Chapel Hill, 1986), 88–90.

37. Harris, *Day of the Carpetbagger*, 597; Currie-McDaniel, *Carpetbagger of Conscience*, 65; *North Carolina Standard*, December 11, 1867; *St. Landry Progress*, December 28, 1867; Charles William Gross, "Black Newspapers in Texas 1868–1970" (Ph.D. diss., University of Texas at Austin, 1972), 58; Abbott, "Jason Clarke Swayze," 344; Michael W. Fitzgerald, *The Union League Movement in the Deep South: Politics and Agricultural Change during Reconstruction* (Baton Rouge, 1989), 34–36. Republican editors involved in the Union Leagues included James Newcomb in Texas, Jason Clarke Swayze in Georgia, James Hunnicutt in Virginia, John Smith in Mississippi, and Albert Griffin in Alabama, all of whom took radical positions on Reconstruction issues.

38. Woody, *Republican Newspapers*, 14–15; *Rutherford Star*, April 27, 1867; Michael Perman, *Reunion Without Compromise: The South and Reconstruction, 1865–1868* (Cambridge, Mass., 1973), 353; *New York Daily Tribune*, October 8, 1867; *Boston Commonwealth*, April 13, 1867; *Nation*, April 25, 1867; Washington *Daily Morning Chronicle*, March 28, April 30, June 20, October 23, 1867 (quote from March 27, 1867); *Charleston Free Press*, April 5, 1868; *Charleston Advocate*, October 12, 1868; *San Antonio Express*, January 21, 1871; *Charleston Daily Republican*, August 19, 1869.

39. *New Orleans Tribune*, December 22, 1867; *Austin Republican*, December 25, 1867; *Wilmington Post*, April 15, 1868; *Nashville Republican*, October 28, 1868; *Charleston Daily Republican*, September 8, 1869, February 15, May 4, 1870. On the pro-Southern bias of the Associated Press, see Summers, *Press Gang*, 218–21.

40. Archie Fisk to John Johnson, August 29, 1868, William E. Chandler Papers; *Vicksburg Weekly Republican*, September 6, 1868; Austin *Daily State Journal*, February 18, 1872; Greensboro *New North State*, November 23, 1871; Richard Lee Hoffman, "The Republican Party in North Carolina, 1867–1871" (master's thesis, University of North Carolina, 1960), 28; *Sumter County Republican*, June 13, 1868.

41. *New York Daily Tribune*, July 22, 1867; Thomas Tullock to James Edmunds, September 19, 1867, in Robert S. Schenck Papers, Rutherford B. Hayes Presidential Library, Fremont, Ohio; W. E. Chandler to William Claflin, December 19, 1868, Claflin Family Papers.

4. Patronage Saves the Republican Press

1. Thompson quoted in Jeanette M. Bergeron, "Reconstruction Journalism in South Carolina" (master's thesis, University of South Carolina, 1974), 20; James E. Sefton, *The United States Army and Reconstruction, 1865–1877* (Baton Rouge, 1967), 55–56; C. Mildred Thompson, *Reconstruction in Georgia: Economic, Social, Political* (New York, 1915), 140–42; J. G. de Roulhac Hamilton, *Reconstruction in North Carolina* (New York, 1914), 167; William L. Richter, *The Army in Texas during Reconstruction, 1865–1870* (College Station, Tex., 1987), 177–78, 251 n.16; Robert H. Woody, *Republican Newspapers of South Carolina* (Charlottesville, 1936), 6; Charles Francis Ritter, "The Press in Florida, Louisiana, and South Carolina and the End of Reconstruction, 1865–1877: Southern Men with Northern Interests" (Ph.D. diss., Catholic University of America, 1976), 35–36; John Allen Meador, "Florida Political Parties, 1865–1877" (Ph.D. diss., University of Florida, 1974), 135; figures on U.S. War Department advertising gained from *The Biennial Register of All Officers and Agents . . . 1867* (Washington, D.C., 1868), 257–73.

2. William C. Harris, The *Day of the Carpetbagger: Republican Reconstruction in Mississippi* (Baton Rouge, 1979), 15–18; Sefton, *United States Army*, 151–52; Walter Lynwood Fleming, *Civil War and Reconstruction in Alabama* (New York, 1905), 485–86; Rhoda Coleman Ellison, *History and Bibliography of Alabama Newspapers in the Nineteenth Century* (University, Ala., 1954), 145; *Moulton Advertiser*, September 7, 1867; Moulton *Union*, February 24, 1868.

3. John Hayes to Nathaniel Banks, February 5, 1867, Nathaniel Banks Papers, LC; Norfolk *True Southerner*, April 12, 1866; *McMinnville Enterprise*, May 25, June 22, 1867; *Memphis Morning Post*, January 27, 1868; Nashville *Press and Times*, August 16, 1867; Thomas S. Staples, *Reconstruction in Arkansas, 1862–1874* (New York, 1923), 147–48; Harris, *Day of the Carpetbagger*, 106–7; James W. Garner, *Reconstruction in Mississippi* (New York, 1901), 233.

4. Sefton, *United States Army*, 148–50; Thompson, *Reconstruction in Georgia*, 177, 347; Jerrell H. Shofner, *Nor Is It Over Yet: Florida in the Era of Reconstruction, 1863–1877* (Gainesville, 1974), 162; John Pope to Edward McPherson, August 17, 1867, Edward McPherson Papers, LC; Montgomery *Daily State Sentinel*, August 14, 28, 29, November 24, 1867, April 4, 1868. The two Alabama papers that changed hands were the Wetumpka *Elmore Standard* and the *Tuscaloosa Observer*. See Ellison, *Alabama Newspapers*, 198; Montgomery *Daily State Sentinel*, August 30, 1867; *Elmore Standard*, October 25, 1867.

5. Culver H. Smith, *The Press, Politics, and Patronage: The American Government's Use of Newspapers, 1789–1875* (Athens, Ga., 1977), 238–39.

6. Richard H. Abbott, *Republican Party and the South, 1855–1877: The First Southern Strategy* (Chapel Hill, 1986), 92; Charles Whittlesey to Edward McPherson, March 4, 1867, McPherson Papers.

7. Whittlesey listed for Virginia the Alexandria *Virginia State Journal*, Richmond *New Nation, Winchester Journal*, and Harrisonburg *American Union;* for North Carolina the Raleigh *North Carolina Standard*, Hendersonville *Henderson Pioneer*, and *Greensboro*

Union Register; for Georgia the Augusta *Loyal Georgian,* Griffin *American Union,* and *Savannah Republican;* for Texas the *San Antonio Express,* Austin *Southern Intelligencer,* and *McKinney Messenger;* for Louisiana the *New Orleans Tribune, New Orleans Christian Advocate,* and *Homer Iliad;* for Alabama the Mobile *Nationalist* and *Huntsville Advocate;* and for the other three states the *New South* of Beaufort, South Carolina; the *Fort Smith New Era* in Arkansas; and an unnamed paper in Jacksonville, Florida.

8. See the notices announcing these papers in McPherson Papers, March–July 1867; Washington *Daily Morning Chronicle,* March 20, April 12, 1867. On the *Charleston Advocate,* see H. Judge Moore to W. H. Seward, October 9, 1867, R.G. 59, National Archives. McPherson did award two Tennessee papers—the *McMinnville Enterprise* and the Jonesborough *Union Flag*—printing for the first session of the Fortieth Congress. A complete list of papers across the country that received U.S. printing patronage for the Thirty-ninth and subsequent Congresses may be found in the volumes of the *Biennial Register.*

9. John Bryant to Harper and Brothers, April 1, 1867, John E. Bryant Papers, Duke University, Durham, N.C.; R. J. Hinton to L. Barnes, May 18, 1867, Benjamin Butler Papers, LC; *Biennial Register, 1867,* 270; Smith, *The Press, Politics, and Patronage,* 255; James Dugan to McPherson, October 29, 1867, and J. R. Smith to McPherson, January 10, 1868, McPherson Papers; *Savannah Daily Republican,* August 3, 1867; *Houston Union* quoted in Austin *Daily State Journal,* January 12, 1871.

10. Washington *Daily Morning Chronicle,* July 11, 1867; *Savannah Daily Republican,* August 15, 1867; Macon *American Union,* April 18, 1872; Amos Akerman to H. M. Turner, November 16, 1871, in Akerman Papers, University of Virginia, Charlottesville.

11. Alexandria *Rapides Gazette,* November 9, 1872; Ellison, *Alabama Newspapers,* 63; E. Merton Coulter, *The South During Reconstruction, 1865–1877* (Baton Rouge, 1947), 288.

12. Jean-Charles Houzeau, *My Passage at the New Orleans Tribune: A Memoir of the Civil War Era,* ed. and with an introduction by David C. Rankin, trans. by Gerard F. Denault (Baton Rouge, 1984), 53; Mobile *Nationalist,* June 7, 1866 (first quote), March 15, 1866 (second quote); Inez Burns, *History of Blount County, Tennessee: From War Trail to Landing Strip, 1795–1955* (Nashville, 1957), 61, 211, 227–28.

13. It is difficult to determine whether the editors and proprietors of some of these papers were white or black. From 1865 to 1866, the publisher of the Charleston *South Carolina Leader,* Timothy Hurley, was white, as were its first two editors, Allen Coffin and H. Judge Moore. Moore also edited the *Charleston Advocate* in 1867. By the fall of 1866, two black men, Richard H. Cain and Alonzo Ransier, were editing the *Leader,* and in 1867 they joined some other blacks in forming a joint stock company that took control of the paper. See Woody, *Republican Newspapers,* 11–13; H. Judge Moore to W. H. Seward, October 9, 1867, R.G. 59, National Archives.

In June 1867, the Raleigh *Weekly Republican's* publisher and editor was Frank Pearson, an African American Union Army veteran. Apparently later in the year another black man, Daniel Battle, replaced Pearson in both roles. See Raleigh *Weekly Republican,* June 29, 1867; Elizabeth Reid Murray, *Wake: Capital County of North Carolina,* vol. 1 (Raleigh, 1983), 565. Joseph Wilson, editor of the Norfolk *Union Republican,* was black, although at least one member of the paper's board of directors was white. See Eric Foner, *Freedom's Lawmakers: A Directory of Black Officeholders during Reconstruction* (New York, 1993), 234; P. H. Whitehurst to Thaddeus Stevens, March 22, 1867, Stevens Papers, LC.

14. The longest-lived of these African American papers were two from Louisiana, the New Orleans *Louisianan* and the Baton Rouge *Grand Era;* each lasted from 1870 to 1877.

15. Macon *American Union,* January 8, 1869; Harrisonburg *American Union,* February 9, 1867; Richmond *New Nation,* July 19, 1866; Jackson *Weekly Mississippi Pilot,* July 7, 1872; Corpus Christi *Nueces Valley,* July 6, 1872; Rutherfordton *Rutherford Star,* March 2, 1867; Montgomery *Daily State Sentinel,* October 15, 22, 1867.

16. Griffin *American Union,* November 1, 8, December 20, 1867; Rutherfordton *Rutherford Star,* October 16, 1869; Harrisonburg *American Union,* February 16, 1867; Maryville *Soldier's Gazette,* August 26, 1870; Mobile *Nationalist,* June 7, 1866; Gallatin *Sumter County Republican,* June 13, 1868; Randolph B. Campbell, *Grass-Roots Reconstruction in Texas, 1865–1880* (Baton Rouge, 1997), 41; Richard H. Abbott, "Jason Clarke Swayze, Republican Editor in Reconstruction Georgia, 1867–1873," *Georgia Historical Quarterly* 79 (1992): 344; Michael W. Fitzgerald, *The Union League Movement in the Deep South: Politics and Agricultural Change during Reconstruction* (Baton Rouge, 1989), 34–36.

17. Harrisonburg *American Union,* October 27, 1866; Charleston *South Carolina Leader,* October 7, 21, 1865; Charleston *Free Press,* April 5, 1868.

18. Harris, *Day of the Carpetbagger,* 598.

19. Ellison, *Alabama Newspapers,* 198; *McMinnville Enterprise,* June 22, 1867; *Journal of the Proceedings of the Constitutional Convention of the State of Mississippi in 1868* (Jackson, 1871), 192; Washington *Daily Morning Chronicle,* July 11, 1867; *Philadelphia Press,* July 22, 1867.

20. Fitzgerald, *Union League Movement,* 185; Richard H. Abbott, "The Republican Party Press in Reconstruction Georgia, 1867–1874," *Journal of Southern History* 61 (1995): 751; W. McKee Evans, *Ballots and Fence Rails: Reconstruction on the Lower Cape Fear* (New York, 1966), 220; Mark Wahlgren Summers, *The Press Gang: Newspapers and Politics, 1865–1877* (Chapel Hill, 1994), 211.

21. Austin *Daily State Journal,* May 2, 1871, February 18, 1872; Greensboro *New North State,* November 23, 1871; Greensboro *Republican Gazette,* November 4, 1869; G. T. Ruby to W. E. Chandler, July 20, 1872, in James A. Padgett, ed., "Reconstruction Letters from North Carolina, Part V," *North Carolina Historical Review* 19 (1942): 74–75; *Weekly Mississippi Pilot,* July 7, 1872.

22. *Debates and Proceedings of the Constitutional Convention of Virginia . . . 1867* (Richmond, 1868), 103; *Journal of the Proceedings of the Constitutional Convention of the State of Mississippi,* 19, 115; *Journal of the Proceedings of the Convention Begun January 20, 1868, Tallahassee, Florida* (Tallahassee, 1868), 12, 119; *Official Journal of the Proceedings of the Convention for Framing a Constitution for the State of Louisiana, 1867–1868* (New Orleans, 1868), 12, 18; *Ordinances Passed by the Constitutional Convention at Austin, Texas, June 1, 1868* (Austin, 1870), 5–6, 16; Staples, *Reconstruction in Arkansas,* 228.

23. *Journal of the Proceedings of . . . Florida,* 127; *Ordinances Passed . . . at Austin,*

Texas, 57–58, 121; Staples, *Reconstruction in Arkansas*, 230; *Official Journal of the Proceedings of . . . Louisiana*, 196; Mississippi Auditor's Report published in *Journal of the House of Representatives of Mississippi, 1870* (Jackson, 1870), 125–278.

24. John J. Palmer to H. H. Wells, March 3, May 4, 1868, Wells Papers, Virginia State Archives, Richmond; State of Virginia, *Auditor's Journal, 1869*, Virginia State Archives, 823, 843, 863, 886, 1038.

25. *Public Laws of the State of North Carolina, 1868–1869* (Raleigh, 1869), 618; *Laws of the State of Florida, First Session . . . 1868*, (Tallahassee, 1868), 161; Woody, *Republican Newspapers*, 48–54; Ella Lonn, *Reconstruction in Louisiana after 1868* (New York, 1918), 86–87; Joe Gray Taylor, *Louisiana Reconstructed, 1863–1877* (Baton Rouge, 1974), 198–99. The figures on printing expenditures for Georgia are drawn from the yearly reports of Georgia's comptroller general. See also Thompson, *Reconstruction in Georgia*, 226–27. Georgia's Governor Bullock found another way to subsidize his party's leading newspaper: he awarded the contract for the state-owned railroad's printing needs, such as tickets and timetables, to Samuel Bard, publisher of the Atlanta *New Era*. The state paid Bard an average of $1,000 a month for this service. See his printer's book for 1870, in Business Records, 1783–1930, Georgia Department of Archives and History, Atlanta.

26. *Memphis Morning Post*, January 2, 1868; Atlanta *New Era*, August 5, 1868.

27. Carolyn DeLatte, "The St. Landry Riot: A Forgotten Incident of Reconstruction Violence," *Louisiana History* 67 (1976): 242; Frank B. Williams, "John Eaton, Jr., Editor, Politician, and School Administrator, 1865–1870," *Tennessee Historical Quarterly* 10 (1951): 300–301.

28. *Acts of the General Assembly of Alabama, 1868* (Montgomery, 1868), 226–27; Staples, *Reconstruction in Arkansas*, 308; Charles W. Ramsdell, *Reconstruction in Texas* (New York, 1910), 299; *Laws of the State of Florida, First Session, 1868*, 161; John S. Reynolds, *Reconstruction in South Carolina, 1865–1877* (Columbia, 1905), 125; Garner, *Reconstruction in Mississippi*, 325–26; Harris, *Day of the Carpetbagger*, 610.

29. *Memphis Morning Post*, January 2, 1868; Demopolis *Southern Republican*, various issues, 1869 to 1871; *Calvert Tribune* quoted in *Daily Austin Republican*, November 15, 1870; Greensboro *New North State*, November 23, 1871; Austin *Daily State Journal*, September 17, 1871.

30. *Acts Passed by the General Assembly of the State of Louisiana . . . 1868* (New Orleans, 1868), 8–12; *New Orleans Republican*, April 15, November 30, 1870; Alexandria *Rapides Gazette*, December 13, 1873.

31. *New Orleans Tribune*, January 12, 26, 1869; *Helena Clarion*, March 3, 1869, October 14, 1871.

32. Bergeron, "Reconstruction Journalism in South Carolina," 39; Batesville *North Arkansas Times*, February 17, 1869; *Memphis Post*, February 21, 1868; *New Orleans Tribune*, December 17, 1867; *McMinnville Enterprise*, May 25, 1867; Jacksonville *Florida Union*, October 24, 1868; *Meridian Chronicle*, January 22, 1868; Jackson *Daily Pilot*, April 12, 1871; *Vicksburg Daily Times*, April 13, 1873; Corpus Christi *Nueces Valley*, October 1, 1870; Austin *Daily State Journal*, May 10, 1870; Summers, *Press Gang*, 210–11.

33. Taylor, *Louisiana Reconstructed*, 198–99; *Memphis Post*, January 27, 1868; *McMinnville Enterprise*, May 25, 1867; Demopolis *Southern Republican*, March 17, 1869.

34. *Acts of the General Assembly of Alabama, 1868*, 227; *Official Journal of the Proceedings of . . . Louisiana*, 12, 24, 63 (quote from 55); *Journal of the Proceedings of . . . Mississippi*, 95; Atlanta *Daily New Era*, March 4, 1868; *Debates and Proceedings of the Constitutional Convention of Virginia . . . 1867*, 124.

35. Ramsdell, *Reconstruction in Texas*, 299; *Journal of the Senate of Mississippi, 1870* (Jackson, 1870), 502, 504; Woody, *Republican Newspapers*, 28n; *New Orleans Republican*, November 30, 1870.

36. Shelbyville *Republican*, April 30, 1869; Alexandria *Rapides Gazette*, February 1, 15 (quotes), 1873; Carrollton *Louisiana State Register*, March 12, 1870.

37. Alexandria *Rapides Gazette*, November 9, 1872, February 15, 1873; Carrollton *Louisiana State Register*, March 12, 1870; Helena *Clarion*, October 14, 1871; Ritter, "The Press in Florida, Louisiana, and South Carolina," 37; William L. Scruggs to Columbus Delano, January 8, 1871, Delano Family Papers, LC; John Pope to Robert Schenk, May 20, 1867, Robert S. Schenck Papers, Rutherford B. Hayes Presidential Library, Fremont, Ohio; Joseph Brown to W. D. Kelley, July 1, 1867, Joseph Brown Papers, University of Georgia, Athens; J. E. Bryant to Edward McPherson, July 30, 1867, McPherson Papers. For another discussion of Southern Republican publishers' dependence on governmental patronage, see Summers, *Press Gang*, 209–18.

38. Chattanooga *Daily Republican*, April 7, 1868, April 13, 1869; Williams, "John Eaton, Jr.," 295; Austin *Daily State Journal*, October 23, 1870.

39. Washington *Daily Morning Chronicle*, June 19, October 23, 1867.

5. The Geographic Breadth of the Southern Republican Press

1. The basic source I used for counting Republican and Democratic newspapers in the South during Reconstruction was George P. Rowell's *American Newspaper Directory*, which appeared first in 1869 and annually thereafter. I developed a list of Republican Party papers that existed prior to 1869 by using a number of sources, including the papers themselves, which often mentioned other Republican sheets, and the large secondary literature available on the Republican Party in the South during Reconstruction. My reading of Republican papers also helped me to identify party journals that did not appear in Rowell or were not identified as Republican. Since I did not undertake a similar search for Democratic papers from 1865 to 1869, I have certainly undercounted the total Democratic newspapers for the Reconstruction years.

2. Usually Rowell published circulation figures with an indication that the numbers were approximate. Sometimes the publishers refused to furnish him with any numbers at all, while many must have exaggerated the circulations they reported to him. In 1871, for instance, Samuel Bard claimed a highly unlikely circulation of fourteen hundred for his weekly *True Georgian*. It is also hard to believe that Joel Griffin's Fort Valley *Southwest Georgian* achieved the circulation of eight hundred that he reported in 1872. The

Notes to Chapter Five

publisher of the *Memphis Post* told Rowell his circulation was fifteen hundred, a figure ten times higher than the number he revealed to his brother; see Walter J. Fraser, "Lucien Bonaparte Eaton: Politics and the Memphis *Post*, 1867–1869," *West Tennessee Historical Society Papers* 20 (1966): 22 n. Also see Mark Wahlgren Summers, *The Press Gang: Newspapers and Politics, 1865–1877* (Chapel Hill, 1994), 214–15, for his discussion of Republican newspaper circulation.

3. Allen W. Trelease, "Who Were the Scalawags?" *Journal of Southern History* 29 (1963): 445–68, has a useful map locating counties with significant white support for the Republican Party. In the ensuing discussion of the distribution of Republican papers in each state and their relation to the distribution of the state's Republican vote, I have used statistics on voter registration and on elections in annual editions of the *Tribune Almanac and Political Register* and in W. D. Burnham, *Presidential Ballots, 1836–1892*, 2 vols. (Baltimore, 1955).

4. Ralph Morrow, *Northern Methodism and Reconstruction* (East Lansing, 1956), 40, 55, 125; Fayette Copeland, "The New Orleans Press and Reconstruction," *Louisiana Historical Quarterly* 30 (1947): 307; Ted Tunnell, *Crucible of Reconstruction: War, Radicalism and Race in Louisiana* (Baton Rouge, 1984), 23–24, 117; Geraldine Mary McTigue, "Forms of Racial Interaction in Louisiana, 1860–1880" (Ph.D. diss., Yale University, 1975) 4, 166, 175.

5. *Official Journal of the Proceedings of the Convention for Framing a Constitution for the State of Louisiana, 1867–1868* (New Orleans, 1868), 196; Washington *Daily Morning Chronicle,* April 12, 1867; Tunnell, *Crucible of Reconstruction*, 224.

6. *Acts Passed by the General Assembly of the State of Louisiana . . . 1868*, 8–12; Ella Lonn, *Reconstruction in Louisiana after 1868* (New York, 1918), 86–87.

7. Tunnell, *Crucible of Reconstruction*, 19–20.

8. The *Tribune* suspended publication on April 25, 1868. It was later revived and was published irregularly until 1871. See Jean-Charles Houzeau, *My Passage at the New Orleans Tribune: A Memoir of the Civil War Era*, ed. and with an introduction by David C. Rankin, trans. by Gerard F. Denault (Baton Rouge, 1984), 72n. In 1869, Newman left New Orleans for Washington, where he became the United States Senate chaplain. Thomas Conway, a friend of carpetbag governor Henry Clay Warmoth, continued to publish Newman's paper as the *New Orleans Advocate and Journal of Education* until 1871.

9. Robert T. Clark Jr., "Reconstruction and the New Orleans German Colony," *Louisiana Historical Quarterly* 23 (1940): 502; Eric Foner, *Freedom's Lawmakers: A Directory of Black Officeholders during Reconstruction* (New York, 1993), 148. Menard also published the *Radical Standard* in Carrollton.

10. Joe Gray Taylor, *Louisiana Reconstructed, 1863–1877* (Baton Rouge, 1974), 158; Tunnell, *Crucible of Reconstruction*, 175. The maps in Tunnell, *Crucible of Reconstruction*, 176–80, and the large regional map of Louisiana parishes on the inside front cover of Roger W. Shugg, *Origins of Class Struggle in Louisiana* (Baton Rouge, 1939), proved very helpful in analyzing sources of Republican strength in Louisiana. See also Frank Joseph Wetta, "The Louisiana Scalawags" (Ph.D. diss., Louisiana State University, 1977), 277–81.

11. Tunnell, *Crucible of Reconstruction,* 175, 187; Samuel C. Hyde Jr., *Pistols and Politics: The Dilemma of Democracy in Louisiana's Florida Parishes, 1810-1899* (Baton Rouge, 1996), 2-5; Foner, *Freedom's Lawmakers,* 31-32.

12. Tunnell, *Crucible of Reconstruction,* 15, 21, and maps, 12-14, 176-80.

13. Hyde, *Pistols and Politics,* 170, 173; Carolyn DeLatte, "The St. Landry Riot: A Forgotten Incident of Reconstruction Violence," *Louisiana History* 67 (1976): 41-49.

14. William C. Harris, *The Day of the Carpetbagger: Republican Reconstruction in Mississippi* (Baton Rouge, 1979), 97. R. J. Moseley to William H. Seward, April 1, 1867; James Dugan to Edward McPherson, [1867], Edward McPherson Papers, LC. *Meridian Chronicle,* April 4, 1868; Michael W. Fitzgerald, *The Union League Movement in the Deep South: Politics and Agricultural Change during Reconstruction* (Baton Rouge, 1989), 105.

15. J. N. Osborn to Edward McPherson, January 6, 1868; James Dugan to McPherson, January 20, February 19, 1868; E. Stafford to McPherson, September 10, 1868, McPherson Papers. A. C. Fisk to William E. Chandler, July 4, 24, August 24, 1868, William E. Chandler Papers, LC.

16. Walker, Atkins and Co. to Edward McPherson, June 27, 1870, McPherson Papers; J. B. Raymond to O. C. French, August 3, 1872, in William E. Chandler Papers; Harris, *Day of the Carpetbagger,* 598.

17. Harris, *Day of the Carpetbagger,* 414, 598; *Vicksburg Daily Times,* July 17, 29, 1870.

18. O. S. Lee to W. E. Chandler, August 18, 1872; J. B. Raymond to O. C. French, August 3, 1872; O. C. French to W. E. Chandler, August 6, 1872, William E. Chandler Papers. *Weekly Mississippi Pilot,* July 7, 1872; James W. Garner, *Reconstruction in Mississippi* (New York, 1901), 325-26; Harris, *Day of the Carpetbagger,* 598.

19. See the statistics on county populations and voting in David G. Sansing, "The Role of the Scalawag in Mississippi Reconstruction" (Ph.D. diss., University of Southern Mississippi, 1969).

20. Carl H. Moneyhon, *Republicanism in Reconstruction Texas* (Austin, 1980), 47, 67; *Free Man's Press,* October 24, 1868. Keith moved the *Freedman's Press* to Galveston in the fall of 1868 and renamed it the *Free Man's Press.* It disappeared shortly thereafter. See Charles William Gross, "Black Newspapers in Texas 1868-1970" (Ph.D. diss., University of Texas at Austin, 1972), 55-61.

21. *General Laws of the Twelfth Legislature* (Austin, 1870), 70-75; *General Laws of the Thirteenth Legislature* (Austin, 1871), 31.

22. Dale A. Somers, "James P. Newcomb: The Making of a Radical," *Southwest Historical Quarterly* 72 (1969): 449-69; Charles W. Ramsdell, *Reconstruction in Texas* (New York, 1910), 286; Moneyhon, *Republicanism in Reconstruction Texas,* 109. The other two dailies were Flake's Galveston *Bulletin,* which survived until 1873, and the Brownsville *Ranchero,* which was Republican from 1871 to 1875. Regarding the use of "scalawag," see introduction, note 10.

23. On the characteristics of this district see Moneyhon, *Republicanism in Reconstruction Texas,* 13, 120. I have also utilized the maps in Moneyhon's book on pp. 13, 48, 125, 127, 132, and 190 in my ensuing discussion of sources of white and black votes for the

Republican Party. See also Randolph B. Campbell, *Grass-Roots Reconstruction in Texas, 1865–1880* (Baton Rouge, 1997), 186–87, for McClellan County.

On Richard Nelson, see Gross, "Black Newspapers in Texas," 65–66, and Foner, *Freedom's Lawmakers*, 160. The other two African American newspapers in Galveston were the *Galveston Republican*, published briefly in 1871 by a Jamaican immigrant, Frank Webb, and the *Standard*, published by George T. Ruby from 1872 to 1873. On Webb, see Austin *Daily State Journal*, December 1, 1870. Ruby played an important role in Texas Reconstruction politics; see Carl H. Moneyhon, "George T. Ruby and the Politics of Expediency in Texas," in *Southern Black Leaders of the Reconstruction Era*, ed. Howard Rabinowitz (Urbana, 1982), 363–92.

24. Moneyhon, *Republicanism in Reconstruction Texas*, 14, and maps in this book. On the establishment of the *National Index*, see Hiram Lorance and others to Edward McPherson, September 24, 1867, McPherson Papers.

25. Moneyhon, *Republicanism in Reconstruction Texas*, 15–16, and maps in this book on election returns. A. B. Norton of *Norton's Union Intelligencer* had originally published the *Southern Intelligencer* in Austin, and in 1868 ran the Jefferson *Union Intelligencer*. He ran unsuccessfully for Congress in 1872.

26. James Marten, *Texas Divided: Loyalty and Dissent in the Lone Star State, 1856–1874* (Lexington, Ky., 1990), 26, 113; Moneyhon, *Republicanism in Reconstruction Texas*, 14–15, 122, and maps in this book.

27. Marten, *Texas Divided*, 62–63, and maps in Moneyhon, *Republicanism in Reconstruction Texas*; Campbell, *Grass-Roots Reconstruction in Texas*, 203–4, 206–8, 212–14.

28. Frank B. Williams, "John Eaton, Jr., Editor, Politician, and School Administrator, 1865–1870," *Tennessee Historical Quarterly* 10 (1951): 300–301; *Public Acts of the General Assembly of the State of Tennessee . . . 1868* (Nashville, 1868), 40–41. In 1868, Ruhm and Bailey, publishers of the German-language Nashville *Staats-Zeitung*, began publishing a paper in English, the *Nashville Daily Republican*; Bailey also published the Gallatin *Sumter County Republican* in 1868 and apparently the *Lebanon Record*, since most of that paper's printed matter came from the *Daily Republican*.

29. On East Tennessee, see Vernon M. Queener, "A Decade of East Tennessee Republicanism," *East Tennessee Historical Society Publications* 14 (1942): 59–85.

30. On Middle Tennessee, see Stephen V. Ash, *Middle Tennessee: Society Transformed, 1860–1870* (Baton Rouge, 1988), esp. 240–52; on Nashville, see Howard N. Rabinowitz, *Race Relations in the Urban South* (New York, 1978), 17, 264–65.

31. Thomas S. Staples, *Reconstruction in Arkansas, 1862–1874* (New York, 1923), 228; *Acts of the General Assembly of Arkansas . . . 1868* (Little Rock, 1868), 42–43.

32. George H. Thompson, *Arkansas and Reconstruction: The Influence of Geography, Economics, and Personality* (Port Washington, N.Y., 1976), 18, 72, maps 70, 74, tables 72–73; Carl H. Moneyhon, *The Impact of the Civil War and Reconstruction on Arkansas* (Baton Rouge, 1994), map 4.

33. Thompson, *Arkansas and Reconstruction*, 16–17, maps 27, 70, 74, table 72–73; Moneyhon, *Impact of the Civil War*, 96, 102, 243.

34. Thompson, *Arkansas and Reconstruction*, 9–13, maps 27, 67, 70, 74, table 72–73.

35. Robert H. Woody, *Republican Newspapers of South Carolina* (Charlottesville, 1936), 6, 12, 18; Morrow, *Northern Methodism and Reconstruction*, 46, 55; Foner, *Freedom's Lawmakers*, 176; Woody, *Republican Newspapers*.

36. Woody, *Republican Newspapers*, 12, 14–18; Foner, *Freedom's Lawmakers*, 176; Alonzo Webster to Edward McPherson, December 21, 1868, McPherson Papers.

37. Woody, *Republican Newspapers*, 25–33; William L. King, *The Newspaper Press of Charleston, S.C.* (Charleston, 1882), 186–87; Jonathan Morris to William E. Chandler, October 3, 1868, William E. Chandler Papers.

38. Woody, *Republican Newspapers*, 34–37.

39. Ibid., 20–25, 48–50.

40. Ibid., 42–47. In 1869, the owner of the Darlington *Southerner* sought and obtained the right to publish the U.S. laws. See J. M. Brown to B. F. Whittemore, July 20, 1869, and Giles A. Smith to Edward McPherson, February 9, 1870, both in McPherson Papers. The paper maintained this privilege through five consecutive congressional sessions, indicating that the Republican Party found it trustworthy. Although its publisher identified the Darlington paper in Rowell's newspaper directory as Democratic, Robert Woody, in his history of Republican newspapers in South Carolina, regarded it as Republican in all but name. He cites the Charleston *Daily News* as describing the *Southerner* in 1869 as Republican "on account of its tone and temper and not on account of any formal profession of party faith." See Woody, *Republican Newspapers*, 19 n.

41. Woody, *Republican Newspapers*, 44–45, 47–48. In 1873 Republicans twice tried and failed to establish a Republican paper in Abbeville.

42. *Acts of the General Assembly of Alabama, 1868* (Montgomery, 1868), 226–27.

43. See map of Alabama showing blacks as a percentage of population by county in Peter Kolchin, *First Freedom: The Responses of Alabama's Blacks to Emancipation and Reconstruction* (Westport, Conn., 1972), 13; William McKinley Cash, "Alabama Republicans during Reconstruction: Personal Characteristics, Motivations, and Political Activity of Party Activists, 1867–1880" (Ph.D. diss., University of Alabama, 1973), 115–16; Rabinowitz, *Race Relations in the Urban South*, 273. The *State Sentinel* was edited by John Hardy, who was also a member of the state house of representatives. Arthur Bingham, a longtime resident of Talladega who had helped organize the Union League there, was editor of the *Alabama State Journal* from 1872 to 1875. See John W. Dubose, *Alabama's Tragic Decade: Ten Years of Alabama, 1865–1874* (Birmingham, 1940), 138, 406; Fitzgerald, *Union League*, 62, 103.

44. See maps in Sarah Woolfolk Wiggins, *The Scalawag in Alabama Politics, 1865–1881* (University, Ala., 1977), 70, 72. On Moseley, see Thomas M. Owen, *History of Alabama and Dictionary of Alabama Biography*, 4 vols. (Chicago, 1921), 4:1252; on Burton, see William Warren Rogers Jr., *Black Belt Scalawag: Charles Hayes and the Southern Republicans in the Era of Reconstruction* (Athens, Ga., 1993), 45.

45. Walter Lynwood Fleming, *Civil War and Reconstruction in Alabama* (New York, 1905), 753–54. The other African American papers in Mobile were the *Herald*, the *Repub-*

lican, and the *Watchman*. See Allen Woodrow Jones, "Alabama," in *The Black Press in the South, 1865–1979*, ed. Henry Lewis Suggs (Westport, Conn., 1983), 24–26.

46. Cash, "Alabama Republicans during Reconstruction," 130, 135; Michael W. Fitzgerald, "Radical Republicanism and the White Yeomanry during Alabama Reconstruction, 1865–1868," *Journal of Southern History* 54 (1988): 565–84; Wiggins, *Scalawag*, 6–7. Robert A. Moseley also published the Selma *National Republican*.

47. *Biographical Congressional Directory, 1774 to 1911* (Washington, D.C., 1913), 766; James Lawrence Lancaster, "The Scalawags of North Carolina, 1850–1868," (Ph.D. diss., Princeton University, 1974), 18–90; Otto Olsen, *Carpetbagger's Crusade: The Life of Albion Winegar Tourgee* (Baltimore, 1965), 61.

48. *Public Laws of the State of North Carolina . . . 1868–1869* (Raleigh, 1869), 618; *Public Laws of the State of North Carolina . . . 1869–1870*, 319; Olsen, *Carpetbagger's Crusade*, 74.

49. W. McKee Evans, *Ballots and Fence Rails: Reconstruction on the Lower Cape Fear* (New York, 1966), 219–21.

50. Alan D. Watson, *A History of New Bern and Craven County* (New Bern, N.C., 1987), 433, 436–39, 472–73; Elizabeth City *North Carolinian*, July 1, 1869.

51. On Republican strength in western North Carolina, see Paul D. Escott, *Many Excellent People: Power and Privilege in North Carolina, 1850–1900* (Chapel Hill, 1985), 152; Lancaster, "Scalawags of North Carolina," ii–iii, 276, 545.

52. Rabinowitz, *Race Relations in the Urban South*, 10; Paul Escott, "White Republicanism and Ku Klux Klan Terror: The North Carolina Piedmont during Reconstruction," in *Race, Class and Politics in Southern History: Essays in Honor of Robert F. Durden*, ed. Jeffrey Crow, Paul D. Escott, and Charles L. Flynn Jr. (Baton Rouge, 1989), 5–34.

53. Lancaster, "Scalawags of North Carolina," 543, 544; G. W. Brooks to Edward McPherson, February 3, 1872, McPherson Papers.

54. Lancaster, "Scalawags of North Carolina," 545; Eugene B. Drake to Benjamin F. Butler, June 2, 1874, in James A. Padgett, ed., "Reconstruction Letters from North Carolina, Part VIII," *North Carolina Historical Review* 20 (1943): 47–48.

55. In 1868, none of Virginia's public printing went to Republican publishers. See John J. Palmer to Francis Pierpont, March 3, 1868; J. E. Goode to Henry H. Wells, April 10, 1868; and John J. Palmer to Wells, May 4, 1868, all in Wells Papers, Virginia State Archives, Richmond. In 1869 and 1870, the state auditor recorded some insignificant payments to the *State Journal*. See the State Auditor's Journals, Virginia State Archives. On the number of Virginia Republican papers, see editions of Rowell's newspaper directory and the *Fredericksburg Ledger*, November 17, 1871, January 19, 1872. Republicans were unable to control city government in Richmond, depriving its papers there of any local patronage. Rabinowitz, *Race Relations in the Urban South*, 14.

56. Richmond *Daily State Journal*, February 3, 1870. J. R. Hathaway to Edward McPherson, November 14, 1870; J. T. Daniels and others to McPherson, November 17, 1870; James Platt to McPherson, November 16, 1870, McPherson Papers.

57. Rabinowitz, *Race Relations in the Urban South*, 14, 264, 267, 275–76; on the *Petersburg Times*, see William D. Henderson, *The Unredeemed City: Reconstruction in*

Petersburg, Virginia: 1865–1874 (Washington, D.C., 1977), 82–83. On the *Lynchburg Press*, see John L. Lewis to Edward McPherson, March 18, 1871; Alexander Rives to McPherson, May 19, December 7, 1871, November 30, 1873; John Wright to McPherson, June 22, December 8, 1871, McPherson Papers, and Steven Elliott Tripp, *Yankee Town, Southern City: Race and Class Relations in Civil War Lynchburg* (New York, 1997), 199. On Sener, see *A Biographical Congressional Directory, 1774–1911*, 984, and Sener to Edward McPherson, November 16, December 5, 1870, McPherson Papers.

58. See maps in Richard Lowe, *Republicans and Reconstruction in Virginia, 1856–1870* (Charlottesville, 1991), 100, 123, 127, 178, for information on county population and voting.

59. In 1867, the Boston-based New England Emigrant Aid Company bought the *Florida Union*, and its agent who had arranged the purchase, Edward M. Cheney, became the editor. See Richard H. Abbott, *Cotton and Capital: Boston Businessmen and Antislavery Reform, 1854–1868* (Amherst, Mass., 1991), 201; Boston *Daily Advertiser*, November 4, 1867; Pleasant Daniel Gold, *History of Duval County* (St. Augustine, Fla., 1929), 159.

60. Peter D. Klingman, *Josiah Walls: Florida's Black Congressman of Reconstruction* (Gainesville, 1976), 21–22; *Laws of the State of Florida, First Session, 1868* (Tallahassee, 1868), 161; *Florida Union*, August 20, 1868.

61. *Laws of the State of Florida, First Session, 1868*, 34; ibid., *1871*, 25; *Florida Union*, August 20, September 23, November 11, 1868, April 26, 1876, January 19, 1877; Joe M. Richardson, "Jonathan C. Gibbs: Florida's Only Negro Cabinet Member," *Florida Historical Quarterly* 42 (1964): 365. See list of newspapers designated by McLin in Jacksonville *New South*, April 7, 1875.

62. Gold, *History of Duval County*, 128, 155, 169. See maps in Edward C. Williamson, *Florida Politics in the Gilded Age, 1877–1893* (Gainesville, 1976), 10, 18.

63. See maps in Williamson, *Florida Politics*, 10, 18.

64. Ruth Currie-McDaniel, *Carpetbagger of Conscience: A Biography of John Emory Bryant* (Athens, Ga., 1987), 90–91, 100; Georgia House of Representatives, *Journal, 1868* (Atlanta, 1869), 148; and Augusta *Daily Press*, February 9, 19, 1869.

65. For an overview of the Republican press in Georgia, see Richard H. Abbott, "The Republican Party Press in Reconstruction Georgia, 1867–1874," *Journal of Southern History* 61 (1995): 725–60.

66. Richard H. Abbott, "Jason Clarke Swayze, Republican Editor in Reconstruction Georgia, 1867–1873," *Georgia Historical Quarterly* 79 (1992): 349, and "Republican Party Press," 752–53; Richard Whiteley to Edward McPherson, September 19, 28, 1873, McPherson Papers.

6. The Ideology of the Republican Press

1. *Charleston Republican*, August 28, 1869; Richard Lowe, "The Republican Party in Antebellum Virginia, 1856–1860," *Virginia Magazine of History and Biography* 81 (1973): 265; Donovan H. Bond, "How the Wheeling *Intelligencer* Became a Republican Organ,"

Notes to Chapter Six

West Virginia History 11 (1950): 160–61; *New York Daily Tribune*, May 17, 1867; Beaufort *Free South* quoted in Jeanette M. Bergeron, "Reconstruction Journalism in South Carolina" (master's thesis, University of South Carolina, 1974), 20; Charleston *South Carolina Leader*, October 7, 1865; *Dardanelle Times*, December 2, 1869; *Nashville Republican*, October 7, 1868.

2. *Little Rock Republican*, April 9, 1869; Demopolis *Southern Republican*, August 31, 1871; *Walterboro News*, October 11, 1873; *New Bern Daily Times* quoted in Raleigh *Carolina Era*, October 26, 1871; *Wilmington Post*, November 23, 1867; *Florida Union*, September 30, 1868.

3. *Louisiana State Register*, November 12, 1870; *Alabama State Journal*, March 11, 1870; *Little Rock Republican*, November 12, 1868; *Great Republic*, May 23, 1867; Alan Conway, *The Reconstruction of Georgia* (Minneapolis, 1966), 145.

4. *New Bern Republican*, May 23, 1867; *New Orleans Republican*, September 23, 1870; Richmond *State Journal*, June 15, 1869; *Wilmington Post*, October 29, 1867; *Richmond Republic*, January 11, 1866; Demopolis *Southern Republican*, May 26, 1869; Raleigh *Carolina Era*, October 26, 1871; *Charleston Republican*, October 4, 1869; Mobile *Nationalist*, September 27, 1866; Greensboro *New North State*, October 17, 1872.

5. *Weekly Austin Republican*, March 11, 1868; *Woodville Republican*, October 30, 1869; *Wilmington Post*, October 26, 1867; *Richmond Register*, January 20, 1868; *New Nation*, March 22, August 30, 1866; Richmond *State Journal*, April 21, 1871; *Meridian Chronicle*, March 24, 1868; *Friar's Point Delta*, May 26, October 27, 1869; *Austin Republican*, March 11, 1868.

6. *Little Rock Republican*, February 27, 1868; Greensboro *New North State*, November 7, 1872; Macon *American Union*, April 14, 1868; *Asheville Pioneer*, August 29, 1867.

7. *Richmond Register*, January 22, 1868; *Atlanta Daily New Era*, May 31, 1868; Demopolis *Southern Republican*, August 11, 1869; Greensboro *New North State*, November 7, 1872; Austin *State Journal*, July 11, 1871.

8. *Knoxville Whig*, November 11, 1863 (first quote), March 1, 1865 (second quote).

9. *Chattanooga Daily Gazette*, February 8, 1865; Jonesborough *Union Flag*, October 6, 1865.

10. Fred W. Allsopp, *History of the Arkansas Press for a Hundred Years and More* (Little Rock, 1922), 419; Augusta *Daily Loyal Georgian*, June 1, 1867; Macon *American Union*, September 11, 1868. Swayze's intemperate editorials have led some historians to suggest that Republican editors were just as vitriolic as their Democratic counterparts. See, for example, Eric Foner, *Reconstruction: America's Unfinished Revolution, 1863–1877* (New York, 1988), 348, and Carl R. Osthaus, *Partisans of the Southern Press: Editorial Spokesmen of the Nineteenth Century* (Lexington, Ky., 1994), 128–29. Swayze was the most outspoken editor I encountered; none of the other editors whose papers I read resorted to such bombastic language. For more information on this colorful journalist, see Richard H. Abbott, "Jason Clarke Swayze, Republican Editor in Reconstruction Georgia, 1867–1873," *Georgia Historical Quarterly* 79 (1992).

11. Osthaus, *Partisans of the Southern Press*, 129; *Knoxville Daily Chronicle*, May 3, 1870; Elizabeth City *North Carolinian*, October 27, 1870; *Woodville Republican*, January 15, 1870; *Little Rock Republican*, April 8, 1869 (first quote), May 12, 1868 (second quote). In his history of South Carolina's Republican press, Robert H. Woody concluded that "one of the noticeable characteristics of the Republican press was its relatively dignified tone, its adherence to principle rather than attacks on character . . . by and large, their plane of conduct was superior to that of the more important Democratic papers." See Robert H. Woody, *Republican Newspapers of South Carolina* (Charlottesville, 1936), 58.

12. Greensboro *New North State*, November 21, 1871; Raleigh *Carolina Era*, June 29, 1871; Jacksonville *New South*, March 27, May 5, 1875; Harrisonburg *American Union*, September 29, 1866; *Sumter County Republican*, June 13, 1868; *Athens Republican*, September 27, 1867; *Aiken Tribune*, November 8, 1873; Camden *South Arkansas Journal*, March 25, 1868; *St. Landry Progress*, August 31, 1867.

13. For papers quoting Lincoln, for example, see Jacksonville *Florida Republican*, Nashville *Colored Tennessean*, Greensboro *Union Register*, Opelika *East Alabama Monitor*, Jackson *Daily Times*, *Vicksburg Republican*; for some papers quoting Grant, see Demopolis *Southern Republican*, *Woodville Republican*.

14. *Nashville Republican*, November 5, 1868; Jacksonville *New South*, March 27, 1875; *Savannah Daily Herald*, April 16, 1865; *Charleston Republican*, November 20, 1869; *Charleston Advocate*, April 6, 1867, September 12, 1868; Clarksville *Weekly Patriot*, October 16, 1867; Jean-Charles Houzeau, *My Passage at the New Orleans Tribune: A Memoir of the Civil War Era*, ed. and with an introduction by David C. Rankin, trans. by Gerard F. Denault (Baton Rouge, 1984), 87–88; *New Orleans Tribune*, September 8, 1866.

15. *Philadelphia Press*, July 22, 1867; *Charleston Free Press*, April 4, 1868.

16. *Memphis Post*, January 15, 1866; Houzeau, *My Passage at the New Orleans Tribune*, 90–92; *Charleston Republican*, September 6, 1869; Otto Olsen, *Carpetbagger's Crusade: The Life of Albion Winegar Tourgee* (Baltimore, 1965), 62; *Livingston Messenger* quoted in Mobile *Nationalist*, October 3, 1867; Selma *Republican Union Advocate* quoted in Mobile *Nationalist*, May 2, 1867; *Wilmington Post* quoted in James Lawrence Lancaster, "The Scalawags of North Carolina, 1850–1868," (Ph.D. diss., Princeton University, 1974), 191; Thomas S. Staples, *Reconstruction in Arkansas, 1862–1874* (New York, 1923), 173–74.

17. Jacksonville *Florida Union*, July 23, 1868; *Little Rock Republican*, April 8, 1868; *New Orleans Republican*, October 12, 1870; Austin *Journal*, September 1, 1871, January 10, 1872; Nashville *Press and Times*, August 7, 1865.

18. Chattanooga *Republican*, October 8, 1867; Greensboro *New North State*, May 30, 1872; Elizabeth City *North Carolinian*, October 7, December 2, 1869; *Wilmington Post*, May 30, 1869; *New Bern Republican*, May 16, 1867; Clarksville *Weekly Patriot*, October 16, 1867; *Woodville Republican*, October 30, 1869; *Charleston Republican*, August 19, 1869; Demopolis *Southern Republican*, May 26, 1869; *Columbia Daily Union*, March 18, April 10, October 21, 1870; *Tallahassee Sentinel* quoted in John Allen Meador, "Florida Political Parties, 1865–1877" (Ph.D. diss., University of Florida, 1974), 179–80.

Notes to Chapter Six

19. Jackson *Mississippi Pilot* quoted in *Charleston Republican*, October 8, 1869; Greensboro *New North State*, March 28, 1872; *Salem Advocate* quoted in Greensboro *Republican*, July 14, 1870; *Little Rock Republican*, April 27, 1868; *Woodville Republican*, October 16, 1869; Richmond *New Nation*, March 22, 1866; *Huntsville Advocate* quoted in Mobile *Nationalist*, July 2, 1868.

20. Greenville *New Era*, October 7, 1865; Elizabeth City *North Carolinian*, May 25, 1871; *San Antonio Express*, December 30, 1867, August 6, 1868; Nashville *Press and Times*, November 25, 1866; *Charleston Republican*, August 21, 1869; Greensboro *New North State*, November 23, 1871; New Orleans *National Republican*, July 24, 1872; Raleigh *Carolina Era*, June 22, 1871; *South Carolina Republican*, October 10, 1868.

21. *San Antonio Express*, July 20, 1869; *Little Rock Republican*, March 5, 1868; *Sumter County Republican*, July 4, August 8, 1868; Austin *Southern Intelligencer*, April 10 (quote), May 2, 1867; *Flake's Bulletin* quoted in *Austin Republican*, August 8, 1867; Murfreesboro *Freedom's Watchman*, October 16, 1867; Nashville *Press and Times*, March 11, September 9, November 18, December 16, 1866, January 25, 1867 (quote); Austin *State Journal*, April 6, 1870. On African American editors and equal rights, see William A. Haskins, "Rhetorical Vision of Equality: Analysis of the Rhetoric of the Southern Black Press during Reconstruction," *Communication Quarterly* 29 (1981): 116–22. Historian Mark Summers has commented on the religious themes that appeared in Republican rhetoric on progress. See Mark Summers, *Railroads, Reconstruction, and the Gospel of Prosperity: Aid under the Radical Republicans, 1865–1877* (Princeton, N.J., 1984), 17–18.

22. *Asheville Pioneer*, May 20, 1869; *Louisiana State Register*, March 12, 1860; Chattanooga *Daily Republican*, November 23, 1867; *San Antonio Express*, December 22, 1867; Austin *State Journal*, October 15, 1871; *New Bern Republican*, July 16, 1867; *Aiken Tribune*, April 18, 1874.

23. Chattanooga *Republican*, February 5, 1868; *Flake's Bulletin* quoted in Murfreesboro *Freedom's Watchman*, January 1, 1868; *San Antonio Express*, July 20, 1869; *St. Landry Progress*, August 3, 1867; *Wilmington Post*, July 30, 1868.

24. *Memphis Post*, January 16, 1866; Nashville *Weekly Press and Times*, February 11, 1866; Raleigh *North Carolina Standard*, January 23, 1867; Montgomery *Daily State Journal*, July 27, 1867; *San Antonio Express*, January 24, 1868, July 20, 1869; *Friar's Point Delta*, February 24, 1869; *Little Rock Republican*, December 12, 1867, February 19, 1868, February 7, September 17, 1870; Salem *People's Press*, July 23, 1869; *New Orleans Republican*, March 3, 1870; Austin *State Journal*, May 29, 1872; *New Bern Weekly Times*, August 28, 1873; Alrutheus A. Taylor, *The Negro in Tennessee, 1865–1880* (Washington, D.C., 1941), 29–30, 163, 167, 231–32.

25. Chattanooga *Republican*, July 21, 1869; *Charleston Republican*, August 23, 1869; *San Antonio Express*, August 5, 1869; Elizabeth City *North Carolinian*, July 29, 1869; Jacksonville *Florida Union*, June 26, 1876; William C. Harris, *Day of the Carpetbagger: Republican Reconstruction in Mississippi* (Baton Rouge, 1979), 503–4. John Price of the *Little Rock Republican* initially approved of bringing Chinese labor to Arkansas but changed his mind after African American editor Tabbs Gross criticized him for this view. See Daniel F.

Littlefield Jr. and Patricia Washington McGraw, "The *Arkansas Freeman*, 1869–1870: Birth of the Black Press in Arkansas," *Phylon* 40 (March 1979), 80; *Little Rock Republican*, June 14, 1869, February 7, 1870.

26. Raleigh *North Carolina Standard*, October 10, 1866; *Little Rock Republican*, February 19, 1868; *Memphis Post* quoted in *Little Rock Republican*, December 12, 1867; *Wilmington Post*, July 26, 1868; *Alabama State Journal*, February 6, 1869; *Knoxville Chronicle*, May 28, 1870; *Chattanooga Daily Republican*, November 5, 1868; *Charleston Daily Republican*, October 21, 1869; Corpus Christi *Nueces Valley*, July 20, 1872; Williamsburg *Virginia Gazette*, March 25, 1869; *Friar's Point Delta*, August 18, 1869; Canton *American Citizen*, October 10, 1874.

27. *New Bern Daily Republican*, December 23, 1868; *Wilmington Post*, December 14, 1867; *Louisiana State Register*, April 16, 1870; Augusta *Daily Loyal Georgian*, June 6, 18, July 27, 1867; Griffin *American Union*, November 22, 1867, January 10, 1868; Houzeau, *My Passage at the New Orleans Tribune*, 87–88.

28. *San Antonio Express*, March 2, 1868; *Austin Republican*, December 11, 1867; *Chattanooga Republican*, May 7, 1868; *Decatur Republican* quoted in Shelbyville *Republican*, October 11, 1868; *Little Rock Republican*, February 1, 1868; *Wilmington Post*, October 5, 1867; Jacksonville *Florida Union*, August 27, 1868.

29. Jacksonville *Florida Union*, August 27, 1868; *Little Rock Republican*, March 5, 1867; Atlanta *Daily Opinion*, November 11, 1867; Augusta *National Republican*, June 16, 1868.

30. *Austin Republican*, September 26, 1868; Harrisonburg *American Union*, February 24, 1866; Williamsburg *Virginia Gazette*, April 15, 1869.

31. *Austin Republican*, September 16, 1868; *Lebanon Record*, September 26, 1868; *Wilmington Post*, July 26, 1868; Greensboro *New North State*, August 22, 1872; *Chattanooga Republican*, May 7, 1868; *Athens Republican*, February 20, 1868; *Little Rock Republican*, December 20, 1867; *Selma Press*, March 25, 1871; Montgomery *Daily State Sentinel*, August 9, 1867.

32. *McMinnville Enterprise*, February 5, 1870; Mobile *Nationalist*, May 3, 1866; Montgomery *Daily State Sentinel*, January 7, 1868.

33. *New Bern Republican*, July 16, 1867; *Alabama State Journal*, May 6, 1870; Wetumpka *Elmore Standard*, May 29, 1867.

34. Foner, *Reconstruction*, 323–24.

35. For the Stafford quote, see Harris, *Day of the Carpetbagger*, 348. See next chapter for further discussion of the issues of equal accommodations and integrated schools.

36. Richard Lowe, *Republicans and Reconstruction in Virginia, 1856–1870* (Charlottesville, 1991), 73; Nashville *Press and Times*, May 6, June 24, 1866; *McMinnville Enterprise*, May 11, 25, 1867; Harrison *Unconditional*, July 16, 1867; *Athens Republican*, August 13, September 10, October 29, 1868; Jonesborough *Union Flag*, February 18, 1870; *Knoxville Daily Chronicle*, May 14, 18, 1870.

37. Nashville *Press and Times*, September 9, November 18, 1866; Greenville *New Era*, February 14, 1867; *Knoxville Whig*, March 18, 1868.

38. *Fort Smith New Era*, December 12, 1863, September 3, October 8, 1864, April 1, 29, July 1, 1865; *Little Rock Republican*, December 4, 5, 1867, February 27, March 10, 1868.

39. Austin *Southern Intelligencer*, January 3, 1867; *San Antonio Express*, July 20, August 26, September 17 (quote), 1867; February 4, 1868.

40. Decatur *Republican* quoted in Shelbyville *Republican*, September 11, 1868; *Selma Press*, August 7, 1869; Opelika *East Alabama Monitor*, January 8, 1869; Moulton *Union*, February 24, 1868; *Huntsville Advocate*, August 4, 11, November 17, 1871; *Alabama State Journal*, July 3, 1869, June 16, 23, July 21, 1871, March 2, 1875; William McKinley Cash, "Alabama Republicans during Reconstruction: Personal Characteristics, Motivations, and Political Activity of Party Activists, 1867–1880" (Ph.D. diss., University of Alabama, 1973), 9, 125–26, 19, 180.

41. *New Bern Republican*, October 1, 1868; *Wilmington Post*, October 5, 1867; Elizabeth City *North Carolinian*, May 11, September 21, 1871; *Rutherford Star*, July 11, 1869.

42. *Norfolk Day Book*, September 15, 1871; Harrisonburg *American Union*, April 27, 1867; Richmond *State Journal*, April 6, 1871; *Louisiana State Register*, July 23, 1870; Canton *American Citizen* quoted in Demopolis *Southern Republican*, June 29, 1870.

43. *Charleston Daily Republican* quoted in Bergeron, "Reconstruction Journalism in South Carolina," 3; *St. Landry Progress*, August 3, 1867; *New Bern Daily Republican*, May 14, 1867; Jonesborough *Flag*, July 16, 1869.

44. *Nashville Republican*, September 12, 1868; Jacksonville *Florida Union*, July 23, 1868; see also Murfreesboro *Freedom's Watchman*, October 16, 1867.

45. Not all Republican newspapers addressed the question of suffrage for women, but of the sixteen I identified that did, only one opposed it.

46. Nashville *Press and Times*, January 21, 1866; Atlanta *German Gazette* published in *Little Rock Republican*, September 8, 1871; Murfreesboro *Freedom's Watchman*, October 16, 1867; *San Antonio Express*, October 21, 1867; Jacksonville *Florida Union*, May 6, 1868; *Nashville Republican*, October 6, 1868; Williamsburg *Virginia Gazette*, April 15, 1869; Richmond *State Journal*, May 3, 1871.

47. For example, see Memphis *Die Neue Zeit*, Austin *Texas Staats Zeitung*, Austin *Vorwarts*, Brenham *Texas Volksbote*, Galveston *Unabhangige*, New Braunfels *Vorwarts*, San Antonio *Freie Presse*, Atlanta *Deutsche Zeitung*, New Orleans *Deutsche Zeitung*, New Orleans *Le Sud*, New Orleans *Mitrailleuse*, St. Martinsville *Echo*.

48. Raleigh *North Carolina Standard*, October 30, 1867; *Asheville Pioneer*, November 7, 1867; *Knoxville Whig*, April 1, 1868; Charlotte *Union Republican*, April 1, 1868.

49. Hampton *True Southerner*, November 24, 1865; *Wilmington Post*, November 26, 1867; Corpus Christi *Nueces Valley*, September 28, 1872; Augusta *Loyal Georgian*, June 22, 1867; *Columbus Press*, July 4, 1874. See also Summers, *Railroads, Reconstruction*, 15–16.

50. *Nashville Republican*, September 12, 1868; Augusta *Loyal Georgian*, June 22, 1867; *Southern Celt* quoted in *Charleston Daily Republican*, May 7, 1870; *Winchester Journal*, May 3, 10, 1867; Harrisonburg *American Union*, April 6, 1867; Richmond *New Nation*, June 18, 1868.

51. Carl H. Moneyhon, *Impact of the Civil War and Reconstruction on Arkansas* (Baton Rouge, 1994), 244; Otto Olsen, "Reconsidering the Scalawags," *Civil War History* 12 (1966): 307–15; Lancaster, "Scalawags of North Carolina," 233–35; Foner, *Reconstruction*, 320; *Friar's Point Delta*, November 24, 1869; *New Orleans Republican*, August 13, 1870; *New Orleans Tribune*, October 31, 1867; *Southwest Georgian* quoted in Macon *American Union*, October 27, 1870; Mobile *Nationalist*, February 4, 1868.

52. *Rutherford Star*, April 22, 1871; Charleston *South Carolina Republican*, February 5, 1870; *Lebanon Record*, May 22, 1869; *Southwest Georgian* quoted in Macon *American Union*, October 27, 1870.

53. *Woodville Republican*, January 29, 1870; Elizabeth Studley Nathans, *Losing the Peace: Georgia Republicans and Reconstruction, 1865–1871* (Baton Rouge, 1968), 42–44; Foner, *Reconstruction*, 326–67.

54. *Winchester Journal*, May 21, 1867; *Fredericksburg Ledger*, October 28, 1870, October 20, 1871; Richmond *State Journal*, November 4, 1870; *Little Rock Republican*, February 5, 18, 25, 1868.

55. *Winchester Journal*, September 13, October 18, 1867; Jacksonville *Florida Union*, April 4, 1868; Mobile *Nationalist*, February 4, 1868; *McMinnville Enterprise*, December 14, 1867.

56. *Winchester Journal*, June 15, 1866; Jacksonville *Florida Union*, April 4, 1868; *Richmond Register*, February 10, 1868; Mobile *Nationalist*, April 11, May 2, 1867; *Vicksburg Daily Times*, October 31, 1871; *Woodville Republican*, October 16, 1869; *Columbus Press*, July 28, 1874; *Friar's Point Delta*, November 10, 1869.

57. *Walterboro News*, March 7, 1874; Jacksonville *Florida Union*, May 2, 1868; Jackson *Daily Pilot* quoted in Harris, *Day of the Carpetbagger*, 631; *Little Rock Republican*, October 8, 1868, July 10, 1869; *Lexington Advertiser*, February 27, 1874; *Columbus Press*, July 18, 1874. For an insightful and informative evaluation of Republican tax policies, see J. Mills Thornton III, "Fiscal Policy and the Failure of Radical Reconstruction in the Lower South," in *Region, Race, and Reconstruction: Essays in Honor of C. Vann Woodward*, ed. J. Morgan Kousser and James M. McPherson (New York, 1982).

58. Richmond *New Nation*, April 2, 1866; *Winchester Journal*, May 21, September 13, 1867; Atlanta *New Era*, March 20, 1868; Atlanta *Daily Opinion*, March 24, 1868.

59. For an illuminating discussion of the Republicans' interest in promoting economic prosperity as the key to political success, see Summers, *Railroads, Reconstruction*, esp. 7–31.

60. Editors of most of the Republican papers I examined hoped the plantation system would give way to small farms. Almost none of them, however, proposed any program to produce such a result.

61. Demopolis *Southern Republican*, January 5, 1870; *Alabama State Journal*, January 15, 1870; Harris, *Day of the Carpetbagger*, 487–89; *New Orleans Tribune*, May 26, July 10, 1867; *St. Landry Progress*, August 3, 1867; Richmond *State Journal*, February 8, April 14, 1870; *Fredericksburg Ledger*, October 29, 1872; Corpus Christi *Nueces Valley*, October 22,

1870; *Tallahassee Sentinel* quoted in Peter D. Klingman, *Josiah Walls: Florida's Black Congressman of Reconstruction* (Gainesville, 1976), 23.

62. Summers, *Railroads, Reconstruction*, 8–10, 33–37, 39; Harris, *Day of the Carpetbagger*, 540; Jerrell H. Shofner, *Nor Is It Over Yet: Florida in the Era of Reconstruction, 1863–1877* (Gainesville, 1974), 211; *Charleston Daily Republican*, September 6, 1869; Meador, "Florida Political Parties," 179–80.

7. Differences in Approach

1. *Alabama State Journal*, April 7, 1871; James Marten, *Texas Divided: Loyalty and Dissent in the Lone Star State, 1856–1874* (Lexington, Ky., 1990), 143.

2. *New Orleans Tribune*, September 10, 1864, May 6, July 13, 16, 22, August 31, 1865; William P. Connor, "Reconstruction Rebels: The *New Orleans Tribune* in Post-War Louisiana," *Louisiana History*, 21 (1980): 171–77.

3. *St. Landry Progress*, July 27, August 10, September 14, 1867; Hampton *True Southerner*, December 21, 1865; Mobile *Nationalist*, October 11, 1866.

4. *Fort Smith New Era*, September 2, 1865; Michael W. Fitzgerald, *The Union League Movement in the Deep South: Politics and Agricultural Change during Reconstruction* (Baton Rouge, 1989), 124n; *Knoxville Whig*, August 10, 1864; Nashville *Press and Times*, July 10, 1867; Jonesborough *Union Flag*, August 16, 1867; *McMinnville Enterprise*, November 9, 1867.

5. Hampton *True Southerner*, December 21, 1865; *Wilmington Post*, August 7, 1867; *Asheville Pioneer*, October 3, 1867; Augusta *Loyal Georgian*, June 15, 1867; Montgomery *Alabama State Sentinel*, January 9, 29, 1868; Steven Elliott Tripp, *Yankee Town, Southern City: Race and Class Relations in Civil War Lynchburg* (New York, 1997), 199; Harrisonburg *American Union*, November 16, 1867.

6. *Winchester Journal*, August 14, 1868; *Louisiana State Register*, May 28, 1870; Raleigh *North Carolina Standard*, September 2, 1868; *Sumter County Republican*, July 4, 1868; *San Antonio Express*, January 11, 1868.

7. Otto Olsen, *Carpetbagger's Crusade: The Life of Albion Winegar Tourgee* (Baltimore, 1965), 76; Mobile *Nationalist*, April 5, 12, 1866.

8. Charleston *South Carolina Leader*, October 21, 1865, July 14, November 17, December 8, 23, 1866; *Charleston Advocate*, June 1, 1867, October 17, 1868; Columbia *South Carolina Republican*, June 19, 1869, February 5, October 29, 1870; *Charleston Daily Republican*, February 1, 2, 1870.

9. Augusta *Loyal Georgian*, July 25, 1867; *Winchester Journal*, July 5, 1867, February 7, 1868; Raleigh *North Carolina Standard*, March 4, April 25, 1866, January 2, 1867; William McKinley Cash, "Alabama Republicans during Reconstruction: Personal Characteristics, Motivations, and Political Activity of Party Activists, 1867–1880" (Ph.D. diss., University of Alabama, 1973), 77; Richmond *New Nation*, September 20, November 15, 29, 1866, February 28, 1867; Mobile *Nationalist*, October 10, 24, 1867; *Fort Smith New Era*, May 27,

1867; *Little Rock Republican,* February 5, 1868; *San Antonio Express,* August 12, 29, 1867; Griffin *American Union,* November 15, 1867; Olsen, *Carpetbagger's Crusade,* 63, 104.

10. *Knoxville Whig,* June 7, 1865; *McMinnville Enterprise,* November 9, 1867; Jonesborough *Union Flag,* August 16, 1867; *Chattanooga Republican,* October 8, 1867; *Memphis Post,* March 18, 1866, April 3, 1868; *Nashville Republican,* October 27, 1868; *Athens Republican,* August 13, 1868.

11. *Meridian Chronicle,* April 21, 1868; William C. Harris, *Day of the Carpetbagger: Republican Reconstruction in Mississippi* (Baton Rouge, 1979), 197 n.82.

12. *New Orleans Tribune,* October 19, November 25 (quote), 1866; New Orleans *Louisianan,* May 11, 1871; *St. Landry Progress,* April 11, 1868. A number of other African American papers in the South also opposed disfranchisement. See Alrutheus A. Taylor, *The Negro in Tennessee, 1865–1880* (Washington, D.C., 1941), 70; Thomas B. Alexander, *Political Reconstruction in Tennessee* (Nashville, 1950), 272 n.11; Harris, *Day of the Carpetbagger,* 230; Julius Eric Thompson, "Mississippi," in *The Black Press in the South,* ed. Henry Lewis Suggs (Westport, Conn., 1983), 179.

13. *New Orleans Tribune,* May 21, June 8, 11 (quote), 1865, April 21, 26, May 9, 21, July 21, November 5, 1867; Connor, "Reconstruction Rebels," 166–69; Caryn Cosse Bell, *Revolution, Romanticism, and the Afro-Creole Protest Tradition in Louisiana, 1718–1868* (Baton Rouge, 1998), 264. For the paper's remarks on arming blacks, see *New Orleans Tribune,* June 7, August 31, 1865, August 31, September 16, December 4, 9, 30, 1866.

14. New Orleans *Louisianan,* January 1, 12, 19, April 9, May 4, 28, June 22, 25, July 9, 1871; Austin *Freedman's Press,* August 22, 1868; *Galveston Republican* quoted in *Louisianan,* January 19, February 12, 1871; Mobile *Nationalist,* April 18, 1867; Savannah *Freedmen's Standard,* February 16, 1868; Little Rock *Arkansas Freeman,* October 5, 1869; Alexander, *Political Reconstruction in Tennessee,* 205.

15. Austin *State Journal,* May 5, 1870; *Little Rock Republican,* February 25, 1868; *Knoxville Whig,* November 20, 1867; Charlotte *Union Republican,* April 1, 1868; *Rutherford Star,* February 27, 1869; Horace W. Raper, *William W. Holden: North Carolina's Political Enigma* (Chapel Hill, 1985), 299; *Charleston Republican,* September 20, 1869; Harris, *Day of the Carpetbagger,* 465; *Vicksburg Times,* July 14, 1874; *Vicksburg Weekly Republican,* October 25, 1868; *Little Rock Republican,* February 25, 1868.

16. *Charleston Advocate,* April 6, 1867; *Charleston Daily Republican,* December 15, 1869, January 1, 1870; *Little Rock Republican,* July 24, 1871; Nashville *Press and Times,* June 6, 1867; *Winchester Journal,* May 16, 1867; Richmond *New Nation,* May 2, 1867; Jackson *Pilot,* January 1, 1873; *Vicksburg Times,* May 7, 1873; Murfreesboro *Freedom's Watchman,* November 6, 1867.

17. Mobile *Nationalist,* May 3, 17, 1866, June 6, 1867; *New Orleans Tribune,* June 2, 1867; Richard H. Abbott, "Jason Clarke Swayze, Republican Editor in Reconstruction Georgia, 1867–1873," *Georgia Historical Quarterly* 79 (1992): 351–52.

18. Richmond *New Nation,* July 5, 1866; *Austin Republican,* July 8, 1868; *New Orleans Republican,* May 19, August 2, 1870; Nashville *Press and Times,* August 7, 1867; *Nashville Republican,* August 20, 1868.

19. Richmond *New Nation,* May 2, 1867; *Alabama State Journal,* April 10, 1869; Howard N. Rabinowitz, *Race Relations in the Urban South* (New York, 1978), 288; *St. Landry Progress,* November 9, 1867; Griffin *American Union,* November 15, 1867, April 27, 1868; *Charleston Daily Republican,* June 24, 27, July 1, 1870; Fitzgerald, *Union League,* 63; *Little Rock Republican,* August 13, 1870. For other papers concerned about black officeholding, see Jacksonville *Florida Union,* August 20, 1868; Elizabeth City *North Carolinian,* August 11, 1870; *Wilmington Post,* July 11, 1869; *Austin Republican,* December 25, 1867; *Louisiana State Register,* July 9, 1870; *New Orleans Republican,* March 13, May 1, 1870.

20. *New Orleans Tribune,* August 31, 1866; *St. Landry Progress,* August 3, 1867.

21. *South Carolina Leader,* October 21, 1865; *Charleston Advocate,* November 7, 1868.

22. *Charleston Daily Republican,* October 5, 11, 15, 16, 20, 27, 28, 29, November 12, 13, 22, 26, 1869, May 5, 1870; *Southern Celt* reprinted in *Charleston Daily Republican,* May 7, 1870; Thomas Holt, *Black over White: Negro Political Leadership in South Carolina during Reconstruction* (Urbana, Ill., 1977), 154–63. Michael Fitzgerald has discussed the role the Union League played in helping workers in Mississippi and Alabama resist planter dominance. See his *The Union League Movement in the Deep South,* passim.

23. Richmond *State Journal,* April 25, May 5, 8, 18, June 9, August 15, 1871; *Lebanon Record,* March 3, 1869.

24. Memphis *Union Appeal* quoted in Stephen V. Ash, *When the Yankees Came: Conflict and Chaos in the Occupied South, 1861–1865* (Chapel Hill, 1995), 182; *Philadelphia Press* quoted in Norfolk *New Regime,* January 23, 1865. For discussion of class conflict in Virginia during the Civil War, see Stephen V. Ash, "White Virginians under Federal Occupation, 1861–1865," *Virginia Magazine of History and Biography* 98 (1990): 184.

25. *Brownlow's Knoxville Whig and Rebel Ventilator* quoted in James B. Campbell, "East Tennessee during the Federal Occupation, 1863–1865," *East Tennessee Historical Society Publications* 19 (1947): 66–67; Nashville *Daily Times and True Union* quoted in Ash, *When the Yankees Came,* 182; *Fort Smith New Era* quoted in Ash, *When the Yankees Came,* 176. For a discussion of class awareness in Arkansas, see Carl H. Moneyhon, *The Impact of the Civil War and Reconstruction on Arkansas* (Baton Rouge, 1994), 52–58, 95–96, 102, 110, 121–22, 159–60; on class issues in Tennessee, see Stephen V. Ash, *Middle Tennessee: Society Transformed, 1860–1870* (Baton Rouge, 1988), 45–51, 157–72.

26. Olsen, *Carpetbagger's Crusade,* 62–65, 86; James Lawrence Lancaster, "The Scalawags of North Carolina, 1850–1868," (Ph.D. diss., Princeton University, 1974), 227, 451 n.78; Paul Escott, "White Republicanism and the Ku Klux Klan Terror: The North Carolina Piedmont during Reconstruction," in Jeffrey Crow, Paul D. Escott, and Charles L. Flynn Jr., *Race, Class and Politics in Southern History: Essays in Honor of Robert F. Durden* (Baton Rouge, 1989), 24–25, 31; *Wilmington Post* quoted in Elizabeth City *North Carolinian,* May 11, 1871; W. McKee Evans, *Ballots and Fence Rails: Reconstruction on the Lower Cape Fear* (New York, 1966), 234. For a discussion of class consciousness in North Carolina, see two works by Paul Escott, "White Republicanism and the Ku Klux Klan Terror" and *Many Excellent People: Power and Privilege in North Carolina, 1850–1900* (Chapel Hill, 1985).

27. Michael Perman, *The Road to Redemption: Southern Politics, 1869–1879* (Chapel Hill, 1984), 23–26. Perman's book has proved invaluable in tracing the development of Republican factionalism as it emerged over the course of Reconstruction. I have relied on it extensively in writing this chapter and the following one.

28. *New Orleans Tribune,* June 11 (first quote), June 12 (second quote), 1867; Macon *American Union,* January 10, 1868 (first quote), August 20, 1869 (second quote); *Little Rock Republican,* June 22, 1868; *San Antonio Express,* August 26, 1867; *Rutherford Star,* September 4, 1869.

29. Perman, *Road to Redemption,* 23–26.

30. Jean Folkerts, "Functions of the Reform Press," *Journalism History* 12 (1985): 22–25.

31. Richard H. Abbott, "The Republican Party Press in Reconstruction Georgia, 1867–1874," *Journal of Southern History* 61 (1995): 736–47.

32. C. E. Harper, "The Country Press of Louisiana, 1860–1910" (master's thesis, Louisiana State University, 1929), 119; Frank Allen Dennis, "West Tennessee Newspapers during the Civil War, 1860–1865" (Ph.D. diss., Mississippi State University, 1970), 150–54, 167, 171, 174; Atlanta *New Era,* April 2, 5, December 1, 1868; Ronald H. Limbaugh, *Rocky Mountain Carpetbaggers: Idaho's Territorial Governors, 1863–1890* (Moscow, Ida., 1982), 90; Macon *American Union,* June 6, 1872; Fred W. Allsopp, *History of the Arkansas Press for a Hundred Years and More* (Little Rock, 1922), 464–65; Samuel Bard to Edward M. Morgan, July 10, 1872, William E. Chandler Papers; *Bainbridge Weekly Sun,* September 24, 1873, April 1, December 24, 1874; Rhoda Coleman Ellison, *History and Bibliography of Alabama Newspapers in the Nineteenth Century* (University, Ala., 1954), 132–33.

33. Ruth Currie-McDaniel, *Carpetbagger of Conscience: A Biography of John Emory Bryant* (Athens, Ga., 1987), 206 n.59; Abbott, "Republican Party Press," 732–36; Atlanta *New Era,* January 7, February 22, 23, 29, March 3, 6, 20, 21, 22, 1868.

34. Atlanta *New Era,* July 14 (third and fourth quotes), August 5 (first quote), 1868, January 26 (second quote), May 12 (fifth quote), 1869; Abbott, "Republican Party Press," 747–48; Atlanta *Daily True Georgian,* December 24, 1870; Currie-McDaniel, *Carpetbagger of Conscience,* 130; Montgomery *Alabama State Journal,* February 5, 1876. For Republican attacks on Bard, see the *New Era,* April 24, 30, May 5, 15, 28, 1869; *New Orleans Republican,* December 15, 1870; *Alabama State Journal,* March 31, 1871; Valentine Dell to Edward McPherson, April 2, 1869, Edward McPherson Papers, LC.

35. *Austin Republican,* July 18, August 8, October 9, 1867, January 15, 1868; James M. Smallwood, *Time of Hope, Time of Despair: Black Texans during Reconstruction* (Port Washington, N.Y., 1981), 133; Carl H. Moneyhon, *Republicanism in Reconstruction Texas* (Austin, 1980), 65, 75, 98, 144–45, 155, 175, 291; Earl W. Fornell, "Ferdinand Flake: German Pioneer Journalist of the Southwest," *American-German Review* 21 (1955): 27.

36. Michael Perman contends that the Republicans made only a limited effort to implement the radical or "expressive" approach toward building their party, generally using it to make "desperate appeals" to white workers at election time. Although he is correct in noting that Republicans made "no sustained effort to win the confidence and allegiance

of the white masses through a series of measures or programs," I believe he is wrong to assert that "southern Republicanism was unwilling to depict itself as a class party." There is much evidence that its editors did exactly that, especially in the early days of Reconstruction. See Perman, *Road to Redemption*, 105.

37. On the role Northern Republicans played in supporting the moderate wing of their party in the South, see Richard H. Abbott, *The Republican Party and the South, 1855–1877: The First Southern Strategy* (Chapel Hill, 1986).

38. W. H. Christy to Edward McPherson, March 22, April 6, 1867, May 21, 1868; O. P. Morton to McPherson, March 22, 1867; Edward M. Cheney to McPherson, April 25, May 13, 1867; John A. Bingham to McPherson, May 24, 1867; Thomas Durant to McPherson, June 25, 1867; William Dockray to McPherson, December 28, 1868, McPherson Papers. Jerrell H. Shofner, *Nor Is It Over Yet: Florida in the Era of Reconstruction, 1863–1877* (Gainesville, 1974), 165–74, 188–89; Canter Brown Jr., *Ossian Bingley Hart: Florida's Loyalist Reconstruction Governor* (Baton Rouge, 1997), 175–92; Peter D. Klingman, *Josiah Walls: Florida's Black Congressman of Reconstruction* (Gainesville, 1976), 23; Charles Francis Ritter, "The Press in Florida, Louisiana, and South Carolina and the End of Reconstruction, 1865–1877: Southern Men with Northern Interests" (Ph.D. diss., Catholic University of America, 1976), 143, 151; Jacksonville *Florida Union*, March 7, 1868.

39. Thomas Durant to Charles Sumner, March 5, 1867, March 4, 1868; Benjamin Butler and others to McPherson, [March 1867]; J. B. Roudanez to McPherson, April 16, 1867, McPherson Papers. Thomas J. Durant to Benjamin Butler, March 9, 1867, Benjamin Butler Papers, LC; Washington *Daily Morning Chronicle*, April 12, 1867; *New Orleans Tribune*, May 19, 21, July 2, July 3, 1867; Ralph Morrow, *Northern Methodism and Reconstruction* (East Lansing, 1956), 40, 55, 221; Robert T. Clark Jr., "Reconstruction and the New Orleans German Colony," *Louisiana Historical Quarterly* 23 (1940): 502, 505; Henry Clay Warmoth, *War, Politics, and Reconstruction: Stormy Days in Louisiana* (New York, 1930), 51–58.

40. Bell, *Revolution, Romanticism*, 268–74; *New Orleans Tribune*, May 24, 25, June 8, November 28, 1867; F. Wayne Binning, "Carpetbaggers' Triumph: The Louisiana State Election of 1868," *Louisiana History* 14 (1973): 35. In December 1868, Roudanez revived the *Tribune*, but it lasted only a few months. See J. C. Laizer to Edward McPherson, December 26, 1868, McPherson Papers; Connor, "Reconstruction Rebels," 180. On the *St. Landry Progress*, see Carolyn DeLatte, "The St. Landry Riot: A Forgotten Incident of Reconstruction Violence," *Louisiana History* 67 (1976): 41–51, and Geraldine Mary McTigue, "Forms of Racial Interaction in Louisiana, 1860–1880," (Ph.D. diss., Yale University, 1975), 291–300.

41. *New Bern Republican*, May 9, June 11, 27, July 6, September 24, October 1, 21, November 15, 17, 18, 25, 1868; Lancaster, "Scalawags of North Carolina," 213.

42. Albion Tourgee to Benjamin Wade, March 29, 1867, Benjamin Wade Papers, LC; Edward McPherson to G. W. Brooks, March 4, 1867, and Brooks to McPherson, March 18, 1867, McPherson Papers; Olsen, *Carpetbagger's Crusade*, 42–74.

43. Robert Francis Engs, *Freedom's First Generation: Black Hampton, Virginia, 1861–1890* (Philadelphia, 1979), 93–94; Suggs, ed., *The Black Press in the South*, 379; Richmond *Register*, January 6, 1868; William D. Henderson, *The Unredeemed City: Reconstruction in Petersburg, Virginia: 1865–1874* (Washington, D.C., 1977), 82–83; Richard Lowe, *Republicans and Reconstruction in Virginia, 1856–1870* (Charlottesville, 1991), 85; Harrisonburg *American Union*, April 6, 27, 1867.

44. James W. Hunnicutt to Charles Sumner, [July 1867], Charles Sumner Papers, Houghton Library, Harvard University; Lowe, *Republicans and Reconstruction in Virginia*, 137, 143, 149, 156–57.

45. Griffin *American Union*, October 11, 1867; *Daily Loyal Georgian*, June 7, 1867; Rufus Bullock and others to Edward McPherson, March 19, 1867, and E. H. Pughe to McPherson, April 6, 1867, McPherson Papers.

46. Joseph Brown to John Sherman, April 6, 1867, John Sherman Papers, LC; William Scruggs to Edward McPherson, January 14, 1868, McPherson Papers; Abbott, "Republican Party Press," 739, 746–47.

47. *Huntsville Advocate* quoted in Nashville *Press and Times*, June 16, 1866, March 21, 1867; Decatur *Alabama Republican* quoted in Shelbyville *Republican*, September 11, 1868; Sarah Woolfolk Wiggins, *The Scalawag in Alabama Politics, 1865–1881* (University, Ala., 1977), 6–7, 33; *Alabama State Sentinel*, June 12, 15, 29, July 2, 11 (quote), 1867, January 23, February 6, 11, 1868; prospectus for *East Alabama Monitor* published in *Alabama State Sentinel*, July 26, 1867; *East Alabama Monitor*, May 16, 1868, January 8, 1869.

48. *Austin Republican*, September 4 (quote), October 9, 19, November 27, December 25, 1867, January 15, 1868.

49. Harris, *Day of the Carpetbagger*, 229, 231.

50. On the *Missionary Record*, see Robert H. Woody, *Republican Newspapers of South Carolina* (Charlottesville, Va., 1936), 15–16.

51. Jacksonville *Florida Union*, November 14, 1868.

52. Cash, "Alabama Republicans during Reconstruction," 180–82; Opelika *East Alabama Monitor*, November 21, 1868, January 15, 1869; *Selma Press* reprinted in *East Alabama Monitor*, February 19, 1869; *Selma Press*, September 11, 1869, January 22, 1870; Mobile *Nationalist*, November 1, 1868; Fitzgerald, *Union League*, 45–46, 188.

53. New Bern *Daily Republican*, November 15, 1868; *Wilmington Post*, November 5, 1868; *Rutherford Star*, December 12, 1868.

54. Atlanta *New Era*, November 3, 1870; *Fredericksburg Ledger*, May 24, September 27, November 3, 1870; Richmond *Daily State Journal*, May 26, 1871; Jack P. Maddex Jr., *The Virginia Conservatives, 1867–1879: A Study in Reconstruction Politics* (Chapel Hill, 1970), 109; Moneyhon, *Republicanism in Reconstruction Texas*, 174.

55. Montgomery *Alabama State Sentinel*, March 18, 1868; Griffin *American Union*, April 24, June 5, 12, 1868; Fort Valley *Southwest Georgian* quoted in Macon *American Union*, October 27, 1870; *Little Rock Republican*, April 3, 1868.

56. *Columbia Daily Union*, November 11, 1872; *Vicksburg Daily Times*, August 1, 1874; Jacksonville *Florida Union*, August 10, 1876.

57. For a fuller discussion of Swayze's editorial perambulations, see Abbott, "Jason Clarke Swayze," passim. Michael Perman identified Swayze as a centrist based on opinions he expressed in 1872, after abandoning his radical phase. See Perman, *Road to Redemption*, 102.

58. In his perceptive analysis of Southern Reconstruction politics, Michael Perman has noted that the centrist Republicans' strategy was based on a belief that if leading whites could be enticed into Republican ranks, the masses of whites would follow. Hence, as Perman says, they neglected grass-roots and issue-oriented mobilization of voters in favor of courting an elite. See Perman, *Road to Redemption*, 106–7.

59. Republicans in Alabama repealed suffrage restrictions in 1868; Louisiana followed two years later. See Perman, *Road to Redemption*, 26.

60. Lowe, *Republicans and Reconstruction in Virginia*, 161–74; Richmond *Independent Republican*, June 12, 19, 26, 1869; *Winchester Journal*, April 2, 16, 1869; Williamsburg *Virginia Gazette*, June 17, 24, July 1, 1869; Richmond *Daily State Journal*, May 10, 31, 1869.

61. Alexander, *Political Reconstruction in Tennessee*, 200–225; Shelbyville *Republican*, November 4, 13, 1868.

62. Alexander, *Political Reconstruction in Tennessee*, 215–17, 274 n.1; James C. Parker, "Tennessee Gubernatorial Elections, I: 1869, The Victory of the Conservatives," *Tennessee Historical Quarterly* 33 (1974): 38–42; Jonesborough *Union Flag*, May 28, July 16, 1869; Huntington *West Tennessean*, June 24, 1869; Chattanooga *Daily Republican*, February 12, 1869, *Athens Republican*, April 29, 1869; Clarksville *Weekly Patriot*, June 23, 1869; *Lebanon Record*, May 29, 1869.

63. Alexander, *Political Reconstruction in Tennessee*, 215–17, 274 nn. 1, 11, 15; Parker, "Tennessee Gubernatorial Elections," 42; Chattanooga *Daily Republican*, August 5, 1869; Huntington *West Tennessean*, June 24, 1869; *Public Acts of the General Assembly of the State of Tennessee, 1st Session, 36th General Assembly, 1869* (Nashville, 1870), 3.

64. Shannon, "Tennessee," in *The Black Press in the South*, ed. Suggs, 317–19; Taylor, *The Negro in Tennessee*, 69–70; *Maryville Republican*, October 7, 1876. McConnell established a strongly Republican paper in Maryville, the *Soldier's Gazette*, that challenged Scott's paper. It was out of business in less than a year. Shannon, "Tennessee," 318–19; *Soldier's Gazette*, May 7, August 26, December 8, 1870.

65. Harris, *Day of the Carpetbagger*, 141–42, 148, 186, 196–98, 205–17; *Meridian Chronicle*, November 14, December 5, 12, 24, 1868; *Vicksburg Republican*, July 14, September 6, 1868.

66. Harris, *Day of the Carpetbagger*, 224–31, 237–39, 244–45, 257.

67. Moneyhon, *Republicanism in Reconstruction Texas*, 83–92.

68. See references to Flake's paper in *Austin Republican*, July 18, August 8, September 4, 1867; *San Antonio Express*, July 16, November 21, 1867, June 19, 1868, January 20, 1869.

69. *Austin Republican*, November 27, 1867, March 25, April 22, May 13, 20, June 17, July 8, 1868; *San Antonio Express*, May 15, 23, December 20, 1868, January 9, 20, 1869.

70. Charles W. Ramsdell, *Reconstruction in Texas* (New York, 1910), 243–55.

71. Moneyhon, *Republicanism in Reconstruction Texas*, 103–22; *San Antonio Express*, June 29, July 2, 3, 1868.

72. Woody, *Republican Newspapers*, 43; *Charleston Republican*, August 26, October 11, 1869, May 3, 1870; Francis Butler Simkins and Robert H. Woody, *South Carolina during Reconstruction* (Chapel Hill, 1932), 448–53; *Selma Press*, September 11, 1869; *Alabama State Journal*, November 6, December 25, 1869; Elizabeth City *North Carolinian*, July 14, 1870; *Rutherford Star*, September 4, 1869.

73. Atlanta *New Era*, July 13 (quote), 14, 1869; Currie-McDaniel, *Carpetbagger of Conscience*, 97–103; Elizabeth Studley Nathans, *Losing the Peace: Georgia Republicans and Reconstruction, 1865–1871* (Baton Rouge, 1968), 147–58.

74. Macon *American Union*, December 18, 1868 (first quote), April 30 (second quote), 1869; Atlanta *New Era*, February 28 (fourth quote), March 28 (third quote), 1869.

75. Currie-McDaniel, *Carpetbagger of Conscience*, 105–13; Atlanta *Daily True Georgian*, June 28, 1870.

76. Thomas S. Staples, *Reconstruction in Arkansas, 1862–1874* (New York, 1923), 341, 375–76; Allsopp, *History of the Arkansas Press*, 362; Little Rock *Morning Journal*, May 17 (quote), June 2, 1869; Daniel F. Littlefield Jr. and Patricia Washington McGraw, "The Arkansas Freeman, 1869–1870: Birth of the Black Press in Arkansas," *Phylon* 40 (March 1979): 75–85; *Arkansas Freeman*, October 5, 1869.

77. *Little Rock Republican*, January 22 (second quote), February 24 (first quote), April 11, September 26 (third quote), 1870; Allsopp, *History of the Arkansas Press*, 617; Staples, *Reconstruction in Arkansas*, 380–83.

8. Continuing Factionalism

1. Michael Perman, *The Road to Redemption: Southern Politics, 1869–1879* (Chapel Hill, 1984), 50–56.

2. Allen W. Trelease, *White Terror: The Ku Klux Klan Conspiracy and Southern Reconstruction* (New York, 1971), 63, 67, 71, 97, 117, 154, 191, 234; on the Democratic press inciting violence, see 104–5, 135, 139, 207, 253, 308. On the Democratic press and the Klan, see also Carl R. Osthaus, *Partisans of the Southern Press: Editorial Spokesmen of the Nineteenth Century* (Lexington, Ky., 1994), 130–32.

3. *Charleston Daily Republican*, September 20, 1869; *Selma Press*, February 25, 1871; *Huntsville Advocate*, July 21, 1871; Raleigh *Carolina Era*, October 26, 1871; *Greensboro Register*, July 14, 1869; *Columbia Daily Union*, February 15, 1872.

4. Eric Foner, *Reconstruction: America's Unfinished Revolution, 1863–1877* (New York, 1988), 443–44; *Wilmington Post*, December 9, 1869; Demopolis *Southern Republican*, February 22, 1871; *Asheville Pioneer*, April 18, 1872.

5. *Memphis Post*, January 27, 1868; Elizabeth City *North Carolinian*, September 15, 1870, May 25, 1871; Raleigh *New Era* quoted in *Asheville Pioneer*, June 22, 1871; Demopolis *Southern Republican*, February 22, 1871; *Alabama State Journal*, May 5, September 1, 1871; Helena *Weekly Clarion*, October 14, 1871; *San Antonio Express*, March 18, 1868, September

10, 1871 (quote); Austin *State Journal*, March 11, May 8, 1870. Law enforcement was a particular concern in Texas, which faced frontier violence as well as Klan activity. In Corpus Christi, the editor of the *Nueces Valley* praised the state's Republican government for adopting strong measures to deal with crime along the Mexican border. See *Nueces Valley*, September 24, November 12, 19, 1870, August 24, 1872.

6. *Rutherford Star*, August 27, 1870; Paul Escott, "White Republicanism and the Ku Klux Klan Terror: The North Carolina Piedmont during Reconstruction," in Jeffrey Crow, Paul D. Escott, and Charles L. Flynn Jr., *Race, Class and Politics in Southern History: Essays in Honor of Robert F. Durden* (Baton Rouge, 1989), 31; Macon *American Union*, April 16, 1869; Atlanta *New Era*, April 24 (first quote), 28 (second quote), 1869; Trelease, *White Terror*, 377.

7. Foner, *Reconstruction*, 439–41; *Knoxville Whig*, March 25, 1868; Shelbyville *Republican*, September 11, 1868; Murfreesboro *Freedom's Watchman*, March 4, 1868; *Sumter County Republican*, August 1, 8, 1868; *Athens Republican*, August 27, September 27, 1868.

8. Nashville *Press and Times*, August 7, 1867, January 15, 28, February 5, March 26, 1868; *Nashville Republican*, July 18, August 20, 25 (quotes), 29, September 8, 1868; *Athens Republican*, April 29, 1869; Thomas B. Alexander, *Political Reconstruction in Tennessee* (Nashville, 1950), 176–98.

9. Thomas S. Staples, *Reconstruction in Arkansas, 1862–1874* (New York, 1923), 288–89, 300–302; Little Rock *Morning Republican*, October 28, 29, 30, November 2, 16, 19, December 28, 1868, January 2, 13, 18, 20, 21, 22, 28, 1869.

10. Foner, *Reconstruction*, 441–42; *Wilmington Post*, November 28, 1869; *North Carolina Standard*, September 15, October 27, December 22, 1869, April 13, July 13, 1870; *Rutherford Star*, October 9, November 6, 1869, June 25, 1870; Elizabeth City *North Carolinian*, October 13, 1870.

11. *Selma Press*, November 20, 1869, April 16, 1870 (quote); *Alabama State Journal*, May 15 (quote), November 20, 1869, April 15, August 12, 19, 1870; Demopolis *Southern Republican*, August 18, September 1, 1869, April 6, 13, 27, July 30 (first quote), September 7 (second quote), 1870; Sarah Woolfolk Wiggins, "Alabama: Democratic Bulldozing and Republican Folly," in *Reconstruction and Redemption in the South*, ed. Otto Olsen (Baton Rouge, 1980), 57; *Columbia Daily Union*, August 27, 1872.

12. Foner, *Reconstruction*, 454–56.

13. *Charleston Daily Republican*, September 11, 1869 (quote), May 28, 1870; *Alabama State Journal*, March 25, 1870, May 5, 1871; Elizabeth City *North Carolinian*, May 25, 1871; *New Orleans Republican*, April 19, 1870; *Selma Press*, May 6, 1871.

14. Demopolis *Southern Republican*, November 9, 1870; *Mobile Herald*, April 24, 1872; *Selma Press*, May 6, 1871; Opelika *Weekly Era and Whig*, April 14, 1871; *New Orleans Louisianan*, March 26, 1871; *New Orleans Republican*, October 22, 1870; *Louisiana State Register*, May 6, 1871; Alexandria *Rapides Gazette*, November 22, December 13, 1873.

15. Jackson *Pilot*, January 25, 27, March 9, 10, 17, April 1, 1871; *Vicksburg Times*, July 18, 1871; Richmond *State Journal*, April 22, 1871; Atlanta *New Era*, June 3, 1870, March 16, April 4, 18, May 25, 1871; Ruth Currie-McDaniel, *Carpetbagger of Conscience: A Biography*

of John Emory Bryant (Athens, Ga., 1987), 115; Macon *American Union*, March 2, 1871; Jeanette M. Bergeron, "Reconstruction Journalism in South Carolina" (master's thesis, University of South Carolina, 1974), 84; Charles Francis Ritter, "The Press in Florida, Louisiana, and South Carolina and the End of Reconstruction, 1865–1877: Southern Men with Northern Interests" (Ph.D. diss., Catholic University of America, 1976), 155.

16. *Fredericksburg Ledger,* December 8, 1871; New Orleans *Louisianan,* December 18, 1870; New Orleans *Republican Standard,* December 22, 1870; *Alabama State Journal,* August 18, 1871; *Arkansas Freeman,* October 5, 1869.

17. *Wilmington Post,* December 19, 1869; *North Carolina Standard,* November 17, 1869; Raleigh *Carolina Era,* December 14, 1871; Greensboro *New North State,* May 30, 1872; *Rutherford Star,* December 14, 1871.

18. Atlanta *New Era,* March 16, 1871; Macon *American Union,* April 1, 1870; *Alabama State Journal,* November 20, 1869; Demopolis *Southern Republican,* July 21, 1869, February 9, October 26, 1870; *Huntsville Advocate,* April 19, 1872.

19. *New Orleans Republican,* September 16, 1870; New Orleans *National Republican,* July 17, 1872; *Louisiana State Register,* January 14, 1871; Corpus Christi *Nueces Valley,* August 26, 1871; Austin *State Journal,* March 18, 1872; *Columbia Daily Union,* January 13, 1872.

20. *Fort Smith New Era,* September 25, 1872; *Hot Springs Courier,* October 6, 1870; *Little Rock Republican,* September 8, 30, 1871.

21. Foner, *Reconstruction,* 488–511.

22. Little Rock *Morning Republican,* September 26, 1870; Fred W. Allsopp, *History of the Arkansas Press for a Hundred Years and More* (Little Rock, 1922), 361–62; Martha Ann Ellenberg, "Reconstruction in Arkansas" (Ph.D. diss., University of Missouri, 1967), 220; Staples, *Reconstruction in Arkansas,* 380–87.

23. Little Rock *Morning Republican,* August 21, September 21, 1871; Allsopp, *History of the Arkansas Press,* 617; Staples, *Reconstruction in Arkansas,* 311–12; Carl H. Moneyhon, *The Impact of the Civil War and Reconstruction on Arkansas* (Baton Rouge, 1994), 258–62; George H. Thompson, *Arkansas and Reconstruction: The Influence of Geography, Economics, and Personality* (Port Washington, N.Y., 1976), 127, 132, 273 n.20.

24. Joe Gray Taylor, *Louisiana Reconstructed, 1863–1877* (Baton Rouge, 1974), 209–12; Ted Tunnell, *Crucible of Reconstruction: War, Radicalism and Race in Louisiana* (Baton Rouge, 1984), 164–69.

25. A. E. Perkins, "James Henri Burch and Oscar James Dunn in Louisiana," *Journal of Negro History* 22 (1937): 321, 322, 327; New Orleans *Louisianan,* November 27, 1870, March 26, May 21, June 1, August 9, September 17, 21, November 16, 1871, January 4, 1872.

26. Taylor, *Louisiana Reconstructed,* 227–36; Alexandria *Rapides Gazette,* April 13, May 11, June 1, September 14, 1872; the *New Orleans Republican* is quoted in the *Rapides Gazette,* August 3, 1872. Lonn has a list of some other papers supporting Warmoth in 1872; many of them were Democratic. Ella Lonn, *Reconstruction in Louisiana after 1868* (New York, 1918), 166 n.1. After 1872 the *Deutsche Zeitung* became a Democratic paper. See

Robert T. Clark Jr., "Reconstruction and the New Orleans German Colony," *Louisiana Historical Quarterly* 23 (1940): 522.

27. Carl H. Moneyhon, *Republicanism in Reconstruction Texas* (Austin, 1980), 153–81; *Nueces Valley,* April 29, August 24, 1872; *San Antonio Express,* June 12, 1872; Paul Casdorph, *A History of the Republican Party in Texas* (Austin, 1965), 23–24.

28. Jerrell H. Shofner, *Nor Is It Over Yet: Florida in the Era of Reconstruction, 1863–1877* (Gainesville, 1974), 281; Richard H. Abbott, "Jason Clarke Swayze, Republican Editor in Reconstruction Georgia, 1867–1873," *Georgia Historical Quarterly* 79 (1992): 363; *Huntsville Advocate,* May 3, 17, August 16, 1872.

29. Alrutheus A. Taylor, *The Negro in Tennessee, 1865–1880* (Washington, D.C., 1941), 227; Foner, *Reconstruction,* 369–71.

30. *New Orleans Tribune,* January 7, 10, 1869; *Louisiana State Register,* June 18, 1870; Murfreesboro *Freedom's Watchman,* November 6, 1867; Nashville *Press and Times,* June 6, November 12, 1867; *Charleston Daily Republican,* December 15, 1869, January 24, 1870; Jackson *Pilot,* February 22, 1873; William C. Harris, *Day of the Carpetbagger: Republican Reconstruction in Mississippi* (Baton Rouge, 1979), 446.

31. Foner, *Reconstruction,* 504–5, 532–34, 553–56.

32. Macon *American Union,* January 25, 1872; New Orleans *Louisianan,* January 28, 1872; *Mobile Herald,* January 23, 1872; Talladega *Our Mountain Home,* June 24, August 5, 12, 1874; *Vicksburg Times,* March 26, 1875; *Columbus Press,* June 20, 1874; *Walterboro News,* July 6, 1874; Jacksonville *New South,* September 26, 1874, February 17, 1875; *Columbia Daily Union,* February 15, 1872.

33. *Alabama State Journal,* August 21, 1874; William McKinley Cash, "Alabama Republicans during Reconstruction: Personal Characteristics, Motivations, and Political Activity of Party Activists, 1867–1880" (Ph.D. diss., University of Alabama, 1973), 371; *Huntsville Advocate,* June 18, 1874; *Knoxville Chronicle,* September 11, 1874; *Asheville Pioneer,* November 7, December 12, 1874; Otto Olsen, *Carpetbagger's Crusade: The Life of Albion Winegar Tourgee* (Baltimore, 1965), 192; *Loudon Times,* June 6, 1874; *Fredericksburg Ledger,* May 26, August 14, October 20, 1874; *Bainbridge Sun,* July 30, August 13 (quote), September 18, 1874; Howard N. Rabinowitz, *Race Relations in the Urban South* (New York, 1978), 290. See the discussion of the impact of civil rights legislation on Republican Party fortunes in Perman, *Road to Redemption,* 138–41, and William Gillette, *Retreat from Reconstruction, 1869–1879* (Baton Rouge, 1979), 259–79.

34. *Wilmington Post,* July 11, 1869; Griffin *American Union,* October 11, 1867; Rabinowitz, *Race Relations in the Urban South,* 289; see also Jacksonville *Florida Union,* August 20, 1868; Elizabeth City *North Carolinian,* August 11, 1870; *Little Rock Republican,* August 13, 1870.

35. Henry Clay Warmoth, *War, Politics, and Reconstruction: Stormy Days in Louisiana* (New York, 1930), 51–59; *St. Landry Progress,* November 9, 1867; New Orleans *Louisianan,* June 22, 1871; *New Orleans Republican,* May 1, 1870; *Rapides Gazette,* March 30, 1872; Tunnell, *Crucible of Reconstruction,* 166–67.

36. Jacksonville *New South*, August 5, 1874; *Charleston Republican*, July 1, 1870; Jackson *Pilot*, February 12, August 17, 1871; Harris, *Day of the Carpetbagger*, 267.

37. Allen Woodrow Jones, "Alabama," in *The Black Press in the South, 1865–1979*, ed. Henry Lewis Suggs (Westport, Conn., 1983), 24–27; Loren Schenwinger, *James T. Rapier and Reconstruction* (Chicago, 1978), 67–77, 114; Peter D. Klingman, *Josiah Walls: Florida's Black Congressman of Reconstruction* (Gainesville, Fla., 1976), 53–54; Edward A. Miller Jr., *Gullah Statesman: Robert Smalls from Slavery to Congress, 1839–1915* (Columbia, S.C., 1995), 74.

38. Foner, *Reconstruction*, 537–39; Taylor, *Louisiana Reconstructed*, 298, 301; *Vicksburg Plain Dealer* quoted in James W. Garner, *Reconstruction in Mississippi* (New York, 1901), 293 n.1; Richmond *Daily State Journal*, May 2, 1872; Alexandria *Rapides Gazette*, November 22, 1873; *Columbus Press*, August 7, 1875; *Natchez Post* quoted in *Vicksburg Daily Times*, April 9, 1875; *Vicksburg Daily Times*, September 12, 1871.

39. Mobile *Nationalist*, June 25, 1868; Opelika *East Alabama Monitor*, February 5, 1869; Montgomery *Alabama State Journal*, June 26, 1869; *Louisiana State Register*, January 14, 1871; *Vicksburg Times*, November 8, 1871; New Orleans *National Republican*, July 17, 1872.

40. *Charleston Daily Republican*, April 7, 1870; see also Raleigh *North Carolina Standard*, September 25, 1867; *New Bern Republican*, December 10, 17, 18, 1868; Fort Smith *Arkansas Patriot*, September 23, 1871; Austin *State Journal*, January 28, 1872; Greensboro *New North State*, April 25, 1872; *Columbus Press*, May 16, 1874; and Jacksonville *New South*, November 11, 1874, for a sample of defenses of carpetbaggers.

41. Alexandria *Rapides Gazette*, April 6, 1872; Taylor, *Louisiana Reconstructed*, 480; New Orleans *National Republican*, July 17, 1872.

42. *Flake's Bulletin* quoted in *New Orleans Republican*, August 18, 1870; *Austin Republican*, August 25, 1870; *Houston Union* quoted in Austin *State Journal*, June 5, 1872; *Fort Smith New Era*, July 12, 1872; *Helena Shield* quoted in Batesville *North Arkansas Times*, February 13, 1869; Helena *Weekly Clarion*, March 31, 1869; *Magnolia Flower* quoted in Ellenberg, "Reconstruction in Arkansas," 217; Little Rock *Morning Republican*, February 22, March 6, April 5 (first quote), June 8 (second quote), 1869.

43. Alexander, *Political Reconstruction in Tennessee*, 204–5, 208–9; Sarah Woolfolk Wiggins, *The Scalawag in Alabama Politics, 1865–1881* (University, Ala., 1977), 49, 132–33; Montgomery *Alabama State Journal*, May 22, 1869, June 23, 30, July 21, 1871; *Huntsville Advocate*, August 11, 1871, May 17, August 23, 1872. Figures died in 1873, and his successors brought the *Advocate* back to Republican ranks; the paper closed in 1874. See *Huntsville Advocate*, August 7, 1873, October 1, 1874.

44. Macon *American Union*, May 28, 1872; *Fredericksburg Ledger*, November 17, 1871; *Norfolk Day Book*, July 17, 1869, and *Day Book* quoted in Richmond *Evening State Journal*, September 15, 1871; Raleigh *Weekly North Carolinian*, October 12, 1870; Canter Brown Jr., "Carpetbagger Intrigues, Black Leadership, and a Southern Loyalist Triumph: Florida's Gubernatorial Election of 1872," *Florida Historical Quarterly* 72 (1993–94): 291, 295.

45. Talladega *Our Mountain Home*, April 29, 1874; see also *Little Rock Republican*, June 2, 1869; Jacksonville *Florida Union*, May 5, 1877.

46. *Wilmington Post*, October 5, 1867; *New Bern Republican*, October 1, 1868; *Asheville Pioneer*, August 26, 1869; *Rutherford Star*, September 11, 1869; Elizabeth City *North Carolinian*, May 11, 1871, March 28, 1872; Raleigh *Carolina Era*, October 12, 1871; *Mobile Herald*, December 18, 1871. On the Whigs and the Republican party, see Perman, *Road to Redemption*, 102–7.

47. Austin *Weekly Southern Intelligencer*, March 21, 1867; *San Antonio Express*, April 4, 9, 1869; Austin *State Journal*, August 9, 1870; Moneyhon, *Republicanism in Reconstruction Texas*, 142–43, 174.

48. *Lebanon Record*, June 19, 1869; *Athens Republican*, December 17, 1868, January 14, June 10, 17, 1869; Chattanooga *Daily Republican*, May 12, 18, 1869.

49. *Rutherford Star*, November 27, 1869; *North Carolina Standard*, November 27, 1869; Elizabeth City *North Carolinian*, August 18, 1870.

50. *Alabama State Journal*, December 18, 1869, January 15, 1870; Demopolis *Southern Republican*, January 5, 1870; *Selma Press*, January 29, 1870; *Huntsville Advocate*, May 26, 1871; *Mobile Herald*, September 11, 1871; *Little Rock Republican*, November 11, 12, 14, 1868, March 10, 1869; Thompson, *Arkansas and Reconstruction*, 232–33; *Fort Smith New Era*, March 27, 1872.

51. *Alabama State Journal*, October 23, 1870; Jacksonville *New South*, October 14, 1874.

52. *Huntsville Advocate*, May 26, 1871; *Mobile Herald*, September 11, 1871; Raleigh *North Carolina Standard*, July 22, 1870; Elizabeth City *North Carolinian*, August 18, 1870; New Bern *Republican and Courier*, December 30, 1871; Raleigh *Daily Examiner*, February 27, 1874; Jacksonville *New South*, October 14, 1874.

53. *Asheville Pioneer*, September 16, 1869; Raleigh *Era* quoted in *Wilmington Post*, July 6, 1872; John Allen Meador, "Florida Political Parties, 1865–1877" (Ph.D. diss., University of Florida, 1974), 214; *New Orleans Republican*, August 31, 1870.

54. *Huntsville Advocate*, May 26, 1871; *Mobile Herald*, September 11, 1871.

55. Joe M. Richardson, *The Negro in the Reconstruction of Florida, 1865–1877* (Tallahassee, 1965), 202, 208; Charleston *South Carolina Republican*, November 15, 1870; San Antonio *Express*, September 7, 1871; Jacksonville *New South*, October 14, 1874.

56. *Little Rock Republican*, July 2, August 10, October 8, 1868, June 23, 1869, July 8, 1871; *Columbia Daily Union*, January 4, February 2, 16, 26, 1872.

57. Elizabeth City *North Carolinian*, August 18, 1870; New Bern *Republican and Courier*, December 30, 1871; *Salem Advocate* quoted in *Greensboro Republican*, July 14, 1870; *Alabama State Journal*, June 16, July 21, 1871, March 8, 1872; *Little Rock Republican*, November 18, 1870; *Fort Smith New Era*, September 29, 1870.

58. Perman, *Road to Redemption*, 143–48; Mark Summers, *Railroads, Reconstruction, and the Gospel of Prosperity: Aid under the Radical Republicans, 1865–1877* (Princeton, N.J., 1984), 287.

59. The editor of the *New Orleans Republican* was furious about the Jackson *Mississippi Pilot*'s condemnation of the Republican Party in Louisiana; see *New Orleans Republican*, September 4, 9, 1870. For other comments on Louisiana, see *Alabama State Journal*, September 1, 1871, and *Florida Union* quoted in Jacksonville *New South*, September 23, 1874.

60. *Louisiana State Register,* January 21, February 9, March 21 (quote), 1871; New Orleans *Louisianan,* May 4, 1871; Alexandria *Rapides Gazette,* January 13, March 9, 1872, August 9, November 9, 1873; *New Orleans Republican* quoted in *Rapides Gazette,* November 22, 1873; Taylor, *Louisiana Reconstructed,* 260–66.

61. Shofner, *Nor Is It Over Yet,* 279, 291–93; Ritter, "The Press in Florida, Louisiana, and South Carolina," 152–53; Jacksonville *Florida Union,* April 24, 1876.

62. *Charleston Republican,* June 16, 18, July 5, 1870; Ritter, "The Press in Florida, Louisiana, and South Carolina," 223; Robert H. Woody, *Republican Newspapers of South Carolina* (Charlottesville, Va., 1936), 20–21, 29–30, 35, 39 (quote), 40; *Columbia Daily Union,* January 4, 5, February 22, March 13, May 11, 1872; Aiken *Tribune,* August 1, 1874; *Walterboro News,* July 17, 1874; Foner, *Reconstruction,* 543.

63. *Vicksburg Times,* September 8, 12, 1871, January 13, April 3, 1872, May 4, 22, September 2, 1873, August 27, September 17, October 2 (quote), 1874; Jackson *Pilot,* December 21, 1871; Harris, *Day of the Carpetbagger,* 429; William C. Harris, "Mississippi: Republican Factionalism and Mismanagement," in *Reconstruction and Redemption in the South,* ed. Otto Olsen (Baton Rouge, 1980), 82–93; Canton *American Citizen,* July 11, 1874; *Columbus Press,* February 20, March 13, 1875.

64. W. E. B. DuBois, *Black Reconstruction in America, 1860–1880* (New York, 1935), 624.

9. The Two-Edged Sword of Patronage

1. See Lawrence N. Powell, "Southern Republicanism during Reconstruction: The Contradictions of State and Party Formation," paper presented at the annual meeting of the Organization of American Historians, 1984), esp. 6–20, and Ted Tunnell, *Crucible of Reconstruction: War, Radicalism and Race in Louisiana* (Baton Rouge, 1984), 151–72.

2. Culver H. Smith, *The Press, Politics, and Patronage: The American Government's Use of Newspapers, 1789–1875* (Athens, Ga., 1977), 236; John Bryant to Horace Greeley, February 7, 1867 (draft) in John E. Bryant Papers, Duke University, Durham, N.C. A. C. Fisk to W. E. Chandler, July 24, 1868; John Keffer to Chandler, August 1, 1868; and J. B. Raymond to O. C. French, August 3, 1872, all in William E. Chandler Papers, LC. G. T. Ruby to W. E. Chandler, July 20, 1872, in James A. Padgett, ed., "Reconstruction Letters from North Carolina, Part V," *North Carolina Historical Review* 19 (1942): 74–75; Augusta *Loyal Georgian,* July 28, 1867; *Fredericksburg Ledger,* November 10, 1874.

3. Smith, *The Press, Politics, and Patronage,* 242. J. B. Davis to Edward McPherson, May 11, 1870; D. H. Starbuck to McPherson, September 20, 1870; J. W. Menard to McPherson, November 30, 1870; Alexander Rives to Edward McPherson, May 19, 1871; James P. Newcomb to McPherson, January 7, 1872; Robert Hughes to McPherson, December 2, 1872; G. W. Brooks to McPherson, December 16, 1873; R. F. Lehman to McPherson, December 5, 1874, all in Edward McPherson Papers, LC; *Rutherford Star,* March 16, 1872.

4. *Official Journal of the Proceedings of the Convention for Framing a Constitution for the State of Louisiana, 1867–1868* (New Orleans, 1868), 8, 55, 190, 288; F. Wayne Binning,

Notes to Chapter Nine 251

"Carpetbaggers' Triumph: The Louisiana State Election of 1868," *Louisiana History* 14 (1973): 32, 35–36; *New Orleans Tribune*, November 27, December 7, 17, 27, 29, 1867.

5. *Ordinances Passed by the Constitutional Convention at Austin, Texas, June 1, 1868*, (Austin, 1870), 5–6, 16; Charles W. Ramsdell, *Reconstruction in Texas* (New York, 1910), 205, 258, 259 n.1; Carl H. Moneyhon, *Republicanism in Reconstruction Texas* (Austin, 1980), 87–88; *San Antonio Express*, June 14, 27, August 1, 1868.

6. *Journal of Proceedings of the Constitutional Convention of the State of Mississippi in 1868* (Jackson, 1871), 19, 115, 493–94, 569, 716, 718.

7. Joe M. Richardson, *The Negro in the Reconstruction of Florida, 1865–1877* (Tallahassee, 1965), 209.

8. State of Virginia, *Report of the Auditor of Public Accounts, 1871* (Richmond, 1871), 22, 30, 40; ibid., *1872*, 14.

9. Salem *People's Press*, July 1, 1870; *Journal of the House of Representatives of the General Assembly of North Carolina, 1870–71* (Raleigh, 1871), 36; J. G. de Roulhac Hamilton, *Reconstruction in North Carolina* (New York, 1914), 656; Elizabeth City *North Carolinian*, May 4, 1871.

10. State of Tennessee, *Report of the Comptroller . . . 1867* (Nashville, 1867), 70; ibid., *1869*, 9, 13; ibid., *1877*, 29; Frank B. Williams, "John Eaton, Jr., Editor, Politician, and School Administrator, 1865–1870," *Tennessee Historical Quarterly* 10 (1951): 292, 294, 301; Walter J. Fraser, "Lucien Bonaparte Eaton: Politics and the Memphis *Post*, 1867–1869," *West Tennessee Historical Society Papers* 20 (1966): 22–24, 25–43; *Public Acts of the General Assembly of the State of Tennessee, 1st Session, 36th General Assembly, 1869* (Nashville, 1870), 3; Thomas B. Alexander, *Political Reconstruction in Tennessee* (Nashville, 1950), 234.

11. *Report of the Auditor of the State of Alabama . . . 1869* (Montgomery, 1869), appendix, iv, xl; ibid., *1870*, 21; ibid., *1871*, 47, 49; ibid., *1872*, 40, 41; ibid., *1873*, 21, 23; ibid., *1874*, 27, 29; ibid., *1875*, 10, 11; ibid., *1876*, 7, 9. Fleming gives somewhat different figures, stating that printing expenditures under the Republican administration of William H. Smith totaled $80,279 in 1869–70 and dropped to $49,716 under the Democratic administration of Robert Lindsay, 1871–72. See Walter Lynwood Fleming, *Civil War and Reconstruction in Alabama* (New York, 1905), 576.

12. Reed's remarks may be found in *Journal of the Proceedings of the Assembly of the State of Florida, First Session, 1868* (Tallahassee, 1868), 121–22. The comptroller's reports can be found in the appendices of the Senate Journals for each legislative session. See *Journal of the Proceedings of the Senate, Second Session, 1869*, (Tallahassee, 1869), appendix, 5; ibid., *Third Session, 1870*, appendix, 4, 6, 8, 12, 13; ibid., *Fourth Session, 1871*, appendix, 10; ibid., *Fifth Session, 1872*, appendix, 6–7; ibid., *Sixth Session, 1873*, appendix, 7; ibid., *Seventh Session, 1874*, appendix, 103; ibid., *Eighth Session, 1875*, appendix, 13.

13. Leonard Henderson Sims, "A Study of the Florida Press during the Reconstruction Years, 1865–1870" (master's thesis, University of Florida, 1958), 100–103; Joe M. Richardson, "Jonathan C. Gibbs: Florida's Only Negro Cabinet Member," *Florida Historical Quarterly* 42 (1964): 365; John Wallace, *Carpetbag Rule in Florida* (Jacksonville, 1888),

239; Jacksonville *New South,* September 16, 19, October 3, 1874; Jacksonville *Daily Florida Union,* April 26, 1876.

14. *Tallahassee Floridian* editorial reprinted in Jacksonville *New South,* January 23, 1875; Jacksonville *Florida Union,* January 19, 1877.

15. State of Georgia, *Comptroller General's Report, 1868* (Atlanta, 1869), 11; ibid., *1869,* 12; ibid., *1870,* 12; Alan Conway, *The Reconstruction of Georgia* (Minneapolis, 1966), 212; C. Mildred Thompson, *Reconstruction in Georgia: Economic, Social, Political* (New York, 1915), 227–28; Willard Range, "Hannibal I. Kimball," *Georgia Historical Quarterly* 29 (1945): 54.

16. Elizabeth Studley Nathans, *Losing the Peace: Georgia Republicans and Reconstruction, 1865–1871* (Baton Rouge, 1968), 184; Atlanta *New Era,* February 5, May 30, 1869; Georgia General Assembly, *Report of the Joint Committee to Investigate Charges Against Governor Bullock* (Atlanta, 1870); Conway, *Reconstruction of Georgia,* 185; Georgia General Assembly, *Report of Committee to Investigate the Official Conduct of Rufus B. Bullock* (Atlanta, 1872), 18–19, 188–89. My own estimate of Bullock's payments for publishing proclamations, based on the yearly reports of Georgia's comptroller general, is around $110,000; I estimate that in total Bullock's administration spent around $184,000 on printing.

17. Little Rock *Morning Republican,* July 13, 14, 17 (quote), 1868; Thomas S. Staples, *Reconstruction in Arkansas, 1862–1874* (New York, 1923), 373; Martha Ann Ellenburg, "Reconstruction in Arkansas" (Ph.D. diss., University of Missouri, 1967), 208–9. Price was from Sterling, Illinois, and apparently had served in the Union Army. See *Morning Republican,* June 15, 1870.

18. Little Rock *Morning Republican,* July 21, 23, 24, 1868; Fred W. Allsopp, *History of the Arkansas Press for a Hundred Years and More* (Little Rock, 1922), 24, 362; Staples, *Reconstruction in Arkansas,* 311–12, 375–76.

19. Allsopp, *History of the Arkansas Press,* 361–62; Little Rock *Morning Republican,* November 29, 1870; *Journal of the Senate of Arkansas . . . 1871* (Little Rock, 1871), 35, 500; Staples, *Reconstruction in Arkansas,* 312.

20. Staples, *Reconstruction in Arkansas,* 311–12; State of Arkansas, *Biennial Report of the Auditor to the Governor, 1876* (Little Rock, 1876), 24.

21. Ramsdell, *Reconstruction in Texas,* 299, 305, 313; James M. Smallwood, *Time of Hope, Time of Despair: Black Texans during Reconstruction* (Port Washington, N.Y., 1981), 153; Houston *Telegraph* quoted in *Daily Austin Republican,* September 26, 1870; *Daily Austin Republican,* November 15, 26, 1870; *Daily State Journal,* October 26, November 22, 1870.

22. *Daily Austin Republican,* September 15, November 17, 26, 1870; *Daily State Journal,* May 10, June 15, 1870, September 17, 1871; *San Antonio Express,* November 23, 1871.

23. *Daily State Journal,* September 17, 1871; *San Antonio Express,* November 23, 1871; *Annual Report of Comptroller of Public Accounts, 1869–1870* (Austin, 1871), 5; ibid., *1870–1871,* 24, 25, 27, 32; ibid., *1871–1872,* 22–30; ibid., *1872–1873,* 20–26; ibid., *1873–1874,* 30–41; ibid., *1874–1875,* 37.

24. *Journal of the House of Representatives of Mississippi, 1870* (Jackson, 1870), 635, 752–53; Jackson *Clarion* quoted in Hernando *Press*, July 14, 1870; *Vicksburg Daily Times*, July 17, 1870; Jackson *Daily Pilot*, August 29, 1871; William C. Harris, *Day of the Carpetbagger: Republican Reconstruction in Mississippi* (Baton Rouge, 1979), 414, 598.

25. Auditors' Reports in *Journal of the House of Representatives of the State of Mississippi, 1870* (Jackson, 1870), 122, and ibid., *1872*, 630; James W. Garner, *Reconstruction in Mississippi* (New York, 1901), 316n; Harris, *Day of the Carpetbagger*, 297, 416–17; *Vicksburg Daily Times*, July 8, 1871. William C. Harris puts Mississippi's 1871 printing expenses at $95,861, while Garner uses the figure of $127,848. My examination of the auditor's reports supports Garner's higher amount.

26. Jackson *Mississippi Pilot*, August 26, 30, 31, 1871.

27. Harris, *Day of the Carpetbagger*, 433–35; Jackson *Daily Pilot*, August 10, 15, 1871; *Vicksburg Daily Times*, February 2, April 4, 9, 10, 1872; *Journal of the House of Representatives of Mississippi, 1872*, 290, 570, and appendix, 12–13; Lillian A. Pereyra, *James Lusk Alcorn: Persistent Whig* (Baton Rouge, 1966), 150.

28. J. B. Raymond to O. C. French, August 3, 1872, and French to W. E. Chandler, August 6, 1872, William E. Chandler Papers; John Raymond to Adelbert Ames, May 15, 1872, in McPherson Papers; Harris, *Day of the Carpetbagger*, 417; Pereyra, *James Lusk Alcorn*, 157–59; *Vicksburg Daily Times*, May 7, 1872, April 13, 1873.

29. *Vicksburg Daily Times*, May 16, September 2, 1873, January 16, 1875; Pereyra, *James Lusk Alcorn*, 159; Garner, *Reconstruction in Mississippi*, 297, 316n, 325–26; Harris, *Day of the Carpetbagger*, 471, 598, 610.

30. *Vicksburg Daily Times*, April 13, 1873, July 8, August 24, 27, September 17, October 2 (quote), 1874; Garner, *Reconstruction in Mississippi*, 316n; Harris, *Day of the Carpetbagger*, 597, 658.

31. Harris, *Day of the Carpetbagger*, 659; *Vicksburg Daily Times*, April 26, 1875; *Jackson Daily Times*, July 19, 29, August 20, October 20, 21, 23, November 4, December 2, 1875; Garner, *Reconstruction in Mississippi*, 316n.

32. Robert H. Woody, *Republican Newspapers of South Carolina* (Charlottesville, 1936), 27–30, 34–40.

33. Ibid., 30 n.115, 49–54; *Columbia Daily Union*, January 22, 1872; *Aiken Tribune*, January 17, February 28, 1874.

34. Woody, *Republican Newspapers*, 20–24, 46; Edward A. Miller Jr., *Gullah Statesman: Robert Smalls from Slavery to Congress, 1839–1915* (Columbia, S.C., 1995), 74.

35. Woody, *Republican Newspapers*, 48–50; Miller, *Gullah Statesman*, 69–71.

36. *Report of Comptroller General to the General Assembly of South Carolina, 1872–1873* (Columbia, 1873), 31–55, 85; *Aiken Tribune*, March 15, 1873, January 17, February 28, March 7, 1874; Woody, *Republican Newspapers*, 20–21, 23, 39, 41. See also *Walterboro News*, January 31, 1874, for statement from Woodruff and Jones responding to accusations against them, and *Walterboro News*, March 7, 1874, for a statement from the South Carolina General Assembly regarding these printing charges.

37. Walter Allen, *Governor Chamberlain's Administration in South Carolina: A Chapter of Reconstruction in the Southern States* (New York, 1888), 17–18, 29, 72, 166, 301; *Aiken Tribune*, December 5, 1874; *Annual Report of the Comptroller General of the State of South Carolina, 1875,* 43–67, 82; ibid., *1876,* 23–58.

38. *Report of the Auditor of Public Accounts to the General Assembly, 1866* (New Orleans, 1867), 5; ibid., *1867 and 1868,* 5; Ella Lonn, *Reconstruction in Louisiana after 1868* (New York, 1918), 31, 86–87; Joe Gray Taylor, *Louisiana Reconstructed, 1863–1877* (Baton Rouge, 1974), 198–99; Fayette Copeland, "The New Orleans Press and Reconstruction," *Louisiana Historical Quarterly* 30 (1947): 213–14, 218 n.88; Francis Byers Harris, "Henry Clay Warmoth, Reconstruction Governor of Louisiana," *Louisiana Historical Quarterly* 30 (1947): 368; *New Orleans Republican,* November 30, December 23, 1870.

39. Alexandria *Rapides Gazette,* March 12, 1870, February 11, 1871; Harris, "Henry Clay Warmoth," 555; *San Antonio Express,* November 23, 1871; *New Orleans Republican,* December 23, 1870.

40. Taylor, *Louisiana Reconstructed,* 198–199, 218, 222; Lonn, *Reconstruction in Louisiana after 1868,* 87, 96, 106n; *National Republican,* July 6, 1872; Henry Clay Warmoth, *War, Politics, and Reconstruction: Stormy Days in Louisiana* (New York, 1930), 112, 118, 153; New Orleans *Louisianan,* September 7, December 7, 1871; *Official Journal of the Senate of the State of Louisiana, 1871–1872* (New Orleans, 1872), 14.

41. Alexandria *Rapides Gazette,* February 17, 1872; Taylor, *Louisiana Reconstructed,* 198–99, 222, 262; Lonn, *Reconstruction in Louisiana after 1868,* 106n, 378, 393; *Report of the Auditor of Public Accounts to the General Assembly of Louisiana, 1872* (New Orleans, 1873), 5, 6, 24; ibid., *1877,* 84.

42. Macon *American Union,* August 22, September 12, October 10, December 12, 1872, January 2, 1873.

43. *Huntsville Advocate,* August 7, 1873, October 1, 1874; Talladega *Our Mountain Home,* November 3, 1875; Montgomery *Alabama State Journal,* July 10, 1876.

44. Garner, *Reconstruction in Mississippi,* 390; *Jackson Daily Times,* November 3, 1875.

45. Charles Francis Ritter, "The Press in Florida, Louisiana, and South Carolina and the End of Reconstruction, 1865–1877: Southern Men with Northern Interests" (Ph.D. diss., Catholic University of America, 1976), 238, 275; Jacksonville *Florida Union,* January 5, 10, 16, February 27, July 14, 1877.

46. *Asheville Pioneer,* June 17, 1872; *Fort Smith New Era,* September 9, 1874; Jacksonville *Florida Union,* February 15, 1876.

47. Michael W. Fitzgerald, *The Union League Movement in the Deep South: Politics and Agricultural Change during Reconstruction* (Baton Rouge, 1989), 98; Staples, *Reconstruction in Arkansas,* 365; John Allen Meador, "Florida Political Parties, 1865–1877" (Ph.D. diss., University of Florida, 1974), 168, 170, 173, 175.

48. *Columbus Press,* November 6, 1875; *Jackson Daily Times,* November 14, 1876.

Index

Abbott, Robert, 42
Aberdeen, Miss., 52
abolition, 18
Adams, E. J., 33
Adams, J. S., 154
Advertiser (Lexington, Miss.), 215 (n. 13)
advertising, newspaper, 1, 3, 8–9, 10, 16, 33, 41, 43–44, 45, 50–52, 56, 61–62, 71, 76
African American newspapers, 14–15, 72, 74, 77, 78, 81, 83, 85, 87, 103, 174, 227 (n. 23), 228 (n. 45); advocacy of equal rights in, 32, 33, 35, 36; challenges of operating, 45–46, 60–61, 221 (n. 13), 222 (n. 14); finances of, 42, 43; and racial division in Republican party, 117, 119, 120, 129, 130, 137, 151, 156, 238 (n. 12); and racial violence, 149; on segregation, 107
African Americans: civil rights of, 15, 103–5, 107, 119–20, 121, 124, 126, 129, 131, 132, 140, 143, 144, 148, 153, 184, 247 (n. 33); free, 8, 14, 15, 28, 29, 32, 33, 34, 74, 103; Republican appeals toward, 119–23, 169; Republican position on officeholding by, 122, 124, 129, 140, 151, 153, 154–56, 181, 239 (n. 19); and suffrage, 14, 24, 29–38 passim, 51, 119, 136
agricultural development, Republican proposals for, 115–16
Aiken Tribune (S.C.), 85, 104, 163, 179
Alabama: African American papers in, 155–56; geographical differences in, 21–22; official state papers in, 64, 66, 169–70; racial violence in, 147; radical editors in, 131–32; Republican papers in, 33, 40, 45, 57, 58, 85–87, 140, 153, 182–83; steam power in, 41; Unionist papers in, 23, 26
Alabama Republican (Decatur), 87, 131
Alabama State Journal (Montgomery), 64, 86,
87, 96, 106, 109, 117, 122, 126, 140, 144, 147, 148, 153, 154, 156, 158, 159, 161, 169, 170, 183, 228 (n. 43)
Alabama State Sentinel. See *State Sentinel* (Montgomery, Ala.)
Alcorn, James Lusk, 76, 138, 147, 163, 175, 177
Alcorn, Robert J., 112, 124, 175
Alexandria, Va., 9–10, 16, 23, 24, 25
Alexandria Gazette (La.), 9
American Advocate (Salem, N.C.), 129
American Citizen (Canton, Miss.), 50
American Missionary Association, 34
American Union (Harrisonburg, Va.), 35, 106, 112, 136, 220 (n. 7)
American Union (Macon and Griffin, Ga.), 4, 42, 49, 61, 93, 94, 97, 99, 119, 120, 124, 131, 134, 135, 140, 149, 153, 182, 221 (n. 7)
Ames, Adelbert, 57, 76, 163, 177
amnesty. *See* Confederates, amnesty for former
Andrews, Sidney, 3
Andrews, T. C., 140
Angier, Nedom, 172
Antoine, Caesar Carpentier, 15
Arkansas: Liberal Republicans in, 141–42, 150–51; official state papers in, 38, 63, 64, 66, 172–74; opposition to carpetbaggers in, 157–58; racial violence in, 146; Republican papers in, 40, 42, 45, 57, 58, 71, 81–83; taxes in, 161; Unionists in, 19–20, 23, 24, 25, 29, 30, 34, 39
Arkansas Freeman (Little Rock), 120, 141, 149, 156
Arkansas Patriot (Fort Smith), 99
Arkansas State Journal (Little Rock), 150, 151, 173
Asheville Pioneer (N.C.), 87, 89, 98, 104, 119, 124, 129, 130, 144, 149, 165, 183
Ashley, Samuel, 120

Associated Press, 55, 219 (n. 37)
Athens Republican (Tenn.), 137, 146
Atlanta, Ga., 51, 61
Atlanta Daily Opinion (Ga.), 106, 114, 126, 131
Atlanta Republican (Ga.), 93
Attakapas Register (La.), 53, 74
Augusta, Ga., 32
Augusta Press (Ga.), 126
Austin, Tex., 28, 38, 80
Austin Republican (Tex.), 77, 78, 80, 97, 106, 132, 139, 157, 166, 174

Bailey, William, 80, 227 (n. 28)
Bainbridge Sun (Ga.), 51, 154
Banks, Nathaniel P., 8, 13, 14, 15, 22, 23
Bard, Samuel, 131; on business and finances, 42–43, 217 (n. 30), 224 (n. 2); as official state printer, 64, 65, 68, 93, 171–72, 223 (n. 25); political opinions of, 51–52, 114, 126–27, 140–41, 145, 155, 182–83
Batesville Republican (Ark.), 82
Batterton, Ira, 22, 26
Battle, Daniel, 221 (n. 13)
Baxter, Elisha, 151, 173
Beaufort, S.C., 10, 23, 25, 84
Beaufort Republican (S.C.), 162, 179, 183
Beaufort Standard (S.C.), 156
Bentley, Emerson, 53, 119
Bingham, Arthur, 109, 154, 156, 158, 161, 228 (n. 43)
Bingham, J. B., 17, 18
Blackburn, W. Jasper, 62, 68–69, 72–73, 157
Blackburn's Homer Iliad (Claiborne Parish, La.), 53, 67, 68–69, 72, 73, 75, 129, 152, 221 (n. 7)
black codes, 29, 30, 32, 39, 184
Black Republican (New Orleans, La.), 15
black suffrage. *See* suffrage, African American
boycotts, of Republican merchants, 51–52
"Brindletails" (Ark.), 151, 173
Brooks, B. F. C., 17–18
Brooks, Edward P., 33, 212 (n. 25)
Brooks, Joseph, 150, 151, 173
Brown, Joseph, 126, 131, 140
Brown, William G., 120
Brownlow, William G. ("Parson"), 18–19, 25, 27, 30, 36, 37, 38, 42, 47, 62, 65, 80, 98, 118, 119, 123, 137, 145, 146, 168, 169, 207 (n. 33)
Brownsville Ranchero (Tex.), 226 (n. 22)

Bryant, John Emory, 4, 32, 49, 53, 58, 60, 99, 105, 111, 119, 120, 124, 131, 132, 140, 141, 149
Buck, Alfred E., 62
Bullock, Rufus, 65, 93, 127, 131, 140, 141, 149, 171–72, 223 (n. 25), 252 (n. 16)
Burch, J. Henri, 74, 151
Burnside, Ambrose, 11
Burton, Pierce, 53, 67, 86, 98, 144–45, 147, 148, 160, 169
Butler, Benjamin, 8, 10, 13, 34, 129
Butler County, Ala., 57

Cain, Richard Harvey, 33, 83, 221 (n. 13)
Canaday, William Parker, 88
Carolina Era (Raleigh, N.C.), 89, 144, 149
Carolina New Era (Spartanburg, S.C.), 85
Carolina Printing Company, 178
Carpenter, J. B., 123, 125, 149
Carpenter, Lewis Cass, 50, 62, 84, 135, 148, 162
carpetbaggers, 4, 10, 11, 12, 13, 22, 32, 34, 37, 52, 75, 82, 83, 84, 87, 88, 92, 110, 129, 132, 137, 143, 150, 152, 156, 157, 158, 161, 166, 204 (n. 10), 248 (n. 40)
Carter, George, 181
Casey, James F., 151, 181
Cavalier (Williamsburg, Va.), 205 (n. 8)
Chamberlain, Daniel H., 163, 178, 180
Chandler, William E., 215 (n. 13)
Chapin, A. B., 144, 145
Charleston, S.C., 32, 61
Charleston Advocate (S.C.), 59, 60–61, 83, 100, 121, 122, 132, 221 (n. 13)
Charleston Colored People's Convention, 32, 33
Charleston Courier (S.C.), 11
Charleston Free Press (S.C.), 54, 83, 100, 132
Charleston Journal (S.C.), 33, 60, 83
Charleston Republican (S.C.), 50, 54, 95, 101, 102, 109, 121, 140, 148, 155, 157, 162, 178
Chase, Salmon P., 12, 34
Chattanooga Gazette (Tenn.), 18, 30, 36, 98
Chattanooga Republican (Tenn.), 137
Cheney, Edward M., 41–42, 62, 64, 92, 96, 101, 128, 132, 170, 184
Christy, W. H., 31, 128
Citizen's Guard (New Orleans, La.), 152
civil rights, Republican support of African Americans', 15, 103–5, 107, 119–20, 121, 124, 126, 129, 131, 132, 140, 143, 144, 148, 153, 184, 247 (n. 33). *See also* equal rights, Republican

support for; freedmen, civil rights of; suffrage, African American
Civil Rights Act (1875), 153, 154
Clarion (Jackson, Miss.), 175, 176
Clark, John, 34
Clark, Thomas, 3
Clarksville Patriot (Tenn.), 81, 102, 137
Clayton, Powell, 82, 141, 142, 146, 150, 151, 158, 160, 173
Coffin, Allen, 221 (n. 13)
Colored American (Augusta, Ga.), 32
Colored Citizen (Jackson, Miss.), 138
Colored Tennessean (Nashville), 36, 81
Columbia, S.C., 50
Columbia Union (S.C.), 84, 135, 145, 148, 150, 162, 178
Columbus Index (Miss.), 53
Columbus Press (Miss.), 53, 77, 111, 113, 154, 156, 163, 185
Commercial Bulletin (New Orleans, La.), 13
Confederacy, opposition to. *See* Unionists, wartime Southern white
Confederates: amnesty for former, 14, 137, 141, 142, 149, 150, 151, 156–57; disfranchisement of former, 19, 25, 36, 81, 107, 116, 119, 125, 126, 128, 130, 131, 132, 135, 136, 137, 140, 143, 150, 238 (n. 12), 243 (n. 59); former, 25, 31, 86, 94, 109, 129; newspapers of, 47–48, 56; property confiscation of, 29, 37, 107, 117, 118, 124, 143
Conway, Thomas, 15, 225 (n. 8)
Cook, Thomas M., 11
Corinth News (Miss.), 138
corruption charges against Republicans, 5, 141, 143, 159–67 passim, 184
Courier (Baton Rouge, La.), 74
Cowing, W. J., 9, 10, 35–36
Crane, A. M., 35, 36, 111, 119, 121, 124
Crescent (New Orleans, La.), 13

Daily Evening Herald (Columbia, S.C.), 84
Daily News (Charleston, S.C.), 228 (n. 40)
Daily Press (Augusta, Ga.), 50, 131
Daily Press (Nashville, Tenn.), 17
Daily Progress (Raleigh, N.C.), 33
Daily Register (Mobile, Ala.), 42
Daily Republican (Charleston, S.C.), 119. See also *Charleston Republican*
Daily Republican (Chattanooga, Tenn.), 51, 101, 104. See also *Chattanooga Republican* (Tenn.)

Daily Republican State Journal (Nashville, Tenn.), 137
Daily State Journal. See *State Journal* (Austin, Tex.)
Daily Times (Jackson, Miss.), 177, 178, 183, 185
Daily Times and True Union (Nashville, Tenn.), 17, 123, 207 (n. 33)
Daily Union Banner (Salisbury, N.C.), 27, 209 (n. 8)
Daniels, Edward, 134
Dardanelle Times (Ark.), 96
Darlington, S.C., 42
Davis, Edmund J., 77–80, 139–40, 150, 159, 161, 166, 174
Dell, Valentine, 19, 30, 31, 34, 38, 62, 81, 82, 108, 118, 119, 123, 157, 160, 161, 172, 173, 174, 184
Democratic newspapers, 42, 45, 49, 50, 52–53, 54, 55, 62, 66, 67, 70, 72, 76, 77, 83, 86, 90, 91, 92, 93, 95, 99, 169, 172, 173, 175, 178, 224 (n. 1), 246 (n. 26)
Democrats, 31, 62, 133; effect of, on Republican papers, 169–71, 174–76, 178, 180–81; in elections, 140, 158, 163, 183; as proslavery, 28, 46, 47; on race relations, 107, 124, 143–54 passim; recruitment of, by Republicans, 129, 135–36, 141, 159; on taxes, 161; in Virginia, 25
Denison, George, 13, 14
Denison Cresset (Tex.), 79
Denny, J. W., 64, 84
Dent, Lewis, 138, 140
desegregation, limited Republican support for, 120–21, 124
Deutsche Zeitung (New Orleans, La.), 15, 73, 74, 129, 152, 155, 165, 246 (n. 26)
Die Neue Zeit (Memphis, Tenn.), 17
disfranchisement. *See* Confederates, disfranchisement of former
Donaldsonville Chief (La.), 44, 74
Douglas, Stephen A., 19, 26, 28, 159
Douglass, Frederick, 35
Downey, William B., 108
Dugan, James, 43, 75, 166, 167
Dunn, Oscar, 151, 181
Durand, C. E., 53
Durant, Thomas J., 13, 14, 15, 34
Dyke, Charles, 167, 170, 171

East Alabama Monitor (Opelika), 131, 133, 157
Eaton, John, 37
Eaton, Lucien, 69, 101, 120, 144

economic growth, Republican proposals for, 114–16, 133, 236 (n. 59)
editors, newspaper: career trajectories of, 62; effect of, on public opinion, 1; violence against, 3, 9, 17, 21, 35, 47, 48, 52–53, 69, 78, 99, 129, 130, 218 (nn. 32, 35). *See also* violence
education. *See* schools, Republican support for public
elites: Republican appeals toward white, 135–36, 142, 157, 159, 164, 243 (n. 58); Republican denunciations of control by, 96–98, 110, 123. *See also* scalawags; Unionists; whites, Southern
Elmore Republican (Wetumpka, Ala.), 86
emancipation, 30
Enforcement Acts (1870–71), 148, 149
Ennemoser, Julius, 73
equal accommodations laws. *See* public accommodations laws
Equal Rights (Pontotoc, Miss.), 53, 121
equal rights, Republican support for, 6, 14, 32–33, 102, 103, 107, 110–12, 116, 120, 184. *See also* civil rights, Republican support of African Americans'

Feliciana Republican (St. Francisville, La.), 53, 74
Fernandina Observer (Fla.), 152
Figures, William B., 26, 33, 85, 87, 102, 109, 131, 153, 158, 248 (n. 43)
First Reconstruction Act (March 1867), 39, 56, 58, 60
Fish, William A., 16
Fishback, William M., 19
Fisher, Hiram, 175
Fisk, A. C., 76, 121
Flake, Ferdinand, 28, 33, 47, 127, 139, 152, 166, 174, 243 (n. 64)
Flake's Bulletin (Galveston, Tex.), 28, 33, 38, 77, 127, 132, 157, 226 (n. 22)
Florence Republican (Ala.), 60
Florida: African American candidates in, 155–56; official state papers in, 63, 64, 66, 71, 72, 128–29, 170–71; reform in, 162; Republican papers in, 31, 40, 41, 44, 45, 57, 58, 91–93, 152; Unionists in, 12, 16, 23, 26
Florida Republican (Jacksonville), 152
Florida Sentinel (Tallahassee), 71, 115
Florida Times (Jacksonville), 31, 38, 59, 92, 128
Florida Union (Jacksonville), 12, 23, 30, 31, 37, 42, 51, 56, 62, 64, 92, 96, 101, 109, 128, 132, 135, 162, 170, 171, 183, 184
Flournoy, Robert, 53, 121
Forney, John W., 54, 59, 69
Forsyth, John, 42
Fort Smith (Ark.), 19, 38
Fort Smith Herald (Ark.), 38
Fort Smith New Era (Ark.), 19, 30, 34, 38, 62, 81, 82, 108, 118, 119, 123, 158, 160, 161, 172, 173, 184, 221 (n. 7)
Fort Smith Union (Ark.), 19
Foster, Charles, 11
Fourteenth Amendment, 37, 39, 142, 149, 150
Fowler, John, 148
Fox, Myron, 84
Fredericksburg Ledger (Va.), 53, 91, 134, 149, 154, 158
free blacks. *See* Africans Americans, free
Freedman's Press (Austin, Tex.), 77, 120, 226 (n. 20)
freedmen, civil rights of, 28, 29, 32, 33, 34, 103. *See also* African Americans
Freedmen's Bureau, 15, 31, 32, 34, 35, 61, 86
Freemen's Standard (Savannah, Ga.), 120
Free South (Beaufort, S.C.), 10–11, 12, 56, 95
Free South (New Orleans, La.), 74
free speech, Republican commitment to, 3, 5, 95–96, 100, 102, 158, 183, 184
Free State General Committee, 13
Free State movement, 14
Freie Presse für Texas (San Antonio), 28, 77, 78, 139, 166, 174, 175
French-language newspapers, 14, 110, 180
Friar's Point Delta (Miss.), 77, 97, 112, 113, 124

Galveston, Tex., 28, 47, 78
Galveston Republican (Tex.), 120, 174, 227 (n. 23)
Galveston Standard (Tex.), 43, 227 (n. 23)
Gamble, Robert H., 170
Gazette (Colleton, S.C.), 179
Georgetown Planet (S.C.), 85
Georgia, 4, 11, 16, 21, 22, 23, 26, 32, 40, 41, 49, 57, 58, 59, 64, 71, 72, 93–94, 134, 140–41, 147–48, 153, 171–72
Georgia Equal Rights Association, 32
Georgia Republican (Augusta), 21, 93, 141, 149
German Gazette (Atlanta, Ga.), 110
German-language newspapers, 15, 17, 28, 73, 77, 78, 80, 110, 129, 146, 152

Index

Gibbs, Jonathan, 92, 170
Gilmer, George K., 35–36, 106, 112, 136
Goliad Guard (Tex.), 80
Grand Army of the Republic, 61
Grand Era (Baton Rouge, La.), 74, 151, 222 (n. 14)
Greeley, Horace, 59
Greensboro Union Register (N.C.), 33, 49, 87, 118, 119, 120, 123, 129, 132, 144, 145, 220 (n. 7)
Greenville Republican (S.C.), 85
Griffin, Albert, 34, 49, 119, 120, 124, 131, 133, 156, 219 (n. 37)
Griffin, Joel R., 53, 94, 134, 224 (n. 2)
Grisham, George E., 99, 118
Gross, Tabbs, 120, 141, 156, 233 (n. 25)

Hahn, Michael, 14, 16, 25, 34, 72, 148, 155
Hamilton, Andrew Jackson, 22–23, 27–28, 29, 33, 38, 139
Hamilton, John R., 13
Hamilton, Morgan, 139, 152, 174
Hardy, John, 118, 119, 124, 131, 134, 184, 228 (n. 43)
Hart, Ossian B., 159, 162
Hathaway, John R., 158
Hayes, John E., 12, 32, 59, 125, 131
Henderson Pioneer (N.C.), 27, 220 (n. 7)
Herald (Chattanooga, Tenn.), 126
Herald of the Union (Wilmington, N.C.), 11–12, 205 (n. 12)
Heroes of America, 20, 21
Herzberg, Theodore, 28
Hill, A. C., 13, 16
Hill, A. G., 13
Hilton Head Island, S.C., 10
Holden, Joseph, 147
Holden, William, 21, 24, 27, 37, 38, 39, 48, 62, 64, 87, 88, 89, 110–11, 124, 129, 147, 158, 159, 168
Homer Iliad. See *Blackburn's Homer Iliad* (Claiborne Parish, La.)
Hood, James R., 18, 30, 36, 98
Houston, Sam, 22, 28
Houston, Tex., 28, 78
Houston Star (Tex.), 53
Houston Telegraph (Tex.), 49
Houston Union (Tex.), 59, 78, 139, 152, 157, 174
Houzeau, Jean-Charles, 14, 15, 101, 105, 112, 118, 119, 120, 124, 129
Hubbs, Ethelbert, 88
Hughes, Robert W., 134

Hunnicutt, James W., 35, 47, 50, 53, 97, 114, 118, 119, 120, 121, 122, 124, 130, 136, 219 (n. 37)
Huntsville Advocate (Ala.), 26, 33, 38, 85, 87, 102, 109, 131, 132, 153, 154, 158, 160, 182, 221 (n. 7), 248 (n. 43)
Hurley, Timothy, 221 (n. 13)

Iberville Pioneer (Plaquemine, La.), 73, 74
immigrants, Republican appeals to, 110, 115
Independent Monitor (Tuscaloosa, Ala.), 48
Independent Republican (Richmond, Va.), 136
interracial political alliances, Republican positions regarding, 122, 123, 124, 132, 135, 142, 143, 164
intraparty strife, 117–42
iron-clad oath, 29

Jackson Pilot (Miss.), 62, 64, 132, 138, 149, 153, 155, 163, 176, 177, 178. See also *Mississippi Pilot* (Jackson)
Jacksonville, Fla., 12, 16, 26, 31, 92
Jacksonville Herald (Fla.), 12, 23, 26
Jeffersonian Republican (Pine Bluff, Ark.), 82
John, Palemon, 88, 144, 147, 148, 161
Johnson, Andrew, 17, 18, 25–37 passim, 58
Johnson, G. M., 182
Jones, Alexander H., 27, 38, 62, 87, 89, 119, 124, 130
Jones, A. O., 178, 179, 253 (n. 36)
Joseph, Philip, 156
journalism, partisan nature of, 47
Journal of Freedom (Raleigh, N.C.), 33
Joy, George Mills, 11, 20

Keith, Melville, 77, 120, 226 (n. 20)
Kellogg, William Pitt, 152, 162, 181
Kendrick, W. E., 104
Key of the Gulf (Key West, Fla.), 12
Knoxville Daily Chronicle (Tenn.), 81, 99, 154
Knoxville Whig and Rebel Ventilator (Tenn.), 18, 98, 118, 119, 137, 158
Ku Klux Klan, 52, 53, 83, 137, 142, 143–49, 169, 179, 182, 245 (n. 5)
Ku Klux Klan Act (1871), 148, 149

labor: Republican appeals to, 111–14, 124, 126, 134, 135, 138; unions, 122–23
Lake City Herald (Fla.), 152
Lash, Israel, 62
Latta, James M., 10, 12

Laurensville Herald (S.C.), 3
Lebanon Record (Tenn.), 137, 227 (n. 28)
Le Louisianais (St. James Parish, La.), 74
Lewellen, James W., 34
Lewis, Hiram W., 185
Liberal (Little Rock, Ark.), 141, 173
Liberal Republican Party, 150–53, 158; in Arkansas, 141
Lincoln, Abraham, 2, 13, 14, 23, 27, 28; administration of, 9, 11–12
Lindsay, Robert, 251 (n. 11)
Littlefield, Milton, 89
Little Rock Gazette (Ark.), 173
Little Rock Republican (Ark.), 63, 64, 81, 82, 96, 97, 99, 101, 103, 108, 112, 119, 121, 124, 125, 141, 146, 150, 156, 158, 160, 161, 172, 173, 184
Lively, R. A., 205 (n. 8)
Livingston Messenger (Ala.), 101
Locke, Richard B., 12
Longley, A. B., 132, 139
Longstreet, James, 124, 129
Loudon Republican (Va.), 108
Louisiana: African American candidates in, 151–52, 155; government corruption in, 162; official state papers in, 64, 68, 129, 166, 180–82; Republican papers in, 40, 43, 44, 45, 48, 58, 71, 72–75; Unionists in, 8, 13–16, 19, 23, 24, 25, 34
Louisiana Intelligencer (Monroe), 73, 75
Louisianan (New Orleans), 74, 75, 119, 120, 148, 149, 151, 152, 154, 155, 162, 222 (n. 14)
Louisiana Staats-Zeitung (New Orleans), 15
Louisiana State Register (Carrollton), 43, 50, 68–69, 74, 96, 104, 105, 148, 149, 152, 157, 162
Loyal Georgian (Augusta), 4, 49, 53, 58, 59, 60, 99, 111, 119, 120, 124, 131, 132, 140, 221 (n. 7)
L'Union (New Orleans, La.), 14–15, 60, 206 (n. 21)
Lynch, James, 138
Lynch, John R., 62
Lynchburg Press (Va.), 91, 124

Magnolia Flower (Ark.), 158
Mann, J. C., 105, 134
Maryville Republican (Tenn.), 53, 60, 61, 81, 120, 137, 138
Mason, S. W., 11, 13, 32
May, Thomas P., 13, 14, 16
Maynard, Horace, 109
McClure, John, 184

McConnell, M. L., 137, 243 (n. 64)
McEnery, John, 152
McKinney Messenger (Tex.), 28–29, 79, 221 (n. 7)
McLin, Samuel, 92, 170
McMinnville Enterprise (Tenn.), 67, 137, 221 (n. 8)
McPherson, Edward, 58, 75, 76, 77, 92, 128, 129, 130, 131, 132, 165, 221 (n. 8)
Meade, George Gordon, 57
Meador, C. V., 19
Memphis, Tenn., 17, 18, 31, 65
Memphis Bulletin (Tenn.), 17, 36, 37, 169
Memphis Planet (Tenn.), 81
Memphis Post (Tenn.), 37, 48, 56, 65, 69, 81, 101, 120, 137, 144, 169, 215 (n. 13)
Memphis Weekly Republican (Tenn.), 17, 23, 37
Menard, John Willis, 74, 75, 151, 165, 225 (n. 9)
Mercer, S. C., 17, 18, 36, 64, 101, 103, 118, 120, 121, 122, 123, 137, 145, 146, 158, 207 (n. 33)
Meridian Chronicle (Miss.), 75, 97, 119, 124, 132, 135, 138
Middleton, Lewis, 53
"Minstrels" (Ark.), 151, 173
Missionary Record (Charleston, S.C.), 60–61, 83, 132
Mississippi: constitution of, 138; official state papers in, 57, 63, 64, 66, 67, 166–67, 175–78; racial violence in, 147; Republican papers in, 40, 41, 44, 45, 58, 71, 75–77, 132; Unionists in, 22, 23, 26
Mississippi Pilot (Jackson), 63, 71, 75, 76, 107, 113, 167, 249 (n. 59). See also *Jackson Pilot* (Miss.)
Mississippi State Journal (Jackson), 75, 166
Mobile, Ala., 34, 48, 62, 87
Mobile Herald (Ala.), 148, 149, 154, 156, 159, 160, 228 (n. 45)
mobs. *See* editors, newspaper, violence against; violence
Montgomery Advertiser (Ala.), 169
Montgomery Watchman (Ala.), 156
Moore, H. Judge, 221 (n. 13)
Morrill, William C., 12
Morris, John, 50, 54, 84, 101, 102, 119, 120, 121, 122, 132, 140, 148, 157, 162
Moseley, R. J., 75
Moseley, Robert A., 86, 87, 159, 182
Moses, Franklin, 178, 179
Moses, Robert K., 162

Index

Moulton, Ala., 57
Mountain Echo (Fayetteville, Ark.), 82, 126
Munson, H. H., 11
Murphy, Isaac, 19–20, 24

Nashville, Tenn., 17, 18, 30–31, 36
Nashville Bulletin (Tenn.), 81
Nashville Press (Tenn.), 18, 36, 207 (n. 33)
Nashville Republican (Tenn.), 96, 100, 109, 110, 137, 146, 227 (n. 28)
Nashville Tennessean, 60
Nashville Union (Tenn.), 17, 23, 30, 56
Nason, George W., 105, 133, 161
Natchez Post (Miss.), 156
National Democrat (Little Rock, Ark.), 19
National Index (Tyler, Tex.), 79
Nationalist (Mobile, Ala.), 33–34, 38, 49, 52, 60–61, 85, 87, 118, 119, 120, 124, 131, 132, 135, 156, 211 (n. 24), 221 (n. 7)
National Republican (Augusta, Ga.), 51, 52–53
National Republican (New Orleans, La.), 53, 149, 157, 181
National Republican (Selma, Ala.), 86
National Union (Greeneville, Tenn.), 36
National Union Party, 37, 138
Nelson, Richard, 78
New Bern, N.C., 11, 20, 41, 88
Newbern Daily Progress (N.C.), 11
New Bern Republican (N.C.), 97, 105, 106, 129, 133, 161
New Bern Times (N.C.), 30, 33, 37, 87, 88, 96, 149, 165
Newcomb, James P., 47, 77, 78, 98, 103, 104, 105, 109, 119, 124, 125, 132, 134, 139, 159, 165, 174, 219 (n. 37)
New Era (Atlanta, Ga.), 43, 51, 63, 64, 65, 68, 93, 100, 114, 126, 127, 131, 134, 140, 141, 149, 155, 171, 204 (n. 10), 223 (n. 25)
New Era (Darlington, S.C.), 32, 83
New Era (Gainesville, Fla.), 156
New Era (Greeneville, Tenn.), 30, 36, 37, 81, 137
Newman, John P., 72, 129, 225 (n. 8)
New Nation (Richmond, Va.), 35, 48, 50, 51, 53, 90, 97, 102, 118, 119, 120, 121, 122, 124, 130, 135, 220 (n. 7)
New North State (Greensboro, N.C.), 90, 97, 98, 149
New Orleans, La., 8, 13–16, 17, 24, 31, 49, 51, 61, 68, 73, 74, 120

New Orleans Advocate (La.), 34, 72, 74, 129, 155, 221 (n. 7), 225 (n. 8)
New Orleans Era (La.), 13, 14, 16
New Orleans Republican (La.), 64, 66, 68, 72, 73, 74, 97, 101, 112, 129, 148, 149, 152, 155, 160, 162, 166, 180, 181, 183, 249 (n. 59)
New Orleans Standard (La.), 165
New Orleans Times (La.), 13, 14, 166
New Orleans Tribune (La.), 15, 23, 34, 49, 60–61, 72, 73, 74, 100, 101, 117, 118, 119, 120, 122, 124, 129, 132, 155, 166, 221 (n. 7), 225 (n. 8), 241 (n. 40)
New Regime (Norfolk, Va.), 10, 34, 123
News (Mobile, Ala.), 49
News and Courier (Charleston, S.C.), 178
News and Times (Orangeburg, S.C.), 85
New South (Beaufort, S.C.), 10, 23, 26, 32, 221 (n. 7)
New South (Jacksonville, Fla.), 102, 154, 170
New South (Natchez, Miss.), 77
New South (Port Royal, S.C.), 10, 83
newspapers: ease in publishing of, 41; subscription figures of, 48, 63, 166, 204 (n. 4), 215 (n. 13)
Noble, W. H., 97
Norfolk, Va., 8, 10, 16, 23, 24, 25
Norfolk Day Book (Va.), 10, 90, 158, 168
Norfolk Post (Va.), 34
Norfolk Union (Va.), 10
North, perceived progressiveness of, by Republicans, 101–2
North Arkansas Times, 67
North Carolina: official state papers in, 64, 72, 168; racial violence in, 147; Republican papers in, 40, 44, 45, 58, 87–90, 129–30, 133–34; Unionists in, 11–12, 16, 20–21, 23, 27, 30, 33
North Carolina Standard (Raleigh), 21, 24, 27, 33, 37, 38, 48, 51, 64, 87, 88, 89, 110, 119, 124, 129, 135, 147, 149, 160, 168, 220 (n. 7)
North Carolina Times (New Bern), 11, 20, 88
North Carolinian (Elizabeth City), 42, 88, 144, 147, 160, 161, 168
Northern civilians, Civil War newspapers published by, 8, 9. *See also* carpetbaggers
North Georgia Republican (Dalton), 94
North Louisiana Journal (St. Joseph), 74
Northrop, L. C., 122–23
Norton, A. B., 28, 33, 103
Norton's Union Intelligencer (Dallas, Tex.), 79

Nueces Valley (Corpus Christi, Tex.), 80, 115, 150, 245 (n. 5)

Old Dominion (Norfolk, Va.), 10, 23, 25, 38
Old North State (Beaufort, N.C.), 11
Opelousas, La., 53
opponents, Republican attitude toward, 99–100
Orangeburg News (S.C.), 85, 140
Ord, Edward, 56, 57
Osborn, J. N., 75
Our Mountain Home (Talladega, Ala.), 87, 154, 159, 182

Palmetto Herald (Port Royal, S.C.), 11, 13
Paris Vindicator (Tex.), 79
patent outsides. *See* ready-print
patronage: and federal printing, 7, 9, 10–11, 15, 17, 18, 37–38, 45, 56–59, 71, 73, 76, 82, 85, 89, 91, 93, 128, 129, 130, 131, 132, 143, 166, 173, 204 (n. 5), 220 (n. 7), 221 (n. 8), 224 (n. 37); and judicial printing, 65–66, 92, 93; and local printing, 45, 57, 62, 65–66, 72, 76, 87, 93, 166, 167, 169, 170, 229 (n. 55); and state printing, 45, 57, 62, 63–69, 71, 72, 73, 76, 77, 84, 86, 92, 93, 137, 165–82 passim, 229 (n. 55); value of printing contracts, 59; and War Department, 13, 204 (n. 4). *See also* printing expenditures
Patton, Robert M., 26
Pearson, Frank, 221 (n. 13)
Pease, E. M., 28, 29, 139, 166
Peek, T. C., 146
Peninsula (Fernandina, Fla.), 12, 31
Pennington, J. L., 20–21, 27, 209 (n. 9)
Pensacola Express (Fla.), 152
Pensacola Observer (Fla.), 12, 92, 129
People's Press (Salem, N.C.), 87, 89
Petersburg Times (Va.), 120, 130, 135, 136
Philadelphia Union Pilot (Tenn.), 137
Phillips, J. W., 131, 157
Picayune (New Orleans, La.), 180
Piedmont (N.C.), 20, 21, 41, 42, 71, 89, 90
Pierpont, Francis H., 9–10, 25, 29, 63
Pinchback, P. B. S., 151, 152, 181
Plaquemines Sentinel (St. Sophie, La.), 74
Poiner, Samuel T., 85, 218 (n. 35)
Pontotoc, Miss., 53
Pope, John, 57, 96
Port Royal, S.C., 10, 11
Portsmouth, Va., 10
Powers, Ridgley, 163, 176, 177

Prairie News (Okolona, Miss.), 77
prejudice, racial, Republican opposition to, 104–5. *See also* civil rights, Republican support of African Americans'
Press and Times (Nashville, Tenn.), 17, 23, 30, 36, 38, 56, 64, 81, 101, 103, 118, 119, 121, 137, 145, 158, 168, 169, 207 (n. 33)
Price, John G., 150–51, 233 (n. 25), 252 (n. 17); as carpetbagger, 157–58; on Democrats, 99–100; on freedom of press, 96, 97; and *Little Rock Republican*, 101, 103, 108; as official state printer, 63, 64, 82, 172, 173; on race issues, 121, 124, 146, 156; on taxes, 113–14, 161; on voting, 119, 125, 134, 141
printing expenditures, 41–44, 59, 63, 65, 165–82 passim, 223 (n. 25), 253 (nn. 25, 36). *See also* patronage, and state printing
public accommodations laws, 107, 117, 120, 121, 142, 151, 153, 154, 164. *See also* civil rights, Republican support of African Americans'
Pughe, E. M., 50, 52–53, 126, 131

Quakers, 89, 91
Quitman Banner (Ga.), 51

race riots, 31. *See also* violence
Radical Republicans, 14, 15, 17–18, 19–20, 29, 31, 34–35, 40, 117–25, 129–42 passim, 166, 169, 174, 240 (n. 36), 243 (n. 57)
Radical Standard (Carrollton, La.), 225 (n. 9)
Radical Standard (New Orleans, La.), 74, 75
Radical Unionist Party, 39
Radical Unionists. *See* Radical Republicans
railroads. *See* transportation projects, Republican proposals for
Raleigh, N.C., 20, 21, 23, 24, 27, 47, 48, 89
Raleigh Weekly Republican (N.C.), 60, 221 (n. 13)
Randolph, Benjamin F., 33, 83
Ransier, Alonzo, 33, 221 (n. 13)
Rapides Gazette (Alexandria, La.), 66, 74, 148, 155, 156, 157, 162
Rapides Tribune (La.), 53
Rapier, James T., 43, 62, 155–56
Raymond, John B., 76, 175, 176
ready-print, 43, 50
"Redeemers," 178, 180, 183. *See also* Democrats
Red River News (Natchitoches, La.), 74
Red Shirts, 20
Reed, Harrison, 10–11, 31, 62, 128, 170, 251 (n. 12)

Reid, Whitelaw, 51
Republic (Richmond, Va.), 34, 35, 36
Republican (Mobile, Ala.), 228 (n. 45)
Republican (Shelbyville, Tenn.), 37, 81, 137, 145
Republican Banner (Nashville, Tenn.), 138
Republican Congressional Committee, 55
Republican National Committee, 55, 95
Republican newspapers: African American support for, 49, 52, 54, 60, 103–4, 131; challenges of operating, in the South, 45; interference with delivery of, 50; northern aid for, 54; numbers of, 69, 70–94 passim, 168–82 passim, 224 (nn. 1, 2); survival rates of, 70
Republican Pioneer (Edgard and Bonnet Carre, La.), 74
Republican Printing Company, 178
Republicans: centrists, 125–51 passim, 163, 166, 241 (n. 37); conservative, 125–26, 127, 131, 176; intraparty strife, 117–42; regular, 143
Republican Sentinel (Montgomery, Ala.), 155–56
Republican Standard (New Orleans, La.), 149, 151, 152
Richmond, Va., 35, 53, 229 (n. 55)
Richmond Examiner (Va.), 48
Richmond Register (Va.), 97, 124, 130
Richmond Whig (Va.), 51
Rodgers, S. W., 15
Rollins, Pinckney, 144, 149, 183
Roudanez, Louis Charles, 15, 241 (n. 40)
Rowell, George P., 44
Ruby, George, 43, 227 (n. 23)
Ruhm, John, 80, 137, 146, 227 (n. 28)
Rutherford Star (N.C.), 27, 33, 37, 50, 53, 54, 87, 90, 120, 123, 125, 129, 134, 144, 147, 149, 158, 159

San Antonio Express (Tex.), 28, 38, 49, 77, 78, 103, 109, 119, 124, 132, 139, 152, 159, 161, 165, 166, 174, 175, 221 (n. 7)
Savannah, Ga., 11, 12–13, 16, 21, 26, 61
Savannah Daily Herald (Ga.), 13, 23, 32, 37, 42
Savannah News (Ga.), 13
Savannah Republican (Ga.), 12, 32, 37, 59, 94, 126, 131, 204 (n. 10), 221 (n. 7)
scalawags, 78, 91, 109, 110, 118, 129, 137, 150, 154, 157, 158, 161, 163, 204 (n. 10). *See also* Unionists
Schofield, John, 63

schools, Republican support for public, 102, 103, 111, 114, 115, 125, 132, 133, 134, 157, 159, 160, 161, 162
Scott, Robert K., 68, 84, 162, 178, 179
Scott, William B., 36, 60, 81, 120, 137, 243 (n. 64)
Screws, W. W., 169
Scruggs, William, 106, 114, 126, 131, 134, 149
Sea Coast Republican (Bay St. Louis, Miss.), 77
Sears, Joseph, 10
segregation, racial, 30
Selma Press (Ala.), 133, 147, 148, 149, 160
Sener, James B., 53, 62, 91, 134, 149, 154, 158
Senter, DeWitt, 137, 140, 141, 169
Sequin Journal (Tex.), 49
Seward, William H., 9, 10, 11, 13, 14, 17, 18, 22, 23, 37, 38, 58, 204 (n. 5)
Sheats, Charles C., 62
Sheats, Christopher, 87, 131
Shelby County, Tenn., 65, 66
Sheldon, A. W., 97, 124
Shenandoah Valley, Va., 35, 61, 91
Shepley, George F., 13
Sheridan, Philip, 35
Sherman, William T., 12, 21
Sherman Patriot (Tex.), 79
Shuften, John T., 32, 211 (n. 22)
Siemering, August, 28, 78, 152, 166
Silsby, John, 34, 119
Simms, James M., 120
slavery, efforts to abolish, 18
slaves, former. *See* freedmen, civil rights of
Smalls, Robert, 156, 179
Smith, John, 219 (n. 37)
Smith, Joshua R., 75, 97, 119, 124, 138
Smith, William H., 147, 160, 251 (n. 11)
Soldier's Gazette (Maryville, Tenn.), 243 (n. 64)
South: number of newspapers in, 40; perceived backwardness of, by Republicans, 101–2; racial division in, 46
South Arkansas Journal (Camden), 83
South Carolina, 3; African American papers in, 156; elections in, 140; official state papers in, 64, 68, 178–80; race relations in, 32; reform in, 161, 162; Republican papers in, 40, 45, 58–59, 72, 83–85, 132, 232 (n. 11); Unionists in, 10–11, 16, 21, 23, 26, 38
South Carolina Leader (Charleston), 32–33, 60, 83, 122, 211 (n. 24), 221 (n. 13)
South Carolina Republican (Charleston), 84, 119, 132, 160–61

Southern Celt (Charleston, S.C.), 111, 123
Southerner (Darlington, S.C.), 228 (n. 40)
Southerners, white: perception of Republican Party by, 46–47, 96–98; Republican appeals toward, 61, 110–16. *See also* elites, Republican appeals toward white; scalawags
Southern Intelligencer (Austin, Tex.), 28, 30, 37, 77, 103, 108–9, 221 (n. 7)
Southern Republican (Demopolis, Ala.), 48, 53, 66, 67, 86, 98, 144, 147, 160, 169
Southern Republican Association, 39
Southern Shield (Helena, Ark.), 82
Southern Standard (Beaufort, S.C.), 179
Southwest Georgian (Fort Valley), 53, 94, 134, 224 (n. 2)
Sparnick, Henry, 85, 104, 163, 179, 180
Spartanburg Republican (S.C.), 85
Speed, Frederick, 119, 138
Stafford, Edward, 76, 107, 132, 138, 167
Stanly, Edward, 11
Star (Panola, Miss.), 48
State (Richmond, Va.), 168
State Journal (Austin, Tex.), 64, 67, 69, 78, 80, 98, 101, 124, 150, 165, 173, 174
State Journal (Baton Rouge, La.), 151
State Journal (Richmond, Va.), 90, 97, 120, 134, 136, 149, 156, 168, 229 (n. 55)
State Leader (Jackson, Miss.), 175, 176
State Sentinel (Montgomery, Ala.), 86, 106, 118, 119, 124, 131, 134, 135, 184, 228 (n. 43)
Statesville American (Iredell, N.C.), 90
Stearns, Marcellus, 162, 171
Steele, Holmes, 30, 31
St. Francisville, La., 53
St. Helena, S.C., 32
Stickney, John, 56
Stickney, Lyman, 10–11, 12, 30, 31, 32, 56
St. James Sentinel (St. James Parish, La.), 74
St. Landry Progress (Opelousas, La.), 53, 60, 73, 74, 100, 104, 118, 119, 122, 129, 132, 155
Stokes, John, 64, 122, 140, 147, 159
Stokes, William B., 137
straitest sect Unionists. *See* Unconditional Unionists
suffrage, African American, 14, 24, 29–38 passim, 51, 119, 136. *See also* civil rights, Republican support of African Americans'; freedmen, civil rights of
Sumter County Republican (Gallatin, Tenn.), 55, 227 (n. 28)

Sumter News (S.C.), 67
Sun (Jacksonville, Fla.), 171
Swayze, Jason Clarke, 99, 135, 145, 158, 219 (n. 37), 231 (n. 10), 243 (n. 57); and *American Union*, 4, 49, 50, 53, 61, 94, 119, 120, 124, 131, 140–41, 182; on race issues, 105, 122, 149, 153–55; on Southern whites, 97, 134

Talladega Sun (Ala.), 53
Tallahassee Floridian, 167
Tallahassee Sentinel (Fla.), 71, 92, 102, 129, 152, 170
Tangipahoa Advocate (Amite City, La.), 74
tax structure, Republican critique of, 113, 236 (n. 57)
Tennessee: elections in, 137–38, 158; official papers in, 64, 65, 168–69; race relations in, 38, 145–46; Republican papers in, 40, 41, 44, 58, 62, 71, 80–81; Unionists in, 17–19, 20, 23, 24, 25, 29, 36–37
Tennessee Republican (Huntington), 81
Tennessee Staats Zeitung (Nashville), 80, 137, 227 (n. 28)
Terrebone Patriot (Houma, La.), 74
Terry, Alfred H., 34
Texas: elections in, 138–39, 152; official state papers in, 63, 64, 66, 67, 166, 174–75; Republican papers in, 40, 41, 43, 44, 45, 58, 61, 71, 77–80, 132, 134; Unionists in, 22–23, 27–29, 30, 33, 38
Texas State Gazette (Austin), 38
Texas Volksblatt (Houston), 78
Thompson, James G., 11, 56, 95, 149, 162, 179
Throckmorton, J. W., 28, 29
Tillman, Lewis, 62, 81, 137
Times and Republican (Vicksburg, Miss.), 76. See also *Vicksburg Times* (Miss.)
Tourgee, Albion, 33, 49, 87, 101, 118, 119, 120, 123, 130, 132
Tracy, James G., 78, 134, 139, 152, 166
transportation projects, Republican proposals for, 29, 115–16, 129, 131, 134, 143, 159, 160, 161, 162, 184
treasury agents, federal, 9, 10, 13, 16, 31
Treasury Department, United States, 10–11, 56
Trevigne, Paul, 14, 15
True Delta (New Orleans, La.), 13, 14, 16
True Georgian (Atlanta), 126, 141, 224 (n. 2)
True Republican (Ark.), 172
True Republicans, 136

Index

True Southerner (Hampton, Va.), 35, 52, 53, 118, 120
True Southerner (Norfolk, Va.), 38, 130
True Southerner (Tampa, Fla.), 92, 93
Truman, Benjamin C., 17
Tyler Index (Tex.), 139

Unconditional Unionist (Little Rock, Ark.), 19–20
Unconditional Unionists, 17, 18, 19, 20, 24, 26, 35, 39, 130
Underwood, John C., 7, 34, 35
Union Appeal (Memphis, Tenn.), 123
Union Army, 7, 17, 19, 29, 34, 35, 40–41, 56–57, 73, 76, 88, 212 (n. 25), 221 (n. 13), 252 (n. 17); newspapers published by, 7–8, 10, 11, 12, 13
Union Flag (Jonesborough, Tenn.), 30, 36, 53, 81, 99, 118, 137, 221 (n. 8)
Union-Herald (Columbia, S.C.), 84, 149, 162, 163, 178, 179, 183
Union Intelligencer (Jefferson, Tex.), 53
Unionist governments, efforts to organize in the Confederacy, 16–24 passim, 40
Unionist newspapers, 9, 10, 19, 21, 30–37, 47, 56, 78
Unionists: postwar Southern white, 75, 77, 94, 145, 157; wartime Southern white, 7–39 passim, 49, 72, 74, 75, 80, 82, 85, 87, 89, 108, 109, 125, 132, 157, 169. *See also* scalawags; whites, Southern, Republican appeals toward
Union League, 40, 54, 55, 61, 78, 127, 128, 129, 139, 157, 219 (n. 37), 228 (n. 43), 239 (n. 22)
Union Reform Party (S.C.), 140
Union Republican (Huntsville, Tex.), 79
Union Republican (Norfolk, Va.), 35, 60, 130, 221 (n. 13)
Union Republican Executive Committee, 54, 58, 62
unions, labor, 122–23
United States Army. *See* Union Army

Valley Virginian (Staunton), 168
Vestal, W. I., 20
Vicksburg Daily Times (Miss.), 49, 113, 175. See also *Vicksburg Times* (Miss.)
Vicksburg Herald (Miss.), 22, 23, 26
Vicksburg Plain Dealer (Miss.), 156
Vicksburg Republican (Miss.), 43, 48–49, 55, 75, 76, 119, 121, 124, 132, 138
Vicksburg Times (Miss.), 56–57, 62, 76, 135, 149, 154, 156, 157, 163, 175, 176, 177. See also *Vicksburg Daily Times* (Miss.)
Vidal, Michael, 62, 100, 104, 118, 122, 155
violence, 121, 135, 141, 143, 144, 149, 163, 178, 182, 245 (n. 5). *See also* editors, newspaper, violence against; Ku Klux Klan
Virginia: early Unionist papers in, 7, 8, 9–10; elections in, 63, 136; official state papers in, 68; Republican papers in, 40, 41, 58, 71, 72, 90–91, 130, 134, 168; Unionists in, 16, 20, 23, 24, 25, 29, 34–36
Virginia Gazette (Williamsburg), 136, 205 (n. 8)
Virginia State Journal (Alexandria), 9, 10, 23, 25, 36, 58, 64, 90, 130, 136, 220 (n. 7)
Vorwarts (Austin, Tex.), 80

Waco Register (Tex.), 79
Walker, Gilbert C., 136, 139, 140, 141, 168
Walls, Josiah T., 62, 156
Walterboro News (S.C.), 96, 113, 154
War Department, United States, 9, 56
Warmoth, Henry Clay, 34, 129, 151, 152, 155, 180, 181, 225 (n. 8), 246 (n. 26)
Watchman (Mobile, Ala.), 229 (n. 45)
Webb, Frank, 120, 174, 227 (n. 23)
Webber, A. W., 176
Webber, D. A., 53
Webster, Alonzo, 83, 121
Weekly Era and Whig (Opelika, Ala.), 148
Weekly Intelligencer (Austin, Tex.), 159
Weekly Progress (Raleigh, N.C.), 20, 23, 27
Weekly Republican (Natchitoches, La.), 74
Weekly Spectator (Galveston, Tex.), 78
Weekly Sun (Bainbridge, Ga.), 94
Weekly Times (New Bern, N.C.), 27
Wells, Henry H., 63–64, 136, 168
Wells, James Madison, 25
Western Clarion (Helena, Ark.), 19, 20, 208 (n. 36)
Western Democrat (Charlotte, N.C.), 27, 209 (n. 8)
West Point Times (Miss.), 53
West Tennessean (Huntington), 81, 137
West Virginia, 9, 17, 25
Wheeling, Va., 7, 9, 17
Wheeling Intelligencer (Va.), 7, 95
Whigs, 25, 26, 27, 29, 47, 62, 109, 129, 132, 133, 134, 138, 141, 143, 159, 249 (n. 46)
White, D. B., 35, 36, 120, 130
White League, 178. *See also* violence

Whiteley, Richard, 62, 94, 154
White River Journal (De Vall's Bluff, Ark.), 82
whites, Southern: perception of Republican Party by, 46–47, 96–98; Republican appeals toward, 61, 110–16. *See also* elites, Republican appeals toward white; scalawags
Whitfield, H. B., 113, 154
Whittemore, Benjamin F., 32
Whittlesey, Charles, 58, 120, 134, 220 (n. 7)
Williamsburg Gazette (Va.), 49. See also *Virginia Gazette* (Williamsburg)
Williamsburg Republican (Kingstree, S.C.), 85
Wilmington, N.C., 11, 53
Wilmington Herald (N.C.), 27, 209 (n. 8)
Wilmington Post (N.C.), 52, 53, 88, 89, 96, 97, 101, 105, 111, 120, 124, 129, 134, 149, 154, 168

Wilson, Henry, 54
Wilson, Joseph T., 35, 130, 221 (n. 13)
Winchester Journal (Va.), 35, 111, 119, 121, 124, 130, 135, 136, 220 (n. 7)
Wofford, Jefferson, 138
women's rights, Republican support for, 110, 235 (n. 45)
Woodruff, Josephus, 178, 179, 253 (n. 36)
Woodville Republican (Miss.), 77, 97, 102, 112, 113
working class. *See* labor, Republican appeals to
Worth, Jonathan, 27
Wright, John P., 124

yeoman farmers. *See* labor, Republican appeals to
Yonley, T. D., 19